D0595172

REAL WORLD
GLOBALIZATION

A READER IN ECONOMICS, BUSINESS, AND POLITICS FROM
DOLLARS&SENSE

EDITED BY RAVI BHANDARI AND THE *DOLLARS & SENSE* COLLECTIVE

CONTENTS

Chapter 1

CRITICAL PERSPECTIVES
ON GLOBALIZATION

Article 1.1

THE GOSPEL OF FREE TRADE
The New Evangelists

BY ARTHUR MacEWAN
November 1991, updated July 2009

Free trade! With the zeal of Christian missionaries, for decades the U.S. government has been preaching, advocating, pushing, and coercing around the globe for "free trade."

As the economic crisis emerged in 2007 and 2008 and rapidly became a global crisis, it was apparent that something was very wrong with the way the world economy was organized. Not surprisingly, as unemployment rose sharply in the United States, there were calls for protecting jobs by limiting imports and for the government to "buy American" in its economic stimulus program. Similarly, in many other countries, as unemployment jumped upwards, pressure emerged for protection—and some actual steps were taken. Yet, free trade missionaries did not retreat; they continued to preach the same gospel.

The free-traders were probably correct in claiming that protectionist policies would do more harm than good as a means to stem the rising unemployment generated by the economic crisis. Significant acts of protectionism in one country would lead to retaliation—or at least copying—by other countries, reducing world trade. The resulting loss of jobs from reduced trade would most likely outweigh any gains from protection.

Yet the argument over international economic policies should not be confined simply to what should be done in a crisis. Nor should it simply deal with trade in goods and services. The free-traders have advocated their program as one for long-

1

run economic growth and development, yet the evidence suggests that free trade is not a good economic development strategy. Furthermore, the free-traders preach the virtue of unrestricted global movement of finance as well as of goods and services. As it turns out, the free flow of finance has been a major factor in bringing about and spreading the economic crisis that began to appear in 2007—as well as earlier crises.

The Push

While the U.S. push for free trade goes back several decades, it has become more intense in recent years. In the 1990s, the U.S. government signed on to the North American Free Trade Agreement (NAFTA) and in 2005 established the Central American Free Trade Agreement (CAFTA). Both Republican and Democratic presidents, however, have pushed hard for a *global* free trade agenda. After the demise of the Soviet Union, U.S. advisers prescribed unfettered capitalism for Eastern and Central Europe, and ridiculed as unworkable any move toward a "third way." In low-income countries from Mexico to Malaysia, the prescription has been the same: open markets, deregulate business, don't restrict international investment, and let the free market flourish.

In the push for worldwide free trade, the World Trade Organization (WTO) has been the principal vehicle of change, establishing rules for commerce that assure markets are open and resources are available to those who can pay. And the International Monetary Fund (IMF) and World Bank, which provide loans to many governments, use their financial power to pressure countries around the world to accept the gospel and open their markets. In each of these international organizations, the United States—generally through the U.S. Treasury—plays a dominant role.

Of course, as with any gospel, the preachers often ignore their own sermons. While telling other countries to open their markets, the U.S. government continued, for instance, to limit imports of steel, cotton, sugar, textiles, and many other goods. But publicly at least, free-trade boosters insist that the path to true salvation—or economic expansion, which, in this day and age, seems to be the same thing—lies in opening our market to foreign goods. Get rid of trade barriers at home and abroad, allow business to go where it wants and do what it wants. We will all get rich.

Yet the history of the United States and other rich countries does not fit well with the free-trade gospel. Virtually all advanced capitalist countries found economic success through heavy government regulation of their international commerce, not in free trade. Likewise, a large role for government intervention has characterized those cases of rapid and sustained economic growth in recent decades—for example, Japan after World War II, South Korea in the 1970s through the 1990s, and China most recently.

Free trade does, however, have its uses. Highly developed nations can use free trade to extend their power and control of the world's wealth, and business can use it as a weapon against labor. Most important, free trade can limit efforts to redistribute income more equally, undermine social programs, and keep people from democratically controlling their economic lives.

A Day in the Park

At the beginning of the 19th century, Lowell, Massachusetts became the premier site of the U.S. textile industry. Today, thanks to the Lowell National Historical Park, you can tour the huge mills, ride through the canals that redirected the Merrimack River's power to those mills, and learn the story of the textile workers, from the Yankee "mill girls" of the 1820s through the various waves of immigrant laborers who poured into the city over the next century.

During a day in the park, visitors get a graphic picture of the importance of 19th-century industry to the economic growth and prosperity of the United States. Lowell and the other mill towns of the era were centers of growth. They not only created a demand for Southern cotton, they also created a demand for new machinery, maintenance of old machinery, parts, dyes, *skills*, construction materials, construction machinery, *more skills*, equipment to move the raw materials and products, parts maintenance for that equipment, *and still more skills*. The mill towns also created markets—concentrated groups of wage earners who needed to buy products to sustain themselves. As centers of economic activity, Lowell and similar mill towns contributed to U.S. economic growth far beyond the value of the textiles they produced.

The U.S. textile industry emerged decades after the industrial revolution had spawned Britain's powerful textile industry. Nonetheless, it survived and prospered. British linens inundated markets throughout the world in the early 19th century, as the British navy nurtured free trade and kept ports open for commerce. In the United States, however, hostilities leading up to the War of 1812 and then a substantial tariff made British textiles relatively expensive. These limitations on trade allowed the Lowell mills to prosper, acting as a catalyst for other industries and helping to create the skilled work force at the center of U.S. economic expansion.

Beyond textiles, however, tariffs did not play a great role in the United States during the early 19th century. Southern planters had considerable power, and while they were willing to make some compromises, they opposed protecting manufacturing in general because that protection forced up the prices of the goods they purchased with their cotton revenues. The Civil War wiped out the planters' power to oppose protectionism, and from the 1860s through World War I, U.S. industry prospered behind considerable tariff barriers.

Different Countries, Similar Experiences

The story of the importance of protectionism in bringing economic growth has been repeated, with local variations, in other advanced capitalist countries. During the late 19th century, Germany entered the major league of international economic powers with substantial protection and government support for its industries. Likewise, in 19th-century France and Italy, national consolidation behind protectionist barriers was a key to economic development.

Britain—which entered the industrial era first—is often touted as the prime example of successful development without tariff protection. Yet, Britain embraced free trade only after its industrial base was well established; as in the U.S., the early and important textile industry was erected on a foundation of protectionism. In addition, Britain built its industry through the British navy and the expansion of empire, hardly prime ingredients in any recipe for free trade.

Japan provides an especially important case of successful government protection and support for industrial development. In the post-World War II era, when the Japanese established the foundations for their economic "miracle," the government rejected free trade and extensive foreign investment and instead promoted its national firms.

In the 1950s, for example, the government protected the country's fledgling auto firms from foreign competition. At first, quotas limited imports to $500,000 (in current dollars) each year; in the 1960s, prohibitively high tariffs replaced the quotas. Furthermore, the Japanese allowed foreign investment only insofar as it contributed to developing domestic industry. The government encouraged Japanese companies to import foreign technology, but required them to produce 90% of parts domestically within five years.

The Japanese also protected their computer industry. In the early 1970s, as the industry was developing, companies and individuals could only purchase a foreign machine if a suitable Japanese model was not available. IBM was allowed to produce within the country, but only when it licensed basic patents to Japanese firms. And IBM computers produced in Japan were treated as foreign-made machines.

In the 20th century, no other country matched Japan's economic success, as it moved in a few decades from a relative low-income country, through the devastation of war, to emerge as one of the world's economic leaders. Yet one looks back in vain to find a role for free trade in this success. The Japanese government provided an effective framework, support, and protection for the country's capitalist development.

Likewise, in many countries that have been late-comers to economic development, capitalism has generated high rates of economic growth where government involvement, and not free trade, played the central role. South Korea is a striking case. "Korea is an example of a country that grew very fast and yet violated the canons of conventional economic wisdom," writes Alice Amsden in *Asia's Next Giant: South Korea and Late Industrialization,* widely acclaimed as perhaps the most important analysis of the South Korean economic success. "In Korea, instead of the market mechanism allocating resources and guiding private entrepreneurship, the government made most of the pivotal investment decisions. Instead of firms operating in a competitive market structure, they each operated with an extraordinary degree of market control, protected from foreign competition."

Free trade, however, has had its impact in South Korea. In the 1990s, South Korea and other East Asian governments came under pressure from the U.S. government and the IMF to open their markets, including their financial markets. When they did so, the results were a veritable disaster. The East Asian financial crisis that began in 1997 was a major setback for the whole region, a major disruption of economic growth. After extremely rapid economic growth for three decades, with output expanding at 7% to 10% a year, South Korea's economy plummeted by 6.3% between 1997 and 1998.

Mexico and Its NAFTA Experience

While free trade in goods and services has its problems, which can be very serious, it is the free movement of capital, the opening of financial markets that has sharp, sudden impacts, sometimes wrecking havoc on national economies. Thus, virtually as soon as Mexico, the United States and Canada formed NAFTA at the beginning of 1994, Mexico was hit with a severe financial crisis. As the economy turned downward at the beginning of that year, capital rapidly left the country, greatly reducing the value of the Mexican peso. With this diminished value of the peso, the cost of servicing international debts and the costs of imports skyrocketed—and the downturn worsened.

Still, during the 1990s, before and after the financial crisis, free-traders extolled short periods of moderate economic growth in Mexico —3% to 4% per year—as evidence of success. Yet, compared to earlier years, Mexico's growth under free trade has been poor. From 1940 to 1990 (including the no-growth decade of the 1980s), when Mexico's market was highly protected and the state actively regulated economic affairs, output grew at an average annual rate of 5%.

Most important, Mexico's experience discredits the notion that free-market policies will improve living conditions for the masses of people in low-income countries. The Mexican government paved the way for free trade policies by reducing or eliminating social welfare programs, and for many Mexican workers wages declined sharply during the free trade era. The number of households living in poverty rose dramatically, with some 75% of Mexico's population below the poverty line at the beginning of the 21st century.

China and Its Impact

Part of Mexico's problem and its economy's relatively weak performance from the 1990s onward has been the full-scale entrance of China into the international economy. While the Mexican authorities thought they saw great possibilities in NAFTA, with the full opening of the U.S. market to goods produced with low-wage Mexican labor, China (and other Asian countries) had even cheaper labor. As China also gained access to the U.S. market, Mexican expectations were dashed.

The Chinese economy has surely gained in terms of economic growth as it has engaged more and more with the world market, and the absolute levels of incomes of millions of people have risen a great deal. However, China's rapid economic growth has come with a high degree of income inequality. Before its era of rapid growth, China was viewed as a country with a relatively equal distribution of income. By the beginning of the new millennium, however, it was much more unequal than any of the other most populace Asian countries (India, Indonesia, Bangladesh, Pakistan), and more in line with the high-inequality countries of Latin America. Furthermore, with the inequality has come a great deal of social conflict. Tens of thousands of "incidents" of conflict involving violence are reported each year, and most recently there have been the major conflicts involving Tibetans and Ouigers.

In any case, the Chinese trade and growth success should not be confused with "free trade." Foundations for China's surge of economic growth were established through state-sponsored infra-structure development and the vast expansion of the country's educational system. Even today, while private business, including foreign business, appears to have been given free rein in China, the government still plays a controlling role—including a central role in affecting foreign economic relations.

A central aspect of the government's role in the county's foreign commerce has been in the realm of finance. As Chinese-produced goods have virtually flooded international markets, the government has controlled the uses of the earnings from these exports. Instead of simply allowing those earnings to be used by Chinese firms and citizens to buy imports, the government has to a large extent held those earnings as reserves. Using those reserves, China's central bank has been the largest purchaser of U.S. government bonds, in effect becoming a major financer of the U.S. government's budget deficit of recent years.

China's reserves have been one large element in creating a giant pool of financial assets in the world economy. This "pool" has also been built up as the doubling of oil prices following the U.S. invasion of Iraq put huge amounts of funds in the pockets of oil-exporting countries and firm and individuals connected to the oil industry. Yet slow growth of the U.S. economy and extremely low interest rates, resulting from the Federal Reserve Bank's efforts to encourage more growth, limited the returns that could be obtained on these funds. One of the consequences—through a complex set of connections—was the development of the U.S. housing bubble, as financial firms, searching for higher returns, pushed funds into more and more risky mortgage loans.

It was not simply free trade and the unrestricted flow of international finance that generated the housing bubble and subsequent crisis in the U.S. economy. However, the generally unstable global economy—both in terms of trade and finance—that has emerged in the free trade era was certainly a factor bringing about the crisis. Moreover, as is widely recognized, it was not only the U.S. economy and U.S. financial institutions that were affected. The free international flow of finance has meant that banking has become more and more a global industry. So as the U.S. banks got in trouble in 2007 and 2008, their maladies spread to many other parts of the world.

The Uses of Free Trade

While free trade is not the best economic growth or development policy and, especially through the free flow of finance, can precipitate financial crises, the largest and most powerful firms in many countries find it highly profitable. As Britain preached the loudest sermons for free trade in the early 19th century, when its own industry was already firmly established, so the United States—or at least many firms based in the United States—find it a profitable policy at the beginning of the 21st century. The Mexican experience provides an instructive illustration.

For U.S. firms, access to foreign markets is a high priority. Mexico may be relatively poor, but with a population of 105 million it provides a substantial market. Furthermore, Mexican labor is cheap relative to U.S. labor; and using modern production techniques, Mexican workers can be as productive as workers in the United States. For U.S. firms to obtain full access to the Mexican market, the United States has to open its borders to Mexican goods. Also, if U.S. firms are to take full advantage of cheap foreign labor and sell the goods produced abroad to U.S. consumers, the United States has to be open to imports.

On the other side of the border, wealthy Mexicans face a choice between advancing their interests through national development or advancing their interests through ties to U.S. firms and access to U.S. markets. For many years, they chose the former route. This led to some development of the Mexican economy but also—due to corruption and the massive power of the ruling party, the PRI—huge concentrations of wealth in the hands of a few small groups of firms and individuals. Eventually, these groups came into conflict with their own government over regulation and taxation. Having benefited from government largesse, they came to see their fortunes in greater freedom from government control and, particularly, in greater access to foreign markets and partnerships with large foreign companies. National development was a secondary concern when more involvement with international commerce would produce greater riches more quickly.

In addition, the old program of state-led development in Mexico ran into severe problems. These problems came to the surface in the 1980s with the international debt crisis. Owing huge amounts of money to foreign banks, the Mexican government was forced to respond to pressure from the IMF, the U.S. government, and large international banks which sought to deregulate Mexico's trade and investment. That pressure meshed with the pressure from Mexico's own richest elites, and the result was the move toward free trade and a greater opening of the Mexican economy to foreign investment.

Since the early 1990s, these changes for Mexico and the United States (as well as Canada) have been institutionalized in NAFTA. The U.S. government's agenda since then has been to spread free trade policies to all of the Americas through more regional agreements like CAFTA and ultimately through a Free Trade Area of the Americas. On a broader scale, the U.S. government works through the WTO, the IMF, and the World Bank to open markets and gain access to resources beyond the Western Hemisphere. In fact, while markets remain important everywhere, low-wage manufacturing is increasingly concentrated in Asia—especially China—instead of Mexico or Latin America.

The Chinese experience involves many of the same advantages for U.S. business as does the Mexican—a vast market, low wages, and an increasingly productive labor force. However, the Chinese government, although it has liberalized the economy a great deal compared to the pre-1985 era, has not abdicated its major role in the economy. For better (growth) and for worse (inequality and repression), the Chinese government has not embraced free trade.

Who Gains, Who Loses?

Of course, in the United States, Mexico, China and elsewhere, advocates of free trade claim that their policies are in everyone's interest. Free trade, they point out, will mean cheaper products for all. Consumers in the United States, who are mostly workers, will be richer because their wages will buy more. In Mexico and China, on the one hand, and in the United States, on the other hand, they argue that rising trade will create more jobs. If some workers lose their jobs because cheaper imported goods are available, export industries will produce new jobs.

In recent years this argument has taken on a new dimension with the larger entrance of India into the world economy and with the burgeoning there of jobs based in information technology—programming and call centers, for example. This "out-sourcing" of service jobs has received a great deal of attention and concern in the United States. Yet free-traders have defended this development as good for the U.S. economy as well as for the Indian economy.

Such arguments obscure many of the most important issues in the free trade debate. Stated, as they usually are, as universal truths, these arguments are just plain silly. No one, for example, touring the Lowell National Historical Park could seriously argue that people in the United States would have been better off had there been no tariff on textiles. Yes, in 1820, they could have purchased textile goods more cheaply, but in the long run the result would have been less industrial advancement and a less wealthy nation. One could make the same point with the Japanese auto and computer industries, or indeed with numerous other examples from the last two centuries of capitalist development.

In the modern era, even though the United States already has a relatively developed economy with highly skilled workers, a freely open international economy does not serve the interests of most U.S. workers, though it will benefit large firms. U.S. workers today are in competition with workers around the globe. Many different workers in many different places can produce the same goods and services. Thus, an international economy governed by the free trade agenda will tend to bring down wages for many U.S. workers. This phenomenon has certainly been one of the factors leading to the substantial rise of income inequality in the United States during recent decades.

The problem is not simply that of workers in a few industries—such as auto and steel, or call-centers and computer programming—where import competition is an obvious and immediate issue. A country's openness to the international economy affects the entire structure of earnings in that country. Free trade forces down the general level of wages across the board, even of those workers not directly affected by imports. The simple fact is that when companies can produce the same products in several different places, it is owners who gain because they can move their factories and funds around much more easily than workers can move themselves around. Capital is mobile; labor is much less mobile. Businesses, more than workers, gain from having a larger territory in which to roam.

Control Over Our Economic Lives

But the difficulties with free trade do not end with wages. In both low-income and high-income parts of the world, free trade is a weapon in the hands of business when it opposes any progressive social programs. Efforts to place environmental restrictions on firms are met with the threat of moving production abroad. Higher taxes to improve the schools? Business threatens to go elsewhere. Better health and safety regulations? The same response.

Some might argue that the losses from free trade for people in the United States will be balanced by gains for most people in poor countries—lower wages in the United States, but higher wages in Mexico and China. Free trade, then, would bring about international equality. Not likely. In fact, as pointed out above, free trade reforms in Mexico have helped force down wages and reduce social welfare programs, processes rationalized by efforts to make Mexican goods competitive on international markets. China, while not embracing free trade, has seen its full-scale entrance into global commerce accompanied by increasing inequality.

Gains for Mexican or Chinese workers, like those for U.S. workers, depend on their power in relation to business. Free trade or simply the imperative of international "competitiveness" are just as much weapons in the hands of firms operating in Mexico and China as they are for firms operating in the United States. The great mobility of capital is business's best trump card in dealing with labor and popular demands for social change—in the United States, Mexico, China and elsewhere.

None of this means that people should demand that their economies operate as fortresses, protected from all foreign economic incursions. There are great gains that can be obtained from international economic relations—when a nation manages those relations in the interests of the great majority of the people. Protectionism often simply supports narrow vested interests, corrupt officials, and wealthy industrialists. In rejecting free trade, we should move beyond traditional protectionism.

Yet, at this time, rejecting free trade is an essential first step. Free trade places the cards in the hands of business. More than ever, free trade would subject us to the "bottom line," or at least the bottom line as calculated by those who own and run large companies. ❑

Article 1.2

FREE MARKETS, INTERNATIONAL COMMERCE, AND ECONOMIC DEVELOPMENT

BY ARTHUR MacEWAN
November 2000

The essence of the neo-liberal position on international commerce is the proposition that economic growth will be most rapid when the movement of goods, services, and capital is unimpeded by government regulations. A simple logic lies at the basis of this free trade position. If, for whatever reasons, countries differ in their abilities to produce various goods, then they can all benefit if each specializes in the production of those items it produces most effectively (i.e., at least cost). They can then trade with one another to obtain the entire range of goods they need. In this manner, each country is using its resources to do what it can do best.

As an illustration of this logic, consider two countries, one with an abundance of good farmland and the other with a good supply of energy resources (hydro power, for example). It seems likely that each of these countries will gain from trade if the first specializes in the production of agricultural goods and the latter specializes in the production of manufactures. Moreover, if the governments impose no constraints on international trade, then this specialization is precisely what will occur. Without constraints on trade, people attempting to produce manufactured goods in the country with abundant good farmland will not be able to do so as cheaply as people in the country with a good supply of energy resources—and vice versa for people attempting to produce agricultural goods in the latter country.

The theory appears to run into trouble if one country produces everything more efficiently than the other. Yet the trouble is only apparent, not real. Under these circumstances, all will gain if each country specializes in the production of those goods where it has a *comparative advantage*. For example, let's assume that the country with abundant farmland produces agricultural goods at half what it costs to produce them in the other country. At the same time, this country with abundant farmland has a workforce with great capacity for industrial labor, and it therefore can produce manufactured goods at one-quarter of what it costs to produce them in the other country. Under these circumstances the country's skilled labor force gives it a greater advantage in the production of manufactures than the advantage that its abundant farmland gives it in the production of agricultural goods. Thus it has a *comparative* advantage in the production of manufactures. Similarly, the second country, even though it is less efficient in the production of both categories of goods, has a *comparative* advantage in the production of agricultural goods. To produce manufactures would cost four times as much in this country as in the other, whereas to produce agricultural goods would only cost twice as much. Consequently, both countries can gain if each specializes where it has a comparative advantage, and they then trade to obtain their full set of needs.

The theory of comparative advantage has played an important role in the history of economics, for it has provided an intellectual rationale for free trade policies. An intellectual rationale has been necessary because, whatever the larger efficacy of the policy, free trade is always costly to groups that have prospered under any prior trade restrictions.

Advocates of the neo-liberal position base their policy prescriptions as much on certain myths about history as on the internal coherence of their theory. They argue that their theory is validated by the history of successful economic growth, both in the longer experience of the relatively advanced economies and in the recent experience of successful growth in newly industrialized countries. They cite, in particular, the history of economic development in the United Kingdom, other countries of Western Europe, and the United States, and the more recent experiences of countries in East Asia.

An examination of these experiences, however, quickly demonstrates that the neo-liberal claims are but crude myths, having only a vague connection to reality.

Historical Experience: A Brief Sketch

Virtually all of our experience with economic development suggests that extensive regulation of foreign commerce by a country's government has been an essential foundation for successful economic growth. In the United Kingdom, perhaps the case most frequently cited to demonstrate the success of free trade, textile producers secured protection from import competition at the end of the 17th century, and high tariffs served British manufacturing well through the era of the country's rise to world economic preeminence. At the beginning of the 19th century, the average tariff rate on manufactures was 50%—high by almost any comparative standard. Later in the century, the United Kingdom did eliminate its tariffs on manufactures, but then it had passed the early stage of development and its industry was well established. Moreover, state support for industry in the United Kingdom came through the creation and maintenance of empire.

Tariff protection also played a large role in the emergence of U.S. industry. The textile industry, which was especially important in the country's economic development, got its start when the hostilities leading up to and through the War of 1812 provided implicit protection by limiting international shipping. After the war, the protection became explicit as a tariff was established. According to the World Bank, the average U.S. tariff on manufactures was 40% in 1820. In the last third of the 19th century, with tariff protection well established at an average of around 30% for most of the 1870 to 1910 period, the United States experienced a great industrial expansion. Only after World War II, when U.S. industry's dominant position in the world economy was secure, did a steady and lasting reduction of tariffs take place.

Countries that achieved their developmental advance at a later historical period were generally characterized by a significantly greater role for the state in the regulation of foreign commerce, both with regard to trade and investment. Japan's experience in joining the ranks of advanced capitalist countries provides the prime example and, insofar as any country has broken out of underdevelopment in more recent decades, South Korea would provide the most important case study. In broad terms, the South Korean experience is very similar to that of Japan. From the early 1960s, the South Korean state followed policies of protecting domestic markets, heavily favoring Korean-owned firms, and using state owned industries to develop national production in certain "strategic" sectors.

One of the important aspects of the South Korean experience is that, in protecting and supporting the development of national industry, the government did not by any means encourage Korean firms to abjure exports and follow an "inward looking" policy. On the contrary, the government used a firm's ability to compete in export markets as a measure of whether or not it was succeeding in becoming more efficient. The South Korean experience shows how economic policy can both regulate foreign commerce but at the same time make sure that national firms reap the many advantages associated with international commerce—including, especially, the transfer of knowledge and technology that come with foreign exposure.

Re-examining the Theory

So the neo-liberal theory of international commerce does not sit very well with historical experience, and this lack of congruence between theory and reality suggests that there are some problems with the theory. Indeed, there are several.

Technology in Economic Growth. The theory of free trade is fundamentally flawed because it fails to take account of the ways in which production itself affects technological change. "Learning-by-doing" is a particularly important form of the phenomenon. In a new activity, initial production may be very costly. Yet as time passes and experience accumulates, the people engaged in the activity learn. They change the way they do things, which is to say that they change the technology. Such an activity might never develop were it forced to compete with already established firms in other countries where the learning-by-doing had already taken place. Yet if the activity were protected from foreign competition during an initial phase in which experience could be accumulated, it could develop and become fully competitive.

Yet protection involves costs. Why should society in general bear the costs of protection in order to assure the development of any particular activity? The answer to these questions lies in the concept of *location specific technological externalities.* Different kinds of production activities tend to bring about different kinds of changes in the overall economic environment. In the 18th and 19th century, for example, manufacturing tended to generate new methods of production and a development of skills that had far reaching technological impacts. In the current era, "high tech" production appears to have similar far reaching impacts. Because the gains from these sorts of changes are not confined to the industry or firm where they originate, they are not reflected in the profits of that industry or firm and will not be taken into account as a basis for investment decisions. These positive technological impacts of particular production activity that do not affect the profits and are outside of—or external to—the purview of the people making decisions about that production are "technological externalities." When positive technological externalities exist for a particular activity, then the value of that activity to society will be greater than the private value. Technological externalities are often "location specific," having their greatest impact within relatively close geographic proximity to the site where they are originally generated—or at least having their principal impact within the same national unit.

The U.S. experience with the cotton textile industry, which I have cited above, provides a particularly good example of the generation of location specific technological externalities. The textile industry emerged in the early decades of the 19th century, prospering especially in the Northeastern part of the United States. Mill towns throughout southern New England became centers of growth. Not only did they create a demand for Southern cotton, but they also created a demand for new machinery, maintenance of old machinery, parts, dyes, *skills*, construction materials, construction machinery, *more skills*, equipment to move the raw materials and the products, parts and maintenance for that equipment, *and still more skills*. As centers of economic activity, innovation, and change, mill towns made a contribution to the economic growth of the United States that went far beyond the value of the textiles they produced.

Trade and Employment. The theory of comparative advantage and arguments for free trade rest on the assumption that full employment exists, or at least that the level of employment is independent of the *pattern* of trade and production. In addition, the theory assumes that when patterns of trade and production change, labor will move from one activity to another instantaneously—or at least sufficiently rapidly so as to cause no great welfare loss or disruption of overall demand. In reality, most low income countries are characterized by very high levels of unemployment and underemployment, the pattern of trade and production does affect employment levels (at least in the short run), and labor markets adjust to change relatively slowly.

An illustration of the problems is provided by experience in many low-income countries when trade restrictions on grain imports are lifted. In Mexico, where the internationalization of grain supply was proceeding apace in the 1980s, even before the establishment of the North American Free Trade Agreement (NAFTA), the replacement of peasant grain production by imports has not worked out so favorably. In fact, those parts of agriculture that have expanded in recent years—meat production and vegetable exports, for example—and export manufacturing use relatively small amounts of labor. Peasants displaced by the import of inexpensive U.S. and Canadian grain, instead of finding employment in these sectors, swell the ranks of the unemployed or underemployed, often in cities. Consequently, instead of labor resources being used more efficiently under the pressure of import competition, labor resources are wasted.

Free Trade and Large Firms. The neo-liberal argument for free trade is based on the assumption that if government did not intervene and regulate international commerce, then the economy would operate in a competitive manner with advantageous results... International commerce, however, is often dominated by a relatively small number of very large firms that operate in a monopolistic manner. Competition among them exists, and in some cases is very intense. It is, however, monopolistic competition, not simply the price competition that is assumed in the argument for free trade. The patterns of trade and production engaged in by very large firms are determined as part of their complex global strategies—with results that do not necessarily coincide with either the price competition model of the free trade argument or the long run development interests of a particular country.

Large firms are sensitive to price considerations, and they are often quick to re-locate production to take advantage of low cost resources. Yet resource costs, the foundation of the theory of comparative advantage, are only one element in the strategies of large, internationally integrated firms. The Japanese automobile companies, for example, established their leading role in the industry through a strategy of developing linkages to suppliers in close physical proximity to the central plant. Resource costs were secondary to the issue of strategic control, which had important impacts on technological change and the management of inventory. In the international textile industry, flexibility is a paramount concern in the strategy of large firms, and issues of market proximity and control over product supply stand along side of resource costs as factors determining the location of production. Similarly, in the semiconductor production of the electronics industry, many firms (particularly U.S. firms) have followed a strategy of vertical integration. When companies produce semiconductors for use in their own final products, their location decisions tend to be dominated by concerns about control of the technology and production process; concerns about least-cost siting tend to be secondary. In all of these examples, selected from industries that are both highly international in their operations and in which very large companies play central roles, monopolistic firms employ strategies of control that enhance their own long run profits. There is no reason to expect the outcomes to conform to those envisioned in the theoretical arguments for free trade.

Primary Product Problems. When the argument for free trade was developed in the 19th century, it was a rationalization for the particular character of the international division of labor that emerged so clearly at that time. That division of labor placed a few countries of Europe and North America in the position of specializing in the production and export of manufactured goods, while several other countries—many of which are today's low income countries—specialized in the production and export of primary products. Today, although the international division of labor has changed, there are still many low income countries characterized by primary product specialization.

Primary product specialization is problematic, first of all, because the prices of primary products are highly unstable. Primary products are, by definition, the raw materials that enter at an early stage into the production of other goods. Sugar, for example, is used largely in the manufacture of a great variety of sweets, and the cost of sugar plays a small role in affecting the final price of those sweets. Copper finds its demand as an input to houses, automobiles and other machinery. Like sugar, its cost plays a small role in determining the price of the final products of which it is a part. Grains, vanilla, cocoa, cotton, coffee and several other products fit this pattern. Consequently, the demand for such a product is very insensitive to its price (that is, the demand is very price inelastic). When the supply of a primary product increases—for example, because of good weather and a resulting good crop in some region of the world—prices will decline a great deal as producers compete with one another to unload their surpluses on the very limited market. Conversely, with a small decline in the supply—resulting, perhaps, from bad weather and a resulting crop failure—producers will be able to push up the price a great deal. Even when the average price of a primary product is in some sense "reasonable," price fluctuations create severe cyclical problems that, when the product is important, may disrupt the development of an entire national economy.

An additional problem of specialization in primary products is that in general the average prices of primary products are not "reasonable," in the sense that the demand for the products is subject to long-term downward pressure. Consider, for example, the case of foods—sugar, coffee, cocoa—exported from low income countries to the advanced economies of Europe and North America. As income rises in the advanced countries, the demand for food rises less rapidly. Under these circumstances, insofar as countries rely on primary product exports to the advanced countries for their national income, their national income must grow more slowly than income in those advanced countries.

International Commerce, Income Distribution, and Power

The deregulation of international commerce that is envisioned in the neo-liberal model is largely, if not entirely, a deregulation of business. By removing constraints on the operation of business, it necessarily would give more power to the owners of capital. It would allow business to seek out profits with fewer constraints—on the location of production, on its sources of supply, on characteristics of production, and so on. Power is largely a question of options, and by providing more options to the owners of capital, neo-liberal globalization would give them more power. Most clearly, within a deregulated international environment, owners of capital can resist labor's demands by exercising, or threatening to exercise, their option of shifting production to regions of the world where labor costs are lower. This is not only an option of moving from high wage to low wage countries, from Britain to Sri Lanka, for example. Owners of businesses in Sri Lanka may move, or threaten to move, operations to Britain if productivity is sufficiently higher in the latter country. So the power that business gains vis-a-vis labor by the deregulation of international commerce can be important in low wage and high wage countries.

Power in economic life means primarily an ability to shift more and more of the value produced by society into one's own hands. In this way, neo-liberal globalization is a *de facto* formula for shifting income to the owners of capital, that is, for increasing inequality in the distribution of income. ❏

Excerpted from Chapter 2 of Arthur MacEwan's Neo-Liberalism or Democracy? Economic Strategy, Markets, and Alternatives for the 21st Century, *Zed Books and St. Martin's Press, 1999.*

Article 1.3

DEBUNKING THE "INDEX OF ECONOMIC FREEDOM"

Economic freedom for corporations has little to do with either political freedom or economic growth.

BY JOHN MILLER
March/April 2005

"HAIL ESTONIA!"

> For the first time in the 11 years that the Heritage Foundation and *The Wall Street Journal* have been publishing the Index of Economic Freedom, the U.S. has dropped out of the top 10 freest economies in the world. ...
>
> The 2005 Index, released today, ranks Hong Kong once again as the world's freest economy, followed by Singapore and Luxembourg. But it is Estonia at No. 4 that makes the point. This former Soviet satellite is a model reformer, setting the standard for how fast countries can move ahead in the realm of economic liberalization. ...
>
> The U.S. ... scores well. But worrying developments like Sarbanes-Oxley in the category of regulation and aggressive use of antidumping law in trade policy have kept it from keeping pace with the best performers in economic freedom. Most alarming is the U.S.'s fiscal burden, which imposes high marginal tax rates for individuals and very high marginal corporate tax rates. ...
>
> Policy makers who pay lip service to fighting poverty would do well to grasp the link between economic freedom and prosperity. This year the Index finds that the freest economies have a per-capita income of $29,219, more than twice that of the "mostly free" at $12,839, and more than four times that of the "mostly unfree." Put simply, misery has a cure and its name is economic freedom.
>
> —*Wall Street Journal* op-ed by Mary Anastasia O'Grady,
> January 4, 2005

I must be confused. I somehow thought that an Index of Economic Freedom would showcase countries that are reducing the democratic deficits of the global economy by giving people more control over their economic lives and the institutions that govern them. In the hands of the *Wall Street Journal* and the Heritage Foundation, Washington's foremost right-wing think tank, however, an economic freedom index merely measures corporate and entrepreneurial freedom from accountability. Upon examination, the index turns out to be a poor barometer of either freedom more broadly construed or of prosperity.

The index does not even pretend that its definition of economic freedom has anything to do with political freedom. Take the two city-states, Hong Kong and Singapore, which top the index's list of free countries. Both are only "partially free" according to *Freedom in the World*, an annual country-by-country assessment published by the nonpartisan think tank Freedom House, which the *Journal*'s editors themselves have called "the Michelin Guide to democracy's development." Hong Kong is still without direct elections for its legislature or its chief executive, and a proposed internal security law threatens press and academic freedom as well as political dissent. In Singapore, freedom of the press and the right to demonstrate are limited; films, TV, and other media are censored; preventive detention is legal; and you can do jail time for littering.

Moving further down the list of "free" countries, the rankings are no better correlated with any ordinary definition of "freedom," as economic journalist Robert Kuttner pointed out when the index was first published in 1997. For instance, Bahrain (#20), where the king holds an effective veto over parliament and freedom of expression is limited, ranks higher than Norway (#29), whose comprehensive social insurance and strong environmental regulation drag down its score. Likewise, Kuwait, an emirship no one would term free or democratic, is tied (at #54) with Costa Rica, long the most vigorous democracy in Latin America.

These results are not surprising, however, given the index's premise: the less a government intervenes in the economy, the higher its freedom ranking. Specifically, the index breaks "economic freedom" down into 10 components: trade policy; fiscal burden of government; level of government intervention; monetary policy; financial liberalization; banking and finance policies; labor market policies; enforcement of property rights; business, labor, and environmental regulations; and size of the black market. In other words, minimum-wage laws, environmental regulations, or requirements for transparency in corporate accounting make a country less free, whereas low business taxes, harsh debtor laws, and little or no regulation of occupational health and safety make a country more free.

Consider that the index docks the United States' ranking for passing Sarbanes-Oxley, a law that seeks to improve corporate accounting practices and to make CEOs responsible for their corporations' profit reports. The segment of the U.S. population whose economic freedom this law erodes is tiny, but it's obviously that segment—not workers and not even shareholders—whose freedom counts for the folks at the *Journal* and at Heritage.

The rather objective-looking list that results from assessing the ten components ranks 155 countries from freest (Hong Kong and Singapore) to most repressive (Burma and North Korea). The index then becomes a tool its authors can use to hammer home their message: economic freedom (as they define it) brings prosperity. As they point out, "the freest economies have a per-capita income more than twice that of the 'mostly free' and more than four times that of the 'mostly unfree.'"

Not so fast. For one thing, the index's creators used some oddball methods that compromise its linkage of prosperity to economic freedom.

For instance, according to the index, the fiscal burden of the Swedish and Danish welfare states is smaller than that of the United States, even though U.S. government spending is more than 20 percentage points lower relative to Gross Domestic Product (GDP, or the size of the economy). This bizarre result comes about because the index uses the change in government spending, not its actual level, to calculate fiscal burden.

To measure the tax side of a country's fiscal burden, the index uses the top rate of the personal and corporate income taxes—and that's equally misleading. Besides ignoring the burden of other taxes, these two figures don't get at *effective* tax rates, which also depend on what share of corporate profits and personal income is actually taxed. On paper, U.S. corporate tax rates are higher than those in Europe, as the *Journal* is quick to point out. But nearly half of U.S. corporate profits go untaxed. The average rate of taxation on U.S. corporate profits currently stands at 15%, far below the top corporate tax rate of 35%. And relative to GDP, U.S. corporate income taxes are no more than half those of other OECD countries.

The index's treatment of government intervention is flawed as well, for it fails to count industrial policy as a form of intervention. This is a serious mistake: it means that the index overestimates the degree to which some of the fastest growing economies of the last few decades, such as in Taiwan and South Korea, relied on the market and underestimates the positive role that government played in directing economic development in those countries by guiding investment and protecting infant industries.

The treatment of informal markets is downright strange. The index considers a large informal sector to indicate less economic freedom because government restrictions must have driven that economic activity underground. (Of course, you could take the opposite view: since the informal sector is for the most part unregulated, countries with larger informal sectors are, by the index's definition, more free!) But this way of looking at it biases the index. Developing countries tend to have large informal sectors while developed economies usually have small informal sectors. That means the index systematically lowers the economic freedom index of developing countries while boosting the scores of developed countries, thus artificially correlating income levels with economic freedom. Even right-wing economist Stefan Karlsson of the libertarian Ludwig Von Mises Institute has criticized the index on this point. Thanks in part to this bias, Estonia, Chile, and Bahrain are the only middle-income countries to make it into the top 20.

Whatever the biases in the index do to cement a tight relationship between economic freedom and income, they can't produce a tight correlation between economic freedom and *growth*. The fastest-growing countries are mostly unfree. Take China, India, and Vietnam, three of the fastest-growing countries in the world. They are way down in the rankings, at #112, #118, and #137 respectively. While all three countries have adopted market reforms in recent years that have improved their standing in the index, their trade policies and regulations remain "repressive." And there are plenty of relatively slow growers among the countries high up in the index, including Estonia (#4), the *Journal*'s poster child for economic freedom. How free or unfree a country is according to the index seems to have little to do with how quickly it grows.

An "Index of Economic Freedom" that tells us little about economic growth or political freedom is a slipshod measure that would seem to have no other purpose other than to sell the neoliberal policies that stand in the way of most people gaining control over their economic lives and obtaining genuine economic freedom in today's global economy. ❑

Sources: Mary Anastasia O'Grady, "Hail Estonia!" *Wall Street Journal*, January 4, 2005; *The 2005 Index of Economic Freedom*, Heritage Foundation, 2005; Johan Fernandez, "Malaysia climbs up economic freedom index," *The Star Online*, January 25, 2005; "Freedom & Growth: No Siamese twins," *The Economic Times*, May 27, 2002; Robert Kuttner, "A Weird Set of Values," *The American Prospect*, December 7, 1997; Stefan M. I. Karlsson, "The Failings of the Economic Freedom Index," Ludwig Von Mises Institute, January 21, 2005; "Freedom in the World 2005: Civic Power and Electoral Politics," Freedom House, 2005, freedomhouse.org.

Article 1.4

THE WORLD IS NOT FLAT

How Thomas Friedman gets it wrong about globalization.

BY MARK ENGLER

May 2008

Turn on the TV and flip to a C-SPAN or CNN discussion of the global economy and you are likely to spot the square head and mustachioed face of *New York Times* columnist Thomas Friedman, who will probably be expressing enthusiasm for the business world's newest high-tech innovations. With his best-selling book *The Lexus and the Olive Tree*, Friedman stepped forward in the late 1990s as a leading cheerleader of neoliberal globalization. Then, in the wake of 9/11, he made common cause with White House militarists. He became a high-profile "liberal hawk" and supported the war in Iraq—only to distance himself later in the Bush era and return to championing corporate expansion with a second widely read book on globalization, *The World Is Flat*. For better or for worse, his punditry provides an indispensable guide to how mainstream commentators have tried to defend neoliberalism in the face of challenges from worldwide social movements. Moreover, Friedman's renewed emphasis on corporate globalization in the wake of the botched war in Iraq may also be a significant bellwether for how the Democratic Party—especially the more conservative "New Democrat" wing of the party—crafts a vision for international relations after Bush.

You Can't Stop the Dawn

In Friedman's view, the end of the Cold War left the world with a single, unassailable ideology. "Globalization," he wrote in *The Lexus and the Olive Tree*, "means the spread of free market capitalism to every country in the world." He saw this as an unmitigated good: "[T]he more you open your economy to free trade and competition, the more efficient and flourishing your economy will be." He marveled that "computerization, miniaturization, digitization, satellite communications, fiber optics, and the Internet" were bringing about untold wonders.

Friedman's conversion into the church of corporate expansion took place over many years. His academic training is not in economics, but in Middle Eastern studies. During the 1980s, Friedman was a respected *New York Times* correspondent in Israel and Lebanon, winning two Pulitzer Prizes for his reporting from the region. In 1994, just at the beginning of the Internet boom, he switched to a beat covering the intersection of politics and economics, and his excitement for globalization began to mount in earnest. By the time he became the *Times'* foreign affairs columnist the following year, he was perfectly positioned to evangelize about how unregulated markets and new technology were reshaping global affairs.

Aware that many people saw him as a modern-day Pangloss extolling the best of all possible worlds, Friedman contended in *The Lexus and the Olive Tree* that he was "not a salesman for globalization." But this is precisely what he was. More than any other public personality, he was responsible for portraying neoliberalism as an inevitable and laudable march of progress. "I feel about globalization a lot like I feel about the dawn," he wrote. "[E]ven if I didn't care much for the dawn there isn't much I could do about it. I didn't start globalization, I can't stop it—except at a huge cost to human development." By defining "globalization" as a broad, sweeping phenomenon—political, economic, technological, and cultural—he saw resistance as ridiculous. So when massive protests erupted at the World Trade Organization meetings in Seattle in late 1999, he disgustedly derided the demonstrators as "a Noah's ark of flat-earth advocates, protectionist trade unions and yuppies looking for their 1960s fix."

You might think that the deflating of the dot-com bubble that began in March 2000 would have quelled Friedman's fervor, but you would be wrong. In Friedman's view, the end of the 1990s boom only led to more advancement. "[T]he dot-com bust," he later wrote, "actually drove globalization into hypermode by forcing companies to outsource and offshore more and more functions in order to save on scarce capital." Friedman's cheerleading, too, would go into "hypermode," but not before the columnist took a detour to become one of the country's most prominent liberal hawks in the wake of 9/11. When Friedman did return to the subject of economic globalization with his 2005 book, *The World Is Flat*, he was once again wowed. Over the course of just a few years, he concluded, "we entered a whole new era: Globalization 3.0."

Fueled now by wireless technology and ever-smaller microchips, this wave of capitalism was "shrinking the world from a size small to a size tiny and flattening the playing field at the same time." Hospitals in the United States were sending CT scans to India for analysis; other corporations opened bustling call centers there to handle customer service calls, training their new South Asian employees to speak in American accents; globetrotting columnists could file their stories from the middle of a golf course in China by using their Blackberries. The march of progress was back on.

Friedman is known for conveying complicated ideas through the use of colorful metaphors. Yet his metaphors consistently get so mixed and muddled as to require delicate linguistic untangling. In the course of his two books on globalization, Friedman goes from seeing the world in 3-D to, remarkably enough, seeing it in at least six dimensions. Technological advance, he tells us, has now accelerated so much that we have gone through Globalization versions 1.0 and 2.0 and entered version 3.0. Friedman presents ten "flatteners," four "steroids," and a "triple convergence," plus at least seven releases of "DOScapital." Various steroids and flatteners are meant to have multiplied globalization's effects exponentially. Journalist Matt Taibbi, who has written the most cutting analysis of Friedman's peculiar language, notes, "Friedman's book is the first I have encountered, anywhere, in which the reader needs a calculator to figure the value of the author's metaphors."

If ever Orwell's warnings that "the slovenliness of our language makes it easier for us to have foolish thoughts" and that the world's "present political chaos is connected with the decay of language" apply to anyone, they apply to Friedman. The connection between Friedman's hazy writing and his suspect conclusions about the global economy shows up in the very premise of his second book on globalization. During a meeting between Friedman and Nandan Nilekani in Bangalore, the Infosys CEO offers that "the playing field is being leveled." For Friedman, the tired cliché is a revelation. He mulls it over for hours and then, suddenly, decides: "My God, he's telling me the world is flat!"

Now, it is quite a stretch to take a routine sports metaphor and superimpose it on the globe; there could be few worse metaphors for talking about a global system that is more integrated and networked than ever before. "Friedman is a person who not only speaks in malapropisms, he also hears malapropisms," Taibbi argues. Nilekani off-handedly mentions a level field and Friedman attributes to him the radical idea of a flat world. "This is the intellectual version of Far Out Space Nuts, when NASA repairman Bob Denver sets a whole sitcom in motion by pressing 'launch' instead of 'lunch' in a space capsule. And once he hits that button, the rocket takes off."

It would all be funny if it didn't mask a deeper political problem: For the world's poor, the playing field is far from level. Our world is not flat.

Putting on Reagan's Jacket

With the ideology of neoliberalism steadily losing ground in international discussion, it is important to see how a leading apologist mounts a defense. In Friedman's case, he does so by holding on to dogmatic assumptions, training his sights on high technology, conducting his interviews largely within the insular world of jet-setting corporate elites, and ignoring a world of evidence that would contradict his selective viewpoint.

Some reviewers have applauded Friedman for acknowledging negative aspects of globalization in his books. But for Friedman, this does not mean looking at the realities of exploitation or environmental destruction that have resulted from corporate expansion. Instead, his caveats boil down to two points: that terrorists, too, can use the Internet, and that many countries, especially in "unflat" Africa, are too backward to read the signs that would put them on the high tech, "free trade" superhighway to prosperity. With regard to the latter, it's not that anything is wrong really, only that the process has not gone far enough and fast enough for everyone to benefit yet.

Needless to say, Friedman's is hardly a biting exposé. In fact, it is virtually impossible to find any evidence that might make him skeptical about the fundamental greatness of corporate globalization. In 1999, even *BusinessWeek* argued "The Asian financial crisis of 1997–99 shows that unfettered liberalization of capital markets without proper regulation can lead the world to the brink of disaster." But for Friedman this crisis, too, was all for the best. He writes, "I believe globalization did us all a favor by melting down the economies of Thailand, Korea, Malaysia, Indonesia, Mexico, Russia and Brazil in the 1990s, because it laid bare a lot of the rotten practices and institutions in countries that had prematurely globalized." He slams the countries for corruption and cronyism, suggesting that they deserved their fates. But by "prematurely globalized" he does not mean that these countries should have been more cautious about linking their fates to speculative international markets. Rather, he believes that they had not done enough to "reduce the role of government" and "let markets more freely allocate resources." Friedman's solution to the dangers of unregulated markets is more deregulation, the remedy for the excesses of unfettered capitalism is even more excess. The argument is airtight.

Missing from this account, of course, is any sense of the social impact of the Asian crisis. In the end, wealthy foreign investors were bailed out by the International Monetary Fund and lost little. The real losers were an untold number of middle-class families in places like Thailand and Korea whose savings were wiped out overnight, as well as the poor in places like Indonesia who went hungry when the government cut food subsidies. It takes a very twisted viewpoint to say that the Asian financial crisis did these people a favor.

Friedman holds that the Internet age has created a "flat" world with opportunity for all. Yet he freely admits that the system he describes is founded on the Reagan-Thatcher model of extreme, "trickle down" neoliberalism—one of the most unequal methods of distributing social goods ever devised. Friedman writes: "Thatcher and Reagan combined to strip huge chunks of economic decision-making power from the state, from the advocates of the Great Society and from traditional Keynesian economics, and hand them over to the free market." Countries now have one choice for economic policy: neoliberalism. They must radically deregulate and privatize their economies. Friedman calls this the "Golden Straitjacket." It's "golden" because the model supposedly creates widespread affluence. But it's a "straitjacket" because it radically constricts democracy. Sounding a lot like Ralph Nader, Friedman writes:

Once your country puts [the Golden Straitjacket] on, its political choices get reduced to Pepsi or Coke—to slight nuances of taste, slight nuances of policy, slight alterations in design ... but never any major deviation from the core golden rules. Governments—be they led by Democrats or Republicans, Conservatives or Labourites, Gaullists or Socialists, Christian Democrats or Social Democrats—that deviate too far away from the core rules will see their investors stampede away, interest rates rise, and stock market valuations fall.

The difference between Friedman and Nader is that the *New York Times* columnist approves of this situation. He does not condemn it as an assault on democracy; he says it's just the way things are. Of the Democrats, he writes, "Mr. Clinton effectively kidnapped the Democratic Party ... moved it into the Republican economic agenda—including free trade, NAFTA and the WTO for China—while holding onto much of the Democrats' social agenda." Any Democrat who would try to move it back meets Friedman's wrath. In the new global age, all those to the left of Ronald Reagan on economic policy are simply out of luck.

Sitting On Top Of The World

Friedman's contention that everyone benefits when countries bind themselves into market fundamentalism is based less on a careful review of the evidence than on blind faith. In July of 2006, he made a startling admission during a CNBC interview with Tim Russert. He said:

> We got this free market, and I admit, I was speaking out in Minnesota—my hometown, in fact, and a guy stood up in the audience, said, "Mr. Friedman, is there any free trade agreement you'd oppose?" I said, "No, absolutely not." I said, "You know what, sir? I wrote a column supporting the CAFTA, the Caribbean Free Trade initiative. I didn't even know what was in it. I just knew two words: free trade."

That a nationally prominent columnist would gloat about such ignorance is a sad statement about the health of our political debate. "Free trade" is an incredibly politicized phrase, with little concrete meaning. For instance, CAFTA (which actually stands for the *Central American* Free Trade Agreement) includes provisions designed to protect the monopoly rights of giant pharmaceutical companies rather than to create "free" commerce.

But the larger point is that neoliberal globalization does not make winners of everyone. Its global track record for producing GDP growth is dismal. In fact, its main accomplishment may be to produce inequality. And Friedman's own position amid this global divide is telling. He regularly represents himself as just an average guy from Minnesota trying to make sense of the world. The real picture is far from average. In July 2006, *Washingtonian* magazine reported that in the 1970s Friedman married into one of the 100 richest families in the United States—the Bucksbaums—who have amassed a fortune worth some $2.7 billion, with origins in real estate development. The magazine noted that he lives in "a palatial 11,400-square-foot house, now valued at $9.3 million, on a 7.5-acre parcel just blocks from I-495 and the Bethesda Country Club." Given that the über-rich, those with huge stock portfolios and investments in multinational corporations, have benefited tremendously from corporate globalization, commentators like David Sirota have suggested that Friedman's vast wealth represents an undisclosed conflict of interest in his journalism. It is as if multimillionaire Richard Mellon Scaife were to write about the repeal of the estate tax without disclosing that he stands to profit handsomely from such a policy change.

Whether or not that is the case, Friedman's position at the very pinnacle of global prosperity is certainly reflected in his view of the world. In a telling admission, he relates in *The Lexus and the Olive Tree* that his "best intellectual sources" about globalization are hedge fund managers. Hedge funds are elite, largely unregulated investment pools that handle money for individuals of extremely high net worth. Their managers are among the highest paid individuals in the United States.

In 2006, the top 25 hedge fund managers in the country made in excess of $240 million each. This means they each pulled in $27,000 per hour, 24 hours per day, whether waking or sleeping, whether at the office or teeing off on the ninth hole. Corporate CEOs and hedge fund managers may indeed be well informed about certain aspects of the global economy. But if that is where you get your information, you end up with a very partial view of the world. You get the winner's view.

In an eloquent critique of *The World Is Flat*, Indian eco-feminist Vandana Shiva writes:

> Friedman has reduced the world to the friends he visits, the CEOs he knows, and the golf courses he plays at. From this microcosm of privilege, exclusion, blindness, he shuts out both the beauty of diversity and the brutality of exploitation and inequality …
>
> That is why he talks of 550 million Indian youth overtaking Americans in a flat world, when the entire information technology/outsourcing sector in India employs only a million out of 1.2 billion people. Food and farming, textiles and clothing, health and education are nowhere in Friedman's monoculture of mind locked into IT. Friedman presents a 0.1% picture and hides 99.9%. … In the eclipsed 99.9% are the 25 million women who disappeared in high growth areas of India because a commodified world has rendered women a dispensable sex. In the hidden 99.9% … are thousands of tribal children in Orissa, Maharashtra, Rajasthan who died of hunger because the public distribution system for food has been dismantled to create markets for agribusiness.

A Race to the Top?

The corporate globalization that Friedman champions has alarming changes in store not just for the poor of the global South, but also for working people in the United States and Europe. One of the things that Friedman particularly lauds about Reagan and Thatcher is their success in breaking unions. He writes: "it may turn out that one of the key turning points in American history, going into the millennium, was Ronald Reagan's decision to fire all the striking air traffic controllers in 1981." "No single event," he notes with satisfaction, "did more to alter the balance of power between management and workers." Everyone wins from this, he argues, since "[t]he easier it is to fire workers, the more incentive employers have to hire them." Because America busted its unions and Western European countries did not, he contends, the United States developed a more dynamic economy.

What Friedman fails to note is that real wages for working people in the United States have been largely stagnant since the early 1970s, while working hours have skyrocketed. When compared with workers in Western Europe, the average American works 350 hours more per year, the equivalent of nine extra weeks. A study by the International Labor Organization reported that in 2000 the average U.S. worker put in 199 more hours than in 1973. Dramatizing such realities, a group of union and nonprofit activists now observe "Take Back Your Time Day" every October 24. On that day, if the U.S. workload were on par with the rest of the industrialized world, Americans would have the rest of the year off.

Friedman utters not a word of protest about the trend toward more work; in fact, he celebrates it. He argues that European social democracies are obsolete, even though they are successful capitalist countries. These nations are running on the wrong version of "DOScapital," Friedman contends, and need to shift to U.S. standards. Never mind that economies like Sweden's have performed very well over the past decade, all while maintaining a much higher quality of life for their citizens.

He has a special hatred for the French, who, he writes, "are trying to preserve a 35-hour work week in a world where Indian engineers are ready to work a 35-hour day." In what he calls a "race to the top," Friedman predicts a turbulent decade for Western Europe, as aging, inflexible economies—which have grown used to six-week vacations and unemployment insurance that is almost as good as having a job—become more intimately integrated with Eastern Europe, India and China in a flattening world. … The dirty little secret is that India is taking work from Europe or America not simply because of low wages. It is also because Indians are ready to work harder and can do anything from answering your phone to designing your next airplane or car. They are not racing us to the bottom. They are racing us to the top. … Yes, this is a bad time for France and friends to lose their appetite for hard work—just when India, China and Poland are rediscovering theirs.

It is unclear what Friedman sees as getting to the "top" if paid vacations, unemployment insurance, and retirement—benefits traditionally regarded as signs of a civilized economy—must be sacrificed. But, Friedman tells us, that is the new reality.

Ultimately, the "race to the top" is another of Friedman's botched metaphors. In the long-standing progressive argument that corporate globalization creates a "race to the bottom," it is not Indian or Chinese workers who are doing the racing at all. It's capital. Deregulation allows corporations to wander the globe in search of ever lower wages and laxer environmental standards. The moment workers stand up for their rights, refusing to tolerate a "35-hour day," a company can pick up and move elsewhere. The governments that might curb such abuses are in straitjackets. The unions that workers might have organized themselves into have been busted. All Friedman can offer is this cryptic and seemingly masochistic advice: "When the world goes flat—and you are feeling flattened—reach for a shovel and dig into yourself. Don't try to build walls."

Globalization from Below

An interesting aspect of Friedman's renewed focus on corporate globalization at the end of the Bush era is that governments and international financial institutions have faded from his picture of the integrating world. Even corporations are becoming less relevant. In his view, the new era of "Globalization 3.0" is all about *individuals*. Today, it is up to all people to pull themselves up by their bootstraps. He writes, "every person now must, and can, ask: Where do *I* as an individual fit into the global competition and opportunities of the day, and how can *I*, on my own, collaborate with others globally?"

Conveniently enough, accepting this idea makes it impossible to oppose neoliberalism. In a world of extreme individualism, no one in particular is responsible for setting the rules of the world order. It is pointless to protest governments or international financial institutions. Globalization is unstoppable because people want it.

These arguments are not new. With scant evidence, Friedman has long claimed that there is a "groundswell" of people throughout the developing world demanding corporate globalization. Of course, the massive protests of the past decade would seem to contradict his assertion. But he does not see this as a problem. He dismisses global justice activism by arguing, "from its origins, the movement that emerged in Seattle was primarily a Western-driven phenomenon." The backlash that does exist in poorer countries, he argues, is not rational politics but simple lawlessness: "what we have been seeing in many countries, instead of popular mass opposition to globalization, is wave after wave of crime—people just grabbing what they need, weaving their own social safety nets and not worrying about the theory or the ideology." In the end, Friedman seems ideologically incapable of accepting that people in the global South could organize their own movements or articulate a coherent politics of resistance.

Today, with much of the world in open rebellion against neoliberalism, this fiction is getting harder and harder to maintain. That Friedman has perpetually failed to spot the vibrant network of grassroots organizations that has built a worldwide campaign against the Washington Consensus is not a sign of widespread support for corporate globalization. It is an indictment of his reporting. Well before Seattle, there had been protests of millions of people throughout the global South against the "Golden Straitjacket."

These have continued into the new millennium. In their book *Globalization from Below*, Jeremy Brecher, Tim Costello, and Brendan Smith note that in just a two-month period, in May and June of 2000, there were six general strikes against the impact of neoliberalism. In India, as many as 20 million farmers and workers struck, protesting their government's involvement with the WTO and the IMF. Twelve million Argentineans went on strike in response to fiscal austerity policies imposed by the IMF. Nigeria was paralyzed by strikes against neoliberal price hikes on fuel. South Koreans demanded a shorter workweek and the full protection of part-time and temporary employees by the country's labor laws. Finally, general strikes in South Africa and Uruguay protested increasing unemployment rates, which resulted from IMF austerity policies. All of these escaped Friedman's notice.

In truth, they are only suggestions of wider resistance. The people of Latin America have certainly not joined the groundswell of support for neoliberal ideology. In country after country they have ousted conservative governments since 2000 and elected more progressive leaders, redrawing the region's political map. The columnist has yet to comment.

There is a way in which Friedman perfectly matches the politics of our times. "Like George Bush, he's in the reality-making business," Matt Taibbi argues. "You no longer have to worry about actually convincing anyone; the process ends when you make the case. Things are true because you say they are. The only thing that matters is how sure you sound when you say it."

As much as he might resemble Bush in this respect, however, Friedman also tells us something important about the post-Bush moment. As a new administration takes over, an increasing number of politicians will seek to move the United States away from the aggressive militarism of imperial globalization and back toward a softer approach to ruling the world. Following Friedman, many will look to revitalize corporate globalization as a model for international affairs. These "New Democrats" will promise a fresh approach to foreign affairs. But really, they will return to something old: a Clintonian model of corporate globalization. Like Friedman, many will proclaim it as the best of all possible worlds, a global order both exciting and unavoidable. It will be up to the world's citizens to demand something better. ❑

Sources: By Thomas Friedman: *The Lexus and the Olive Tree: Understanding Globalization* (Anchor Books, 2000); *The World Is Flat* (Farrar, Straus & Giroux, 2005); "Senseless in Seattle," *New York Times*, December 1, 1999; "Senseless in Seattle II," *New York Times*, December 8, 1999; "A Race To The Top," *New York Times*, June 3, 2005. Other sources: Matt Taibbi, "Flathead: The peculiar genius of Thomas L. Friedman," *New York Press*, April 27, 2005; "The Lessons of Seattle," *BusinessWeek*, December 13, 1999; Robin Broad and John Cavanagh, "The Hijacking of the Development Debate: How Friedman and Sachs Got It Wrong," *World Policy Journal*, Summer 2006; David Sirota, "Caught on Tape: Tom Friedman's Truly Shocking Admission," SirotaBlog, July 24, 2006; Garrett M. Graff, "Thomas Friedman is On Top of the World," *The Washingtonian*, July 2006; David Sirota, "Billionaire Scion Tom Friedman," DailyKos, July 31, 2006; Roger Lowenstein, "The Inequality Conundrum," *New York Times Magazine*, June 10, 2007; Vandana Shiva, "The Polarised World Of Globalisation," ZNet, May 27, 2005; Jeremy Brecher et al., *Globalization from Below* (South End Press, 2000).

Chapter 2

CORPORATE POWER AND THE GLOBAL ECONOMY

Article 2.1

U.S. BANKS AND THE DIRTY MONEY EMPIRE

BY JAMES PETRAS
September/October 2001

Washington and the mass media have portrayed the United States as being in the forefront of the struggle against narcotics trafficking, drug-money laundering, and political corruption. The image is of clean white hands fighting dirty money from the Third World (or the ex-Communist countries). The truth is exactly the opposite. U.S. banks have developed an elaborate set of policies for transferring illicit funds to the United States and "laundering" those funds by investing them in legitimate businesses or U.S. government bonds. The U.S. Congress has held numerous hearings, provided detailed exposés of the illicit practices of the banks, passed several anti-laundering laws, and called for stiffer enforcement by public regulators and private bankers. Yet the biggest banks continue their practices and the sums of dirty money grow exponentially. The $500 billion of criminal and dirty money flowing annually into and through the major U.S. banks far exceeds the net revenues of all the information technology companies in the United States. These yearly inflows surpass the net profits repatriated from abroad by the major U.S. oil producers, military industries, and airplane manufacturers combined. Neither the banks nor the government have the will or the interest to put an end to practices that provide such high profits and help maintain U.S. economic supremacy internationally.

Big U.S. Banks and Dirty Money Laundering

"Current estimates are that $500 billion to $1 trillion in illegal funds from organized crime, narcotics trafficking and other criminal misconduct are laundered
through banks worldwide each year," according to Senator Carl Levin (D-Mich.),
"with about half going through U.S. banks." The senator's statement, however, only
covers proceeds from activities that are crimes under U.S. law. It does not include
financial transfers by corrupt political leaders or tax evasion by overseas businesses,
since in those cases any criminal activity takes place outside the United States.
Raymond Baker, a leading U.S. expert on international finance and guest scholar in
economic studies at the Brookings Institution, estimates the total "flow of corrupt
money ... into Western coffers" from Third World or ex-Communist economies at
$20 to $40 billion a year. He puts the "flow stemming from mis-priced trade" (the
difference between the price quoted, for tax purposes, of goods sold abroad, and
their real price) at a minimum of $80 billion a year. "My lowest estimate is $100
billion per year by these two means ... a trillion dollars in the decade, at least half
to the United States," Baker concludes. "Including other elements of illegal flight
capital would produce much higher figures."

The money laundering business, whether "criminal" or "corrupt," is carried out
by the United States' most important banks. The bank officials involved in money
laundering have backing from the highest levels of the banking institutions. These
are not isolated offenses perpetrated by loose cannons. Take the case of Citibank's
laundering of Raúl Salinas' $200 million account. The day after Salinas, the brother
of Mexico's ex-President Carlos Salinas de Gortari, was arrested and his large-scale
theft of government funds was exposed, his private bank manager at Citibank, Amy
Elliott, said in a phone conversation with colleagues (the transcript of which was
made available to Congressional investigators) that "this goes [on] in the very, very
top of the corporation, this was known ... on the very top. We are little pawns in
this whole thing."

Citibank is the United States' biggest bank, with 180,000 employees worldwide, operating in 100 countries, with $700 billion in known assets. It operates
what are known as "private banking" offices in 30 countries, with over $100 billion
in client assets. Private banking is the sector of a bank which caters to extremely
wealthy clients, with deposits of $1 million or more. The big banks charge custom-
ers for managing their assets and for providing the specialized services of the private
banks. These services go beyond routine banking services like check clearing and
deposits, to include investment guidance, estate planning, tax assistance, off-shore
accounts, and complicated schemes designed to secure the confidentiality of financial transactions. Private banks sell secrecy to their clients, making them ideal for
money laundering. They routinely use code names for accounts. Their "concentration accounts" disguise the movement of client funds by co-mingling them with
bank funds, cutting off paper trails for billions of dollars in wire transfers. And they
locate offshore private investment corporations in countries such as the Cayman

Islands and the Bahamas, which have strict banking secrecy laws. These laws allow offshore banks and corporations to hide a depositor's name, nationality, the amount of funds deposited, and when they were deposited. They do not require any declarations from bank officials about sources of funds.

Private investment corporations (PICs) are one particulary tricky way that big banks hold and hide a client's assets. The nominal officers, trustees, and shareholders of these shell corporations are themselves shell corporations controlled by the private bank. The PIC then becomes the official holder of the client's accounts, while the client's identity is buried in so-called "records of jurisdiction" in countries with strict secrecy laws. The big banks keep pre-packaged PICs on the shelf awaiting activation when a private bank client wants one. The system works like Russian matryoshka dolls, shells within shells within shells, which in the end can be impenetrable to the legal process.

Hearings held in 1999 by the Senate's Permanent Subcommittee on Investigations (under the Governmental Affairs Committee) revealed that in the Salinas case, private banking personnel at Citibank—which has a larger global private banking operation than any other U.S. bank—helped Salinas transfer $90 to $100 million out of Mexico while disguising the funds' sources and destination. The bank set up a dummy offshore corporation, provided Salinas with a secret codename, provided an alias for a third party intermediary who deposited the money in a Citibank account in Mexico, transferred the money in a concentration account to New York, and finally moved it to Switzerland and London.

Instead of an account with the name "Raúl Salinas" attached, investigators found a Cayman Islands account held by a PIC called "Trocca, Ltd.," according to Minority Counsel Robert L. Roach of the Permanent Committee on Investigations. Three Panama shell companies formed Trocca, Ltd.'s board of directors and three Cayman shell companies were its officers and shareholders. "Citibank controls all six of these shell companies and routinely uses them to function as directors and officers of PICs that it makes available to private clients," says Roach. Salinas was only referred to in Citibank documents as "Confidential Client No. 2" or "CC-2."

Historically, big-bank money laundering has been investigated, audited, criticized, and subjected to legislation. The banks have written their own compliance procedures. But the big banks ignore the laws and procedures, and the government ignores their non-compliance. The Permanent Subcommittee on Investigations discovered that Citibank provided "services," moving a total of at least $360 million, for four major political swindlers, all of whom lost their protection when the political winds shifted in their home countries: Raúl Salinas, between $80 and $100 million; Asif Ali Zardari (husband of former Prime Minister of Pakistan), over $40 million; El Hadj Omar Bongo (dictator of Gabon since 1967), over $130 million; Mohammed, Ibrahim, and Abba Sani Abacha (sons of former Nigerian dictator General Sani Abacha), over $110 million. In all cases Citibank violated all of its own procedures and government guidelines: there was no review of the client's background (known as the "client profile"), no determination of the source of the funds, and no inquiry into any violations of the laws of the country where the money originated. On the contrary, the bank facilitated the outflow in its prepackaged format: shell corporations were established, code names were provided, funds were moved through concentration accounts, and the funds were invested in legitimate businesses or in U.S. bonds. In none of these cases did the banks practice "due diligence," taking the steps required by law to ensure that they do not facilitate money laundering. Yet top banking officials have never been brought to court and tried. Even after the arrest of its clients, Citibank continued to provide them with its services, including moving funds to secret accounts.

Another route that the big banks use to launder dirty money is "correspondent banking." Correspondent banking is the provision of banking services by one bank to another. It enables overseas banks to conduct business and provide services for their customers in jurisdictions where the bank has no physical presence. A bank that is licensed in a foreign country and has no office in the United States can use correspondent banking to attract and retain wealthy criminal or corrupt clients interested in laundering money in the United States. Instead of exposing itself to U.S. controls and incurring the high costs of locating in the U.S., the bank will open a correspondent account with an existing U.S. bank. By establishing such a relationship, the foreign bank (called the "respondent") and its customers can receive many or all of the services offered by the U.S. bank (called the "correspondent"). Today, all the big U.S. banks have established multiple correspondent relationships throughout the world so they may engage in international financial transactions for themselves and their clients in places where they do not have a physical presence. The largest U.S. and European banks, located in financial centers like New York or London, serve as correspondents for thousands of other banks. Most of the offshore banks laundering billions for criminal clients have accounts in the United States. Through June 1999, the top five correspondent bank holding companies in the United States held correspondent account balances exceeding $17 billion; the total correspondent balances of the 75 largest U.S. correspondent banks was $34.9 billion. For billionaire criminals an important feature of correspondent relationships is that they provide access to international transfer systems. The biggest banks specializing in international fund transfers (called "money center banks") can process up to $1 trillion in wire transfers a day.

The Damage Done

Hundreds of billions of dollars have been transferred, through the private-banking and correspondent-banking systems, from Africa, Asia, Latin America, and Eastern Europe to the biggest banks in the United States and Europe. In all these regions, liberalization and privatization of the economy have opened up lucrative opportunities for corruption and the easy movement of booty overseas. Authoritarian governments and close ties to Washington, meanwhile, have ensured impunity for most of the guilty parties. Russia alone has seen over $200 billion illegally transferred out of the country in the course of the 1990s. The massive flows of capital out of these regions—really the pillaging of these countries' wealth through the international banking system—is a major factor in their economic instability and mass impoverishment. The resulting economic crises, in turn, have made these countries more vulnerable to the prescriptions of the International Monetary Fund and the World Bank, including liberalized banking and financial systems that lead to further capital flight.

Even by an incomplete accounting (including both "criminal" and "corrupt" funds, but not other illicit capital transfers, such as illegal shifts of real estate or securities titles, wire fraud, etc.), the dirty money coming from abroad into U.S. banks amounted to $3.5 to $6.0 trillion during the 1990s. While this is not the whole picture, it gives us a basis for estimating the significance of the "dirty money factor" in the U.S. economy. The United States currently runs an annual trade deficit of over $400 billion. The gap has to be financed with inflows of funds from abroad—at least a third of which is "dirty money." Without the dirty money the U.S. economy's external accounts would be unsustainable. No wonder the biggest banks in the United States and Europe are actively involved, and the governments of these countries turn a blind eye. That is today's capitalism—built around pillage, criminality, corruption, and complicity. ❑

Sources: "Private Banking and Money Laundering: A Case Study of Opportunities and Vulnerabilities," Permanent Subcommittee on Investigations of the Committee on Governmental Affairs, United States Senate, One Hundred Sixth Congress, November 9-10, 2000; "Report on Correspondent Banking: A Gateway to Money Laundering," Minority Staff of the U.S. Senate Permanent Subcommittee on Investigations, February 2001.

Article 2.2

ENRON IN THE THIRD WORLD

BY THE INSTITUTE FOR POLICY STUDIES
July/August 2002, excerpted October 2003

The Institute for Policy Studies' (IPS) 2002 report, Enron's Pawns: How Public Institutions Bankrolled Enron's Globalization Game, *documents the extent to which Enron's ascendancy depended on public-sector financial assistance and governmental support for energy privatization policies worldwide. Since 1992, the U.S. government, the World Bank, and other government institutions have approved $7.2 billion in public financing for Enron's activities in 29 countries, with U.S. support totaling over $4 billion. These public actors also leveraged Enron's rise by actively promoting the deregulation of developing countries' energy sectors. The devastating consequences for these nations have included price hikes and blackouts more severe than California's and leading on numerous occasions to street rioting and state repression—and sometimes to protesters' deaths.*

The IPS report highlights Enron's misadventures in seven countries while detailing the role of public institutions in the company's activities in the United States and abroad. The excerpts below present the study's key findings and outline the efforts of the World Bank and Enron to forge a common agenda.

The full report can be found on IPS' Sustainable Energy and Economy Network website www.seen.org.

Many public officials have described Enron's demise as the product of corporate misbehavior. This perspective ignores a vital fact: Enron would not have scaled such grand global heights, nor fallen so dramatically, without its close financial relationships with government agencies.

Since 1992, at least 21 agencies, representing the U.S. government, multilateral development banks, and other national governments, helped leverage Enron's global reach by approving $7.219 billion in public financing toward 38 projects in 29 countries.

The now-fallen giant, until recently the country's seventh largest corporation, marched into risky projects abroad, backed by the "deep pockets" of government financing and with the firm, and at times forceful, assistance of U.S. officials and their counterparts in international organizations. Enron's overseas operations rewarded shareholders temporarily but often punished the people and governments of foreign countries with price hikes and blackouts worse than what California suffered in 2001, causing social unrest and riots that were sometimes brutally repressed. For example:

- In the Dominican Republic, eight people were killed when police were brought in to quell riots after blackouts lasting up to 20 hours followed a power price hike that Enron and other private firms initiated. The local population was further enraged by allegations that a local affiliate of Arthur Andersen had undervalued the newly privatized utility by almost $1 billion, reaping enormous profits for Enron.

- In India, police hired by the power consortium of which Enron was a part beat non-violent protesters who challenged the $30 billion agreement—the largest deal in Indian history—struck between local politicians and Enron.

- The president of Guatemala tried to dissolve the Congress and declare martial law after rioting ensued, following a price hike that the government deemed necessary after selling the power sector to Enron.

- In Panama, the man who negotiated the asking price for Enron's stake in power production was the brother-in-law of the head of the country's state-owned power company. Rioting followed suspicions of corruption, Enron's price hikes, and power outages.

- In Colombia, two politicians resigned amid accusations that one was trying to push a cut-rate deal for Enron on the state-owned power company.

While all this was occurring, the U.S. government and other public agencies continued to advocate on Enron's behalf, threatening poor countries like Mozambique with an end to aid if they did not accept Enron's bid on a natural gas field. So linked was Enron with the U.S. government in many people's minds that they assumed, as the late Croatian strongman Franjo Tjudman did, that pleasing Enron meant pleasing the White House. For Tjudman, he hoped that compliance with an overpriced Enron contract might parlay into an array of political favors, from softer treatment at The Hague's War Crimes Tribunal to the entry of his country into the World Trade Organization.

Only when Enron's scandals began to affect Americans did these same government officials and institutions hold the corporation at arm's length. And only when Enron leadership revealed its greed on home turf did it become the biggest corporate scandal in recent U.S. history.

The World Bank, India, and Enron in the 1990s

The history of the United States' experiments with power and energy supplies over the past century has proven that public, regulated power utilities tend to provide both cheaper and more reliable service than their private counterparts. Unregulated utilities not only tend to impose higher prices on household consumers; they also strip away transparency, accountability, and citizen oversight from their operations. Deregulation has proven disastrous in the United States—with the California energy crisis costing the state billions of dollars.

Nevertheless, in 1991, India was willing to take desperate measures to attract foreign investors. Capital was fleeing the country, while foreign exchange reserves were low. The World Bank's largest client at the time, India was getting heavy pressure from the lender to change its policies and allow private capital into certain sectors, particularly its petroleum sector. Prime Minister Narasimha Rao decided to bow to World Bank pressure and allowed foreign direct investment into the country after decades of economic protectionism. Power sector privatization plans drawn up by the World Bank soon followed.

It was shortly thereafter that Enron came calling. Claiming to be one of the "world's leading power companies" (though the company was only six years old and its actual production of power amounted to several hundred megawatts globally), Enron proposed to set up a natural gas power plant in the town of Dabhol, in the western Indian state of Maharashtra... The size of the Dabhol power plant, 2,500 megawatts, would more than double Enron's power production globally.

In the fine print of the memorandum of understanding Enron and General Electric signed with the Maharashtra State Electricity Board (MSEB) on June 20, 1992, was buried the fact that the MSEB would owe Enron $35 billion over the life of the contract, regardless of how much power the state consumed. This deal would have been the single largest purchase in the history of India. After learning of the deal, India's other branches of government began to object, and the squabbles began.

Meanwhile, Enron's Ken Lay and former CEO Rebecca Mark began courting the World Bank, lobbying the Bank for support of their Dabhol project in India. Though the Bank refused to support the project, citing [its] "adverse financial impact" on the MSEB, Enron succeeded in gaining financial backers at the Overseas Private Investment Corporation (OPIC), the Export-Import Bank, and elsewhere.

Lay and Mark also succeeded in garnering other favors, including a formal exchange of staff through the World Bank's Staff Exchange Program and other relationship-building exercises. At the 1996 World Bank annual meetings, NGOs [non-governmental organizations] observed, poverty and social development were not the focus of the meetings. Instead, they reported, "Special pleadings to the Annual Meeting [were] made by corporate presidents, such as Enron's Ken Lay, not by poor people or their representatives... Lay and other corporate representatives have also been pleading their case with the U.S. Congress through a task force on multilateral development banks chaired by Senator Bill Bradley and Representative John Kasich."

Though Lay gained access to top officials at the World Bank, he complained that World Bank officials were blocking guarantees for their projects. His efforts paid off here, too—with three Multilateral Investment Guarantee Agency (MIGA) guarantees in 1996, 1997 and 2001, totalling $80 million, for its power projects in Hainan Island, China; East Java, Indonesia; and Bahia las Minas, Panama.

However, the East Java project, joined at the hip with Suharto, shared the ruler's demise. Enron then filed the first-ever claim to MIGA. In 2000, MIGA paid Enron $15 million for its political risk insurance claim on the cancelled East Java 500-megawatt power plant in Indonesia. MIGA demanded—and received last year—reimbursement from the new Indonesian government, citing the dictates of "international law."

While the World Bank Group—the International Bank for Reconstruction and Development, the IDA, the International Finance Corporation, and MIGA—ultimately provided less financing for Enron-related projects—$761 million for 12 projects over the last decade—than OPIC [which provided $2.62 billion], they played a key role in Enron's global reach in other ways.

Deregulation, the World Bank, and Enron

Deregulation proved to be a more indirect, but extremely helpful, way in which the World Bank advanced Enron's global agenda. Here is how it worked: The World Bank would issue loans for privatization of the energy or the power sector in a developing country or make this a condition of further loans, and Enron would be amongst the first, and often the most successful, bidders to enter the country's newly privatized or deregulated energy markets.

Enron's activities in Argentina, Bolivia, Colombia, Dominican Republic, Guatemala, Mozambique, and Panama reveal ways in which the World Bank acted as a pawn for Enron, allowing the corporation entrée into some of the poorest countries in the world. As in Dabhol, India, the changes the two institutions introduced made things worse for the poor; protests and riots—even deaths—ensued as a result. But in almost all cases, Enron came out unscathed, paying no price in the form of restricted access to future capital, despite a growing list of dubious, and controversial practices. ❑

Article 2.3

THE ECONOMICS AND POLITICS OF DEPROPRIATION IN THE OTHER COLOMBIA

BY PATRICIA M. RODRIGUEZ

November/December 2010

It has rained for days, and the swampy ocean waters that surround this community of displaced fishermen in northern Colombia rise at their own whim, flooding people's houses and making life even harder than usual. Yet most of the families living in this tiny makeshift encampment in Boca de Aracataca in the Magdalena province of Colombia have gathered under a tarp to eloquently tell a group of activists from Witness for Peace, a Washington-based social justice organization, about their problems. "[The foreign companies] kicked us out of our land. We do not have water, electricity, food, nor any help from the government... we need to be respected, we need to be treated as people, and not as animals," says Alicia Camargo, who has been displaced three times already, once very violently, along with family and neighbors.

As it turns out, the source of the problems in this community—and others nearby—is the presence of multinational corporations. In this particular case, it involves a new port expansion project along the Caribbean coast near the otherwise-idyllic city of Santa Marta. The construction of this mega-port has been funded by foreign coal companies that have operated practically unrestrictedly in Colombia for nearly 15 years. When it is finished in 2013, the port will allow U.S.-based company Drummond and Swiss-based Glencore to ship an extra 30 to 60 million tons of coal per year to global markets, in addition to the nearly 69 million tons they already export. The Colombian government allegedly receives a royalty of 10% of this total export profit, but only a handful of people see this money. A large portion of the money is never transferred to the communities that are most impoverished and environmentally affected by corporate presence. Still, foreign direct investment is embraced wholeheartedly by Colombian elites who equate corporate ventures in the agricultural, mineral, and industrial sectors with growth and prosperity.

It is not uncommon to hear about how corporations bring investment to developing countries and even their "willingness" to address problem areas such as environmental contamination and child labor practices. It is sometimes said that corporations' business practices are completely socially responsible and that corporations give back to the communities in which they operate. The media give much less attention to stories about how corporations destroy local lives, directly and indirectly. Yet it happens, and in some cases it leaves a trail of unimaginable destruction and violence. In this Caribbean region of Colombia, to talk of displacement of communities by corporations does not do justice to the reality; rather, locals speak of depropriation, or the takeover of property and livelihoods with complete impunity.

In this corner of the world, multinational corporations in the coal industry like Drummond and Glencore, and in the banana sector, like Dole and Chiquita Brands (among others), are not just operating on the basis of government-granted licenses to exploit natural resources. Through alliances with authorities, legal and otherwise, these companies have crafted what amounts to an informal ownership of the region. They own a large part of the railroads, highways, ports, and mines, and they have little concern for how communities feel about their presence there.

But what is it about the nature of these enterprises and the context in which they operate that make for such dominance, and what facilitates their exploitation of workers and communities? How have local people resisted these infractions, and to what degree, considering the widespread corruption of their political representatives? To answer both these questions, it helps to understand more about the region. Whether due to its strategic location, its natural resources, or its distance from the centers of power in the capital city, Bogotá, this region is often referred to as "the other Colombia." It is an allusion both to its potential and to its stigma as something of a no man's land.

Free Reign in the "Other Colombia"

Multinational companies began to arrive in the Magdalena and Cesar provinces in large part because the location offers such natural advantages. Surrounded in the east by the Sierra Nevada mountains, several municipalities in Magdalena province have direct access to the rivers that originate in these slopes. This makes the land well suited for banana plantations and other kinds of large-scale agriculture, and therefore for elite and corporate interests. It comes as no surprise that one of the U.S.-based companies with most presence throughout Latin America, the United Fruit Company (UFCO), operated in Magdalena since the beginning of the 20th century. As with its operations elsewhere, UFCO labor practices in Colombia were exploitative and repressive. During a strike by UFCO banana workers on December 6, 1928, in which they asked for better treatment and working conditions, an indefinite number of workers were massacred by company and police security forces in Ciénaga. The Nobel Prize-winning Colombian writer Gabriel García Márquez wrote a fictional account of this massacre in One Hundred Years of Solitude. Though UFCO left the Magdalena region in 1950s and moved to other regions of Colombia, it continued subcontracting with local growers.

In the mid to late 1980s, Chiquita Brands (formerly UFCO) and Dole rediscovered the Zona Bananera, or the Caribbean Banana Zone, at a time when local landowners had already been paying a "security fee" to rebel guerrilla groups that operated from the largely uninhabited Sierra Nevada, like the National Liberation Army (ELN). Noticing the potential for exclusive control of land and/or lucrative contracts with local large-scale banana growers, Chiquita and Dole officials negotiated economic deals with the landowners and security deals with the guerrillas. Their aim was to guarantee the companies' unrestricted access to highways and railroads leading to the coastal ports. In just a few years, however, small private security gangs began brutal confrontations with guerrillas in the mountains and the cities. Aware of their stronger firepower, the companies began to pay these small groups for protection instead of the guerrillas. By the late 1990s, these gang-style private security groups multiplied and fought each other for control of the territory (and for the substantial payments from landowners and multinational companies). A handful of gang leaders emerged victorious, and soon formed more structured paramilitary organizations like the powerful United Self-Defense Forces of Colombia (AUC). AUC and other paramilitary groups are known to have solid ties to drug lords as well as to military and high-level state authorities.

One of the AUC leaders in the Caribbean region is Rodrigo Tovar, popularly known as Jorge 40. He was a former army official and comes from one of a handful of powerful traditional families in the region. In the mid 1990s, Jorge 40 began to work under the command of the Castaño family, who founded the AUC when the patriarch Jesús Castaño was kidnapped and assassinated in the mid 1990s by another guerrilla group, the Revolutionary Armed Forces of Colombia (FARC). To garner control, Jorge 40 was known to carry out "cleansings" of local communities in Magdalena and Cesar provinces, targeting anyone suspected of ties to ELN or FARC. In 2000, after a guerrilla attack on a group of business and mafia leaders in the town of Nueva Venezia, Jorge 40 ordered the massacre of 70 people from this community. According to witnesses, the armed paramilitaries then played soccer with victims' severed heads to show the community that they were in complete control. There are several others like Jorge 40 who have ties to the different landowning families and to different companies. In 2007, Chiquita Brands admitted in federal court that it paid nearly $2 million to paramilitary death squads over a period of seven years. On its end, Drummond is currently being sued in a United States court under the Alien Tort Claims Act for having contracted paramilitary forces to kill three union leaders. The violence in the region is widespread, and largely tied to corporate interest in acquiring lands and controlling the regions' vast resources. Between 1997 and 2007, 4,000 people died and at least 500 were disappeared. Moreover, during the height of the violence in between 2003 and 2006, 43,300 families from the region suffered forced displacement from their communities.

On their end, the companies suffered no major consequences from the bloodbath, other than occasionally having to rearrange their deals with different paramilitary leaders. As long as they kept scheduled payments, the companies enjoyed complete control over vast lands. By 2002 Chiquita and Dole decided to divvy up the 10,000 hectares of land in the Zona Bananera: the medium-to-large farms that grew bananas for Dole had their main houses painted red and white, and those that grew bananas for Chiquita were painted blue and white. They also happily shared the railroad. On the other hand, small farms that for one or another reason do not have contracts with these companies have hardly survived. Many peasants have agreed to sell their lands, only to lose most of their money to criminal and paramilitary gangs that extorted them shortly after the sale. Others, out of fear, have simply never returned after their violent displacement by paramilary groups. In the near future, these corporations are likely to continue to buy lands in the region, especially with the impending passage of the free trade agreement (FTA) between the United States and Colombia. While former president Alvaro Uribe championed the push for the FTA deal with the United States, current president Juan Manuel Santos, a former defense minister and a millionaire who has solid ties to many traditional elite Colombian families, is likely to deepen the open-borders approach.

The free reign of foreign coal companies reflects a similar history. The mountainous terrain in neighboring Cesar province contains some of the biggest coal mines in Latin America. Drummond, Prodeco (a subsidiary of Glencore), and now Brazilian-owned Vale, have capitalized on this by buying part of the national railroad company Fenoco, so as to have unrestricted access to the approximately 300 miles of railroad line between the mines and the port of Ciénaga, near Santa Marta. The port installations now cover four kilometers (of a total twelve kilometers) of the coastal shores in Magdalena, but the mega-port currently under construction would extend them by another two kilometers. When the project got under way in 2008, several communities living in the swamps, or ciénaga, near the port were forcibly displaced by armed gunmen, and many ended in the encampment in Boca de Aracataca. The port expansion work has prevented the fishermen from being able to access close-by waters and they now have to fish in far away waters, if their boats are solid enough to make it there. The damage extends far beyond access. For years, the companies have been dumping millions of tons of coal onto communities where the railroad crosses, and into coastal waters. This is due to negligence, as residuals "accidentally" fall out when the coal is carried uncovered or dumped into the shipping containers. This has resulted in severe erosion and environmental contamination of local flora and fish. As if that did not suffice, Drummond was recently conceded the rights to Rio Toribio, including control over the station that supplies clean water to local communities. According to the fishermen, Drummond uses the water to wet down the coal so that it does not ignite in the containers on the way to global markets. This has generated the contamination of river water with coal dust, and has caused a variety of skin and respiratory diseases among the local population.

State Complicity

This depropriation and destruction occurs under the protective eye of the Colombian state. Though laws exist which delimit any alterations to the agro-ecological balance in much of the coastal area, the government blatantly disregards the laws. In December 2007 the national Ministry of Transportation declared that the entire municipality was a public interest zone for purposes of national development, paving the way for the expansion of the port. Though Drummond and Prodeco appear to have followed all the legal steps to begin the expansion project, the process has certainly faltered in many aspects. According to a report prepared by local community leaders, the companies and municipal authorities did not adequately consult local community groups about worrisome environmental and socio-economic effects. Though the royalties for mining concessions and banana profits by law should remain in the communities for social and infrastructural investment, a majority of this money is simply distributed privately to national and municipal authorities. As a community leader from Ciénaga states, "what we have here is a case of mafia triangulation, with companies, the central government, and local authorities keeping the municipal funds for themselves, and thereby diffusing any responsibility that they should have towards communities."

The foreign companies do as they please, with impunity. When unionized coal workers organize to demand respect for their labor rights, or to ask for appropriate paid sick time for work injuries, the companies fire them. Such is the case of Moisés Padilla, a former Drummond employee who belongs to the Sintraminergética (National Union of Industry and Energy Workers) union. He worked for 50 years as a welder (25 at Drummond), and is now incapacitated due to severe respiratory and heart conditions. The company has successfully resisted any outside intervention, despite legal efforts of the union. In a letter to Moisés Padilla, a company representative stated that it was not company policy to consent to third-party involvement, in this case a committee of independent and state officials that could evaluate his injury claims. Union workers have less and less job security, especially since the company has recently created its own union, Sintradrummond. Although the practice was previously prohibited, a recent judicial decision has opened a loophole for companies to begin organizing their own unions. Anibal Perez, another injured worker from Sintraminergética, affirms that "for us to belong to our union is considered by the state practically a crime...the state does not give us the tools and protections to make our voices heard, and the result is that we have communities full of widows, orphans, and sick workers." The union has had five of its leaders killed since 2001, and several others now live in exile after being threatened by paramilitaries.

The companies are also quick to hold on to the façade of being socially and environmentally responsible. One example: Drummond trains a certain number of people from the community to be mine workers, but rarely hires local trainees. Some think this is because it is cheaper for the company to hire migrants from other regions. Similarly, national companies like Augura (Association of Banana Workers of Colombia) organize some of their own workers in seemingly beneficial cooperatives. Though independent on paper, Augura does business strictly with Dole, and prices are arranged between top level managers from Augura and Dole. So even if cooperative workers would truly get a fair trade price for their bananas, the lack of liberty to make autonomous decisions within the company-run cooperatives is problematic at best.

Not that state intervention would do any good. For one thing, much of the state funding for social programs for local communities is channeled to the companies themselves, such as the Augura-run cooperatives. So while the state has funds that it invests in social programs, these are mostly captured by the companies.

Secondly, other state-funded social programs deliver subsidies as if community members were clients. The community at large, whether they belong to the category of low-income families, displaced families, or relatives and victims of violence, barely has access to a program that distributes about $40 every two months; most do not have enough of a connection with municipal authorities to receive even this small benefit. Thirdly, though the laws exist on paper to make the state more responsible and responsive, implementation is a problem. For instance, Colombia has had a Labor Statute since 1991, but the mechanisms for its implementation have not yet been discussed in Congress. Besides, corruption pervades the state. In 2009, a national scandal erupted over a government program aimed at helping struggling farmers, the Agro Ingreso Seguro (AIS) program. The funding (partly from the U.S. Agency for International Development) began in 2006 as part of an effort to ease concern over a potential negative impact of an impending FTA with the United States, but small farmers were not the ones benefiting; the bulk of AIS' $630 million per year was discovered to be going to rich landowners, narco-traffickers, and mobsters.

Organizing an Effective Resistance

Considering the pervasiveness of corporate interests, violence, and state complicity, what can the handful of community leaders, human rights defenders, and union workers do to organize effective resistance? The truth is that they cannot organize freely; their lives are threatened constantly. Despite the threats, is not so hard to understand why those who are still alive publicly denounce the companies, the Colombian government, and the United States for trampling on their dignity. "Our denunciations make us very public personas, and since we do not have money to pay for private security guards, speaking out publicly and internationally ironically gives us some sense of security," says Edgardo Alemán, a local human rights defender.

And so they do challenge, collectively when possible. One of the small victories of the sintramienergética union and other allied groups has been the Collective Labor Agreement signed between the union and Drummond, for the years 2010-2013. Even at quick glance, it is easy to find the voice of the workers, and their concern for community. Article 7 states that when a job opens at Drummond, the company will give preference to skilled members of the local community; upon the death of a worker, the company commits to hiring a family member of the victim. Union leaders concur that the agreement feels more like "our list of demands" than an actual commitment by Drummond representatives. Yet many insist that a more effective interaction between the communities and the companies is the only solution. "We need to guarantee a way to capture the resources, to have a social development policy that favors our communities. If we go through the politicians, we will get nothing," says local activist and economist, Luís Eduardo Rendón.

If the state's lack of responsiveness is any indication, negotiating with the companies might in fact be a viable approach. But the success of that strategy does not depend on the amount of pressure Colombian workers and community leaders exert. In this sense, the context (and place) in which they operate limits their impact. For their voice to mean anything in a system dominated by elite power in Bogotá and abroad, it will take the U.S. government and global citizens en masse to press the companies (American companies!) and the Colombian state to be honest, and to practice their activities legally, with true social responsibility. Perhaps then there can begin to be justice for these communities in the other Colombia. ❑

Sources: Luis E. Barranco, "Como el gobierno nacional convirtió una zona agroecológica en zona de interés público para fines portuarios," *EDUMAG*, Ciénaga, Colombia, 2010; Marcelo Bucheli, *Bananas and Business: The United Fruit Company in Colombia, 1899-2000* (New York University Press, 2005); Peter Chapman, *Bananas: How the United Fruit Company Shaped the World* (Canongate, 2007); Aviva Chomsky, Garry Leech, and Steve Striffler, *Bajo el manto del carbon: Pueblos y multinacionales en las minas de El Cerrejón* (Casa Editorial Pisando Callos, 2007).

Article 2.4

STOP KILLER COKE!

BY MADELEINE BARAN
November/December 2003

O n the morning of December 5, 1996, two members of a paramilitary gang drove a motorcycle to the Carepa Coca-Cola bottling plant in northern Colombia. They fired 10 shots at worker and union activist Isidro Segundo Gil, killing him. Luis Adolso Cardona, a fellow worker, witnessed the assassination. "I was working and I heard the gun shots and then I saw Isidro Gil falling," he said in a recent interview. "I ran, but when I got there Isidro was already dead."

A few hours later, paramilitary officials detained Cardona, but he escaped, fleeing to the police office, where he received protection. Around midnight that night, the paramilitaries looted the local union office and set it on fire. "There was nothing left. Only the walls," said Cardona. The paramilitary group returned to the plant the next week, lined up the 60 unionized workers, and ordered them to sign a prepared letter of resignation from the union. Everyone did. Two months later, all the workers—including those who had never belonged to the union—were fired.

Gil, 27, had worked at the plant for eight years. His wife, Alcira Gil, protested her husband's killing and demanded reparations from Coca-Cola. She was killed by paramilitaries in 2000, leaving their two daughters orphaned. A Colombian judge later dropped the charges against Gil's alleged killers.

Paramilitaries, violent right-wing forces composed of professional soldiers and common thugs, maintain bases at several Coca-Cola bottling facilities in Colombia, allegedly to protect the bottlers from left-wing militants who might target the plants as symbols of globalization.

Activists say at least eight union activists have been killed by paramilitaries at Colombian Coca-Cola facilities since 1989. And plaintiffs in a recent series of lawsuits hold Coca-Cola and two of its bottlers responsible for the violence, alleging "systematic intimidation, kidnapping, detention, and murder of trade unionists in Colombia, South America at the hands of paramilitaries working as agents of corporations doing business in that country."

The murders of Coke bottling workers are part of a larger pattern of antiunion violence in Colombia. Since 1986, over 3,800 trade unionists have been murdered in the country, making it the most dangerous place to organize in the world. Three out of every five people killed worldwide for trade union activities are from Colombia.

Suing Coke and its Bottlers

The Washington, D.C.-based advocacy organization International Labor Rights Fund (ILRF) and the United Steel Workers of America filed four lawsuits in

Federal District Court in July 2001 on behalf of Sinaltrainal (a union representing food and beverage workers in Colombia), five individuals who have been tortured or unlawfully detained for union activities, and the estate of murdered union activist Isidro Gil. The plaintiffs contend Coca-Cola bottlers "contracted with or otherwise directed paramilitary security forces that utilized extreme violence and murdered, tortured, unlawfully detained, or otherwise silenced trade union leaders."

In addition to demanding that Coca-Cola take responsibility for the murder of Colombian union activists, the plaintiffs are asking for compensatory and punitive damages, which by some estimates could range from $50 million to $6 billion.

Coca-Cola's legal defense "is not that the murder and terrorism of trade unionists did not occur," according to an ILRF press release. The company argues that it cannot be held liable in a U.S. federal court for events outside the United States. "Coca-Cola also argues that it does not 'own,' and therefore does not control, the bottling plants in Colombia."

RAY ROGERS' CORPORATE CAMPAIGN STRATEGY

In the Corporate Campaign, Inc., offices near Union Square in Manhattan, Ray Rogers sits at a large table covered in binders detailing the investors, corporate structure, and finances of the Coca-Cola Company. Rogers, 59, is the founder of the progressive labor consulting company Corporate Campaign, Inc., and a veteran of dozens of battles against corporations like Hormel, Con Edison, and General Electric. His trademark strategy, the "corporate campaign," involves identifying and targeting a company's sources of power from as many angles as possible.

"If I'm representing a union and they're in a contract fight or some sort of organizing drive," Rogers said, "I'm going to find a whole series of sensitive issues as they relate to the company. What's their record on the environment? Do they have a bank tied into them? What's the record of the bank on redlining? How do they treat poor communities? What's the safety and health record of the company? Where are they lending their money? What right-wing groups are they tied into?"

Rogers famously used these tactics in 1980 to force the anti-union J.P. Stevens textile company to sign a collective bargaining agreement with the Amalgamated Clothing and Textile Workers Union. In that campaign, Rogers first publicized the textile company's exploitative workplace practices, then exposed its connections with other major corporations—most importantly, the Metropolitan Life Insurance Company. Top MetLife corporate officers who had business dealings with J.P. Stevens were forced to resign, and investor confidence in J.P. Stevens plummeted. Once the textile company realized the extent to which the campaign was hurting both its reputation and its profits, it agreed to union demands. The victory led many other unions and progressive groups to incorporate Rogers' tactics into their own struggles.

In late March, a judge dismissed Coca-Cola from the lawsuits—on grounds that the firm does not have control over the labor practices of its bottlers—but allowed the case against the bottlers to go forward. A request for an appeal is pending.

According to Daniel Kovalik, assistant general counsel for the United Steelworkers of America and co-counsel for the plaintiffs: "In the short run, [the court decision] means that we can't proceed against Coke, but it doesn't necessarily mean that in the long run. I am absolutely confident that we'll win the appeal."

Kovalik maintains that Coca-Cola is liable for its bottlers' actions. For one thing, the 20 Colombia bottlers are deeply entwined in Coke's core economic activities. Coca-Cola provides syrup to the bottlers, who mix, bottle, package, and ship the drinks to wholesalers and retailers throughout Colombia. The bottlers are integral to the beverage giant's operations in the country.

Moreover, Coca-Cola and its bottlers have deep financial links. In May, Coca-Cola FEMSA, a bottling company, acquired Pan American Beverages, Latin America's largest bottler and a defendant in the case. In the year before it was acquired, sales of Coca-Cola represented 89% of Pan American's $2.35 billion net

---

"You can't confront powerful institutions and expect to gain any meaningful concessions unless you're backed by significant force and power yourself," Rogers said. "The corporate campaign is really a mechanism to confront power with power."

Some dismiss Rogers' style as too uncompromising and say his tactics force him into polarizing positions—either total victory or total defeat, a style of campaigning that leaves no room for the compromises that are sometimes necessary in union battles. They say Rogers' brash tactics harm unions at the bargaining table. Former United Auto Workers organizer Jerry Tucker adds, "Ray doesn't have a lot of sense of the internal workings of unions."

Rogers acknowledges that collective bargaining is not his specialty, but states, "We go in there and back up the union leadership with publicity and resources. Bargaining does not go on when the union has no power behind it."

Rogers' defenders argue that opposition to the corporate campaign model stems from union leaders' rigid resistance to nontraditional strategies. Referring to Rogers' critics within the labor movement, labor historian Peter Rachleff said, "[they] hate people who are independent, who they can't control, who can walk out the door and get another job. They believe in organization from the top down."

Many have nothing but praise for Rogers' bold tactics. "Ray is a corporate-buster without peer," says Jim Guyette, who worked with Rogers during the 1985-1986 Hormel strike in Austin, Minn. Labor journalist Tom Robbins agrees. "He has a formula down," he says. Rogers sees that "there's a connection between the shareholders and the corporate responsibility to workers."

And according to Rogers, given the dominance of corporations worldwide, the need to analyze corporate structures and connections and to deploy that analysis in the growing battle against corporate power is more urgent than ever.

sales. The acquisition made Mexico-based Coca-Cola FEMSA the largest Coca-Cola bottler in Latin America. The Coca-Cola Company owns a 30% equity stake in Coca-Cola FEMSA, according to the bottling company, and several of its executives also work for Coke.

The plaintiffs are now considering whether to add Coca-Cola FEMSA as a defendant in the lawsuits. If they do, Coca-Cola will be put in the uncomfortable position of trying to prove that Coca-Cola FEMSA and the Coca-Cola Company—despite their shared name, shared executives, and Coke's part-ownership of FEMSA—are completely independent from one another.

Coca-Cola did not return calls for comment, but has stated in the past that Pan American Beverages was an independent company. More recently, Coca-Cola has denied allegations that its bottlers tolerate or assist in acts of violence against union activists. In a statement released in July, Coca-Cola said the allegations are "nothing more than a shameless effort to generate publicity using the name of our Company, its trademark and brands."

Kovalik argues that the corporation's communications with shareholders contradict these public statements and suggest that the firm in fact can, and should, investigate and put a stop to the killings. He plans to submit Coca-Cola documents as legal evidence, including a letter to a shareholder that reads: "We require that everyone within the Coca-Cola system abide by the laws and regulations of the countries in which they do business. We demand integrity and honesty in business at the Coca-Cola Company...."

"They can't be able to profit from these bottlers and say that they don't have control over these situations," says Kovalik.

Taking Down a Corporate Giant

The Stop Killer Coke campaign may prove to be the biggest test yet of the corporate campaign model pioneered by labor consultant Ray Rogers (see "Ray Rogers' Corporate Campaign Strategy"). As the public face of the ILRF lawsuits, the Stop Killer Coke campaign aims to put public pressure on Coca-Cola to acknowledge its role in the killings and to persuade the company to stop collaborating with violent paramilitary organizations.

It's one part of a massive coalition gearing up for a multi-front attack on Coca-Cola. The anti-Coke effort, launched by the lawsuits against Coca-Cola and its bottlers, has grown to include the Stop Killer Coke campaign, consumer and student groups, and labor organizations like the Teamsters and the AFL-CIO. These various groups share the same primary goal: to damage the soft-drink giant's reputation in order to force the company to acknowledge its role in the Colombian killings. With the launch of the Stop Killer Coke campaign this summer, the movement is picking up momentum.

Rogers plans to expand the campaign far beyond the plaintiffs' allegations to encompass "at least a dozen issues" including the lack of health care for Coca-Cola workers in Africa; the corporation's water use in India, which causes groundwater destruction; and more. He has spent the last several months researching Coke's corporate structure and intricate financial dealings.

Rogers often refers to his strategic style as "divide and conquer" because it aims to isolate companies from investors, creditors, politicians, and consumers. In the most successful corporate campaigns, the target corporation's relationship with the business world breaks down, as other companies, banks, and executives decide that the benefits of the business relationship are not worth the risk of being the target of a high-profile campaign. Eventually, the company, isolated and weak, caves in to the campaign's demands in order to end the media blitz and restore its position in the business world.

"A corporation is really nothing more than a coalition of individual and institutional economic and political interests, some more vital and vulnerable than others, that can be challenged and attacked, divided and conquered," Rogers said. "I know enough now to know exactly where the Achilles heel of Coca-Cola is. I'm so confident about where we're going with this thing."

That Achilles heel appears to be Coke's relationship with SunTrust Bank, its main creditor. Many of Coca-Cola's top shareholders own significant amounts of SunTrust stock, and their boards overlap—three current or former Coke CEOs sit on SunTrust's board of directors and two current or former SunTrust CEOs sit on Coke's board. "In almost 30 years of studying corporate structures, I have never seen a more intimate or incestuous relationship," said Rogers.

Rogers plans to expose the relations between SunTrust and Coca-Cola, then use information on Coke's human rights and environmental practices to drive SunTrust into a financial and public relations disaster. If the plan works, investors will lose confidence in SunTrust; key executives will resign rather than face negative media attention; and unions, progressive groups, and consumers will close their accounts. Given the deep ties between the two companies, whatever hurts SunTrust will hurt Coke. Backed into such a position, Coca-Cola would be forced to acknowledge and end its ties to paramilitaries in order to stabilize its main creditor and regain investor and consumer confidence.

The campaign faces an uphill battle. Coca-Cola has virtually unlimited resources to fight lawsuits and conduct its own media blitz. Also, Coca-Cola, like most major companies, now has years of experience fighting high-profile consumer campaigns. The beverage giant has a truly global reach, producing over 300 brands in more than 200 countries, with more than 70% of its income coming from outside the United States. If the campaign hopes to damage Coca-Cola financially, it will have to attract international support.

Despite these serious obstacles, Rogers is optimistic. "We're going to move very quickly on this thing," he said. "I think they're going to find themselves involved in something that they're going to find a total nightmare." Terry Collingsworth, executive director of the ILRF, is also confident. "Ray's like the classic pit bull," he said. "Once he bites into you, he won't let go. Ray's not going to walk away from this until he's won."

The battle is already heating up, with activists in Latin America, Turkey, Ireland, and Australia leading anti-Coke campaigns with Stop Killer Coke materials. Student organizations like United Students Against Sweatshops are starting campaigns to ban Coke from campuses. University College Dublin, Ireland's largest university, voted recently to remove all Coca-Cola products from the campus. Meanwhile, Bard College in New York has decided against renewing Coke's contract with the school when it expires in May. At Carnegie Mellon in Pittsburgh, students staged a "Coke dump," spilling soda into the streets to call attention to the plight of Colombian union activists. Union involvement is also growing. United Auto Workers Local 22 in Detroit, recently ordered 4,000 "Coke Float" flyers, which explain the campaign. The union will hand them out to workers as they leave their plant.

In the meantime, violence against union activists in Colombia continues. On September 10, 2003, David Jose Carranza Calle, the 15-year-old son of Sinaltrainal's national director, was kidnapped by paramilitaries. According to Sinaltrainal, four masked men forced the younger Carranza into a truck and tortured him, asking for the whereabouts of his father. At the same time, his father, Limberto Carranza, received a phone call from an unidentified individual who said, "Unionist son of a bitch, we are going to break you. And if you won't break, we will attack your home." The kidnappers freed Carranza Calle over three hours later. But unionists in Colombian bottling plants, including Coca-Cola facilities, are far from safe. ❑

For more information on the Coca-Cola campaign, go to www. killercoke.org.

Article 2.5

BANKRUPTCY AS CORPORATE MAKEOVER

ASARCO demonstrates how to evade environmental responsibility.

BY MARA KARDAS-NELSON, LIN NELSON, AND ANNE FISCHEL
May/June 2010

> "At around noon [every] July and August…our folks would bring us into the
> house, because the smoke, the pollution, the sulfur, would settle into our
> community for about two or three hours…when there was no breeze to take that
> away. When we would breathe that, we could not be outside because we were
> constantly coughing. So nobody can tell me that there was no ill effect on the
> majority of the folks that lived in Smeltertown."
>   —Daniel Solis, resident of Smeltertown, a Mexican-American
>   neighborhood in El Paso, Texas located next to an ASARCO smelter.

After five long years in court, the bankruptcy of the American Smelting and Refining Company, or ASARCO, has finally been determined.

Hailed as one of the earliest and largest multinational corporations and responsible for the employment of hundreds of thousands, ASARCO has a long history of polluting both the environment and the workplace. After racking up billions in environmental damages, the company filed for bankruptcy in 2005.

It has been billed as the largest environmental bankruptcy in United States history; 90 communities from 21 states will share a $1.79 billion settlement to cover the costs of environmental monitoring and cleanup and limited compensation to some of its workers. This figure, however, represents less than one percent of the funds originally identified as needed by claimants.

The ASARCO case emerged in the context of a diminished and disabled "Superfund," as the federal environmental program established to deal with hazardous waste sites is known. The fund was originally created by Congress to hold companies accountable for environmental damage and to ensure that communities are not left with large bills and no means to pay them. But years of corporate pressure on Capitol Hill has depleted Superfund, placing the financial burden of environmental cleanups on taxpayers, rather than on corporations.

This use of bankruptcies to avoid responsibility, coupled with a cash-strapped Superfund, offers a chilling glimpse into the world of corporate irresponsibility allowable under U.S. bankruptcy provisions and environmental policy. As the case closes, ASARCO is transforming from an aging corporation weighed down by shuttered factories and contaminated communities into a lean and profitable company. This is setting a precedent for how others can use legal loopholes to evade liability and undermine government protections.

Damaging Health and Environment, Yet Shaping Environmental Policy

ASARCO began operations in the late 1890s, mining, smelting, and refining essential ores (first lead, then copper) in order to provide base materials for industrial production. By the mid-20ᵗʰ century, the company had expanded to include holdings and operations in Latin America, Australia, Canada, Africa, and the Philippines. In 1914 company workers unionized through the Western Federation of Miners, which later became the Mine, Mill & Smelterworkers, eventually merging with the United Steelworkers in the 1960s. In its heyday, ASARCO operated in close to 90 U.S. communities in 22 states, employing thousands.

By the mid-1970s, employees and communities were growing concerned about environmental and public health risks resulting from company operations. Researchers, health departments, unions, and workers began tracking the impact of exposure to arsenic, lead, cadmium, and sulfur dioxide, all byproducts of the smelting process. In Tacoma, WA, site of one of ASARCO's largest smelting operations, dissident workers launched "The Smelterworker" newsletter, one of the first union-based occupational health efforts in the country. The Puget Sound Air Pollution Control Agency began to voice similar concerns when ASARCO's lobbying regarding federal laws and regulations successfully slowed development of a federal arsenic standard.

Health concerns also emerged in El Paso, Texas, site of a large ASARCO smelter that had polluted both sides of the U.S.-Mexico border. In 1970, following passage of the Clean Air Act, the City of El Paso sued ASARCO over its sulfur dioxide emissions. During the process of discovery, ASARCO submitted documentation of its emissions to the City for the first time. These reports showed that between 1969 and 1971, 1,012 metric tons of lead, 508 metric tons of zinc, eleven metric tons of cadmium, and one metric ton of arsenic had been released during operations.

By 1969 the city had a higher concentration of airborne lead than any other in the state. In the early 1970s a research team from the Centers for Disease Control (CDC), led by Dr. Philip Landrigan, confirmed a pattern of smelter-sourced lead threatening the children on the U.S. side.

Chronic arsenic exposure can lead to skin pigmentation, numbness, cardiovascular disease, diabetes, vascular disease, and a variety of cancers, including skin, kidney, bladder, lung, prostate and liver.

Lead exposure can result in damage to the kidneys, liver, brain, nerves, and other organs, and the development of osteoporosis, reproductive disorders, seizures, mental retardation, behavioral and learning disorders, lowered IQ, high blood pressure and elevated risk of heart disease.

The studies conducted by the CDC linked the high levels of lead in air, soil, and dust to the ASARCO smelter. They also linked the lead in soil and dust to elevated lead levels in children's blood. Landrigan's research team administered IQ tests and reaction time tests, and found significant differences in performance between lead-impacted children and those with lower blood levels. This pathbreaking research transformed scientific thinking about the impact of lead on children's development, and confirmed numerous dangers, even in children without obvious clinical symptoms.

At the time of research the threshold for lead in blood was 40 micrograms per deciliter. Today it is 10 micrograms per deciliter, and many health researchers and physicians want to see it set even lower. Yet some researchers had asserted that lead from smelters was not harmful to humans, and an El Paso pediatrician, in a study funded by an organization connected to the industry, claimed that levels of 40 to 80 micrograms were acceptable, as long as the children were properly nourished. As a result of the CDC studies, however, "it is now widely accepted in the scientific community that lead is toxic at extremely low levels," according to Landrigan.

Some of the affected children were treated with painful chelation therapy. Daniel Solis, a Smeltertown resident, recalls his siblings' reaction to the treatment:

> They would get hysterical because of how much the treatment would hurt, they would literally go underneath their cribs and they would hold on to the bottom of the bed. I would literally have to go underneath and drag them out…It was excruciating. My mom would cry to see…the pain that her kids would be going through. But we had no other choice, you know, my siblings were that infected with lead that they had to get that treatment.

In 1991, through its subsidiary Encycle, ASARCO received highly hazardous waste, sourced from a Department of Defense site at Rocky Mountain Arsenal in Colorado. Napalm, sarin nerve gas, cluster bombs, and white phosphorous had all been produced at this site, and private pesticide companies also rented space in the facility. At Encycle, hazardous waste labels were removed and materials were shipped to ASARCO facilities in El Paso and in East Helena, Mont. Neither facility was licensed to manage hazardous waste; it is possible that the waste was shipped to other sites as well. In El Paso, workers were not informed of the risks of such incineration and were not trained to deal with these hazardous materials. This lack of protection and withholding of information violates the federal right-to-know workplace law.

The Government Accountability Office (GAO) has verified that from 1991 to 1999, the El Paso and East Helena plants received and incinerated waste meant only for licensed hazardous waste facilities. This illegal disposal potentially exposed hundreds of workers and both communities. In 1998, the federal government fined ASARCO $50 million for these violations and problems at other ASARCO sites. The settlement did not include provisions for testing workers, soil, air, water, or community members for exposure to potential contaminants. The El Paso community was not informed about these illegal activities; the extent of knowledge in East Helena is unclear. The wrist-slap against the company—and the actions that provoked it—became public only through the investigative work of citizen activists in El Paso, leading to a *New York Times* exposé in 2006.

Although many communities endure severe health effects and environmental problems, ASARCO's ties to powerful politicians gave it substantial influence on public health policy. During the George W. Bush years, James Connaughton, one of ASARCO's key attorneys, served as head of the White House Council for Environmental Quality. A key ASARCO scientist was positioned for the federal Lead Advisory Board, while other prominent, independent scientists were pushed to the margins. ASARCO has also promoted the corporate "audit privilege," allowing companies to self-monitor hazards.

Superfund: Hope and Disappointment for Polluted Communities

ASARCO was hardly the only company polluting communities throughout the industrial boom of the 20th century. As research linked contamination to birth defects, higher cancer rates, and other serious illnesses, community advocates and municipal and state leaders took collective action. In 1980, in response to the discovery of hazardous waste at Love Canal, N.Y., Congress passed the Comprehensive Environmental Response, Compensation & Liability Act (CERCLA), better known as "Superfund." The Act made companies legally and financially responsible for environmental degradation that occurred as a result of their operations. Additionally, cleanup costs for "orphan sites" where specific companies could not be identified or held responsible would draw money from the Superfund, made of a series of corporate taxes, or "polluter-pays fees," and supported by government revenue. The legislation authorized the Environmental Protection Agency (EPA) to place heavily contaminated sites on the National Priorities List. If identified as a "Superfund site," a community qualified for enforced cleanup and funds. Since the inception of Superfund, the EPA has identified over 1,200 sites, including 20 ASARCO operations. One in four Americans lives within four miles of a Superfund site.

In 1995, under the watch of President Clinton and a Republican Congress, Superfund's polluter-pays fees expired, thus shifting most of the financial burden onto taxpayers. As of 2010, these fees have yet to be reinstated. By 2003, all corporate funds were exhausted and the Superfund now relies solely on taxpayer-funded government revenues. According to the U.S. Public Interest Research Group, in 1995 taxpayers paid only 18% ($300 million) of the Superfund, but by 2005, they contributed 100%—approximately $1.2 billion.

As a result of under-financing and lack of political will, the number of Superfund sites undergoing cleanup has diminished. While the EPA averaged 87 completed cleanups a year from 1997 to 2000, in 2008 only 30 sites were processed, representing a drop of over 50% in the pace of cleanups. Without polluter-pays fees and in light of the bankruptcy, the affected communities at ASARCO sites are left with few options to ensure comprehensive cleanup and reparations.

Penny Newman of the Center for Community Action & Environmental Justice calls the fund "impotent" without corporate contributions: "It's disingenuous to pretend a program exists without the funding." In spring 2009, the Obama administration directed $600 million in stimulus money to 50 Superfund sites—including the ASARCO site in Tacoma—that have shown significant progress in their cleanups. Obama and the EPA call this a "stopgap measure," setting the restoration of the polluter-pays tax as an important environmental health goal.

The Bankruptcy "Solution"

As environmental and community health concerns mounted, public pressure increased, and projected cleanup costs skyrocketed, ASARCO closed most of its operations. All of ASARCO's sites—operating, shuttered, or in remediation—were affected by the 2005 Chapter 11 bankruptcy filing. The company cited environmental liabilities as a primary explanation for the action.

The bankruptcy was not a last-minute act of desperation. On the contrary, the company had been rearranging itself for some time, shedding liabilities and cutting costs through sales and mergers. In 1999, ASARCO was "bought" by its major subsidiary, Grupo México, a Mexican-based company that is one of the largest metal producers in the world. This sale is significant because ASARCO's assets and records were shifted outside of the United States and therefore no longer under U.S. government jurisdiction; citizens requesting records and remediation from the company now had difficulty doing so. In 2002, ASARCO sold one of its most valuable mining complexes, Southern Peru Copper, to its new parent company, transferring even more valuable resources beyond national boundaries. Fearing a potential bankruptcy, the Department of Justice forced ASARCO to set up a $100 million trust to cover liabilities for impacted U.S. communities.

Chapter 11 of the U.S. Bankruptcy Code permits corporate reorganization and invokes "automatic stay," in which most litigation is put on hold until it can be resolved in court, with creditors ceasing collection attempts. This status allowed ASARCO to legally avoid paying for environmental damage at sites that required it for the duration of the bankruptcy. Additionally, pension payments and other monies owed to workers as negotiated by the United Steelworkers, which represents most employees, were threatened and delayed. As a result of the bankruptcy, the Steelworkers, a member of the bankruptcy creditors' committee, settled with a one-year extension of their collective bargaining agreement.

Complexities stemming from ASARCO's multinational status became more apparent during the 2005-2009 bankruptcy proceedings. During the case, Grupo México, by court ruling, was removed as the controlling agent of ASARCO. As such, Grupo México battled with another corporate suitor, India-based Sterilite/Vedanta Corporation, for control; Grupo México eventually prevailed. This competition prolonged proceedings, as the judge assessed competing purchase offers and changing promises to affected communities and workers.

Through bankruptcy negotiations, ASARCO significantly reduced its debts to damaged communities. The *Tacoma News Tribune* reported that more than a dozen states and the federal government originally collectively filed $6 billion in environmental claims involving 20 ASARCO sites. Other estimates placed cleanup and liability costs as high as $25.2 billion. This figure was subsequently reduced to $3.6 billion in early bankruptcy court proceedings, which was later sliced to the final settlement of $1.79 billion.

In the days following the announcement of the settlement, government spokespeople and community members expressed a mix of relief and disappointment. According to U.S. Associate Attorney General Tom Perrelli, "The effort to recover this money was a collaborative and coordinated response by the states and federal government. Our combined efforts have resulted in the largest recovery of funds to pay for past and future cleanup of hazardous materials in the nation's history. Today is a historic day for the environment and the people affected across the country."

But activists and affected communities insist the ruling did not go far enough. In addition to paying less than originally projected, ASARCO's parent company, Grupo México, faces fewer responsibilities than it did before the bankruptcy. While the company had previously been pegged with penalty payments for the transfer of Southern Peru Copper, the bankruptcy decision, which reinstated Grupo México control, nullified this.

The $1.79 billion settlement will also be unevenly split between affected communities. While Washington State celebrated the perseverance of their attorneys and coordinated work of departments, Texas, which had relatively little sustained support and attention by federal authorities, will not be as well served. The El Paso area has a modest $52 million to address complex and hazardous contamination.

ASARCO's Legacy and Communities' Call for Responsibility

Throughout the bankruptcy proceedings, U.S. Senator Maria Cantwell (D-WA) warned that ASARCO's use of bankruptcy will be imitated by other companies aiming to minimize their liability for environmental and health damages. The *Tacoma News Tribune* has reported that companies in eight of the ten regions under EPA jurisdiction have considered bankruptcy in order to elude responsibility. A 2007 study identified six companies connected to approximately 120 Superfund sites in 28 states filing for bankruptcy, with four of these companies successfully avoiding over half a billion dollars in cleanup costs. In 2009, eleven states involved in the ASARCO bankruptcy and the Justice Department reaffirmed the warning that more companies will follow suit.

Twice Cantwell has introduced bills to curtail companies' use of bankruptcies and other "legal" techniques to avoid responsibility; twice the bills have failed.

Texas State Senator Shapleigh has witnessed the city of El Paso's struggle with the high cost of environmental cleanup and jeopardized public health. Commenting on the bankruptcy and echoing Cantwell's concerns, he warns, "This is a strategy that will be used over and over again in the United States. The corporations will play out this environmental saga…this is the first one."

A Familiar Story

The story of ASARCO is a complicated one. It is a story of environmental degradation, of countless hidden occupational health hazards, of a corporation comfortably connected to federal and state administrations, and of a broken safety net that offers little compensation for communities impacted by a century of industrial operations.

Yet the story of ASARCO is not an unfamiliar one. The company's evasion of corporate responsibility in the face of weakened federal regulations demonstrates how companies can shift billions of dollars of environmental cleanup costs onto affected communities.

The special brew of corporate bankruptcies and an under-funded Superfund leaves us extremely vulnerable to industrial contamination. ASARCO's bankruptcy left thousands of exposed workers and family members, 21 states, two Indian tribal communities, and unions in limbo for years, and now with very limited reparation for life-altering health effects and degraded environments. Despite the company's responsibility for extensive environmental and health damage, the settlement holds them accountable for only a sliver of originally projected cleanup costs. A lack of political will from Congress to ensure corporate funding for Superfund and to pass legislation that tightens legal loopholes has left communities who believed they were protected by the 1980 CERCLA legislation strapped for cash and with few legal protections to enforce corporate responsibility.

Current and former ASARCO employees, affected communities, and allies are organizing to push for corporate accountability and government regulations. In El Paso, as a result of the bankruptcy, the Superfund dysfunction, and the special burden of illegal hazardous waste incineration, community advocates are working to shape a strategy for activating workplace right-to-know for former employees at high risk for illness. They are further insisting on transparency in the cleanup and corporate accountability for public health.

In February 2010, a group of over two dozen organizations and individuals, including current and former ASARCO employees and several Mexican government officials, wrote to the EPA with concerns that the cleanup plan for the El Paso site is "inadequate to protect the health of the [El Paso] community and does not address offsite-pollution in [New Mexico], Mexico and Texas." The current plan only addresses hazards in El Paso, but according to Mariana Chew of the Sierra Club, "Cuidad Juárez in Mexico and Sunland Park in [New Mexico] are the communities most affected by ASARCO's legal and illegal operations and yet are not taken in account." Chew and others are especially concerned about the health of children at an elementary school in Cuidad Juárez that sits just 400 feet downwind from the smelter.

The group demands larger payments from ASARCO, specifically for its illegal incineration of hazardous waste. In the interim, the group claims that federal monies from the Superfund should be used.

The 2010 National Latino Congress has also condemned ASARCO's contamination of the border region and the company's bankruptcy. The Congress, supported by hundreds of organizations and over 40 elected U.S. officials, demanded full disclosure of the illegal incineration of hazardous waste, and comprehensive testing and treatment for workers and community members who may have been exposed.

Meanwhile, in Hayden, Ariz., site of the company's only operating U.S. smelter, ASARCO officials have reassured residents that blowing dust from mine tailings is not a hazard. According to ASARCO vice president Thomas Aldrich, "Across the board these are very low in metals, about what you'd expect here, comparable to the background levels in soil."

Such statements offer little comfort for communities still struggling for information, protection, and accountability. ❑

This article is based on the project "No Borders: Communities Living and Working with Asarco" based at Evergreen and guided by Fischel and Nelson. The project examines the occupational and environmental health and social justice implications of ASARCO's operations with a focus on three communities: Ruston/Tacoma, Wash., Hayden, Ariz. and El Paso, Texas. A documentary film, "Borders of Resistance," to be released in the summer of 2010, documents the El Paso story of community and labor advocates pressing for accountability and health protections. Other films and writing are forthcoming.

Sources: Office of Texas Senator Eliot Shapleigh, "Asarco in El Paso," September 2008; Les Blumenthal, "Asarco Mess Reveals Superfund Failings," *Tacoma News Tribune*, March 21, 2006; Les Blumenthal, "Lawyers Dissect Asarco's cleanup obligation in the US," *Tacoma News Tribune*, May 20, 2006; Les Blumenthal, "Grupo México wins Asarco back in court ruling," *Tacoma News Tribune*, September 3, 2009; Joel Millman, "Asarco Bankruptcy Leaves Many Towns with Cleanup Mess," *Wall Street Journal*, May 24, 2006; Office of U.S. Senator Maria Cantwell, "Cantwell Introduces Legislation to Prevent Corporate Polluters from Evading Toxic Cleanup Responsibilities," June 15, 2006; Center for Health, Environment and Justice, "Superfund: In the Eye of the Storm," March 2009; Center for Health, Environment and Justice, "America's Safety Net in Crisis: 25th Anniversary of Superfund," 2005; *The Smelterworker* rank-and-file union newsletter, circa 1970-75, Tacoma Wash.; Marianne Sullivan, "Contested Science and Exposed Workers: ASARCO and the Occupational Standard for Inorganic Arsenic," *Public Health Chronicles*, July 2007; Ralph Blumenthal, "Copper Plant Illegally Burned Hazardous Waste, EPA Says," *New York Times*, October 11, 2006; Government Accountability Office, "Environmental Liabilities: EPA Should Do More to Ensure That Liable Parties Meet Their Cleanup Obligations," August 2005; Government Accountability Office, "Hazardous Waste: Information about How DOD and Federal and State Regulators Oversee the Off-site Disposal of Waste from DOD Installations," November 2007; Department of Justice, "Largest Environmental Bankruptcy in US History Will Result in Payment of $1.79 Billion Towards Environmental Cleanup and Restoration," December 10 2009;

Seattle and King County Department of Public Health, Arsenic Facts, 2010 (www.kingcounty. gov/healthservices/health/ehs/toxic/ArsenicFacts.aspx); The Center for Health, Environment & Justice, "Letter to the Environmental Protection Agency," February 16 2010; The Center for Health, Environment & Justice, "News Release," February 16 2010; The 2010 National Latino Congress, "Draft Amended ASARCO Resolution," 2010; Interview, Dr. Philip Landrigan, Mt Sinai Medical School, August 27 2009; Interview, Daniel Solis, El Paso, Tex, August 2007.

Chapter 3

TRADE, INVESTMENT, AND DEBT

Article 3.1

WHAT CAUSES EXCHANGE-RATE FLUCTUATIONS?

BY ARTHUR MacEWAN

March/April 2001, updated August 2009

> Dear Dr. Dollar:
> What are the primary forces that cause foreign exchange rates to fluctuate, and what are the remedies to these forces?
>
> —*Mario Anthony, West Palm Beach, Fla.*

A foreign exchange rate is the price, in terms of one currency, that is paid for another currency. For example, at the end of December 2000, in terms of the U.S. dollar, the price of a British pound was $1.50, the price of a Japanese yen was 0.9 cents, and the price of a Canadian dollar was 67 cents. Like any other prices, currency prices fluctuate due to a variety of forces that we loosely categorize as "supply and demand." And as with other prices, the forces of "supply and demand" can have severe economic impacts and nasty human consequences.

Two factors, however, make exchange rates especially problematic. One is that they are subject to a high degree of speculation. This is seldom a significant problem for countries with stable economies—the "developed" countries. But for low-income countries, where instability is endemic, small changes in economic conditions can lead speculators to move billions of dollars in the time it takes to press a button, resulting in very large changes in the prices of currencies. This can quickly and greatly magnify small changes in economic conditions. In 1997 in East Asia, this sort of speculation greatly worsened the economic crisis that arose first in Thailand and then in several other countries. The speculators who drive such crises include bankers and the treasurers of multinational firms, as well as individuals and the operatives of investment companies that specialize in profiting off of the international movement of funds.

The second factor making exchange rates especially problematic is that they affect the prices of many other commodities. For a country that imports a great deal, a drop in the price of its currency relative to the currencies of the countries from which it imports means that a host of imported goods—everything from food to machinery—become more costly. When speculators moved funds out of East Asian countries in 1997, the price of foreign exchange (e.g., the price of the dollar in terms of local currencies) rose, imports became extremely expensive (in local currencies), and both living standards and investment fell dramatically. (Strong speculative movement of funds into a country can also create problems—driving up the price of the local currency, thereby hurting demand for the country's exports, and limiting economic growth.)

In the "normal" course of international trade, short-term exchange-rate fluctuations are seldom large. Consider, for example, trade between the United States and Canada. If people in the United States increasingly buy things from Canada—lumber, vacations in the Canadian Rockies, fish, minerals, auto parts—they will need Canadian dollars to do so. Thus these increased purchases of Canadian goods by people in the United States will mean an increased demand for Canadian dollars and a corresponding increased supply of U.S. dollars. If nothing else changes, the price of the Canadian dollar in terms of the U.S. dollar will tend to rise.

A great deal of the demand and supply of international currencies, however, is not for trade but for investment, often speculative investment. With the strong U.S. stock market in the late 1990s, investors in other countries bought a large amount of assets in the United States. To do so, they demanded U.S. dollars and supplied their own currencies. As a result, the price of the dollar in terms of the currencies of other countries rose substantially, by about 25% on average between the middle of 1995 and the end of 2000. One of the results has been to make imports to the U.S. relatively cheap, and this has been a factor holding down inflation in the United States. Also, as the cost of foreign currency dropped, the cost (in terms of dollars) of hiring foreign workers to supply goods also dropped. The result was more severe competition for many U.S. workers (including, for example, people employed in the production of auto parts, glass goods, textiles, and apparel) and, no surprise, their wages suffered.

There is little point in attempts by governments to constrain the "normal" fluctuations in foreign exchange rates that are associated with trade adjustments (as in the U.S.-Canada example above) or those associated with long-run investment movements (as in the case of the United States during the late 1990s). Although these fluctuations can create large problems—like their impact on U.S. wages—it would be very costly and very difficult, if not impossible, to eliminate them. There are other ways to deal with declining wages.

The experience of the East Asian countries in 1997 is another matter. Speculative investment drove huge exchange-rate changes and (along with other factors) severely disrupted these countries' economies. Between mid-1997 and early 1998, for example, the value of the Thai baht lost close to 60% of its value in terms of the U.S. dollar, and the Malaysian ringgit lost close to 50%. Governments can control such speculative swings by a variety of limits on the quick movement of capital into and out of countries. One mechanism would be a tax on short-term investments. Another would be direct limits on movements of funds. These sorts of controls are not easy to implement, but they have worked effectively in many cases—notably in Malaysia following the 1997 crisis.

It has become increasingly clear in recent years that effective development policies in low-income countries cannot be pursued in the absence of some sort of controls on the movement of funds in and out of those countries. Otherwise, any successful program—whatever its particular aims—can be disrupted and destroyed by the actions of international speculators.

Update, August 2009

The years leading into the economic crisis that appeared in 2007 and 2009 illustrate the way a variety of forces affect the value of the dollar relative to other currencies. Between 1995 and the end of the millennium, the value of the dollar relative to other currencies rose by almost 28%. Many factors were involved, but one important force was the demand by foreign interests for dollars to take part in the stock market boom of that period. After the dot-com stock market bubble of the late 1990s burst, however, the value of the dollar did not fall immediately. The value of the dollar was maintained (and even rose a bit through 2001) as the U.S. economy entered into the 2001 recession; with the recession, there was a fall off in demand for imports—which meant a reduction in the supply of dollars.

Then, however, the value of the dollar began to fall. By early 2008, it was back down to its 1995 level, more than 25% below the 2001 peak. Again, several factors account for the fall. In particular, the vary large trade deficit (imports greater than exports)—which more than doubled between 2001 and 2006—meant a growing supply of dollars relative to the demand for dollars. This was partly offset by the demand of foreign interests—for example, the central banks of China, Japan and other countries—for U.S. government bonds (which financed the growing federal budget deficit). But low interest rates in the United States kept the demand for U.S. assets from outweighing the huge supply of dollars generated by the trade deficit.

Ironically, from early 2008 through the beginning of 2009, as the U.S. economy plunged, the value of the dollar shot back up—rising by 14% between April 2008 and April 2009. The reason was simple: as the instability of world financial markets became increasingly apparent, there was a rush to security. That is, investors moved their money into U.S. government bonds, widely viewed as the most secure way to hold assets (in spite of the very low interest rates). This meant a strong demand for dollars.

These movements in the value of the dollar over the last two decades tell a story of instability in the world economy and in the economic relation of the United States to other countries. This instability in turn, can be extremely disruptive for a variety of industries—and for workers in those industries. ❑

Note: In this discussion of recent experience, the value of the dollar is the "trade-weighted value of the dollar"—that is, the average value of the dollar relative to the values of the currencies of U.S. trading partners.

Article 3.2

IS CHINA'S CURRENCY MANIPULATION HURTING THE U.S.?

BY ARTHUR MacEWAN
November/December 2010

> Dear Dr. Dollar:
> Is it true that China has been harming the U.S. economy by keeping its currency
> "undervalued"? Shouldn't the U.S. government do something about this situation?
> —*Jenny Boyd, Edmond, W.Va.*

The Chinese government, operating through the Chinese central bank, does keep its currency unit—the yuan—cheap relative to the dollar. This means that goods imported *from* China cost less (in terms of dollars) than they would otherwise, while U.S. exports *to* China cost more (in terms of yuan). So we in the United States buy a lot of Chinese-made goods and the Chinese don't buy much from us. In the 2007 to 2009 period, the United States purchased $253 billion more in goods annually from China than it sold to China.

This looks bad for U.S workers. For example, when money gets spent in the United States, much of it is spent on Chinese-made goods, and fewer jobs are then created in the United States. So the Chinese government's currency policy is at least partly to blame for our employment woes. Reacting to this situation, many people are calling for the U.S. government to do something to get the Chinese government to change its policy.

But things are not so simple.

First of all, there is an additional reason for the low cost of Chinese goods— low Chinese wages. The Chinese government's policy of repressing labor probably accounts for the low cost of Chinese goods at least as much as does its currency policy. Moreover, there is a lot more going on in the global economy. Both currency problems and job losses involve much more than Chinese government actions— though China provides a convenient target for ire.

And the currency story itself is complex. In order to keep the value of its currency low relative to the dollar, the Chinese government increases the supply of yuan, uses these yuan to buy dollars, then uses the dollars to buy U.S. securities, largely government bonds but also private securities. In early 2009, China held $764 billion in U.S. Treasury securities, making it the largest foreign holder of U.S. government debt. By buying U.S. government bonds, the Chinese have been financing the federal deficit. More generally, by supplying funds to the United States, the Chinese government has been keeping interest rates low in this country.

If the Chinese were to act differently, allowing the value of their currency to rise relative to the dollar, both the cost of capital and the prices of the many goods imported from China would rise. The rising cost of capital would probably not be a serious problem, as the Federal Reserve could take counteraction to keep interest rates low. So, an increase in the value of the yuan would net the United States some jobs, but also raise some prices for U.S. consumers.

It is pretty clear that right now what the United States needs is jobs. Moreover, low-cost Chinese goods have contributed to the declining role of manufacturing in the United States, a phenomenon that both weakens important segments of organized labor and threatens to inhibit technological progress, which has often been centered in manufacturing or based on applications in manufacturing (e.g., robotics).

So why doesn't the U.S. government place more pressure on China to raise the value of the yuan? Part of the reason may lie in concern about losing Chinese financing of the U.S. federal deficit. For several years the two governments have been co-dependent: The U.S. government gets financing for its deficits, and the Chinese government gains by maintaining an undervalued currency. Not an easy relationship to change.

Probably more important, however, many large and politically powerful U.S.-based firms depend directly on the low-cost goods imported from China. Wal-mart and Target, as any shopper knows, are filled with Chinese-made goods. Then there are the less visible products from China, including a power device that goes into the Microsoft Xbox, computer keyboards for Dell, and many other goods for many other U.S. corporations. If the yuan's value rose and these firms had to pay more dollars to buy these items, they could probably not pass all the increase on to consumers and their profits would suffer.

Still, in spite of the interests of these firms, the U.S. government may take some action, either by pressing harder for China to let the value of the yuan rise relative to the dollar or by placing some restrictions on imports from China. But don't expect too big a change. ❑

Article 3.3

WHERE DO U.S. DOLLARS GO WHEN THE UNITED STATES RUNS A TRADE DEFICIT?

BY ELLEN FRANK
March/April 2004

Dear Dr. Dollar:

Can you explain what trade deficits are? Who owes what to whom or is it just an accounting device?

—*Jack Miller, Indianapolis, Ind.*

Dear Dr. Dollar:

I see that the United States has had a negative international trade balance for years. What happens to those dollars we've sent overseas?

—*Bill Clark, Chillicothe, Ohio*

If Americans collectively import more goods and services from foreigners than we export, we are said to have a trade deficit. Paying for the things we import accounts for most of the flow of dollars out of the United States. However, money flows out of the country for other reasons as well. The U.S. government provides foreign aid and supports overseas military bases; immigrants to the United States send dollars back to their families; foreigners who own U.S. businesses or financial assets take income out of the country.

When these factors are added to the trade deficit, the net outflow of dollars is called the *current account deficit*. In 2002, the U.S. trade deficit amounted to $418 billion, and the current account deficit totaled $480 billion. Data for 2003 is not yet available, but preliminary reports indicate the current account deficit will be at least $550 billion.

Once the dollars leave the country, three things can happen. First, foreigners can use dollars to purchase U.S. assets: stocks, bonds, bank deposits, government debt, real estate, businesses. When Toyota buys land and equipment for a factory in the United States, when a British investment fund buys stock in a U.S. corporation, when a German bank purchases U.S. Treasury bonds, then the United States is said to be "financing" its current account deficit by selling assets. In 2002, foreigners acquired $612 billion in U.S. assets.

The United States has run persistent and increasing current account deficits since the 1980s, and foreigners have used the dollars to stake significant claims on U.S. assets. At the end of 2002, the value of U.S. assets owned by foreigners exceeded the value of foreign assets owned by U.S. residents by $2.4 trillion. This is the reason the United States is often said to be a debtor nation, with a net debt to the rest of the world of $2.4 trillion. But this "debt" is denominated in our own currency. For that reason, it does not pose the same risks for the United

States as developing countries with large debts—which must be repaid in dollars or euro—face.

Foreign central banks provide a second outlet for dollars that leave the United States. The dollar is the most widely used international currency, and many less-developed countries have sizable dollar-denominated debts. Governments sometimes hang on to whatever dollars fall into their hands, parking them in liquid assets like U.S. bank accounts or U.S. government bonds to earn interest. In 2002, foreign governments held almost $95 billion in dollar reserves, which they will use to cover future deficits, repay debts, intervene in financial markets, or simply to exert influence in negotiations with the United States.

If you've followed the arithmetic so far, you will have figured out that in 2002, on balance, more dollars flowed back into the United States to purchase assets then flowed out. This allowed U.S. companies to buy assets overseas, almost $200 billion worth.

As long as the country's large current account deficit is financed by these capital inflows, it is not necessarily a problem. But a third possible consequence of the massive U.S. current account deficit is that foreigners will lose confidence in the U.S. economy and stop purchasing U.S. assets. If this happens, the supply of dollars in the global banking system will exceed demand and the exchange value of the dollar will fall.

Some people believe this is already happening. Over the past few years, the dollar lost about one-third of its value relative to the euro. This could signify that foreigners are shifting from U.S. to euro-based assets. If the era of dollar supremacy is indeed coming to a close, the value of the dollar will continue to fall. What this would mean for the U.S. and world economies is difficult to predict. A sustained loss of confidence in the dollar could have many potentially serious ramifications.

Imports would grow more expensive, infuriating our trading partners, who depend on the U.S. market for their goods. With less foreign demand for U.S. assets, stock prices might tumble and interest rates rise. United States-based banks and corporations would find it harder to buy foreign assets and expand overseas. The dollar has been in trouble before and, in the past, the U.S. government pressured other countries to buy or hold dollars and prop up its value. Whether other countries agree to this will depend, ultimately, on whether the United States and other major economic powers are still talking to one another. ❏

Article 3.4

DOLLAR ANXIETY—REAL REASONS TO WORRY

The advantages of imperial finance have propped up the U.S. economy—but they may not last.

BY JOHN MILLER

January/February 2005

The value of the dollar is falling. Does that mean that our economic sky is falling as well? Not to sound like Chicken Little, but the answer may well be yes. If an economic collapse is not in our future, then at least economic storm clouds are gathering on the horizon.

It's what lies behind the slide of the dollar that has even many mainstream economists spooked: an unprecedented current account deficit—the difference between the country's income and its consumption and investment spending. The current account deficit, which primarily reflects the huge gap between the amount the United States imports and the amount it exports, is the best indicator of where the country stands in its financial relationship with the rest of the world.

At an estimated $670 billion, or 5.7% of gross domestic product (GDP), the 2004 current account deficit is the largest ever. An already huge trade deficit (the amount exports fall short of imports) made worse by high oil prices, along with rock bottom private savings and a gaping federal budget deficit, have helped push the U.S. current account deficit into uncharted territory. The last time it was above 4% of GDP was in 1816, and no other country has ever run a current account deficit that equals nearly 1% of the world's GDP. If current trends continue, the gap could reach 7.8% of U.S. GDP by 2008, according to Nouriel Roubini of New York University and Brad Setser of University College, Oxford, two well-known finance economists.

Most of the current account deficit stems from the U.S. trade deficit (about $610 billion). The rest reflects the remittances immigrants send home to their families plus U.S. foreign aid (together another $80 billion) less net investment income (a positive $20 billion because the United States still earns more from investments abroad than it pays out in interest on its borrowing from abroad).

The current account deficit represents the amount of money the United States must attract from abroad each year. Money comes from overseas in two ways: foreign investors can buy stock in U.S. corporations, or they can lend money to corporations or to the government by buying bonds. Currently, almost all of the money must come from loans because European and Japanese investors are no longer buying U.S. stocks. U.S. equity returns have been trivial since 2000 in dollar terms and actually negative in euro terms since the dollar has lost ground against the euro.

In essence, the U.S. economy racks up record current account deficits by spending more than its national income to feed its appetite for imports that are now half again exports. That increases the supply of dollars in foreign hands.

At the same time, the demand for dollars has diminished. Foreign investors are less interested in purchasing dollar-dominated assets as they hold more of them (and as the self-fulfilling expectation that the value of the dollar is likely to fall sets in). In October 2004, net foreign purchases of U.S. securities—stocks and bonds—dipped to their lowest level in a year and below what was necessary to offset the current account deficit. In addition, global investors' stock and bond portfolios are now overloaded with dollar-denominated assets, up to 50% from 30% in the early '90s.

Under the weight of the massive current account deficit, the dollar has already begun to give way. Since January 2002, the value of the dollar has fallen more than 20%, with much of that dropoff happening since August 2004. The greenback now stands at multiyear lows against the euro, the yen, and an index of major currencies.

Should foreign investors stop buying U.S. securities, then the dollar will crash, stock values plummet, and an economic downturn surely follow. But even if foreigners continue to purchase U.S. bonds—and they already hold 47% of U.S Treasury bonds—a current account deficit of this magnitude will be a costly drag on the economy. The Fed will have to boost interest rates, which determine the rate of return on U.S. bonds, to compensate for their lost value as the dollar slips in value and to keep foreigners coming back for more. In addition, a falling dollar makes imports cost more, pushing up U.S inflation rates. The Fed will either tolerate the uptick in inflation or attempt to counteract it by raising interest rates yet higher. Even in this more orderly scenario of decline, the current expansion will slow or perhaps come to a halt.

Imperial Finance

You can still find those who claim none of this is a problem. Recently, for example, the editors of the *Wall Street Journal* offered worried readers the following relaxation technique—a version of what former Treasury Secretary Larry Summers says is the sharpest argument you typically hear from a finance minister whose country is saddled with a large current account deficit.

First, recall that a large trade deficit requires a large surplus of capital flowing into your country to cover it. Then ask yourself, would you rather live in a country that continues to attract investment, or one that capital is trying to get out of? Finally, remind yourself that the monetary authorities control the value of currencies and are fully capable of halting the decline.

Feel better? You shouldn't. Arguments like these are unconvincing, a bravado borne not of postmodern cool so much as the old-fashioned, unilateral financial imperialism that underlies the muscular U.S. foreign policy we see today.

True, so far foreigners have been happy to purchase the gobs of debt issued by the U.S. Treasury and corporate America to cover the current account deficit. And that has kept U.S. interest rates low. If not for the flood of foreign money, Morgan

Stanley economist Stephen Roach figures, U.S. long-term interest rates would be between one and 1.5 percentage points higher today.

The ability to borrow without pushing up interest rates has paid off handsomely for the Bush administration. Now when the government spends more than it takes in to prosecute the war in Iraq and bestow tax cuts on the rich, savers from foreign shores finance those deficits at reduced rates. And cash-strapped U.S. consumers are more ready to swallow an upside-down economic recovery that has pushed up profit but neither created jobs nor lifted wages when they can borrow at low interest rates.

How can the United States get away with running up debt at low rates? Are other countries' central banks and private savers really the co-dependent "global enablers" Roach and others call them, who happily hold loads of low-yielding U.S.

IF THE UNITED STATES WERE AN EMERGING MARKET

If the United States were a small or less-developed country, financial alarm bells would already be ringing. The U.S. current account deficit is well above the 5%-of-GDP standard the IMF and others use to pronounce economies in the developing world vulnerable to financial crisis.

Just how crisis-prone depends on how the current account deficit affects the economy's spending. If the foreign funds flowing into the country are being invested in export-producing sectors of the economy, or the tradable goods sectors, such as manufacturing and some services, they are likely over time to generate revenues necessary to pay back the rest of the world. In that case, the shortfall is less of a problem. If those monies go to consumption or speculative investment in non-tradable (i.e., non-export producing) sectors such as a real estate, then they surely will be a problem.

By that standard, the U.S. current account deficit is highly problematic. Economists assess the impact of a current account deficit by comparing it to the difference between net national investment and net national savings. (Net here means less the money set aside to cover depreciation.) In the U.S. case, that difference has widened because saving has plummeted, not because investment has picked up. Last year, the United States registered its lowest net national savings rate ever, 1.5%, due to the return of large federal budget deficits and anemic personal savings. In addition, U.S. investment has shifted substantially away from tradable goods as manufacturing has come under heavy foreign competition toward the non-traded goods sector, such as residential real estate whose prices have soared in and around most major American cities.

Capital inflows that cover a decline in savings instead of a surge in investment are not a sign of economic health nor cause to stop worrying about the current account deficit.

assets? The truth is, the United States has taken advantage of the status of the dollar as the currency of the global economy to make others adjust to its spending patterns. Foreign central banks hold their reserves in dollars, and countries are billed in dollars for their oil imports, which requires them to buy dollars. That sustains the demand for the dollar and protects its value even as the current account imbalance widens.

The U.S. strong dollar policy in the face of its yawning current account deficit imposes a "shadow tax" on the rest of the world, at least in part to pay for its cost of empire. "But payment," as Robert Skidelsky, the British biographer of Keynes, reminds us, "is voluntary and depends at minimum on acquiescence in U.S. foreign policy." The geopolitical reason for the rest of the capitalist world to accept the "seignorage of the dollar"—in other words, the advantage the United States enjoys by virtue of minting the reserve currency of the international economy—became less compelling when the United States substituted a "puny war on terrorism" for the Cold War, Skidelsky adds.

The tax does not fall only on other industrialized countries. The U.S. economy has not just become a giant vacuum cleaner that sucks up "all the world's spare investible cash," in the words of University of California, Berkeley economist Brad DeLong, but about one-third of that money comes from the developing world. To put this contribution in perspective: DeLong calculates that $90 billion a year, or one-third of the average U.S. current account deficit over the last two decades, is equal to the income of the poorest 500 million people in India.

The rest of the world ought not to complain about these global imbalances, insist the strong dollar types. That the United States racks up debt while other countries rack up savings is not profligacy but a virtue. The United States, they argue, is the global economy's "consumer of last resort." Others, especially in Europe, according to U.S. policymakers, are guilty of "insufficient consumption": they hold back their economies and dampen the demand for U.S. exports, exacerbating the U.S. current account deficit. Last year U.S. consumers increased their spending three times as quickly as European consumers (excluding Britain), and the U.S. economy grew about two and half times as quickly.

Global Uprising

Not surprisingly, old Europe and newly industrializing Asia don't see it that way. They have grown weary from all their heavy lifting of U.S. securities. And while they have yet to throw them overboard, a revolt is brewing.

Those cranky French are especially indignant about the unfairness of it all. The editors of Le Monde, the French daily, complain that "[t]he United States considers itself innocent: it refuses to admit that it lives beyond its means through weak savings and excessive consumption." On top of that, the drop of the dollar has led to a brutal rise in the value of the euro that is wiping out the demand for euro-zone exports and slowing their already sluggish economic recoveries.

Even in Blair's Britain *The Economist*, the newsweekly, ran an unusually tough-minded editorial warning: "The dollar's role as the leading international currency can no longer be taken for granted. ... Imagine if you could write checks that were accepted as payment but never cashed. That is what [the privileged position of the dollar] amounts to. If you had been granted that ability, you might take care to hang on to it. America is taking no such care. And may come to regret it."

But the real threat comes from Asia, especially Japan and China, the two largest holders of U.S. Treasury bonds. Asian central banks already hold most of their reserves in dollar-denominated assets, an enormous financial risk given that the value of the dollar will likely continue to fall at current low interest rates.

In late November, just the rumor that China's Central Bank threatened to reduce its purchases of U.S. Treasury bonds was enough to send the dollar tumbling.

No less than Alan Greenspan, chair of the Fed, seems to have come down with a case of dollar anxiety. In his November remarks to the European Banking Community, Greenspan warned of a "diminished appetite for adding to dollar balances" even if the current account deficit stops increasing. Greenspan believes that foreign investors are likely to realize they have put too many of their eggs in the dollar basket and will either unload their dollar-denominated investments or demand higher interest rates. After Greenspan spoke, the dollar fell to its lowest level against the Japanese yen in more than four years.

A Rough Ride From Here

The question that divides economists at this point is not whether the dollar will decline more, but whether the descent will be slow and orderly or quick and panicky. Either way, there is real reason to believe it will be a rough ride.

First, a controlled devaluation of the dollar won't be easy to accomplish. Several major Asian currencies are formally or informally pegged to the dollar, including the Chinese yuan. The United States faces a $160 billion trade deficit with China alone. U.S. financial authorities have exerted tremendous pressure on the Chinese to raise the value of their currency, in the hope of slowing the tide of Chinese imports into the United States and making U.S. exports more competitive. But the Chinese have yet to budge.

Beyond that, a fall in the dollar sufficient to close the current account deficit will slaughter large amounts of capital. The *Economist* warns that "[i]f the dollar falls by another 30%, as some predict, it would amount to the biggest default in history: not a conventional default on debt service, but default by stealth, wiping trillions off the value of foreigners' dollar assets."

Even a gradual decline in the value of dollar will bring tough economic consequences. Inflation will pick up, as imports cost more in this bid to make U.S. exports cheaper. The Fed will surely raise interest rates to counteract that inflationary pressure, slowing consumer borrowing and investment. Also, closing the current account deficit would require smaller government deficits. (Although not politically likely, repealing Bush's pro-rich tax cuts would help.)

What will happen is anyone's guess given the unprecedented size of the U.S. current account deficit. But there is a real possibility that the dollar's slide will be anything but slow or orderly. Should Asian central banks stop intervening on the scale needed to finance the U.S. deficit, then a crisis surely would follow. The dollar would drop through the floor; U.S. interest rates would skyrocket (on everything from Treasury bonds to mortgages to credit cards); the stock market and home values would collapse; consumer and investment spending would plunge; and a sharp recession would take hold here and abroad.

The Bush administration seems determined to make things worse. Should the Bush crew push through their plan to privatize Social Security and pay the trillion-dollar transition cost with massive borrowing, the consequences could be disastrous. The example of Argentina is instructive. Privatizing the country's retirement program, as economist Paul Krugman has pointed out, was a major source of the debt that brought on Argentina's crisis in 2001. Dismantling the U.S. welfare state's most successful program just might push the dollar-based financial system over the edge.

The U.S. economy is in a precarious situation held together so far by imperial privilege. Its prospects appear to fall into one of three categories: a dollar crisis; a long, slow, excruciating decline in value of the dollar; or a dollar propped up through repeated interest-rate hikes. That's real reason to worry. ❑

Sources: "Dollar Anxiety," editorial, *Wall Street Journal*, 11/11/04; D. Wessel, "Behind Big Drop in Currency: U.S. Soaks Up Asia's Output," *WSJ*, 12/2/04; J. B. DeLong, "Should We Still Support Untrammeled International Capital Mobility? Or are Capital Controls Less Evil than We Once Believed," *Economists' Voice*, 2004; R. Skidelsky, "U.S. Current Account Deficit and Future of the World Monetary System" and N. Roubini and B. Setser "The U.S. as A Net Debtor: The Sustainability of the U.S. External Imbalances," 11/04, Nouriel Roubini's Global Macroeconomic and Financial Policy site <www.stern.nyu.edu/globalmacro>; Rich Miller, "Why the Dollar is Giving Way," *BusinessWeek,* 12/6/04; Robert Barro, "Mysteries of the Gaping Current-Account Gap," *BusinessWeek*, 12/13/04; D. Streitford and J. Fleishman, "Greenspan Issues Warning on Dollar," *L.A. Times*, 11/20/04; S. Roach, "Global: What Happens If the Dollar Does Not Fall?" Global Economic Forum, Morgan Stanley, 11/22/04; L. Summers, "The U.S. Current Account Deficit and the Global Economy," The 2004 Per Jacobsson Lecture, 10/3/04; "The Dollar," editorial, *The Economist*, 12/3/04; "Mr. Gaymard and the Dollar," editorial, *Le Monde*, 11/30/04.

Article 3.5

"PRESSURE FROM THE BOND MARKET"

BY ARTHUR MACEWAN
May/June 2010

> Dear Dr. Dollar:
>
> *With the crisis in Greece and other countries, commentators have said that governments are "under pressure from the bond market" or that bond markets will "punish" governments. What does this mean?*
> —Nikolaos Papanikolaou, Queens, N.Y.

It means that money is power.

The people and institutions that buy government bonds have the money. They are "the bond market." By telling governments the conditions under which they will make loans (i.e., buy the governments' bonds), they are able to greatly influence governments' policies.

But let's go back to some basics. When a government spends more than it takes in as taxes, it has to borrow the difference. It borrows by selling bonds, which are promises to pay. So the payments for the bonds are loans.

A government might sell a bond that is a promise to pay $103 a year from the date of sale. If bond buyers are confident that this promise will be kept and if the return they can get on other forms of investments is 3%, they will be willing to pay $100 for the bond. That is, they will be willing to loan the government $100 to be paid back in one year with 3% interest. This investment will then be providing the same return as their other investments.

But what if they are not confident that the promise will be kept? What if the investors ("the bond market") think that the government of Greece, for example, may not be able to make the payments as promised and will default on the bonds? Under these circumstances the investors will not pay $100 for the bonds that return $103 next year. They may be willing to pay only $97.

If the government then does meet its promise, the bond will provide a 6.2% rate of return. But if the "bond market's" fear of default turns out to be correct, then these bonds will have a much lower rate of return—or, in the extreme case, they will be a total loss. The "bond market" is demanding a higher rate of return to compensate for the risk. (The 3% - 6.2% difference was roughly the difference between the return on German and Greek bonds in March, when this column was written. By mid-April Greece was paying 9%.)

However, if the Greek government—or whatever government is seeking the loans—can sell these bonds for only $97, it will have to sell more bonds in order to raise the funds it needs. In a year, the payments (that 6.2%) will place a new, severe burden on the government's budget.

So the investors say, in effect, "If you fix your policies in ways that we think make default less likely, we will buy the bonds at a higher price—not $100, but maybe at $98 or $99." It is not the ultimate purchasers of the bonds who convey this message; it is the underwriters, the large investment banks—Goldman Sachs for example. As underwriters they handle the sale of the bonds for the Greek government (and take hefty fees for this service).

Even if the investment banks were giving good, objective advice, this would be bad enough. However, the nature of their advice—"the pressure from the bond market"—is conditioned by who they are and whom they represent.

Foremost, they push for actions that will reduce the government's budget deficit, even when sensible economic policy would call for a stimulus that would be provided by maintaining or expanding the deficit. Also, investment bankers will not tell governments to raise taxes on the rich or on foreign corporations in order to reduce the deficit. Instead, they tend to advocate cutting social programs and reducing the wages of public-sector workers.

It does not require great insight to see the class bias in these sorts of actions.

Yet the whole problem does not lie with the "pressure from the bond market." The Greek government and other governments have followed policies that make them vulnerable to this sort of pressure. Unwilling or unable to tax the rich, governments borrowed to pay for their operations in good times. Having run budget deficits in good times, these authorities are in a poor position to add more debt when it is most needed—in the current recession in particular. So now, when governments really need to borrow to run deficits, they—and, more important, their people—are at the mercy of the "bond markets."

Popular protests can push back, saving some social programs and forcing governments to place a greater burden on the wealthy. A real solution, however, requires long-term action to shift power, which would change government practices and reduce vulnerability to "the pressure from the bond market." ❑

Chapter 4

INTERNATIONAL INSTITUTIONS AND TRADE AGREEMENTS

Article 4.1

THE ABCs OF THE GLOBAL ECONOMY

BY THE *DOLLARS & SENSE* COLLECTIVE

March/April 2000; updated December 2006, August 2009, and October 2011

In the 1960s, U.S. corporations changed the way they went after profits in the international economy. Instead of producing goods in the United States to export, they moved more and more toward producing goods overseas to sell to consumers in those countries and at home. They had done some of this in the 1950s, but really sped up the process in the 1960s.

Before the mid-1960s, free trade probably helped workers and consumers in the United States while disadvantaging workers in poorer countries. Exporters invested their profits at home in the United States, creating new jobs and boosting incomes. The American Federation of Labor-Congress of Industrial Organizations (AFL-CIO) thought this was a good deal and backed free trade.

But when corporations changed strategies, they changed their alliances. By the late 1960s, the AFL-CIO began opposing free trade as it watched jobs go overseas. But unionists did not see that they had to start building alliances internationally. The union federation continued to take money secretly from the U.S. government to help break up red unions abroad, not a good tactic for producing solidarity. It took until the 1990s for the AFL-CIO to reduce (though not eliminate) its alliance with the U.S. State Department. In the 1990s, unions also forged their alliance with the environmental movement to oppose free trade.

But corporations were not standing still; in the 1980s and 1990s they were working to shift the architecture of international institutions created after World War II to work more effectively in the new global economy they were creating. More and more of their profits were coming from overseas—by the 1990s, 30% of U.S. corporate profits came from their direct investments overseas, up from 13% in the 1960s. This includes money made from the operations of their subsidiaries abroad. But the share of corporate profits earned overseas is even higher than that because the 30% figure doesn't include the interest companies earn on money they loan abroad. And the financial sector is an increasingly important player in the global economy.

Financial institutions and other global corporations without national ties now use governments to dissolve any national restraints on their activities. They are global, so they want their governments to be global too. And while trade used to be taken care of through its own organization (GATT) and money vaguely managed through another organization (the International Monetary Fund), the World Trade Organization has erased the divide between trade and investment in its efforts to deregulate investment worldwide.

In helping design some of the global institutions after World War II, John Maynard Keynes assumed companies and economies would operate within national bounds, with the IMF and others regulating exchanges across those borders. The instability created by ruptured borders is made worse by the deregulation sought by corporations, and especially, the financial sector. The most powerful governments of the world seem oblivious to the threat giving into this neoliberal corporate agenda poses to their ability to govern.

The current economic crisis presents us with a world-historical moment in which it is possible to stop the corporate offensive, a moment when the weaknesses of the neoliberal approach have been laid bare. In fact, even amidst the celebration of globalization pre-crisis, the further expansion of this model had already begun to meet with resistance. In the Americas, further progress on a continent-wide free-trade agreement stalled after 2003, although Central America did conclude a new free-trade deal with the United States in 2005. In the summer of 2006, the current round of World Trade Organization talks, launched in Doha, Qatar in 2001, collapsed for good in the face of European refusal to give up its farm supports and the growing recognition among developing countries that further trade liberalization had little to offer them. This economic crisis signals the end of the United States' ability and desire to enable the export-led growth that developing countries have been asked to pin their futures upon. Resistance to neoliberalism in developing countries is likely to increase even more. Amidst the economic rubble of the crisis there is some hope that global institutions just might be reshaped in a liberatory manner.

What follows is a primer on the most important of those institutions.

—*The* Dollars & Sense *collective*

THE INTERNATIONAL MONETARY FUND (IMF) AND WORLD BANK

The basic structure of the postwar international capitalist economy was created in 1944, at an international conference in Bretton Woods, New Hampshire. Among the institutions coming out of this conference were the World Bank and the International Monetary Fund (IMF). For this reason, they are sometimes known as the "Bretton Woods twins." Both institutions engage in international lending. The IMF primarily acts as a "lender of last resort" to countries (usually, but not always, lower-income countries) that have become heavily indebted and cannot get loans elsewhere. The World Bank, meanwhile, focuses primarily on longer-term "development" lending.

At both the World Bank and the IMF, the number of votes a country receives is closely proportional to how much capital it contributes to the institution, so the voting power of rich countries like the United States is disproportionate to their numbers. Eleven rich countries, for example, account for more than 50% of the voting power in the IMF Board of Governors. At both institutions, five powerful countries—the United States, the United Kingdom, France, Germany, and Japan—get to appoint their own representatives to the institution's executive board, with 19 other directors elected by the rest of the 180-odd member countries. The president of the World Bank is elected by the Board of Executive Directors, and traditionally nominated by the U.S. representative. The managing director of the IMF is traditionally a European.

The IMF and the World Bank wield power vastly greater than the share of international lending they account for because private lenders follow their lead in deciding which countries are credit-worthy. The institutions have taken advantage of this leverage—and of debt crises in Latin America, Africa, Asia, and even Europe—to push a "free-market" (or "neoliberal") model of economic development.

The IMF

While the Bretton Woods conference included representatives of the U.S. and British governments, the Americans dominated the outcome. The British delegation (including the legendary economist John Maynard Keynes) argued for an international currency for world trade and debt settlements. The Americans insisted on the U.S. dollar being the de facto world currency (with the dollar's value fixed in terms of gold and the values of other currencies fixed in proportion to the dollar). The British wanted countries that ran trade surpluses and those that ran trade deficits (and became indebted to the "surplus" countries) to share the costs of "adjustment" (bringing the world economy back into balance). The U.S. insisted on a system in which the "deficit" countries would have to do the adjusting, and a central aim would be making sure that the debtors would pay back their creditors at any cost.

The IMF was a key part, from the very start of the "debtor pays" system the U.S. government had insisted on at Bretton Woods. When a country fell heavily into debt, and could no longer get enough credit from private sources, the IMF would step in as the "lender of last resort." This made it possible for the debtor to continue to pay its creditors in the short run. The typical IMF adjustment program, however, demanded painful "austerity" or "shock therapy"—elimination of price controls on basic goods (such as food and fuel), cuts in government spending, services, and employment, and "devaluation" of the country's currency. All three of these austerity measures hit workers and poor people the hardest, the first two for fairly obvious reasons. The impact of currency devaluation, however, requires a little more explanation.

Devaluation meant that the currency would buy fewer dollars—and fewer of every other currency "pegged" to the dollar. This made imports to the country more expensive. (Suppose that a country's peso had been pegged at a one-to-one ratio to the dollar. An imported good that cost $10 would cost 10 pesos. If the currency was devalued to a two-to-one ratio to the dollar, an imported good that cost $10 would now cost 20 pesos.) Devaluation also caused domestic prices to rise, since domestic producers faced less import competition. Meanwhile, it made the country's exports less expensive to people in other countries. The idea was that the country would export more, earn more dollars in return, and—this is the key—be able to pay back its debts to U.S. and European banks. In other words, the people of the country (especially workers and the poor) would consume less of what they produced, and send more of it abroad to "service" the country's debt.

For many years, these kinds of measures were the core of IMF "adjustment" plans. Since the 1970s, however, the IMF broadened its standard program to include deeper "structural" changes to debtor countries' economies. "Structural adjustment programs" (SAPs) included not only the austerity measures described above, but also the elimination of trade barriers and controls on international investment, the privatization of public enterprises, and the "deregulation" of labor markets (including elimination of minimum wage laws, hours laws, occupational safety and health regulations, and protections for unions). These were the basic ingredients for overturning "regulated" (or "interventionist") forms of capitalism in many lower-income countries, and replacing it with "free-market" (or "neoliberal") capitalism. They also prepared the ground for the system of globalized production. This made it easier for multinational companies to locate operations in these countries (thanks to the removal of restrictions on foreign investment), employ a relatively cheap and controllable workforce (thanks to the removal of labor regulations), and export the goods back to their home countries or elsewhere in the world (thanks to the elimination of trade barriers). Structural adjustment programs became the lance-point of "free-market" reform, especially in Latin America during the 1980s debt crisis, but also in other low-income regions.

The World Bank

In its early years, just after World War II, the World Bank mostly loaned money to Western European governments to help rebuild their war-ravaged economies. This was an important factor in the postwar reconstruction of the world capitalist economy. European reconstruction bolstered demand for exported goods from the United States, and ultimately promoted the reemergence of Western Europe as a global manufacturing powerhouse.

During the long period (1968-1981) that former U.S. Defense Secretary Robert S. McNamara headed the World Bank, however, the bank turned toward "development" loans to lower-income countries. McNamara brought the same philosophy to development that he had used as a chief architect of the U.S. war against Vietnam: big is good and bigger is better. Since then, the World Bank has favored large, expensive projects regardless of their appropriateness to local conditions, and with little attention to environmental and social impacts. The Bank has been especially notorious, for example, for supporting large dam projects that have flooded wide areas, deprived others of water, and uprooted the people living in affected regions. The Bank's support for large, capital-intensive "development" projects has also been a disguised way of channeling benefits to large global companies. Many of these projects require inputs—like high-tech machinery—that are not produced in the countries where the projects take place. Instead, they have to be imported, mostly from high-income countries. Such projects may also create long-run dependencies, since the spare parts and technical expertise for proper maintenance may only be available from the companies that produced these inputs in the first place.

While the Bank's main focus is long-term "development" lending, it has also engaged in "structural adjustment" lending. The Bank's structural adjustment policies, much like those from the IMF, have imposed heavy burdens on workers and poor people. In the 1980s and 1990s, during its "structural adjustment era," the Bank went so far as to advocate that governments charge fees even for public primary education. (Predictably, in countries that adopted such policies, many poor families could not afford the fees and school enrollment declined.) The Bank has since publicly called for the abolition of school fees. Critics argue, however, that the shift is at least partly rhetorical. Katarina Tomasevski, founder of the organization Right to Education, argues that the Bank presents itself as opposing fees, but does not oppose hidden charges, as for textbooks, school uniforms, and other costs of attending school.

The World Bank has also made development loans conditional on the adoption of "free-market" policies, like privatization of public services. Most notoriously, the Bank has pushed for the privatization of water delivery. Where privatization of water or other public services has not been possible, the Bank has urged governments to adopt "cost-recovery" strategies—including raising fees on users. Both privatization and cost-recovery strategies have undermined poor people's access to water and other essentials.

Recent developments

Since the 1990s, opposition to World Bank and IMF policies have shaken the two institutions' power—especially in Latin America, the world region to which "neoliberalism" came first and where it went furthest. This is part of a broader backlash against neoliberal policies, which opponents (especially on the Latin American left) blame for persistent poverty and rising inequality in the region. The last decade or so has seen a so-called "pink wave" in Latin America, with "center-left" parties coming to power in Argentina, Bolivia, Brazil, Chile, Ecuador, and Venezuela. (The center-left has since lost the presidency in Chile.) Different governments have adopted different policies in power, some staying close to the neoliberal path, others veering sharply away from it. Venezuela threatened to withdraw from the IMF and World Bank, but has not yet done so. It has, along with several other countries, withdrawn from the World Bank-affiliated International Centre for the Settlement of Investment Disputes (ICSID). The Venezuelan government has also proposed the formation of a new regional lending institution, the Bank of the South, which would be an alternative lender (for both long-term development and short-term "liquidity crises") to the IMF and World Bank.

On the other hand, the IMF has emerged, surprisingly, as a powerful influence in Western Europe. For many years, acute debt crises seemed to be confined to lower-income economies, and most observers did not dream that they could happen in Europe or other high-income regions. (For this reason, the IMF was widely criticized as a hammer that high-income countries used on low-income countries.) During the current economic crisis, however, several Western European countries have fallen deeply into debt. The IMF has stepped in as part of "bailout" programs for Greece, Iceland, and Ireland. True to its origins, it has also pushed for austerity—especially cuts in public spending—in highly indebted countries. Many economists—especially proponents of "Keynesian" views—have argued that weakness in total demand is the main cause of the current economic crisis in Europe and the rest of the world. Under these conditions, they argue, cuts in government spending will only reduce total demand further, and likely cause the crisis to drag on.

Sources: International Monetary Fund, "IMF Members' Quotas and Voting Power, and IMF Board of Governors" (www.imf.org); International Monetary Fund, "IMF Executive Directors and Voting Power" (www.imf.org); World Bank, "Executive Directors and Alternates" (www.worldbank.org); World Bank, "Cost Recovery for Water Supply and Sanitation and Irrigation and Drainage Projects (www.worldbank.org); Zoe Godolphin, "The World Bank as a New Global Education Ministry?" Bretton Woods Project, January 21, 2011 (www.brettonwoodsproject.org); Katerina Tomasevski, "Both Arsonist and Fire Fighter: The World Bank on School Fees," Bretton Woods Project, January 23, 2006 (www.brettonwoodsproject.org); Katerina Tomasevski, "Six Reasons Why the World Bank Should Be Debarred From Education ," Bretton Woods Project, September 2, 2006 (www.brettonwoodsproject.org).

THE MULTILATERAL AGREEMENT ON INVESTMENT (MAI) AND TRADE RELATED INVESTMENT MEASURES (TRIMS)

Where did they come from?

You're probably not the sort of person who would own a chemical plant or luxury hotel, but imagine you were. Imagine you built a chemical plant or luxury hotel in a foreign country, only to see a labor-friendly government take power and threaten your profits. This is the scenario which makes the CEOs of footloose global corporations wake up in the middle of the night in a cold sweat. To avert such threats, ministers of the richest countries met secretly at the Organization for Economic Cooperation and Development (OECD) in Paris in 1997 and tried to hammer out a bill of rights for international investors, the Multilateral Agreement on Investment (MAI).

When protests against the MAI broke out in the streets and the halls of government alike in 1998 and 1999, scuttling the agreement in that form, the corporations turned to the World Trade Organization to achieve their goal.

What are they up to?

Both the MAI and Trade Related Investment Measures (or TRIMs, the name of the WTO version) would force governments to compensate companies for any losses (or reductions in profits) they might suffer because of changes in public policy. Governments would be compelled to tax, regulate, and subsidize foreign businesses exactly as they do local businesses. Policies designed to protect fledgling national industries (a staple of industrial development strategies from the United States and Germany in the 19th century to Japan and Korea in the 20th) would be ruled out.

TRIMs would also be a crowning blow to the control of governments over the movement of capital into or out of their countries. Until fairly recently, most governments imposed controls on the buying and selling of their currencies for purposes other than trade. Known as capital controls, these curbs significantly impeded the mobility of capital. By simply outlawing conversion, governments could trap investors into keeping their holdings in the local currency. But since the 1980s, the IMF and the U.S. Treasury have pressured governments to lift these controls so that international companies can more easily move money around the globe. Corporations and wealthy individuals can now credibly threaten to pull liquid capital out of any country whose policies displease them.

Malaysia successfully imposed controls during the Asian crisis of 1997 and 1998, spurring broad interest among developing countries. The United States wants to establish a new international discussion group—the Group of 20 (G-20), consisting of ministers from 20 developing countries handpicked by the United States—to consider reforms. Meanwhile, it continues to push for the MAI-style liberation of capital from any control whatsoever.

Why should you care?

It is sometimes said that the widening chasm between the rich and poor is due to the fact that capital is so easily shifted around the globe while labor, bound to family and place, is not. But there is nothing natural in this. Human beings, after all, have wandered the earth for millennia—traversing oceans and continents, in search of food, land, and adventure—whereas a factory, shipyard, or office building, once built, is almost impossible to move in a cost effective way. Even liquid capital (money) is less mobile than it seems. To be sure, a Mexican can fill a suitcase with pesos, hop a plane and fly to California, but once she disembarks, who's to say what the pesos will be worth, or whether they'll be worth anything at all? For most of this century, however, capitalist governments have curbed labor's natural mobility through passports, migration laws, border checkpoints, and armed border patrols, while capital has been rendered movable by treaties and laws that harmonize the treatment of wealth around the world. The past three decades especially have seen a vast expansion in the legal rights of capital across borders. In other words, labor fights with the cuffs on, while capital takes the gloves off.

WORLD INTELLECTUAL PROPERTY ORGANIZATION (WIPO) AND TRADE-RELATED ASPECTS OF INTELLECTUAL PROPERTY RIGHTS (TRIPS)

One of the less familiar members of the "alphabet soup" of international economic institutions, the World Intellectual Property Organization (WIPO) has governed "intellectual property" issues since its founding in 1970. In the old days, "intellectual property" only covered property rights over inventions, industrial designs, trademarks, and artistic and literary works. But WIPO has been busy staking out a brave new world of property rights, especially in the electronic domain. Now "intellectual property" includes computer programs, electronic images, and digital recordings, as well as pharmaceuticals and even biological processes and genetic codes.

The 1996 WIPO treaty outlaws the "circumvention" of electronic security measures. It makes it illegal, for example, to sidestep the security measures on a website (such as those requiring that users register or send payment in exchange for access). The treaty also prevents programmers from cracking open commercial software to view the underlying code. Similar restrictions had already gone into effect in the United States, thanks to the Digital Millennium Copyright Act (DMCA). These laws prevent programmers from crafting their own programs so that they are compatible with existing software, and prevent innovation in the form of "reengineering"—drawing on one design as the basis of another. Reengineering has been at the heart of many countries' economic development, including the United States'. In the 19th century, for example, Lowell, Massachusetts, textile manufacturers built their looms based on English designs.

In recent years, WIPO has faced a turf war over the intellectual property issue with none other than the World Trade Organization (WTO). Wealthy countries are attempting an end run around WIPO because it lacks enforcement power and because some poor countries have resisted its agenda. But the mass media, information technology, drug, and biotechnology industries in wealthy countries stand to lose a great deal from "piracy" and to gain a fortune in fees and royalties if given more extensive property rights. So they have introduced, under the name "Trade-Related Aspects of Intellectual Property Rights" (TRIPs), extensive provisions on intellectual property into recent WTO negotiations.

TRIPs would put the muscle of trade sanctions behind intellectual property rights. It would also stake out new intellectual property rights over plant, animal, and even human genetic codes. The governments of some developing countries have objected, warning that private companies based in rich countries will declare ownership over the genetic codes of plants long used for healing or crops within their countries—what activists have called "biopiracy." By manipulating just one gene of a living organism, a company can be declared the sole owner of an entire plant variety.

These proposals may seem like a new frontier of property rights, but except for the issue of ownership of life forms, TRIPs actually defend the old regime of property rights. It is because current electronic, chemical, and biological technology make virtually unlimited production and free distribution possible that the fight for private property has become so extreme.

THE WORLD TRADE ORGANIZATION (WTO)
Where did it come from?

Since the 1950s, government officials from around the world have met irregularly to hammer out the rules of a global trading system. Known as the General Agreements on Trade and Tariffs (GATT), these negotiations covered, in excruciating detail, such matters as what level of taxation Japan could impose on foreign rice, how many American automobiles Brazil could allow into its market, and how large a subsidy France could give its vineyards. Every clause was carefully crafted, with constant input from business representatives who hoped to profit from expanded international trade.

The GATT process however, was slow, cumbersome and difficult to monitor. As corporations expanded more rapidly into global markets they pushed governments to create a more powerful and permanent international body that could speed up trade negotiations as well as oversee and enforce provisions of the GATT. The result is the World Trade Organization, formed out of the ashes of GATT in 1995.

The WTO's ministerial meetings have been the target of massive anti-globalization protests. Over 50,000 people went to Seattle in 1999 to say no to the WTO's corporate agenda, successfully shutting down the first day of the ministerial meeting. African, Caribbean, and other least-developed country representatives walked out of the meeting. The WTO held its 2001 ministerial meeting in Doha, Qatar, safe from protest. The WTO initiated a new round of trade talks it promised would address thee need s of developing countries. The Doha Development round was in fact continued the WTO's pro-corporate agenda. Two years later "the Group of 20 developing countries" at the Cancún ministerial refused to lower trade barriers in their countries trade until the United States and EU cleaned up their unfair global agricultural systems. By the summer of 2006, five years after it began, the Doha round had collapsed and the WTO suspended trade negotiations.

What is it up to?

The WTO functions as a sort of international court for adjudicating trade disputes. Each of its 153 member countries has one representative, who participates in negotiations over trade rules. The heart of the WTO, however, is not its delegates, but its dispute resolution system. With the establishment of the WTO, corporations now have a place to complain to when they want trade barriers—or domestic regulations that limit their freedom to buy and sell—overturned.

Though corporations have no standing in the WTO—the organization is, officially, open only to its member countries—the numerous advisory bodies that provide technical expertise to delegates are overflowing with corporate representation. The delegates themselves are drawn from trade ministries and confer regularly with the corporate lobbyists and advisors who swarm the streets and offices of Geneva, where the organization is headquartered. As a result, the WTO has become, as an anonymous delegate told the *Financial Times,* "a place where governments can collude against their citizens."

Lori Wallach and Michelle Sforza, in their book *The WTO: Five Years of Reasons to Resist Corporate Globalization*, point out that large corporations are essentially "renting" governments to bring cases before the WTO, and in this way, to win in the WTO battles they have lost in the political arena at home. Large shrimping corporations, for example, got India to dispute the U.S. ban on shrimp catches that were not sea-turtle safe. Once such a case is raised, the resolution process violates most democratic notions of due process and openness. Cases are heard before a tribunal of "trade experts," generally lawyers, who, under WTO rules, are required to make their ruling with a presumption in favor of free trade. The WTO puts the burden squarely on governments to justify any restriction of what it considers the natural order of things. There are no amicus briefs (statements of legal opinion filed with a court by outside parties), no observers, and no public records of the deliberations.

The WTO's rule is not restricted to such matters as tariff barriers. When the organization was formed, environmental and labor groups warned that the WTO would soon be rendering decisions on essential matters of public policy. This has proven absolutely correct. The organization has already ruled against Europe for banning hormone-treated beef and against Japan for prohibiting pesticide-laden apples. Also WTO rules prohibit selective purchasing laws, even those targeted at human rights abuses. In 1998 the WTO court lodged a complaint against the Massachusetts state law that banned government purchases from Burma in an attempt to punish its brutal dictatorship. Had the WTO rules been in place at the time, the anti-Apartheid divestment movement would have violated them as well.

Why should you care?

At stake is a fundamental issue of popular sovereignty—the rights of the people to regulate economic life, whether at the level of the city, state, or nation. The U.S. does not allow businesses operating within its borders to produce goods with child labor, so why should we allow those same businesses—Disney, Gap, or Walmart—to produce their goods with child labor in Haiti and sell the goods here?

THE INTERNATIONAL LABOR ORGANIZATION (ILO)

Where did it come from?

The ILO was established in 1919 in the wake of World War I, the Bolshevik revolution in Russia, and the founding of the Third (Communist) International, a world federation of revolutionary socialist political parties. Idealistic motives mingled with the goal of business and political elites to offer workers an alternative to revolution, and the result was an international treaty organization (established by agreement between governments) whose main job was to promulgate codes of practice in work and employment.

After World War II the ILO was grafted onto the U.N. structure, and it now serves a wide range of purposes: drafting conventions on labor standards (182 so far), monitoring their implementation, publishing analyses of labor conditions around the world, and providing technical assistance to national governments.

Why should you care?

The ILO's conventions set high standards in such areas as health and safety, freedom to organize unions, social insurance, and ending abuses like workplace discrimination and child labor. It convenes panels to investigate whether countries are upholding their legal commitment to enforce these standards, and by general agreement their reports are accurate and fair. ILO publications, like its flagship journal, *The International Labour Review,* its *World Labor and Employment Reports,* and its special studies, are of very high quality. Its staff, which is headquartered in Geneva and numbers 1,900, has many talented and idealistic members. The ILO's technical assistance program is minuscule in comparison to the need, but it has changed the lives of many workers.

(You can find out more about the ILO at its website: www.ilo.org.)

As a rule, international organizations are reflections of the policies of their member governments, particularly the ones with the most clout, such as the United States. Since governments are almost always biased toward business and against labor, we shouldn't expect to see much pro-labor activism in official circles. The ILO provides a partial exception to this rule, and it is worth considering why. There are probably four main reasons:

- The ILO's mission explicitly calls for improvements in the conditions of work, and the organization attracts people who believe in this cause. Compare this to the mission of the IMF (to promote the ability of countries to repay their international debts) or the WTO (to expand trade), for instance.
- Governments send their labor ministers (in the U.S., the Secretary of Labor) to represent them at the ILO. Labor ministers usually specialize in social protection issues and often serve as liaisons to labor unions. A roomful of labor ministers will generally be more progressive than a similar gaggle of finance (IMF) or trade (WTO) ministers.
- The ILO's governing body is based on tripartite principles: representatives from unions, employers, and government all have a seat at the table. By institutionalizing a role for non-governmental organizations, the ILO achieves a greater degree of openness and accountability.
- Cynics would add that the ILO can afford to be progressive because it is largely powerless. It has no enforcement mechanism for its conventions, and some of the countries that are quickest to ratify have the worst records of living up to them.

The ILO has significant shortcomings as an organization. Perhaps the most important is its cumbersome, bureaucratic nature: it can take forever for the apparatus to make a decision and carry it out. (Of course, that beats the IMF's approach: decisive, reactionary, and authoritarian.) The experience of the ILO tells us that creating a force capable of governing the global economy will be extremely difficult, and that there are hard tradeoffs between democracy, power, and administrative effectiveness. But it also demonstrates that reforming international organizations—changing their missions and governance systems—is worth the effort, especially if it brings non-governmental activists into the picture. ❑

Sources: David Mermelstein, ed., *The Economic Crisis Reader* (Vintage, 1975); Susan George and Fabrizio Sabelli, *Faith and Credit: The World Bank's Secular Empire* (Penguin Books, 1994); Hans-Albrecht Schraepler, *Directory of International Economic Organizations* (Georgetown University Press, 1997); Jayati Ghosh, Lectures on the history of the world economy, Tufts University, 1995; S.W. Black, "International Monetary Institutions," *The New Palgrave: A Dictionary of Economics*, John Eatwell, Murray Milgate, and Peter Newman, eds. (The Macmillan Press Limited, 1987).

ARTICLE 4.2

THE ABCs OF FREE-TRADE AGREEMENTS
AND OTHER REGIONAL ECONOMIC BLOCS
BY THE *DOLLARS & SENSE* COLLECTIVE
January/February 2001; updated, December 2006 and October 2011

In the United States, the corporate media have framed the debate over "globalization" largely as a struggle between cosmopolitan advocates and their provincial opponents. The pro-globalization types are celebrated as champions not only of a "global marketplace," but also of a worldwide community of peoples brought together by communications, transportation, and commerce, a "global village." Meanwhile, "anti-globalization" protesters face not only tear gas and truncheons, but also accusations of protectionism, isolationism, and disregard for those outside the United States.

International institutions—like the World Trade Organization (WTO), International Monetary Fund (IMF), and World Bank—as well as regional associations—such as the North American Free Trade Agreement (NAFTA), the European Union (EU), the Association of Southeast Asian Nations (ASEAN), and now the Central American Free Trade Agreement (CAFTA)—are primarily concerned with granting capital the freedom to move from country to country. It is true that many opponents of globalization have invoked national sovereignty as a first line of defense against this new wave of aggressive capitalist expansion. In some cases, this reaction has been accompanied by ugly nativist impulses, which join hostility towards international institutions and multinational corporations with hostility towards "foreign" workers. To its credit, however, much of the "global economic justice" movement has deftly avoided the nativist pitfall—avowing a solidarity that crosses all lines of nation and national origin, that stands up "for humanity and against neoliberalism."

Already, part of the movement is grappling with the problematic defense of national sovereignty, advocating instead a brand of grassroots democracy that does not exist very often in either international institutions or national states. Many activists even reject the "anti-globalization" label that has been hung on them, posing their own vision of "globalization from below" against a "globalization dominated by capital." Today, goods and capital pass freely across national frontiers while people run a gauntlet of border patrols and barbed wire. "Globalization from below" turns this status quo, which combines the worst of both worlds, on its head. Instead of the free movement of capital across national borders, "globalization from below" champions the free movement of people. Instead of equal treatment for all investors, no matter where they are investing, it demands equal human and civil rights for all people, no matter where they are living. Instead of greater worldwide integration of multinational corporations, it raises the banner of greater international solidarity among popular movements and organizations.

Instead of the "race to the bottom," it calls for an "upward harmonization." Instead of the rule of capital, the rule of the people. Instead of more inequality, less. Instead of less democracy, more.

That is an appealing vision for the future. At this point, however, "globalization dominated by capital" is still on the march—operating through both global institutions and regional associations. A decade of protests against the WTO and IMF (not only in the United States, but across the world) has shown that resistance is not futile. The immediate effect, however, may be to channel the globalization agenda back into regional "free-trade" agreements. Ultimately, the forces of resistance will need to be far greater to turn the tide. In the meantime, here's what we're up against.

THE NORTH AMERICAN FREE TRADE AGREEMENT (NAFTA)

The North American Free Trade Agreement (NAFTA) came into effect on January 1, 1994. The agreement eliminated most barriers to trade and investment among the United States, Canada and Mexico. For some categories of goods—certain agricultural goods, for example—NAFTA promised to phase out restrictions on trade over a few years, but most goods and services were to be freely bought and sold across the three countries' borders from the start. Likewise, virtually all investments—financial investments as well as investments in fixed assets such as factories, mines, or farms (foreign direct investment)—were freed from cross-border restrictions.

NAFTA, however, made no changes in the restrictions on the movement of labor. Mexican—and, for that matter, Canadian—workers who wish to come to the United States must enter under the limited immigration quotas or illegally. Thus NAFTA gave new options and direct benefits to those who obtain their income from selling goods and making investments, but the agreement included no parallel provision for those who make their incomes by working.

Supporters of NAFTA have argued that both firm owners and workers in all three countries can gain from the removal of trade and investment barriers. For example, the argument goes, U.S. firms that produce more efficiently than their Mexican counterparts will have larger markets, gain more profits, generate more jobs, and pay higher wages. The prime examples would include information technology firms, bio-tech firms, larger retailers, and other U.S. corporations that have an advantage because of skilled U.S. labor or because of experience in organization and marketing. On the other hand, Mexican firms that can produce at low cost because of low Mexican wages will be able to expand into the U.S. market. The main example would be assembly plants or *maquiladoras*.

Critics of the agreement have focused on problems resulting from extreme differences among the member countries in living standards, wages, unionization, environmental laws, and social legislation. The options that NAFTA creates for business firms put them at a great advantage in their dealings with workers and communities. For example, U.S. unions are weakened because firms can more easily shut down domestic operations and substitute operations in Mexico. With the government suppressing independent unions in Mexico, organization of workers in all three countries is undermined. (Actually, the formal Mexican labor laws are probably as good or better than those in the United States but they are usually not enforced.) While NAFTA may mean more jobs and better pay for computer software engineers in the United States, auto-assembly and parts workers in the United States, for example, see their wages stagnate or fall. Similarly, the greater freedom of international movement that NAFTA affords to firms gives them greater bargaining power over communities when it comes to environmental regulations. One highly visible result has been severe pollution problems in Mexican *maquiladora* zones along the U.S. border.

An additional and important aspect of NAFTA is that it creates legal mechanisms for firms based in one country to contest legislation in the other countries when it might interfere with their "right" to carry out their business. Thus, U.S. firms operating in Mexico have challenged stricter environmental regulations won by the Mexican environmental movement. In Canada, the government rescinded a public-health law restricting trade in toxic PCBs as the result of a challenge by a U.S. firm; Canada also paid $10 million to the complaining firm, in compensation for "losses" it suffered under the law. These examples illustrate the way in which NAFTA, by giving priority to the "rights" of business, has undermined the ability of governments to regulate the operation of their economies in an independent, democratic manner.

Finally, one of NAFTA's greatest gifts to business has been the removal of restrictions on the movement of financial capital. The immediate result for Mexico was the severe financial debacle of 1994. Investment funds moved rapidly into Mexico during the early 1990s, and especially after NAFTA went into effect. Without regulation, these investments were able to abandon Mexico just as rapidly when the speculative "bubble" burst, leading to severe drops in production and employment.

FTAA AND CAFTA: EXTENDING THE FREE TRADE AGENDA TO THE WESTERN HEMISPHERE

After the implementation of NAFTA, it looked like the Americas were on a fast track to a hemisphere-wide free-trade zone. In 1994, Clinton proposed to have the world's largest trading block in place by 2005. Instead, the Free Trade Area of the Americas (FTAA) stalled in its tracks when, in 1997, Congress denied Clinton "fast-track" negotiating authority. Bush revived the fast-track push in 2001 and succeeded in getting fast-track legislation through both the House of Representatives and the U.S. Senate in 2002.

What would a realized FTAA look like? There are two near-certainties. First, labor and environmental standards are unlikely to be on the agenda unless popular movements force the issue. Canadian Trade Minister Pierre Pettigrew, for example, told Parliament that labor and environmental side agreements like those in NAFTA would only impede negotiations (Canada chaired the FTAA negotiations process until late 1999 and remains an important booster of the pact). Second, the United States, which accounts for 70% of the hemispheric economy, would dominate any hemisphere-wide economic bloc. As a Brazilian businessman succinctly put it at a July 2000 meeting of the Common Market of the South (Mercado Comun del Sur, or Mercosur), Latin America's largest trading bloc, "Who rules in FTAA is the U.S."

While 2005 came and went without the FTAA, the U.S. Congress did approve by the narrowest of margins the Central American Free Trade Agreement (CAFTA). CAFTA is now in effect for trade between the United States and El Salvador, Honduras, Nicaragua, and Guatemala. The Dominican Republic has also ratified the agreement but Washington has held off on implementing the agreement in a bid to increase protections for large pharmaceutical companies from generic competition. Costa Rica signed the agreement but has yet to ratify it. Economic size alone assures that U.S. interests dominate the agreement. The combined economic output of the countries in Central America is smaller than the total income of just two U.S.-based agribusiness companies that will benefit from the accord: Cargill and Archer Daniels Midland.

CAFTA, modeled after the North American Free Trade Agreement, has all the shortcomings of NAFTA and will do more to hamper sustainable development and no more to further human rights and labor abuses in Central America than NAFTA did in Mexico. A recent report from the "Stop CAFTA Coalition" documents the problems evident already just one year into the agreement. First, there are few signs that CAFTA is creating the promised regional textile complex to offset competition from China. Central American garment exports continue to lose market share to their Asian competitors. In addition, CAFTA is contributing to making difficult conditions in the Central American countryside yet worse. U.S. imports of fresh beef, poultry, and dairy products have increased dramatically, displacing local producers, and food prices have risen. Promised monies to contend with the disruption of rural life have not been forthcoming. Finally, CAFTA has done nothing to improve human rights or extend labor rights in Central America. In El Salvador government crackdowns on peaceful demonstrations have increased at the same time that exports have declined. And CAFTA poses yet another danger. Its rules, buried in the technical language of the investment chapter of the agreement, would make it more difficult for the six Central American nations to escape their heavy debt burdens or recover from a debt crisis.

THE EUROPEAN UNION (EU)

The European Union (EU) forms the world's largest single market. From its beginnings in 1951 as the six-member European Coal and Steel Community, the association has grown both geographically (now including 15 countries in Central and Western Europe, with plans to expand into Eastern Europe) and especially in its degree of unity. Eleven of the EU's members now share a common currency (the euro), and all national border controls on goods, capital, and people were abolished between member countries in 1993.

Open trade within the EU poses less of a threat for wages and labor standards than NAFTA or the WTO. Even the poorer member countries, such as Spain, Portugal, and Greece, are fairly wealthy and have strong unions and decent labor protections. Moreover, most EU countries, including top economic powers like France, Germany, Italy, and the United Kingdom, are ruled by parties (whether "socialist," social democratic, or labor) with roots in the working-class movement. This relationship has grown increasingly distant in recent years; still, from the perspective of labor, the EU represents a kind of best-case scenario for freeing trade. The results are, nonetheless, cautionary.

The main thrust of the EU, like other trade organizations, has been trade. Labor standards were never fully integrated into the core agenda of the EU. In 1989, 11 of the then-12 EU countries signed the "Charter of the Fundamental Social Rights of Workers," more widely known as the "Social Charter." (Only the United Kingdom refused to sign.) Though the "Social Charter" did not have any binding mechanism—it is described in public communications as "a political instrument containing 'moral obligations'"—many hoped it would provide the basis for "upward harmonization," that is, pressure on European countries with weaker labor protections to lift their standards to match those of member nations with stronger regulations. The 11 years since the adoption of the "Social Charter" have seen countless meetings, official studies, and exhortations but few appreciable results.

Since trade openness was never directly linked to social and labor standards and the "Social Charter" never mandated concrete actions from corporations, European business leaders have kept "Social Europe" from gaining any momentum simply by ignoring it. Although European anti-discrimination rules have forced countries like Britain to adopt the same retirement age for men and women, and regional funds are dispersed each year to bring up the general living standards of the poorest nations, the social dimension of the EU has never been more than an appendage for buying off opposition. As a result, business moved production, investment, and employment in Europe toward countries with low standards, such as Ireland and Portugal.

The EU also exemplifies how regional trading blocs indirectly break down trade regulations with countries outside the bloc. Many Europeans may have hoped that the EU would insulate Europe from competition with countries that lacked social, labor, and environmental standards. While the EU has a common external tariff, each member can maintain its own non-tariff trade barriers. EU rules requiring openness between member countries, however, made it easy to circumvent any EU country's national trade restrictions. Up until 1993, member states used to be able to block indirect imports through health and safety codes or border controls, but with the harmonization of these rules across the EU, governments can no longer do so. Since then, companies have simply imported non-EU goods into the EU countries with the most lax trade rules, and then freely transported the goods into the countries with higher standards. (NAFTA similarly makes it possible to circumvent U.S. barriers against the importation of steel from China by sending it indirectly through Mexico.) EU members that wished to uphold trade barriers against countries with inadequate social, labor, and environmental protections ended up becoming less important trading hubs in the world economy. This has led EU countries to unilaterally abolish restrictions and trade monitoring against non-EU nations. The logic of trade openness seems to be against labor and the environment even when the governments of a trading bloc individually wish to be more protective.

THE EUROZONE

The process of European economic integration, which began with the formation of the six-country European Coal and Steel Community in 1951, culminated with the establishment of a common currency (the euro) between 1999 and 2002. Of the 27 European Union (EU) member countries, only 17 have adopted the euro as their currency (joined the "eurozone"). One of the most important EU economies, the United Kingdom, for example, has retained its own national currency (the pound). The countries that did adopt the euro, on the other hand, retired their national currencies. There is no German deutschmark, French franc, or Italian lira anymore. These currencies, and the former national currencies of other eurozone countries, stopped circulating in 2001 or 2002, depending on the country. Bank balances held in these currencies were converted to euros. People holding old bills and coins were also able to exchange them for euros.

The creation of the euro seemed to cap the rise of Europe, over many years, from the devastation of the Second World War. Step by step, Western Europe had rebuilt vibrant economies. The largest "core" economy, Germany, had become a global manufacturing power. Even some countries with historically lower incomes, like Ireland, Italy, and Spain, had converged toward the affluence of the core countries. The euro promised to be a major new world currency, ultimately with hundreds of millions of users in one of the world's richest and seemingly most stable regions. Some commentators viewed the euro as a potential rival to the dollar as a key currency in world trade, and as a "reserve" currency (in which individuals, companies, and national banks would hold financial wealth).

The adoption of the euro meant a major change in the control over monetary policy for the eurozone countries. Countries that have their own national currencies generally have a central bank (or "monetary authority") responsible for policies affecting the country's overall money supply and interest rates. In the United States, for example, the Federal Reserve (or "the Fed") is the monetary authority. To "tighten" the money supply, the Fed sells government bonds to "the public" (really, to private banks). It receives money in return, and so reduces the amount of money held by the public. The Fed may do this at the peak of a business-cycle boom, in order to combat or head off inflation. Monetary tightening tends to raise interest rates, pulling back on demand for goods and services. Reduced overall demand, in turn, tends to reduce upward pressure on prices. To "loosen" the money supply, on the other hand, the Fed buys government bonds back from the banks. This puts more money into the banks' hands, which tends to reduce interest rates and stimulate spending. The Fed may do this during a business-cycle downturn or full-blown recession, in order to raise output and employment. As these examples suggest, monetary policy can be an important lever through which governments influence overall demand, output, and employment. Adopting the euro meant giving up control over monetary policy, a step many EU countries, like the UK, were not willing to make.

For eurozone countries, monetary policy is made not by a national central bank, but by the European Central Bank (ECB). ECB policy is made by 23-member "governing council," including the six members of the bank's executive board and the directors of each of the 17 member countries' central banks. The six executive-board members, meanwhile, come from various eurozone countries. (The members in late 2011 are from France, Portugal, Italy, Spain, Germany, and Belgium.) While all countries that have adopted the euro are represented on the governing council, Germany has a much greater influence on European monetary policy than other countries. Germany's is the largest economy in the eurozone. Among other eurozone countries, only France's economy is anywhere near its size. (Italy's economy is less than two-thirds the size of Germany's, in terms of total output; Spain's, less than half; the Netherlands', less than one-fourth.) German policymakers, meanwhile, have historically made very low inflation rates their main priority (to the point of being "inflation-phobic"). In part, this harkens back to a scarring period of "hyperinflation" during the 1920s. Even during the current crisis, as economist Paul Krugman puts it, "what we're seeing is an ECB catering to German desires for low inflation, very much at the expense of making the problems of peripheral economies much less tractable."

For countries, like Germany, that have not been hit so hard by the current crisis, the "tight money" policy is less damaging than for the harder-hit countries. With Germany's unemployment rate at 6.5% and the inflation rate at only 2.5%, as of October 2011, an insistence on a tight money policy does reflect an excessive concern with maintaining very low inflation and insufficient concern with stimulating demand and reducing unemployment. If this policy torpedoes the economies of other European countries, meanwhile, it may drag the whole of Europe—including the more stable "core" economies—back into recession.

For the harder-hit countries, the results are disastrous. These countries are mired in a deep economic crisis, in heavy debt, and unable to adopt a traditional "expansionary" monetary policy on their own (since the eurozone monetary policy is set by the ECB). For them, a looser monetary policy could stimulate demand, production, and employment, even without causing much of an increase in inflation. When an economy is producing near its full capacity, increased demand is likely to put upward pressure on prices. (More money "chasing" the same amount of goods can lead to higher inflation.) In Europe today, however, there are vast unused resources—including millions of unemployed workers—so more demand could stimulate the production of more goods, and need not result in rising inflation.

Somewhat higher inflation, moreover, could actually help stimulate the harder-hit European economies. Moderate inflation can stimulate demand, since it gives people an incentive to spend now rather than wait and spend later. It also reduces the real burdens of debt. Countries like Greece, Ireland, Italy, Portugal, and Spain are drowning in debt, both public and private. These debts are generally specified in nominal terms—as a particular number of euros. As the price level increases, however, it reduces the real value of a nominal amount of money. Debts can be paid back in euros that are worth less than when the debt was incurred. As real debt burdens decrease, people feel less anxious about their finances, and may begin to spend more freely. Inflation also redistributes income from creditors, who tend to be wealthier and to save more of their incomes, to debtors, who tend to be less wealth and spend most of theirs. This, too, helps boost demand.

The current crisis has led many commentators to speculate that some heavily indebted countries may decide to abandon the euro. This need not mean that they would repudiate (refuse to pay) their public debt altogether. They could, instead, convert their euro debts to their new national currencies. This would give them more freedom to pursue a higher-inflation policy, which would reduce the real debt burden. (Indeed, independent countries that owe their debt in their own currency need not ever default. A country that controls its own money supply can "print" more money to pay back creditors—with the main limit being how the money supply can be expanded without resulting in unacceptably high inflation. Adopting the euro, however, deprived countries in the eurozone of this power.) The current crisis, some economists argue, shows how the euro project was misguided from the start. Paul Krugman, for example, argues that the common currency was mainly driven by a political (not economic) aim—the peaceful unification of a region that had been torn apart by two world wars. It did not make much sense economically, given the real possibility for divergent needs of different national economies. Today, it seems a real possibility that the eurozone, at least, will come apart again.

Sources: Paul Krugman, "European Inflation Targets," *New York Times* blog, January 18, 2011 (krugman.blogs.nytimes.com); European Central Bank, Decision-making, Governing Council (www.ecb.int/); European Central Bank, Decision-making, Executive Board (www.ecb.int/); Federal Statistical Office (Statistisches Bundesamt Deutschland), Federal Republic of Germany, Short-term indicators, Unemployment, Consumer Price Index (www.destatis.de); Paul Krugman, "Can Europe Be Saved?" *New York Times*, January 12, 2011 (nytimes.com).

THE ASSOCIATION OF SOUTH EAST ASIAN NATIONS (ASEAN)
AND ASIA-PACIFIC ECONOMIC COOPERATION (APEC)

Founded in 1967 at the height of the Vietnam War, the Association of South East Asian Nations (ASEAN) sought to promote "regional security" for its five original members (Indonesia, Malaysia, Philippines, Singapore, and Thailand). After 1975, it focused on counteracting the spread of communism following the defeat of the U.S. military in Vietnam. Beginning in the 1980s, and especially since the collapse of the Soviet Union, the ASEAN agenda turned from fighting communism to "accelerating economic growth" through cooperation and trade liberalization. At the same time, the organization added the remaining countries of Southeast Asia (Brunei Darussalam, Cambodia, Laos, Myanmar, and even Vietnam) to its member list. Today ASEAN oversees a cohesive geographical region with a population of nearly 500 million (about twice that of the United States) and combined output of nearly $750 billion (about one-tenth that of the United States).

ASEAN has pushed for member countries to open up to international trade and capital. While Singapore grew rapidly beginning in the 1960s, and Indonesia, Malaysia, and Thailand grew quickly beginning in the 1970s, high levels of Japanese foreign direct investment pushed the growth rates of these Southeast Asian economies to near double-digit levels in the late 1980s. Still, in the 1990s, increased competition from other developing countries and regional trading partnerships (such as NAFTA and the EU) threatened the stability of these export economies. In 1992, ASEAN adopted its own "free trade" agreement. AFTA, the ASEAN Free Trade Area, lowered tariffs among member nations, and promoted intra-regional trade which now stands at about 25% of the exports of these nations, about twice the level in the early 1970s. In response to the Asian economic crisis, ASEAN member nations agreed at their 1998 summit to further open up their economies, especially their manufacturing sectors, to foreign investment. Ignoring the calls of grassroots movements for controls or taxes on international capital movements, the summit implemented plans allowing 100% foreign ownership of enterprises in member countries, duty-free imports of capital goods, and a minimum for corporate tax breaks of three years.

The ASEAN tradition of "non-intervention" in the internal political affairs of its member states meant that the organization turned a blind eye to the repression of pro-democracy movements in Myanmar, Indonesia, Cambodia, and other countries in the region. Nor has ASEAN insisted that member nations meet International Labor Organization (ILO) core labor conventions. Member states have failed to sign and even denounced conventions recognizing the freedom of workers to organize trade unions, abolishing child and forced labor, and outlawing discrimination in employment. At times, they have brutally attacked trade union movements. ASEAN has also failed to intervene in regional environmental problems, witnessed by its inability in 1999 to fashion an effective regional response to Indonesia's uncontrolled forest fires. The ASEAN reaction to the December 1999 WTO conference was no different. Leaders of ASEAN nations objected to U.S. calls to include core labor standards as part of trade agreements, insisting that they were an attempt to protect U.S. jobs. And Rodolfo Severino, secretary-general of ASEAN, complained that the United States and other rich countries had not lived up to the WTO textile agreement that would allow ASEAN garment exporters greater access to First World markets.

It is China's entry into the WTO, however, that has most threatened ASEAN interests. China had already replaced Southeast Asia as the favorite location of Japanese foreign direct investment, and Chinese exporters of toys, textiles, and other low-wage manufactured products have put ASEAN exporters under pressure. Unfortunately, the ASEAN response to Chinese competition has been to further liberalize its own rules on foreign direct investment.

Chinese competition for the ASEAN nations and the rest of the developing world intensified in January 2005, when the Multifiber Agreement (MFA), the 30-year-old the quota system for that guaranteed a share of the world's clothing market for dozens of poor countries, expired. Chinese-produced garments have flooded world markets undercutting garment producers across the globe. China increased it garments exports to the U.S. market by $6 billion in 2005, increasing its market share from 15% to nearly 27%. Cambodia and Indonesia maintained their market shares, but most Southeast garment producing nations lost market share to China in 2005. But hardest hit by the by the expiration of the MFA has been garment producers in former major quota holders, like Hong Kong, Taiwan, and South Korea, as well as garment producers in Mexico, and sub-Saharan African, despite those nations' trade preferences. The phasing out of the MFA has already cost Africa more than 250,000 jobs over the last few years, reports the International Textile, Garment and Leather Workers' Federation. Most jobs have been lost in Lesotho, South Africa, Swaziland, Nigeria, Ghana, Mauritius, Zambia, Madagascar, Tanzania, Malawi, Namibia and Kenya.

Long before this year's WTO conference, ASEAN member states recognized that their economic interests went well beyond the boundaries of Southeast Asia. In the late 1980s, Prime Minister Mahathir Mohammed of Malaysia called for the formation of a pan-Asian regional economic bloc to include, along with the ASEAN countries, Japan, China, Korea, Taiwan, and Hong Kong, the largest investors in Southeast Asia. Mahathir's proposal was met with stiff opposition from the West. At the United States' insistence, the Asia-Pacific Economic Cooperation forum (including the United States, Canada, Australia, New Zealand, and Korea, along with ASEAN members Brunei Darussalam, Indonesia, Malaysia, and the Philippines) was formed. The Asia-Pacific Economic Cooperation (APEC) today consists of 21 members, having added Chile, China, Hong Kong, Taiwan, Mexico, Papua New Guinea, Peru, Russia, and Vietnam to its 12 founding members. Unlike ASEAN, APEC members do not form a cohesive region other than bordering on the Pacific. APEC has no formal criteria for membership, but actual or promised trade liberalization is a de facto condition for entry. While commitments made by APEC members are formally voluntary and nonbinding, APEC pressures governments to remove trade and investment restrictions faster than they would following their own agenda.

APEC is heavily influenced by large corporations. In 1996 it even adopted "APEC means business" as its official slogan. While APEC is not an official trading bloc, APEC's push for lower tariffs has proceeded further and faster than the WTO's free-trade agenda. APEC is calling for free trade among APEC nations by 2010 for "developed nations" and 2020 for "developing nations." In addition, APEC pushes labor market policies guaranteed to impose hardships on workers. For instance, in response to the Asian economic crisis, APEC counseled member countries to "maintain flexibility in domestic labor markets," advice sure to mean lower wages and more layoffs for workers already suffering from the effects of the Asian economic crisis. And while pledging to promote "environmentally sustainable development," APEC has done little to combat the depletion of national resources and deforestation, especially in developing nations. APEC has also insisted that member economies harmonize food and product safety standards, which means high standards are likely to be replaced by the lowest common denominator. ❑

Sources: Brian Hanson, "What Happened to Fortress Europe?: External Trade Policy Liberalization in the European Union," International Organization, 52, no. 1 (Winter 1998), 55-86; Linda Lim, "ASEAN: New Modes of Economic Cooperation," in *Southeast Asia in the New World Order*, Wurfel and Burton; ASEAN Web, www.asean.or.id; APEC Secretariat, www.apecsec.org.sg,; SAY NO TO APEC (www.apec.gen.nz).

Article 4.3

ECONOMIC DEBACLE IN ARGENTINA: THE IMF STRIKES AGAIN
BY ARTHUR MACEWAN
March/April 2002

In the days just before Christmas [2001], with increasing cutbacks in social programs and an official unemployment rate approaching 20%, Argentinians took to the streets in protest. At the time, Argentina was in the midst of its fourth year of recession. The immediate spark for the unrest was the government's latest economic policies, which restricted the amount of money people could withdraw from their bank accounts. Political demonstrations and the looting of grocery stores quickly spread across the country.

The government declared a state of siege, but police often stood by and watched the looting "with their hands behind their backs." There was little the government could do. Within a day after the demonstrations began, principal economic minister Domingo Cavallo had resigned; a few days later, the president, Fernando de la Rúa, stepped down.

In the wake of the resignations, a hastily assembled interim government immediately defaulted on $155 billion of Argentina's foreign debt, the largest debt default in history. The new government also promised a public works jobs program and announced plans to issue a new currency, the argentino, that would circulate alongside the Argentine peso and the U.S. dollar. As economic instability deepened, however, the argentino plan was abandoned. And the new public works program did little to address the fact that per capita income had dropped by 14% since 1998. Unable to win the popular support it needed, the new government quickly dissolved. The current president, Eduardo Duhalde, was sworn in on January 1; he was the fifth president to serve in two weeks.

As of this writing (mid-February [2002]), Argentina still faces widespread political and economic uncertainty. In the short run, many anticipate more unemployment, severe inflation, or both. Also, Argentina's currency remains highly unstable. After experimenting with several different exchange rates, the Duhalde government is now permitting the peso to "float." The peso has already dropped from its previous value (one to the dollar) down to two to the dollar on the open market, and further devaluation is widely anticipated.

Argentina's experience leading into the current debacle provides one more lesson regarding the perils of "free market" ideology, and specifically the economic policies that the International Monetary Fund (IMF) pushes on governments around the globe. In Argentina, as in other places, these policies have been embraced by local elites, who see their fortunes (both real and metaphoric) as tied to the deregulation of commerce and the curtailment of social programs. Yet the claims that these policies bring economic growth and widespread well-being have been thoroughly discredited, as events in Argentina have shown.

From Good to Bad to Ugly

Not long ago, Argentina was the poster child for the conservative economic policies of the IMF. From the late 1980s onward, a series of loans gave the IMF the leverage to guide Argentine policymakers in privatizing state enterprises, liberalizing foreign trade and investment, and tightening government fiscal and monetary policy. During the 1990s, the country's economy seemed to do well, with real per capita income growing at the very rapid annual rate of about 4.5%.

The rapid economic growth through most of the 1990s, however, was built on weak foundations. That growth, while substantial, appears to have resulted largely from an increasing accumulation of international obligations (debt to private banks, the IMF, and foreign governments, as well as direct foreign investment), fortuitous expansion of foreign markets for Argentine exports, and short-term injections of government revenues from the sale of state enterprises. Before the end of the decade, things began to fall apart.

Argentina's current problems are all the more severe because in the early 1990s, in the name of fighting inflation, the government created a "currency board." The board was charged with regulating the country's currency so that the Argentine peso would exchange one-to-one with the U.S. dollar. To assure this fixed exchange rate, the board kept a supply of dollars on reserve, and could not expand the supply of pesos without an equivalent increase in the dollars that it held. The currency board system appeared attractive because of absurd rates of inflation in the 1980s, with price increases of up to 200% a month. By restricting the growth of the money supply, the system brought inflation rates to heel.

Although the currency board system had virtually eliminated inflation in Argentina by the mid-1990s, it had also eliminated flexibility in monetary policy. When the current recession began to develop in the late 1990s, the government could not stimulate economic activity by expanding the money supply.

Worse yet, as the economy continued to spiral downward, the inflow of dollars slowed, forcing the currency board to restrict the country's money supply even further. And still worse, in the late 1990s, the U.S. dollar appreciated against other currencies, which meant (because of the one-to-one rule) that the peso also increased in value. As a result, the price of Argentine exports rose, further weakening world demand for Argentina's goods.

As Argentina entered into the lasting downturn of the period since 1998, the IMF continued, unwavering, in its financial support. The IMF provided "small" loans, such as $3 billion in early 1998 when the country's economic difficulties began to appear. As the crisis deepened, the IMF increased its support, supplying a loan of $13.7 billion and arranging $26 billion more from other sources at the end of 2000. As conditions worsened further in 2001, the IMF pledged another $8 billion.

However, the IMF coupled its largesse with the condition that the Argentine government maintain its severe monetary policy and continue to tighten its fiscal policy by eliminating its budget deficit. (The IMF considers deficit reduction to be the key to macroeconomic stability and, in turn, the key to economic growth.)

The Argentine government undertook deficit reduction with a vengeance. With the economy in a nosedive and tax revenues plummeting, the only way to balance the budget was to drastically cut government spending. In early July 2001, just before making a major government bond offering, Argentine officials announced budget cuts totaling $1.6 billion (about 3% of the federal budget), which they hoped would reassure investors and allow interest rates to fall. Apparently, however, investors saw the cuts as another sign of worsening crisis, and the bonds could only be sold at high interest rates (14%, as compared to 9% on similar bonds sold just a few weeks before the announcement of budget cuts). By December, the effort to balance the budget required cuts that were far more severe; the government announced a drastic reduction of $9.2 billion in spending, or about 18% of its entire budget.

With these cutbacks, the government both eviscerated social programs and reduced overall demand. In mid-December, the government announced that it would cut the salaries of public employees by 20% and reduce pension payments. At the same time, as the worsening crisis raised fears that Argentina would abandon the currency board system and devalue the peso, the government moved to prevent people from trading their pesos for dollars by limiting bank withdrawals. These steps were the final straws, and in the week before Christmas, all hell broke loose.

Who Benefits from IMF Policies?

Argentina is just the latest example of how IMF policies have failed to establish the basis for long-term economic growth in low-income countries. IMF policies usually do succeed in curtailing inflation, as they did in Argentina in the mid-1990s, because sharp cuts in government spending and restrictions on the money supply tend to yield reduced price increases. Also, as the Argentine case illustrates, adopting IMF programs can open the door to large influxes of foreign loans—from the Fund itself, the World Bank, the governments of the United States and other high-income countries, and (with the IMF's approval) internationally operating banks. But nowhere, including Argentina, has the IMF policy package led to stable, sustained economic expansion.

What IMF policies do often lead to, though, is growing inequality. Officially, the IMF laments that its policies—specifically reductions in government spending—have a severe negative impact on low-income groups (because they generate high rates of unemployment and lead to the gutting of social programs). Yet, IMF officials rationalize their mania for spending cuts in times of crisis by claiming that balanced budgets are the foundation of long-term economic stability and growth.

Nonsense. In recessions, moderate government deficits, like those in Argentina in recent years, are a desirable policy because they boost spending, which counteracts the downturn; balanced budgets in such circumstances tend to exacerbate down-turns. Also, curtailing social spending—on education, health care, infrastructure projects—cuts the legs out from under long-term economic progress.

Yet the IMF sticks to its policies, probably because those policies serve impor-tant and powerful interests in the U.S. and world economies. The IMF is controlled by the governments of the high-income countries that finance its operations. The U.S. government, with over 18% of the voting shares in the Fund, has by far the greatest influence. Indeed, over the years, the IMF has operated largely as a branch of the U.S. foreign policy apparatus, attempting to create a context that assures the well-being of U.S. interests—which is to say the interests of U.S.-based internation-ally operating firms. Since the same context serves the interests of firms based in Europe, Japan, and elsewhere, the U.S. government generally has the support of its allied governments in directing the IMF.

To serve those interests, the IMF tells governments that a key to economic growth lies in providing unrestricted access for imports and foreign investment. In fact, virtually all experience suggests the opposite. Britain, the United States, Japan, the countries of Western Europe, Taiwan, South Korea—all built the foundations for successful economic growth not on "free trade," but on government regulation of trade. The IMF gets around the inconvenient facts of history by conflating free trade with extensive engagement in the international economy. But the two are not the same. Yes, successful development has always been accompanied by extensive international engagement, but through regulated commerce, not free trade.

During the 1980s and 1990s, the IMF pushed governments in low-income countries to liberalize their capital markets, claiming that capital controls were anathema to development. Then came 1997, when the open capital markets of East Asian countries were instruments of disaster. In the aftermath of 1997, it seemed clear that the real winners from open capital markets were financial firms based in the United States and other high-income countries.

These same financial firms have also been the winners of another component in the IMF policy package. "Fiscal responsibility," according to the IMF, means that governments must give the highest priority to repaying their international debts. However, experience does not support the contention that, when governments fail to pay foreign debts, they bring on financial disaster. Instead, experience suggests that, at times, defaulting on foreign debt—can be an effective, positive policy option. It is the banks operating out of New York and other financial centers, not people in low-income countries, that gain from giving first priority to debt repayment.

The IMF's advocacy of privatization offers one more way to open the world econ-omy more fully to U.S.-based firms. When state enterprises in low-income countries are sold, they are often bought by large internationally operating firms, able to move in quickly with their huge supply of capital. Of course, in Argentina and elsewhere, local business groups have often benefited directly from privatization, sometimes on their own and sometimes as junior partners of firms based abroad. Either way, this enlargement of the private sphere works in favor of private firms. The problem here is not that privatization is always inappropriate, but simply that, contrary to IMF nostrums, it is not always appropriate. Privatization is especially problematic when it only replaces an inefficient government monopoly with a private monopoly yielding huge profits for its owners. Moreover, the record from Mexico City to Moscow demonstrates that privatization is often a hugely corrupt process.

Forging an Argentine Alternative?

The recent political upheaval in Argentina lends new strength to the argument that IMF policies not only fail to bolster economic development but also lead to social and political disintegration. It also provides new opportunities to call for alternative strategies that support democratic, egalitarian forms of economic development. Such strategies would promote investment in social programs and other public services, the expansion of government revenues (raising taxes), and regulations to keep the private sector from being guided simply by private profits. These strategies, unlike those of the IMF, would establish a foundation for long-run economic expansion— and economic equality.

Could such strategies succeed in Argentina? The demonstrations that brought down the de la Rúa government seem to have brought together unemployed people, workers, and large segments of the middle class, at least for a time. Sporadic rioting continues, and in Buenos Aires, scores of neighborhood-based assemblies, attracting thousands of participants, are calling for a more democratic political system as well as issuing demands for economic change.

Nonetheless, positive changes will be difficult to attain. Although the Argentine government did default on the debt (a key element in repudiating the policies of the IMF), it did so as an act of desperation, not in a controlled manner that might yield the greatest advantage. Also, while deputy economic minister Jorge Todesca has been harshly critical of the IMF, he is also trying to appease foreign investors, saying that the government is "not thinking of" nationalizing the banking system or establishing price controls.

Externally, there are substantial political barriers to an alternative model of economic growth. At the end of December, even as a new spate of rioting broke out in Buenos Aires, President Bush told the Argentine government to seek guidance from the IMF and "to work closely with" the Fund in developing its economic plans. In early February, the finance ministers of the G-7 (the world's seven wealthiest industrial nations) rejected Argentina's request for a $20 billion loan, saying that the IMF must be on board in order to bring about a "sustainable" plan. At this writing, Argentina's current economic minister, Jorge Remes Lenicov, is meeting with IMF officials in Washington, D.C.

And the IMF is unlikely to change its program in any significant way. Indeed, as Argentinians took to the streets in response to their long suffering under the aegis of the IMF, the IMF disclaimed all responsibility. "The economic program of Argentina was designed by the government of Argentina and the objective of eliminating the budget deficit was approved by the Congress of Argentina," declared the IMF's spokesperson on December 21. Continued pressure from the U.S. government, combined with the IMF's persistence in pursuing its discredited policies, will make progressive change difficult.

Also, powerful elites in Argentina will reinforce the barriers to change. In spite of the current difficulties, Argentina's economic policies of the past 15 years have delivered substantial benefits to the country's business elite, especially those whose incomes derive from the financial sector and primary product exports (grain and beef). Those policies have allowed the elite to strengthen their position in their own country and to secure their roles as junior partners with U.S.-based and other internationally operating firms. Changing policies will therefore require shifting the balance of power within Argentina, and that will be no easy task. ❏

A version of this article originally appeared in Foreign Policy in Focus *(fpif.org), January 2, 2002.*

Article 4.4

WOUNDED TIGER
Ireland submits to the IMF.

BY DAN READ
July/August 2011

Guinness is, apparently, now good for public relations. President Barack Obama, in his recent visit to Ireland, seemed to develop a fondness for the drink, or at least put on a brave face when he posed for the cameras with a pint in his hand. Less than twenty-four hours later, though, he had departed the country, after promising to do "everything that we can to be helpful" on Ireland's economic woes that have led to not just one, but potentially two bailouts by the International Monetary Fund (IMF).

The initial three-year Extended Fund Facility granted by the IMF in December 2010 amounted to a loan of over 22.5 billion euros (roughly $32 billion). Coupled with loans from the European Union and state intervention from Dublin, the grand total comes to around $121 billion. The extraordinary price tag came with conditions: Ireland has had to make structural adjustments to its economy that align with IMF goals.

On the surface there is a lot of financial jargon involving "debt restructuring" that will ostensibly render the Irish economy "solvent" once again. The practical implications of these vague and somewhat strange phrases are spelled out in a National Recovery Plan enacted by the government and endorsed by the IMF.

The plan aims to cut government spending by over $21 billion within three years, with $8.5 billion being taken out of the public sector in 2011 alone.

Government pay and staffing levels are thus being downscaled, with the state payroll having already been slashed in 2010 to the tune of over $2 billion. Wages for "new entrants" have also been hit with a blanket 10% reduction, with recruitment to the state sector limited to 3,300 new personnel each year. In conjunction with measures to fire existing staff, the government hopes to have a leaner, less well-paid public sector, with fewer than 294,000 employees by 2014. Taking public-sector employment figures for late 2008, this entails a decline of 75,100 employees.

Downgrading for Growth

In their online press releases, the IMF has lauded the plan for laying the foundations for recovery while still paying "due regard to a social safety net." The safety net is looking a little worn, however. Some measures proposed by the plan involved the withdrawal of $144 million from state pension funds, as well as raising the retirement age to 66 in 2014, to 67 in 2021, and to 68 in 2028. Furthermore, for 2011 alone $1.1 billion is to be taken from Social Protection (welfare), which will see a total cut of $4.3 billion by 2014.

The plan paves new ground for political institutions worldwide in that it openly admits the measures "will negatively affect the living standards of citizens," but claims that this is necessary to "to return [the Irish] economy to a sustainable medium-term economic growth path."

The state sector employs workers from a diverse set of industries, ranging from hospital nurses to postmen to police officers. Policies threatening these workers' jobs have prompted renewed militancy on the part of trade unions and leftist political organizations.

"We have had several huge workers demonstrations in the past couple of years," Macdara Doyle, a spokesman for the Irish Congress of Trade Unions (ICTU), told *Dollars & Sense*. "These were some of the largest in Europe—I mean, if you factor in the overall size of the population of Ireland, one hundred thousand or so people on the streets of Dublin is like several million in London and Paris."

The ICTU has not been slow to note a mounting pressure on working families. Speaking to a meeting of trade unionists in April, the congress's economic advisor, Paul Sweeney, took note of a deteriorating economic situation made worse by a global rise in food and oil prices.

Coupled with a recent rise in interest rates for Ireland's existing consumer debts, Sweeney cited "extra hardship for people all over the country" due to people "being squeezed on too many fronts. There is a limit to the burden of austerity that any society, or household, can tolerate."

Yet the Dail, the principal house of Ireland's parliament, seemed more than willing to engage in economic austerity measures even before the IMF received its not-so-warm welcome last December. The national budget for 2010 detailed "savings" on expenditure to the tune of $4.3 billion. Of this sizeable sum, $1.1 billion was taken from "Social and Family Affairs"—in part welfare measures such as benefit payments to the unemployed—alongside $576 million from child care and health services.

"We have actually had four austerity budgets in this country," says Doyle of the ICTU, "December's bailout was actually triggered by the European Central Bank [ECB] in response to a broken and busted banking system that has brought down the whole country. We were in debt to the ECB to the tune of around 130 billion euros [$187 billion], and the government just kept going to them for aid until the ECB just said 'No, we can't do this anymore, this debt needs to be restructured.'"

IMF spokesmen are in agreement with Doyle on this point. In a document released shortly after the December bailout, the IMF emphasized the flaws of "an oversized banking system" that had become "overly dependent on financing from the European Central Bank."

The paradox here is that the ECB is still intimately involved in the recovery process and remains an important participant in the Extended Fund Facility. What has changed, however, is that the IMF intervention seems to have mollified the ECB into acting as creditors to what they might otherwise have viewed as a lost cause.

Fewer Resources

The case of Ireland's banks is similar to the British or American experience—except that the Irish government does not have the capital reserves to implement extensive banking bailouts. Figures compiled by the World Bank during the height of the recession in 2009 show Irish GDP sitting at just over $227 billion. The corresponding figure for the UK showed British GDP leagues ahead at over $2.1 trillion.

THE WRONG MEDICINE: WHY FISCAL AUSTERITY IS A BAD IDEA FOR A SLUMPING ECONOMY

As protesters take to the streets in Europe to oppose government spending cuts, proponents of austerity in the United States and Europe claim that immediate moves to reduce government deficits are the way to renewed economic growth. Accepting a little pain now, they argue, will reduce the pain in the long run.

Those familiar with Keynesian economic theory will find the austerity-to-growth claims surprising. Fiscal austerity, or a "contractionary fiscal policy," means either spending cuts or tax increases, or a combination of the two. Reductions in government spending reduce total demand directly. Government spending on real goods and services is just as much a part of total demand as private consumption or investment spending. Spending cuts can also reduce demand indirectly, as those who would have received income as a result of government spending cut back on their spending as well. Tax increases reduce demand by reducing the disposable incomes of private individuals, who then spend less. Either way, lower demand for goods and services can translate into less output and employment.

How, then, is fiscal contraction supposed to lead to growth? Austerity proponents argue that balancing government budgets and reducing public debt will boost private-sector "confidence." As public debt increases, the argument goes, people may become wary about spending, since they will be on the hook (through taxes) to pay down that debt in the future. Individuals and firms will spend more freely now if they do not have future taxes hanging over their heads.

The pro-austerity faction has relied heavily on a few recent studies, especially one by Harvard economists Alberto Alesina and Silvia Ardagna claiming to have identified 26 cases in which fiscal contraction led to renewed growth. This conclusion, however, has not stood up to careful scrutiny. Economists Arjun Jayadev and Mike Konczal, after studying the cases that Alesina and Ardagna describe, find that "in virtually none did the country a) reduce the deficit when the economy was in a slump and b) increase growth rates while reducing the debt-to-GDP ratio."

In 20 of the 26 cases, Jayadev and Konczal argue, the government did not carry out a fiscal contraction during the low (or "slump") phase of a business cycle. (Budgets are much easier to balance, and debt easier to pay down, during the "boom" phase of a business cycle. With output and incomes

Unsurprisingly, the United States won first with a GDP of well over $14 trillion. If the response to the crisis has been somewhat similar in these countries, the facts on the ground show that the Irish economy, despite its reputation as a "Celtic Tiger" in the 1990s, is simply unable to cope with the aftershocks of recession.

What prompted the crisis is, again, a somewhat familiar story: Ireland's former prosperity has been attributed to a housing bubble that lifted the country from depression in the late 1980s into the lofty heights of financial stardom less than ten

high, total tax revenue is bound to be high as well, while expenditures on things like unemployment insurance are bound to be low.) Out of the six remaining cases, they find, the rate of economic growth actually declined in five. Looking at a broader sample of countries engaging in austerity, Jayadev and Konczal find that, in most cases, deficit cutting during a slump results in lower growth. Even in most of the cases where the growth rate did increase, the ratio of debt to gross domestic product actually increased as well. This suggests that, even if fiscal austerity had some effect in reducing the growth of total debt, it also resulted in such weak overall economic growth that the debt burden (relative to GDP) continued to rise.

Austerity can actually undermine a country's ability to reduce its government deficit and debt, and increase the interest rates a government is forced to pay on its debt. A government's ability to borrow depends on the size and stability of the economy that it has the power to tax. By cutting demand, a government may prolong a slump. The longer the slump goes on, the longer tax revenues will remain below normal, and the longer the government will have above-normal expenditures on items like unemployment insurance. If investors conclude that the slump is bound to go on for a long time, and that the government will therefore be a bad credit risk for the foreseeable future, they will demand a higher interest rate (to compensate them for that risk). This, too, will tend to increase the government's debt burden.

Austerity advocates present themselves as tough-minded and pragmatic—not flinching from the painful sacrifices necessary for a better future. The facts might suggest, instead, that fiscal austerity during a slump amounts to cutting off one's nose to spite one's face. Except that, as the protests raging in Europe show, it is other people's noses that the pro-austerity faction aims to lop off.

—Alejandro Reuss

Sources: Arjun Jayadev and Mike Konczal, "The Boom Not the Slump: Not the Right Time for Austerity," The Roosevelt Institute, August 23, 2010; Alberto Alesina and Silvia Ardagna, "Large Changes in Fiscal Policy: Taxes Versus Spending," NBER Working Paper No. 15438, 2009; Andrew G. Biggs, Kevin A. Hassett, and Matthew Jensen, "A Guide for Deficit Reduction in the United States Based on Historical Consolidations That Worked," American Enterprise Institute, December 2010; International Monetary Fund, "Will It Hurt? Macroeconomic Effects of Fiscal Consolidation," World Economic Outlook, Chapter 3, October 2010; Paul Krugman, "Does Fiscal Austerity Reassure Markets?" June 13, 2010 (krugman.blogs.nytimes.com).

years later. This claim is further substantiated by a 6.5% annual GDP growth rate between 1991 and 2007. *The Economist* had this to say in May 1997: "just yesterday, it seems, Ireland was one of Europe's poorest countries. Today it is about as prosperous as the European average and getting richer all the time."

Yet *The Economist* in its optimism overlooked some important facts. At the time of the article, house prices were already soaring dramatically; between 1992 and 2006 they rose by around 300%. In a story that is no doubt familiar, Irish banks were all too willing to lend at low interest rates while believing it safe to imitate the behavior of their American and British counterparts. But the property boom—and with it the banks' reckless lending and low interest rates—was not to last, and despite its former prosperity, Dublin is not the financial hub that London or New York can claim to be.

If the Dail cannot match Westminster in financial prosperity, however, it can match it in how it handles recession, and that's by passing the burden onto ordinary people. The Value Added Tax (VAT) has been hiked in both countries, despite the fact that, in Ireland in particular, a burden on the spending of the individual consumer is also an extra weight on small businesses, which are typically more dependent on the internal market than larger franchises with potential holdings overseas. "Obviously, it depends on what kind of small business we are talking about," said Sean Murphy, deputy chief executive for Chambers Ireland, Ireland's largest business advocacy organization, "but on the domestic side we are seeing a lowering of consumer confidence which is going to be affecting them. Outside of that, we can see that Irish exports are growing, but when dealing with the internal market and VAT rises and so on, things are not going so well."

A Second Bailout?

So far, talk of a second bailout in 2013 has been confined to supposition that the government will be forced to default on existing debts despite the implementation of the recovery plan. An additional bailout has therefore been raised as a possibility for boosting revenue, although the economic "adjustments" involved may differ in severity from those contained in the National Recovery Plan.

The possible additional bailout comes recommended by former IMF deputy director Donal Donovan. Donovan claimed last March that the country would need assistance until at least 2015, with further "debt restructuring" on the agenda should the economy prove "insolvent."

The Irish people themselves appear to disagree. The United Left Alliance (ULA), an umbrella organization of leftist groups founded last November, has already started to make waves on the political scene after winning five seats in the Dail in March.

"The only people who are in denial about a second bailout actually happening are the main political parties," Michael O'Brien, a member of the ULA's national interim steering committee, told *Dollars & Sense*. "It could be said that the reason why the original terms brought in last December were so harsh is that the IMF knew there would be a default, but not an immediate one, it's just that in the three-year period the first bailout is in effect foreign investors will be able to get more of a hold over the Irish banking sector before a second bailout becomes necessary."

"Both the left and the right don't seem to want to talk about this, but unless we reject these harsh terms we will certainly default, and that's when a second bailout becomes likely. Even if we reduce ourselves to serfdom there will be a default."

O'Brien is also a believer in Irish economist Richard Douthwait's theory that duplicity is integral to the IMF's strategy. If the IMF apparently believes a default will occur, then why have they bothered with a bailout in the first place? Douthwait believes, as does O'Brien, that the secret lies in the interests of foreign depositors in Irish banks. Writing in the magazine *Construct Ireland*, Douthwait poses the question: "If a default is inevitable, why is Ireland being paid, via the bailout money, not to default now? The answer is clear. A default now would mean that the foreign banks and other institutions which have lent to Ireland would suffer massive losses and might need to be rescued by the governments of the countries in which they are based. Big firms with deposits in Irish banks in excess of the 100,000 euros [$145,000] state guarantee would suffer big losses too. Indeed, if the two major banks collapsed, the government could find itself unable to honour its deposit guarantees at all."

Donovan, Douthwait, and O'Brien seem set on the belief that a second bailout will therefore be necessary, although they clearly have differing opinions as to why. Douthwait and O'Brien believe the priority of the IMF and ECB is to safeguard foreign deposits, or permit them to withdraw in time in order to avert further losses while adopting a wait-and-see approach to the Irish recovery. The IMF's Donovan, however, is slightly more optimistic. The British newspaper The Guardian quotes Donovan as being amenable to the notion of writing off some of Ireland's debt, provided that the nation continues to follow the measures prescribed by the National Recovery Plan. Once this is done, he argues, the ECB may be more willing to let Ireland off the hook, at least to a degree.

PIIGS

But talk of partial relief at some point in the future does little for those already facing unemployment and falling living standards. Moreover, economists at the IMF and elsewhere seem to have developed a contemptuous attitude towards Ireland and other countries still reeling from the economic crisis—an attitude that hardly endears them to the populations they claim to be helping.

Over the years, economists have referred to the weaker economies of Europe, such as Italy, as being "sick" or otherwise suffering some kind of ailment. The acronym "PIIGS" (as in Portugal, Ireland, Italy, Greece, and Spain) is now in use by economists and pundits to describe the economically troubled parts of the continent.

Being referred to as a pig is hardly likely to prompt a positive reaction, yet hardship and the contempt of powerful foreigners is not something that is new to Ireland. In the past, the Irish have often dealt with economic woes by moving abroad; almost a million Irish headed to the United States during the Potato Famine of the late 1840s. Although the Irish are now in different straits, their tried-and-tested method of seeking greener pastures abroad has resurfaced.

The ICTU has estimated that perhaps a thousand citizens leave the country each week, although according to Doyle "some of them are immigrants anyway." According to the Economic and Social Research Institute, a Dublin-based research organization, 60,000 people left the country in the twelve months leading up to April 2010 alone. Over the course of 2010 and 2011 this trend has only continued.

"The problem," said Doyle, "is that we are losing a lot of people who are very qualified and very skilled; the kind of people you need to help an economy recover."

Economic Freedom

The Irish socialist James Connelly once said that half-measures on the road to independence would ensure "England will still rule" through "the whole array of commercial institutions she has planted in this country and watered with the tears of our mothers and the blood of our martyrs."

Prophetic words, yet Connelly could not have envisaged the future scale of the problem. What Ireland now faces is not so much a single foreign aggressor but multiple economic ties to a globe-spanning organization imposing privation through financial means.

With the National Recovery Plan viewed more as a National Austerity Plan by large segments of the population, unemployment at over 13%, and discontent on the rise, the days of Irish prosperity appear to be over. The demand for a politically and economically free Ireland, as put forth by the likes of Connelly before his execution by the British in 1916, still remains valid. ❑

Sources: Irish Congress of Trade Unions (www.ictu.ie); International Monetary Fund (imf.org); "National Recovery Plan 2010-2014," An Roinn Airgeadais Department of Finance (www.budget. gov.ie); United Left Alliance (unitedleftalliance.org); Chambers Ireland (www.chambers.ie); Dáil Éireann (www.oireachtas.ie); Central Statistics Office Ireland (www.cso.ie); Economic and Social Research Institute (www.esri.ie); Richard Douthwait, "Ireland's inevitable default," Construct Ireland, May 9, 2011 (www.constructireland.ie); Lisa O'Carroll, "Ireland will need another bailout, says former IMF director," *The Guardian*, April 7, 2011 (www.guardian.co.uk); "Ireland Shines," *The Economist*, May 15, 1997 (economist.com).

Chapter 5

LABOR IN THE INTERNATIONAL ECONOMY

Article 5.1

INTERNATIONAL LABOR STANDARDS

BY ARTHUR MacEWAN
September/October 2008

Dear Dr. Dollar:

U.S. activists have pushed to get foreign trade agreements to include higher labor standards. But then you hear that developing countries don't want that because cheaper labor without a lot of rules and regulations is what's helping them to bring industries in and build their economies. Is there a way to reconcile these views? Or are the activists just blind to the real needs of the countries they supposedly want to help?

—*Philip Bereaud, Swampscott, Mass.*

In 1971, General Emilio Medici, the then-military dictator of Brazil, commented on economic conditions in his country with the infamous line: "The economy is doing fine, but the people aren't."

Like General Medici, the government officials of many low-income countries today see the well-being of their economies in terms of overall output and the profits of firms—those profits that keep bringing in new investment, new industries that "build their economies." It is these officials who typically get to speak for their countries. When someone says that these countries "want" this or that— or "don't want" this or that—it is usually because the countries' officials have expressed this position.

Do we know what the people in these countries want? The people who work in the new, rapidly growing industries, in the mines and fields, and in the small shops and market stalls of low-income countries? Certainly they want better conditions—more to eat, better housing, security for their children, improved health and safety. The officials claim that to obtain these better conditions, they must "build their economies." But just because "the economy is doing fine" does not mean that the people are doing fine.

In fact, in many low-income countries, economic expansion comes along with severe inequality. The people who do the work are not getting a reasonable share of the rising national income (and are sometimes worse off even in absolute terms). Brazil in the early 1970s was a prime example and, in spite of major political change, remains a highly unequal country. Today, in both India and China, as in several other countries, economic growth is coming with increasingly severe inequality.

Workers in these countries struggle to improve their positions. They form—or try to form—independent unions. They demand higher wages and better working conditions. They struggle for political rights. It seems obvious that we should support those struggles, just as we support parallel struggles of workers in our own country. The first principle in supporting workers' struggles, here or anywhere else, is supporting their right to struggle—the right, in particular, to form independent unions without fear of reprisal. Indeed, in the ongoing controversy over the U.S.-Colombia Free Trade Agreement, the assassination of trade union leaders has rightly been a major issue.

Just how we offer our support—in particular, how we incorporate that support into trade agreements—is a complicated question. Pressure from abroad can help, but applying it is a complex process. A ban on goods produced with child labor, for example, could harm the most impoverished families that depend on children's earnings, or could force some children into worse forms of work (e.g., prostitution). On the other hand, using trade agreements to pressure governments to allow unhindered union organizing efforts by workers seems perfectly legitimate. When workers are denied the right to organize, their work is just one step up from slavery. Trade agreements can also be used to support a set of basic health and safety rights for workers. (Indeed, it might be useful if a few countries refused to enter into trade agreements with the United States until we improve workers' basic organizing rights and health and safety conditions in our own country!)

There is no doubt that the pressures that come through trade sanctions (restricting or banning commerce with another country) or simply from denying free access to the U.S. market can do immediate harm to workers and the general populace of low-income countries. Any struggle for change can generate short-run costs, but the long-run gains—even the hope of those gains—can make those costs acceptable. Consider, for example, the Apartheid-era trade sanctions against South Africa. To the extent that those sanctions were effective, some South African workers were deprived of employment. Nonetheless, the sanctions were widely supported by mass organizations in South Africa. Or note that when workers in this country strike or advocate a boycott of their company in an effort to obtain better conditions, they both lose income and run the risk that their employer will close up shop.

Efforts by people in this country to use trade agreements to raise labor standards in other countries should, whenever possible, take their lead from workers in those countries. It is up to them to decide what costs are acceptable. There are times, however, when popular forces are denied even basic rights to struggle. The best thing we can do, then, is to push for those rights—particularly the right to organize independent unions—that help create the opportunity for workers in poor countries to choose what to fight for. ❑

Article 5.2

SWEATSHOPS 101

Lessons in Monitoring Apparel Production Around the World

BY DARA O'ROURKE
September/October 2001

Navy blue sweatshirts bearing a single foreign word, "Michigan," and a well-known logo, the Nike swoosh, were piled high in a small room off the main factory floor. After cutting, stitching, and embroidering by the 1,100 workers outside, the sweatshirts landed in the spot-cleaning room, where six young Indonesian women prepared the garments for shipment to student stores and NikeTowns across America. The women spent hour after hour using chemical solvents to rid the sweatshirts of smudges and stains. With poor ventilation, ill-fitting respiratory protection, no gloves, and no chemical hazard training, the women sprayed solvents and aerosol cleaners containing benzene, methylene chloride, and perchloroethylene, all carcinogens, on the garments.

It used to be that the only thing people wondered when you wore a Harvard or Michigan sweatshirt was whether you had actually gone there. More and more, though, people are wondering out loud where that sweatshirt was made, and whether any workers were exploited in making it. Students, labor activists, and human-rights groups have spearheaded a movement demanding to know what really lies beneath their university logos, and whether our public universities and private colleges are profiting from global sweatshop production.

Where Was That T-Shirt Made?

So far, few universities have been able to answer these questions. Universities generally don't even know where their products are produced, let alone whether workers were endangered to produce them. Indeed, with global out-sourcing many brand name companies cannot trace the supply chains which lead to the student store, and are blissfully ignorant of conditions in these factories.

Under pressure from student activists across the country, a small group of university administrators decided it was time to find out more about the garments bearing their schools' names and logos. As part of a collaborative research project, called the "Independent University Initiative" (IUI), funded by Harvard University, the University of Notre Dame, Ohio State University, the University of California, and the University of Michigan, I joined a team investigating where and under what conditions university garments were being made. The team included staff from the business association Business for Social Responsibility, the non-profit Investor Responsibility Research Center, and the accounting firm PricewaterhouseCoopers (PwC). PwC was responsible for auditing the labor conditions in each of the factories included in the study. At the request of student activists, I joined the team as an outside evaluator.

The IUI research team evaluated garment manufacturing for the top apparel companies licensing the logos of these five universities. It looked at factories subcontracted by nine companies, including adidas, Champion, and Nike. The nine alone outsource university apparel to over 180 factories in 26 countries. This may sound like a lot, but it is actually the tip of the global production iceberg. Americans bought about $2.5 billion worth of university-logo garments in 1999. Overall, however, U.S. apparel sales totaled over $180 billion. There are an estimated 80,000 factories around the world producing garments for the U.S. market. The university garment industry is important not so much for its size, but for the critical opening it provides onto the larger industry.

The research team visited factories in the top seven countries producing apparel for the nine companies: China, El Salvador, Korea, Mexico, Pakistan, Thailand, and the United States. It inspected 13 work sites in all. I personally inspected factories for the project in China and Korea, and then inspected factories in Indonesia on my own to see what things looked like outside the official process. Through this research I discovered not only exploitative and hazardous working conditions, but also an official monitoring process designed to gloss over the biggest problems of the apparel industry. PwC auditors found minor violations of labor laws and codes of conduct, but missed major labor problems including serious health and safety hazards, barriers to freedom of association, and violations of overtime and wage laws. This was a learning experience I call "Sweatshops 101."

Lesson #1: Global Outsourcing

The garment industry is extremely complicated and highly disaggregated. The industry has multiple layers of licensees, brokers, jobbers, importer-exporters, component suppliers, and subcontractors on top of subcontractors.

The University of Michigan does not manufacture any of the products bearing its name. Nor does Notre Dame nor Harvard nor any other university. These schools simply license their names to apparel makers and other companies for a percentage of the sale—generally around 7% of the retail price for each T-shirt, sweatshirt, or key chain. Until recently, the universities had little interest in even knowing who produced their goods. If they tracked this at all, it was to catch companies using their logos without paying the licensing fee.

Sometimes the companies that license university names and logos own the factories where the apparel is produced. But more often the licensees simply contract production out to factories in developing countries. Nike owns none of the hundreds of factories that produce its garments and athletic shoes.

A sweatshirt factory itself may have multiple subcontractors who produce the fabric, embroider the logo, or stitch sub-components. This global supply chain stretches from the university administration building, to the corporate office of the licensee companies, to large-scale factories in China and Mexico, to small scale sub-contractor factories everywhere in between, and in some cases, all the way to women stitching garments in their living rooms.

Lesson #2: The Global Shell Game

The global garment industry is highly mobile, with contracts continuously shifting from subcontractor to subcontractor within and between countries. Licensees can move production between subcontractors after one year, one month, or even as little as one week.

It took the university research team three months to get from the licensee companies a list of the factories producing university-logo garments. However, because the actual factories producing university goods at any one time change so fast, by the time I had planned a trip to China and Korea to visit factories, the lists were essentially obsolete. One licensee in Korea had replaced eight of its eleven factories with new factories by the time I arrived in town. Over a four month period, the company had contracted with twenty one different factories. A range of factors—including price competition between contractors, changes in fashions (and factories capable of filling orders), fluctuations in exchange rates, and changing import quotas for different countries—is responsible for this constant state of flux.

Even after double-checking with a licensee, in almost every country the project team would arrive at the factory gates only to be told that the factories we planned to inspect were no longer producing university goods. Of course, some of this may have been the licensees playing games. Faced with inspections, some may have decided to shift production out of the chosen factory, or at least to tell us that it had been shifted.

Some of the largest, most profitable apparel firms in the world, known for their management prowess, however, simply did not know where their products were being produced. When asked how many factories Disney had around the world, company execs guessed there were 1,500 to 1,800 factories producing their garments, toys, videos, and other goods. As it turns out, they were only off by an order of magnitude. So far the company has counted over 20,000 factories around the world producing Disney-branded goods. Only recent exposés by labor, human rights, and environmental activists have convinced these companies that they need better control over their supply chains.

Lesson #3: Normal Operating Conditions

The day an inspector visits a factory is not a normal day. Any factory that has prior knowledge of an inspection is very likely to make changes on the day of the visit.

In a Nike-contracted shoe factory in Indonesia I visited in June 2000, all of the workers in the hot press section of the plant (a particularly dangerous area) were wearing brand new black dress shoes on the day of our inspection. One of the workers explained they had been given the shoes that morning and were expected to return them at the end of the shift. Managers often give workers new protective equipment—such as gloves, respirators, and even shoes—on the day of an inspection. However, as the workers have no training in how to even use this equipment, it is common to see brand-new respirators being worn below workers' noses, around their necks, or even upside down.

At one factory the university team visited in Mexico, the factory manager wanted to guarantee that the inspectors would find his factory spotless. So he locked all of the bathrooms on the day of the inspection. Workers were not allowed to use the bathrooms until the project team showed up, hours into the work day.

Licensees and subcontractors often try to subvert monitoring. They block auditors from inspecting on certain days or from visiting certain parts of a plant, claim production has moved, feign ignorance of factory locations, keep multiple sets of books on wages and hours, coach workers on responses to interviews, and threaten workers against complaining to inspectors. The university research team was unable to get around many of these obstructions.

Lesson #4: Conditions in University Factories

Factories producing university apparel often violate local laws and university codes of conduct on maximum hours of work, minimum and overtime wages, freedom of association, and health and safety protections.

In a 300-worker apparel plant in Shanghai, the university team found that many of the workers were working far in excess of maximum overtime laws. A quick review of timecards found women working over 315 hours in a month and 20 consecutive days without a day off. The legal maximum in China is only 204 hours per month, with at least one day off in seven. A sample of 25 workers showed that the average overtime worked was 101 hours, while the legal limit is 36 hours per month. One manager explained these gross violations with a shrug, saying, "Timecards are just used to make sure workers show up on time. Workers are actually paid based on a piece rate system."

The factory also had a wide range of health and safety problems, including a lack of guarding on sewing and cutting machines, high levels of cotton dust in one section of the plant, several blocked aisles and fire exits, no running water in certain toilets, no information for workers on the hazardous chemicals they were using, and a lack of protective equipment for the workers.

Living conditions for the workers who lived in a dormitory on site were also poor. The dormitory had 12 women packed into each room on six bunk beds. Each floor had four rooms (48 women) and only one bathroom. These bathrooms had only two shower heads and four toilet stalls each, and no dividers between them.

And what of workers' rights to complain or demand better conditions? The union in this factory was openly being run by the management. While 70% of workers were "members" of the union, one manager explained, "We don't have U.S.-style unions here." No workers had ever tried to take control of this group or to form an independent union.

Lesson #5: The Challenges of Monitoring

Finding a dozen factories is relatively easy compared to the job of tracking the thousands of rapidly changing factories that produce university goods each year. Systematically monitoring and evaluating their practices on wages, hours, discrimination, and health and safety issues is an even bigger challenge.

Most universities don't have the capacity to individually monitor the conditions in "their" factories, so some are joining together to create cooperative monitoring programs. The concept behind "independent monitoring" is to have a consulting firm or non-governmental organization inspect and evaluate a factory's compliance with a code of conduct. There are now two major university monitoring systems. The Fair Labor Association (FLA) now has over 157 universities as members, and the Worker Rights Consortium (WRC) has over 80 affiliated universities. (The four smaller monitoring initiatives are Social Accountability International (SA8000), the Ethical Trading Initiative, the Clean Clothes Campaign, and the Worldwide Responsible Apparel Production (WRAP) program.)

The FLA emerged from the Clinton-convened "White House Apparel Industry Partnership" in 1998. It is supported by a small group of apparel companies including Nike, Reebok, Adidas, Levi-Strauss, Liz Claiborne, and Philips Van Heusen. Students and labor-rights advocates have criticized the group for being industry-dominated and for allowing companies to monitor only 10% of their factories each year, to use monitors that the companies pay directly, to control when and where monitors inspect, and to restrict the information released to the public after the audits.

The United Students Against Sweatshops (USAS) and UNITE (the largest garment-workers' union in the United States) founded the WRC in 1999 as an alternative to the FLA. The WRC promotes systems for verifying factory conditions after workers have complained or after inspections have occurred, and to create greater public disclosure of conditions. The WRC differs from the FLA in that it refuses to certify that any company meets a code of conduct. The group argues that because of the problems of monitoring, it is simply not possible to systematically monitor or certify a company's compliance. Some universities and companies have criticized the WRC as being a haphazard "gotcha" monitoring system whose governing body excludes the very companies that must be part of solving these problems.

Both groups profess to support the International Labour Organization's core labor standards, including upholding workers' rights to freedom of association and collective bargaining, and prohibiting forced labor, child labor, and discrimination in the workplace. The WRC, however, goes further in advocating that workers be paid a "living wage," and that women's rights receive particular attention. Both programs assert a strong role for local NGOs, unions, and workers. However, the two have widely varying levels of transparency and public disclosure, and very different systems of sanctions and penalties.

Lesson #6: How Not to Monitor

Corporate-sponsored monitoring systems seem almost designed to miss the most critical issues in the factories they inspect. Auditors often act as if they are on the side of management rather than the workers.

PricewaterhouseCoopers (PwC) is the largest private monitor of codes of conduct and corporate labor practices in the world. The company performed over 6,000 factory audits in the year 2000, including monitoring for Nike, Disney, Walmart, and the Gap. (PwC recently announced that they were spinning off their labor monitoring services into a firm called Global Social Compliance.) PwC monitors for many of the top university licensees, and was hired as the monitor for the university project. Like other corporate monitors, the company has been criticized for covering up problems and assuaging the public conscience about sweatshop conditions that have not really been resolved.

PwC's monitoring systems epitomize current corporate monitoring efforts. The firm sends two auditors—who are actually financial accountants with minimal training on labor issues—into each factory for eight hours. The auditors use a checklist and a standard interview form to evaluate legal compliance, wages and benefits, working hours, freedom of association and collective bargaining, child labor, forced labor, disciplinary practices, and health and safety.

On the university project, PwC auditors failed to adequately examine any major issue in the factories I saw them inspect. In factories in Korea and Indonesia, PwC auditors completely missed exposure to toxic chemicals, something which could eventually cost workers their lives from cancer. In Korea, the auditors saw no problem in managers violating overtime wage laws. In China, the auditors went so far as to recommend ways for the managers to circumvent local laws on overtime hours, essentially providing advice on how to break university codes of conduct. And the auditors in Korea simply skipped the questions on workers' right to organize in their worker interviews, explaining, "They don't have a union in this factory, so those questions aren't relevant."

The PwC auditing method is biased towards managers. Before an inspection, PwC auditors send managers a questionnaire explaining what will be inspected. They prepare managers at an opening meeting before each inspection. In the Chinese factory, they asked managers to enter wages and hours data into the PwC spreadsheet. Even the worker interviews were biased towards the managers. PwC auditors asked the managers to help them select workers to be interviewed, had the managers bring their personnel files, and then had the managers bring the workers into the office used for the interviews. The managers knew who was being interviewed, for how long, and on what issues. Workers knew this as well, and answered questions accordingly.

The final reports that PwC delivered to its clients gave a largely sanitized picture of the factories inspected. This is unsurprising, considering PwC's business interest in providing companies with "acceptable" audits.

Where to Begin?

Universities face increasing public pressure to guarantee that workers are not being injured or exploited to produce their insignia products. They have no system, however, to track apparel production around the world, and often no idea where their production is occurring. Monitoring systems are still in their fledgling stages, so universities are starting from a difficult position, albeit one they have profited from for years.

What can universities do about this? They should do what they are best at: produce information. They should take the lead in demanding that corporations—beginning with those they do business with—open themselves up to public inspection and evaluation. Universities have done this before, such as during the anti-apartheid campaign for South Africa. By doing this on the sweatshop issue, universities could spur a critical dialogue on labor issues around the world.

To start, the universities could establish a central coordinating office to collect and compare information on factory performance for member universities' licensees. (The WRC has proposed such a model.) This new office would be responsible for keeping records on licensee compliance, for making this information available over the internet, for registering local NGOs and worker organizations to conduct independent verifications of factory conditions, and for assessing sanctions.

Such a program would allow universities to evaluate different strategies for improving conditions in different parts of the world. This would avoid the danger of locking in one code of conduct or one certification system. In place of sporadic media exposés embarrassing one company at a time, we would have an international system of disclosure and learning—benchmarking good performers, identifying and targeting the worst performers, and motivating improvement.

It is clearly not enough to expose one company at a time, nor to count on industry-paid consulting firms to monitor labor conditions. The building blocks of a new system depend on information. This fits the mission of universities. Universities should focus on information gathering and dissemination, and most importantly, on learning. If the universities learn nothing else from "Sweatshops 101," it is that they still have a lot of homework to do—and their next test will be coming soon. ❑

Article 5.3

NIKE TO THE RESCUE?

Africa needs better jobs, not sweatshops.

BY JOHN MILLER
September/October 2006

"In Praise of the Maligned Sweatshop"
WINDHOEK, Namibia—Africa desperately needs Western help in the form of schools, clinics and sweatshops.

On a street here in the capital of Namibia, in the southwestern corner of Africa, I spoke to a group of young men who were trying to get hired as day laborers on construction sites.

"I come here every day," said Naftal Shaanika, a 20-year-old. "I actually find work only about once a week."

Mr. Shaanika and the other young men noted that the construction jobs were dangerous and arduous, and that they would vastly prefer steady jobs in, yes, sweatshops. Sure, sweatshop work is tedious, grueling and sometimes dangerous. But over all, sewing clothes is considerably less dangerous or arduous—or sweaty—than most alternatives in poor countries.

Well-meaning American university students regularly campaign against sweatshops. But instead, anyone who cares about fighting poverty should campaign in favor of sweatshops, demanding that companies set up factories in Africa.

The problem is that it's still costly to manufacture in Africa. The headaches across much of the continent include red tape, corruption, political instability, unreliable electricity and ports, and an inexperienced labor force that leads to low productivity and quality. The anti-sweatshop movement isn't a prime obstacle, but it's one more reason not to manufacture in Africa.

Imagine that a Nike vice president proposed manufacturing cheap T-shirts in Ethiopia. The boss would reply: "You're crazy! We'd be boycotted on every campus in the country."

Some of those who campaign against sweatshops respond to my arguments by noting that they aren't against factories in Africa, but only demand a "living wage" in them. After all, if labor costs amount to only $1 per shirt, then doubling wages would barely make a difference in the final cost.

One problem ... is that it already isn't profitable to pay respectable salaries, and so any pressure to raise them becomes one more reason to avoid Africa altogether.

One of the best U.S. initiatives in Africa has been the African Growth and Opportunity Act, which allows duty-free imports from Africa—and thus has stimulated manufacturing there.

—Op-ed by Nicholas Kristof, *New York Times*, June 6, 2006

Nicholas Kristof has been beating the pro-sweatshop drum for quite a while. Shortly after the East Asian financial crisis of the late 1990s, Kristof, the Pulitzer Prize-winning journalist and now columnist for the *New York Times*, reported the story of an Indonesian recycler who, picking through the metal scraps of a garbage dump, dreamed that her son would grow up to be a sweatshop worker. Then, in 2000, Kristof and his wife, *Times* reporter Sheryl WuDunn, published "Two Cheers for Sweatshops" in the *Times Magazine*. In 2002, Kristof's column advised G-8 leaders to "start an international campaign to promote imports from sweatshops, perhaps with bold labels depicting an unrecognizable flag and the words 'Proudly Made in a Third World Sweatshop.'"

Now Kristof laments that too few poor, young African men have the opportunity to enter the satanic mill of sweatshop employment. Like his earlier efforts, Kristof's latest pro-sweatshop ditty synthesizes plenty of half-truths. Let's take a closer look and see why there is still no reason to give it up for sweatshops.

A Better Alternative?

It is hardly surprising that young men on the streets of Namibia's capital might find sweatshop jobs more appealing than irregular work as day laborers on construction sites.

The alternative jobs available to sweatshop workers are often worse and, as Kristof loves to point out, usually involve more sweating than those in world export factories. Most poor people in the developing world eke out their livelihoods from subsistence agriculture or by plying petty trades. Others on the edge of urban centers work as street-hawkers or hold other jobs in the informal sector. As economist Arthur MacEwan wrote a few years back in *Dollars & Sense*, in a poor country like Indonesia, where women working in manufacturing earn five times as much as those in agriculture, sweatshops have no trouble finding workers.

But let's be clear about a few things. First, export factory jobs, especially in labor-intensive industries, often are just "a ticket to slightly less impoverishment," as even economist and sweatshop defender Jagdish Bhagwati allows.

Beyond that, these jobs seldom go to those without work or to the poorest of the poor. One study by sociologist Kurt Ver Beek showed that 60% of first-time Honduran *maquila* workers were previously employed. Typically they were not destitute, and they were better educated than most Hondurans.

Sweatshops don't just fail to rescue people from poverty. Setting up export factories where workers have few job alternatives has actually been a recipe for serious worker abuse. In *Beyond Sweatshops*, a book arguing for the benefits of direct foreign investment in the developing world, Brookings Institution economist Theodore Moran recounts the disastrous decision of the Philippine government to build the Bataan Export Processing Zone in an isolated mountainous area to lure foreign investors with the prospect of cheap labor. With few alternatives, Filipinos took jobs in the garment factories that sprung up in the zone. The manufacturers typically paid less than the minimum wage and forced employees to work overtime in factories filled with dust and fumes. Fed up, the workers eventually mounted a series of crippling strikes. Many factories shut down and occupancy rates in the zone plummeted, as did the value of exports, which declined by more than half between 1980 and 1986.

Kristof's argument is no excuse for sweatshop abuse: that conditions are worse elsewhere does nothing to alleviate the suffering of workers in export factories. They are often denied the right to organize, subjected to unsafe working conditions and to verbal, physical, and sexual abuse, forced to work overtime, coerced into pregnancy tests and even abortions, and paid less than a living wage. It remains useful and important to combat these conditions even if alternative jobs are worse yet.

The fact that young men in Namibia find sweatshop jobs appealing testifies to how harsh conditions are for workers in Africa, not the desirability of export factory employment.

Oddly, Kristof's desire to introduce new sweatshops to sub-Saharan Africa finds no support in the African Growth and Opportunity Act (AGOA) that he praises. The Act grants sub-Saharan apparel manufacturers preferential access to U.S. markets. But shortly after its passage, U.S. Trade Representative Robert Zoellick assured the press that the AGOA would not create sweatshops in Africa because it requires protective standards for workers consistent with those set by the International Labor Organization.

Antisweatshop Activism and Jobs

Kristof is convinced that the antisweatshop movement hurts the very workers it intends to help. His position has a certain seductive logic to it. As anyone who has suffered through introductory economics will tell you, holding everything else the same, a labor standard that forces multinational corporations and their subcontractors to boost wages should result in their hiring fewer workers.

But in practice does it? The only evidence Kristof produces is an imaginary conversation in which a boss incredulously refuses a Nike vice president's proposal to open a factory in Ethiopia paying wages of 25 cents a hour: "You're crazy! We'd be boycotted on every campus in the country."

While Kristof has an active imagination, there are some things wrong with this conversation.

First off, the antisweatshop movement seldom initiates boycotts. An organizer with United Students Against Sweatshops (USAS) responded on Kristof's blog: "We never call for apparel boycotts unless we are explicitly asked to by workers at a particular factory. This is, of course, exceedingly rare, because, as you so persuasively argued, people generally want to be employed." The National Labor Committee, the largest antisweatshop organization in the United States, takes the same position.

Moreover, when economists Ann Harrison and Jason Scorse conducted a systematic study of the effects of the antisweatshop movement on factory employment, they found no negative employment effect. Harrison and Scorse looked at Indonesia, where Nike was one of the targets of an energetic campaign calling for better wages and working conditions among the country's subcontractors. Their statistical analysis found that the antisweatshop campaign was responsible for 20% of the increase in the real wages of unskilled workers in factories exporting textiles, footwear, and apparel from 1991 to 1996. Harrison and Scorse also found that "antisweatshop activism did not have significant adverse effects on employment" in these sectors.

Campaigns for higher wages are unlikely to destroy jobs because, for multinationals and their subcontractors, wages make up a small portion of their overall costs. Even Kristof accepts this point, well documented by economists opposed to sweatshop labor. In Mexico's apparel industry, for instance, economists Robert Pollin, James Heintz, and Justine Burns from the Political Economy Research Institute found that doubling the pay of nonsupervisory workers would add just $1.80 to the production cost of a $100 men's sports jacket. A recent survey by the National Bureau of Economic Research found that U.S. consumers would be willing to pay $115 for the same jacket if they knew that it had not been made under sweatshop conditions.

Globalization in Sub-Saharan Africa

Kristof is right that Africa, especially sub-Saharan Africa, has lost out in the globalization process. Sub-Saharan Africa suffers from slower growth, less direct foreign investment, lower education levels, and higher poverty rates than most every other part of the world. A stunning 37 of the region's 47 countries are classified as "low-income" by the World Bank, each with a gross national income less than $825 per person. Many countries in the region bear the burdens of high external debt and a crippling HIV crisis that Kristof has made heroic efforts to bring to the world's attention.

But have multinational corporations avoided investing in sub-Saharan Africa because labor costs are too high? While labor costs in South Africa and Mauritius are high, those in the other countries of the region are modest by international standards, and quite low in some cases. Take Lesotho, the largest exporter of apparel from sub-Saharan Africa to the United States. In the country's factories that subcontract with Wal-Mart, the predominantly female workforce earns an average of just $54 a month. That's below the United Nations poverty line of $2 per day, and it includes regular forced overtime. In Madagascar, the region's third largest exporter of clothes to the United States, wages in the apparel industry are just 33 cents per hour, lower than those in China and among the lowest in the world. And at Ramatex Textile, the large Malaysian-owned textile factory in Namibia, workers only earn about $100 per month according to the Labour Resource and Research Institute in Windhoek. Most workers share their limited incomes with extended families and children, and they walk long distances to work because they can't afford better transportation.

On the other hand, recent experience shows that sub-Saharan countries with decent labor standards *can* develop strong manufacturing export sectors. In the late 1990s, Francis Teal of Oxford's Centre for the Study of African Economies compared Mauritius's successful export industries with Ghana's unsuccessful ones. Teal found that workers in Mauritius earned ten times as much as those in Ghana— $384 a month in Mauritius as opposed to $36 in Ghana. Mauritius's textile and garment industry remained competitive because its workforce was better educated and far more productive than Ghana's. Despite paying poverty wages, the Ghanaian factories floundered.

Kristof knows full well the real reason garment factories in the region are shutting down: the expiration of the Multifiber Agreement last January [2008]. The agreement, which set national export quotas for clothing and textiles, protected the garment industries in smaller countries around the world from direct competition with China. Now China and, to a lesser degree, India, are increasingly displacing other garment producers. In this new context, lower wages alone are unlikely to sustain the sub-Saharan garment industry. Industry sources report that sub-Saharan Africa suffers from several other drawbacks as an apparel producer, including relatively high utility and transportation costs and long shipping times to the United States. The region also has lower productivity and less skilled labor than Asia, and it has fewer sources of cotton yarn and higher-priced fabrics than China and India.

If Kristof is hell-bent on expanding the sub-Saharan apparel industry, he would do better to call for sub-Saharan economies to gain unrestricted access to the Quad markets—the United States, Canada, Japan, and Europe. Economists Stephen N. Karingi, Romain Perez, and Hakim Ben Hammouda estimate that the welfare gains associated with unrestricted market access could amount to $1.2 billion in sub-Saharan Africa, favoring primarily unskilled workers.

But why insist on apparel production in the first place? Namibia has sources of wealth besides a cheap labor pool for Nike's sewing machines. The *Economist* reports that Namibia is a world-class producer of two mineral products: diamonds (the country ranks seventh by value) and uranium (it ranks fifth by volume). The mining industry is the heart of Namibia's export economy and accounts for about 20% of the country's GDP. But turning the mining sector into a vehicle for national economic development would mean confronting the foreign corporations that control the diamond industry, such as the South African De Beers Corporation. That is a tougher assignment than scapegoating antisweatshop activists.

More and Better African Jobs

So why have multinational corporations avoided investing in sub-Saharan Africa? The answer, according to international trade economist Dani Rodrik, is "entirely due to the slow growth" of the sub-Saharan economies. Rodrik estimates that the region participates in international trade as much as can be expected given its economies' income levels, country size, and geography.

Rodrik's analysis suggests that the best thing to do for poor workers in Africa would be to lift the debt burdens on their governments and support their efforts to build functional economies. That means investing in human resources and physical infrastructure, and implementing credible macroeconomic policies that put job creation first. But these investments, as Rodrik points out, take time.

In the meantime, international policies establishing a floor for wages and safeguards for workers across the globe would do more for the young men on Windhoek's street corners than subjecting them to sweatshop abuse, because grinding poverty leaves people willing to enter into any number of desperate exchanges. And if Namibia is closing its garment factories because Chinese imports are cheaper, isn't that an argument for trying to improve labor standards in China, not lower them in sub-Saharan Africa? Abusive labor practices are rife in China's export factories, as the National Labor Committee and *BusinessWeek* have documented. Workers put in 13- to 16-hour days, seven days a week. They enjoy little to no health and safety enforcement, and their take-home pay falls below the minimum wage after the fines and deductions their employers sometimes withhold.

Spreading these abuses in sub-Saharan Africa will not empower workers there. Instead it will take advantage of the fact that they are among the most marginalized workers in the world. Debt relief, international labor standards, and public investments in education and infrastructure are surely better ways to fight African poverty than Kristof's sweatshop proposal. ❏

Sources: Arthur MacEwan, "Ask Dr. Dollar," *Dollars & Sense*, Sept–Oct 1998; John Miller, "Why Economists Are Wrong About Sweatshops and the Antisweatshop Movement," *Challenge*, Jan–Feb 2003; R. Pollin, J. Burns, and J. Heintz, "Global Apparel Production and Sweatshop Labor: Can Raising Retail Prices Finance Living Wages?" Political Economy Research Institute, Working Paper 19, DATE; N. Kristof, "In Praise of the Maligned Sweatshop,"*New York Times*, June 6, 2006; N. Kristof, "Let Them Sweat," *NYT* , June 25, 2002; N. Kristof, "Two Cheers for Sweatshops," *NYT* , Sept 24, 2000; N. Kristof, "Asia'[s Crisis Upsets Rising Effort to Confront Blight of Sweatshops," *NYT*, June 15, 1998; A. Harrison and J. Scorse, "Improving the Conditions of Workers? Minimum Wage Legislation and Anti-Sweatshop Activism," *Calif. Management Review*, Oct 2005; Herbert Jauch, "Africa's Clothing and Textile Industry: The Case of Ramatex in Namibia," in *The Future of the Textile and Clothing Industry in Sub-Saharan Africa*, ed. H. Jauch and R. Traub-Merz (Friedrich-Ebert-Stiftung, 2006); Kurt Alan Ver Beek, "Maquiladoras: Exploitation or Emancipation? An Overview of the Situation of Maquiladora Workers in Honduras," *World Development*, 29(9), 2001; Theodore Moran, *Beyond Sweatshops: Foreign Direct Investment and Globalization in Developing Countries* (Brookings Institution Press, 2002); "Comparative Assessment of the Competitiveness of the Textile and Apparel Sector in Selected Countries," in *Textiles and Apparel: Assessment of the Competitiveness of Certain Foreign Suppliers to the United States Market*, Vol. 1, U.S. International Trade Commission, Jan 2004; S. N. Karingi, R. Perez, and H. Ben Hammouda, "Could Extended Preferences Reward Sub-Saharan Africa's Participation in the Doha Round Negotiations?," *World Economy*, 2006; Francis Teal, "Why Can Mauritius Export Manufactures and Ghana Can Not?," *The World Economy*, 22 (7), 1999; Dani Rodrik, "Trade Policy and Economic Performance in Sub-Saharan Africa," Paper prepared for the Swedish Ministry for Foreign Affairs, Nov 1997.

Article 5.4

OUTSIZED OFFSHORE OUTSOURCING

The scope of offshore outsourcing gives some economists and the business press the heebie-jeebies.

BY JOHN MILLER
September/October 2007

At a press conference introducing the 2004 *Economic Report of the President*, N. Gregory Mankiw, then head of President Bush's Council of Economic Advisors, assured the press that "Outsourcing is probably a plus for the economy in the long run [and] just a new way of doing international trade."

Mankiw's comments were nothing other than mainstream economics, as even Democratic Party-linked economists confirmed. For instance Janet Yellen, President Clinton's chief economist, told the *Wall Street Journal*, "In the long run, outsourcing is another form of trade that benefits the U.S. economy by giving us cheaper ways to do things." Nonetheless, Mankiw's assurances were met with derision from those uninitiated in the economics profession's free-market ideology. Sen. John Edwards (D-N.C.) asked, "What planet do they live on?" Even Republican House Speaker Dennis Hastert (Ill.) said that Mankiw's theory "fails a basic test of real economics."

Mankiw now jokes that "if the American Economic Association were to give an award for the Most Politically Inept Paraphrasing of Adam Smith, I would be a leading candidate." But he quickly adds, "the recent furor about outsourcing, and my injudiciously worded comments about the benefits of international trade, should not eclipse the basic lessons that economists have understood for more than two centuries."

In fact Adam Smith never said any such thing about international trade. In response to the way Mankiw and other economists distort Smith's writings, economist Michael Meeropol took a close look at what Smith actually said; he found that Smith used his invisible hand argument to favor domestic investment over far-flung, hard-to-supervise foreign investments. Here are Smith's words in his 1776 masterpiece, *The Wealth of Nations*:

> By preferring the support of domestic to that of foreign industry, he [the investor] intends only his own security; and by directing that industry in such a manner as its produce may be of the greatest value, he intends only his own gain, and he is in this, as in many other cases, led by an invisible hand to promote an end, which was no part of his intention.

Outsized offshore outsourcing, the shipping of jobs overseas to take advantage of low wages, has forced some mainstream economists and some elements of the business press to have second thoughts about "free trade." Many are convinced that the painful transition costs that hit before outsourcing produces any ultimate benefits may be the biggest political issue in economics for a generation. And some recognize, as Smith did, that there is no guarantee unfettered international trade will leave the participants better off even in the long run.

Keynes's Revenge

Writing during the Great Depression of the 1930s, John Maynard Keynes, the pre-eminent economist of the twentieth century, prescribed government spending as a means of compensating for the instability of private investment. The notion of a mixed private/government economy, Keynes's prosthesis for the invisible hand of the market, guided U.S. economic policy from the 1940s through the 1970s.

It is only fitting that Paul Samuelson, the first Nobel Laureate in economics, and whose textbook introduced U.S. readers to Keynes, would be among the first mainstream economist to question whether unfettered international trade, in the context of massive outsourcing, would necessarily leave a developed economy such as that of the United States better off—even in the long run. In an influential 2004 article, Samuelson characterized the common economics wisdom about outsourcing and international trade this way:

> Yes, good jobs may be lost here in the short run. But ...the gains of the winners
> from free trade, properly measured, work out to exceed the losses of the losers. ...
> Never forget to tally the real gains of consumers alongside admitted possible
> losses of some producers. ... The gains of the American winners are big enough
> to more than compensate the losers.

Samuelson took on this view, arguing that this common wisdom is "dead wrong about [the] *necessary* surplus of winning over losing" [emphasis in the original]. In a rather technical paper, he demonstrated that free trade globalization can sometimes

---

OFFSHORED? OUTSOURCED? CONFUSED?

The terms "offshoring" and "outsourcing" are often used interchangeably, but they refer to distinct processes:

Outsourcing – When a company hires another company to carry out a business function that it no longer wants to carry on in-house. The company that is hired may be in the same city or across the globe; it may be a historically independent firm or a spinoff of the first company created specifically to outsource a particular function.

Offshoring or *Offshore Outsourcing* – When a company shifts a portion of its business operation abroad. An offshore operation may be carried out by the same company or, more typically, outsourced to a different one.

ATTRIBUTES OF JOBS OUTSOURCED

- No Face-to-Face Customer Servicing Requirement
- High Information Content
- Work Process is Telecommutable and Internet Enabled
- High Wage Differential with Similar Occupation in Destination Country
- Low Setup Barriers
- Low Social Networking Requirement

---

give rise to a situation in which "a productivity gain in one country can benefit that country alone, while permanently hurting the other country by reducing the gains from trade that are possible between the two countries."

Many in the economics profession do admit that it is hard to gauge whether intensified offshoring of U.S. jobs in the context of free-trade globalization will give more in winnings to the winners than it takes in losses from the losers. "Nobody has a clue about what the numbers are," as Robert C. Feenstra, a prominent trade economist, told *BusinessWeek* at the time.

The empirical issues that will determine whether offshore outsourcing ultimately delivers, on balance, more benefits than costs, and to whom those benefits and costs will accrue, are myriad. First, how wide a swath of white-collar workers will see their wages reduced by competition from the cheap, highly skilled workers who are now becoming available around the world? Second, by how much will their wages drop? Third, will the U.S. workers thrown into the global labor pool end up losing more in lower wages than they gain in lower consumer prices? In that case, the benefits of increased trade would go overwhelmingly to employers. But even employers might lose out depending on the answer to a fourth question: Will cheap labor from abroad allow foreign employers to out-compete U.S. employers, driving down the prices of their products and lowering U.S. export earnings? In that case, not only workers, but the corporations that employ them as well, could end up worse off.

Bigger Than A Box

Another mainstream Keynesian economist, Alan Blinder, former Clinton economic advisor and vice-chair of the Federal Reserve Board, doubts that outsourcing will be "immiserating" in the long run and still calls himself "a free-trader down to his toes." But Blinder is convinced that the transition costs will be large, lengthy, and painful before the United States experiences a net gain from outsourcing. Here is why.

First, rapid improvements in information and communications technology have rendered obsolete the traditional notion that manufactured goods, which can generally be boxed and shipped, are tradable, while services, which cannot be boxed, are not. And the workers who perform the services that computers and satellites have now rendered tradable will increasingly be found offshore, especially when they are skilled and will work for lower wages.

Second, another 1.5 billion or so workers—many in China, India, and the former Soviet bloc—are now part of the world economy. While most are low-skilled workers, some are not; and as Blinder says, a small percentage of 1.5 billion is nonetheless "a lot of willing and able people available to do the jobs that technology will move offshore." And as China and India educate more workers, offshoring of high-skill work will accelerate.

Third, the transition will be particularly painful in the United States because the U.S. unemployment insurance program is stingy, at least by first-world standards, and because U.S. workers who lose their jobs often lose their health insurance and pension rights as well.

How large will the transition cost be? "Thirty million to 40 million U.S. jobs are potentially offshorable," according to Blinder's latest estimates. "These include scientists, mathematicians and editors on the high end and telephone operators, clerks and typists on the low end."

Blinder arrived at these figures by creating an index that identifies how easy or hard it will be for a job to be physically or electronically "offshored." He then used the index to assess the Bureau of Labor Statistics' 817 U.S. occupational categories. Not surprisingly, Blinder classifies almost all of the 14.3 million U.S. manufacturing jobs as offshorable. But he also classifies more than twice that many U.S. service sector jobs as offshorable, including most computer industry jobs as well as many others, for instance, the 12,470 U.S. economists and the 23,790 U.S. multimedia artists and animators. In total, Blinder's analysis suggests that 22% to 29% of the jobs held by U.S. workers in 2004 will be potentially offshorable within a decade or two, with nearly 8.2 million jobs in 59 occupations "highly offshorable." Table 1 provides a list of the broad occupational categories with 300,000 or more workers that Blinder considers potentially offshorable.

Mankiw dismissed Blinder's estimates of the number of jobs at risk to offshoring as "out of the mainstream." Indeed, Blinder's estimates are considerably larger than earlier ones. But these earlier studies either aim to measure the number of U.S. jobs that will be outsourced (as opposed to the number at risk of being outsourced), look at a shorter period of time, or have shortcomings that suggest they underestimate the number of U.S. jobs threatened by outsourcing. (See "Studying the Studies.")

Global Arbitrage

Low wages are the reason U.S. corporations outsource labor. Table 2 shows just how large the international wage differentials were for computer programmers in 2002. Programmers in the United States make wages nearly *ten times* those of their counterparts in India and the Philippines, for example.

Today, more and more white-collar workers in the United States are finding themselves in direct competition with the low-cost, well-trained, highly educated workers in Bangalore, Shanghai, and Eastern and Central Europe. These workers

TABLE 1: MAJOR OCCUPATIONS RANKED BY OFFSHORABILITY

Occupation	Category	Index Number	Number of Workers
Computer programmers	I	100	389,090
Telemarketers	I	95	400,860
Computer systems analysts	I	93	492,120
Billing and posting clerks and machine operators	I	90	513,020
Bookkeeping, accounting, and auditing clerks	I	84	1,815,340
Computer support specialists	I and II	92/68	499,860
Computer software engineers: Applications	II	74	455,980
Computer software engineers: Systems software	II	74	320,720
Accountants	II	72	591,311
Welders, cutters, solderers, and brazers	II	70	358,050
Helpers—production workers	II	70	528,610
First-line supervisors/managers of production and operating workers	II	68	679,930
Packaging and filling machine operators and tenders	II	68	396,270
Team assemblers	II	65	1,242,370
Bill and account collectors	II	65	431,280
Machinists	II	61	368,380
Inspectors, testers, sorters, samplers, and weighers	II	60	506,160
General and operations managers	III	55	1,663,810
Stock clerks and order fillers	III	34	1,625,430
Shipping, receiving, and traffic clerks	III	29	759,910
Sales managers	III	26	317,970
Business operations specialists, all other	IV	25	916,290

Source: Alan Blinder, "How Many U.S. Jobs Might Be Offshorable?" *CEPS Working Paper* #142, March 2007, figures from Bureau of Labor Statistics and author's judgments.

often use the same capital and technology and are no less productive than the U.S. workers they replace. They just get paid less.

This global labor arbitrage, as Morgan Stanley's chief economist Stephen Roach calls it, has narrowed international wage disparities in manufacturing, and now in services too, by unrelentingly pushing U.S. wages down toward international norms. ("Arbitrage" refers to transactions that yield a profit by taking advantage of a price differential for the same asset in different locations. Here, of course, the "asset" is wage labor of a certain skill level.) A sign of that pressure: about 70% of laid-off workers in the United States earn less three years later than they did at the time of the layoff; on average, those reemployed earn 10% less than they did before.

And it's not only laid-off workers who are hurt. A study conducted by Harvard labor economists Lawrence F. Katz, Richard B. Freeman, and George J. Borjas finds that every other worker with skills similar to those who were displaced also loses out. Every 1% drop in employment due to imports or factories gone abroad shaves 0.5% off the wages of the remaining workers in that occupation, they conclude.

Global labor arbitrage also goes a long way toward explaining the poor quality and low pay of the jobs the U.S. economy has created this decade, according to Roach. By dampening wage increases for an ever wider swath of the U.S. workforce, he argues, outsourcing has helped to drive a wedge between productivity gains and wage gains and to widen inequality in the United States. In the first four years of this decade, nonfarm productivity in the United States has recorded a cumulative increase of 13.3%—more than double the 5.9% rise in real compensation per hour over the same period. ("Compensation" includes wages, which have been stagnant for the average worker, plus employer spending on fringe benefits such as health

TABLE 2: AVERAGE SALARIES OF PROGRAMMERS

Country	Salary Range
Poland and Hungary	$4,800 to $8,000
India	$5,880 to $11,000
Philippines	$6,564
Malaysia	$7,200
Russian Federation	$5,000 to $7,500
China	$8,952
Canada	$28,174
Ireland	$23,000 to $34,000
Israel	$15,000 to $38,000
USA	$60,000 to $80,000

Source: CIO magazine, November 2002, from Merrill Lynch Smart Access Survey.

insurance, which has risen even as, in many instances, the actual benefits have been cut back.) Roach reports that the disconnect between pay and productivity growth during the current economic expansion has been much greater in services than in manufacturing, as that sector weathers the powerful forces of global labor arbitrage for the first time.

Doubts in the Business Press?!

Even in the business press, doubts that offshore outsourcing willy-nilly leads to economic improvement have become more acute. Earlier this summer, a *BusinessWeek* cover story, "The Real Cost of Offshoring," reported that government statistics have underestimated the damage to the U.S. economy from offshore outsourcing. The problem is that since offshoring took off, *import* growth, adjusted for inflation, has been faster than the official numbers show. That means improvements in living standards, as well as corporate profits, depend more on cheap imports, and less on improving domestic productivity, than analysts thought.

Growing angst about outsourcing's costs has also prompted the business press to report favorably on remedies for the dislocation brought on by offshoring that deviate substantially from the non-interventionist, free-market playbook. Even the most unfazed pro-globalization types want to beef up trade adjustment assistance for displaced workers and strengthen the U.S. educational system. But both proposals are inadequate.

More education, the usual U.S. prescription for any economic problem, is off the mark here. Cheaper labor is available abroad up and down the job-skill ladder, so even the most rigorous education is no inoculation against the threat of offshore outsourcing. As Blinder emphasizes, it is the need for face-to-face contact that stops jobs from being shipped overseas, not the level of education necessary to perform them. Twenty years from now, home health aide positions will no doubt be plentiful in the United States; jobs for highly trained IT professionals may be scarce.

Trade adjustment assistance has until now been narrowly targeted at workers hurt by imports. Most new proposals would replace traditional trade adjustment assistance and unemployment insurance with a program for displaced workers that offers wage insurance to ease the pain of taking a lower-paying job and provides for portable health insurance and retraining. The pro-globalization research group McKinsey Global Institute (MGI), for example, claims that for as little as 4% to 5% of the amount they've saved in lower wages, companies could cover the wage losses of all laid-off workers once they are reemployed, paying them 70% of the wage differential between their old and new jobs (in addition to health care subsidies) for up to two years.

While MGI confidently concludes that this proposal will "go a long way toward relieving the current anxieties," other globalization advocates are not so sure. They recognize that economic anxiety is pervasive and that millions of white-collar workers now fear losing their jobs. Moreover, even if fears of actual job loss are overblown, wage insurance schemes do little to compensate for the downward pressure offshoring is putting on the wages of workers who have not been laid off.

Other mainstream economists and business writers go even further, calling for not only wage insurance but also taxes on the winners from globalization. And globalization has produced big winners: on Wall Street, in the corporate boardroom, and among those workers in high demand in the global economy.

Economist Matthew Slaughter, who recently left President Bush's Council of Economic Advisers, told the *Wall Street Journal*, "Expanding the political support for open borders [for trade] requres making a radical change in fiscal policy." He proposes eliminating the Social Security-Medicare payroll tax on the bottom half of workers—roughly, those earning less than $33,000 a year—and making up the lost revenue by raising the payroll tax on higher earners.

The goal of these economists is to thwart a crippling political backlash against trade. As they see it, "using the tax code to slice the apple more evenly is far more palatable than trying to hold back globalization with policies that risk shrinking the economic apple."

Some even call for extending global labor arbitrage to CEOs. In a June 2006 *New York Times* op-ed, equity analyst Lawrence Orlowski and New York University

STUDYING THE STUDIES

When economist Alan Blinder raised alarm bells in 2006 about the potentially large-scale offshoring of U.S. jobs, his results were inevitably compared to earlier research on offshore outsourcing. Three studies have been especially influential. The 2002 study (revised in 2004) by Forrester Research, a private, for-profit market research firm, which estimated that 3.3 million U.S. service sector jobs would move offshore by 2015, caused perhaps the biggest media stir. It was picked up by *BusinessWeek* and the *Wall Street Journal*, and hyped by Lou Dobbs, the CNN business-news anchor and outspoken critic of offshoring.

Forrester researcher John McCarthy developed his estimate by poring over newspaper clippings and Labor Department statistics on 505 white-collar occupations and then making an educated guess about how many jobs would be shipped offshore by 2015.

The Forrester study projects actual offshoring, not the number of jobs at risk of offshoring, so its estimate is rightfully lower than Blinder's. But the ample possibilities for technological change between now and 2015 convince Blinder that the Forrester estimate is nonetheless too low.

A 2003 study by University of California economists Ashok Bardhan and Cynthia Kroll estimated that about 11% of all U.S. jobs in 2001 were vulnerable to offshoring. Bradhan and Kroll applied the "outsourceability attributes" listed in "Attributes of Jobs Outsourced" to occupations where at least some outsourcing either has already taken place or is being planned.

Blinder considers the Bardhan and Kroll estimate for 2001 to be comparable to his estimate that 20% to 30% of the employed labor force will be at risk of offshore outsourcing within the next ten to twenty years, especially considering that Bardhan and Kroll do not allow for outsourcing to spread beyond the occupations it is currently affecting. This is like "looking only slightly beyond the currently-visible tip of the iceberg," according to Blinder.

The McKinsey Global Institute (MGI), a research group known for its unabashedly favorable view of globalization, has done its best to put a positive spin on offshore assistant research director Florian Lengyel argued that offshoring the jobs of U.S. chief executives would reduce costs and release value to shareholders by bringing the compensation of U.S. CEOs (on average 170 times greater than the compensation of average U.S. workers in 2004) in line with CEO compensation in Britain (22 times greater) and in Japan (11 times greater).

Yet others focus on the stunning lack of labor mobility that distinguishes the current era of globalization from earlier ones. Labor markets are becoming increasingly free and flexible under globalization, but labor enjoys no similar freedom of movement. In a completely free market, the foreign workers would come here to do the work that is currently being outsourced. Why aren't more of those workers coming to the United States? Traditional economists Gary Becker and Richard Posner argue the answer is clear: an excessively restrictive immigration policy.

Onshore and Offshore Solidarity

Offshoring is one of the last steps in capitalism's conversion of the "physician, the lawyer, the priest, the poet, the man of science, into its paid wage laborers," as

---

outsourcing. Its 2003 study, which relied on the Forrester offshoring estimates, concluded that offshoring is already benefiting the U.S. economy. For instance, MGI calculates that for every dollar spent on a business process outsourced to India, the U.S. economy gains at least $1.12. The largest chunk—58 cents—goes back to the original employer in the form of cost savings, almost exclusively in the form of lower wages. In addition, 30% of Indian offshoring is actually performed by U.S. companies, so the wage savings translate into higher earnings for those companies. The study also argues that offshore outsourcing frees up U.S. workers to do other tasks.

A second MGI study, in 2005, surveyed dozens of companies in eight sectors, from pharmaceutical companies to insurers. The study predicted that multinational companies in the entire developed world will have located only 4.1 million service jobs in low-wage countries by 2008—a figure equal to only 1% of the total number of service jobs in developed countries.

But the MGI outsourcing studies have serious limitations. For instance, Blinder points out that MGI's analysis looks at a very short time frame, and that the potential for outsourcing in English-speaking countries such as the United States is higher than elsewhere, a fact lost in the MGI studies' global averages.

In their 2005 book *Outsourcing America*, published by the American Management Association, public policy professors Ron Hira and Anil Hira argue that MGI's 2003 report "should be viewed as a self-interested lobbying document that presents an unrealistically optimistic estimate of the impact of offshore outsourcing." For instance, most of the data for the report came from case studies conducted by MGI that are unavailable to the public and unsupported by any model. Moreover, the MGI analysis assumes that the U.S. economy will follow its long-term trend and create 3.5 million jobs a year, enough to quickly reemploy U.S. workers displaced by offshoring. But current U.S. job creation falls far short of that trend. A recent White House fact sheet brags that the U.S. economy has created 8.3 million jobs since August 2003. Still, that is less than 2.1 million jobs a year, and only 1.8 million jobs over the last 12 months.

MGI's Farrell is right about one thing. "If the economy were stronger," she says, "there wouldn't be such a negative feeling" about work getting offshored. But merely assuming high job growth doesn't make it so.

Marx and Engels put it in the *Communist Manifesto* 160 years ago. It has already done much to increase economic insecurity in the workaday world and has become, Blinder suggests, the number one economic issue of our generation.

Offshoring has also underlined the interdependence of workers across the globe. To the extent that corporations now organize their business operations on a global scale, shifting work around the world in search of low wages, labor organizing must also be global in scope if it is to have any hope of building workers' negotiating strength.

Yet today's global labor arbitrage pits workers from different countries against each other as competitors, not allies. Writing about how to improve labor standards, economists Ajit Singh and Ann Zammit of the South Centre, an Indian non-governmental organization, ask the question, "On what could workers of the world unite" today? Their answer is that faster economic growth could indeed be a positive-sum game from which both the global North and the global South could gain. A pick-up in the long-term rate of growth of the world economy would generate higher employment, increasing wages and otherwise improving labor standards in both regions. It should also make offshoring less profitable and less painful.

The concerns of workers across the globe would also be served by curtailing the ability of multinational corporations to move their investment anywhere, which weakens the bargaining power of labor both in advanced countries and in the global South. Workers globally would also benefit if their own ability to move between countries was enhanced. The combination of a new set of rules to limit international capital movements and to expand labor mobility across borders, together with measures to ratchet up economic growth and thus increase worldwide demand for labor, would alter the current process of globalization and harness it to the needs of working people worldwide. ❑

Sources: Alan S. Blinder, "Fear of Offshoring," CEPS Working Paper #119, Dec. 2005; Alan S. Blinder, "How Many U.S. Jobs Might Be Offshorable?" CEPS Working Paper #142, March 2007; N. Gregory Mankiw and P. Swagel, "The Politics and Economics of Offshore Outsourcing," Am. Enterprise Inst. Working Paper #122, 12/7/05; "Offshoring: Is It a Win-Win Game?" McKinsey Global Institute, August 2003; Diane Farrell et al., "The Emerging Global Labor Market, Part 1: The Demand for Talent in Services," McKinsey Global Institute, June 2005; Ashok Bardhan and Cynthia Kroll, "The New Wave of Outsourcing," Research Report #113, Fisher Center for Real Estate and Urban Economics, Univ. of Calif., Berkeley, Fall 2003; Paul A. Samuelson, "Where Ricardo and Mill Rebut and Confirm Arguments of Mainstream Economists Supporting Globalization," *J Econ Perspectives* 18:3, Summer 2004; Alan S. Blinder, "Free Trade's Great, but Offshoring Rattles Me," *Wash. Post,* 5/6/07; Michael Mandel, "The Real Cost of Offshoring," *BusinessWeek,* 6/18/07; Aaron Bernstein, "Shaking Up Trade Theory," *BusinessWeek,* 12/6/04; David Wessel, "The Case for Taxing Globalization's Big Winners," *WSJ,* 6/14/07; Bob Davis, "Some Democratic Economists Echo Mankiw on Outsourcing," *WSJ;* N. Gregory Mankiw, "Outsourcing Redux," gregmankiw.blogspot.com/2006/05/outsourcing-redux; David Wessel and Bob Davis, "Pain From Free Trade Spurs Second Thoughts," *WSJ,* 3/30/07; Ajit Singh and Ann Zammit, "On What Could Workers of the World Unite? Economic Growth and a New Global Economic Order," from *The Global Labour Standards Controversy: Critical Issues For Developing Countries,* South Centre, 2000; Michael Meeropol, "Distorting Adam Smith on Trade," *Challenge,* July/Aug 2004.

Article 5.5

ARE LOW WAGES AND JOB LOSS INEVITABLE?

BY ARTHUR MacEWAN
May/June 2011

> Dear Dr. Dollar:
>
> The main narrative that I hear in mainstream press is that U.S. workers are being undercut and eventually displaced by global competition. I think this narrative has a tone of inevitability, that low wages and job loss are driven by huge impersonal forces that we can't do much about. Is this right?
>
> — *Vicki Legion, San Francisco, Calif.*

Yes, that is the main narrative. But, no, it's not right.

Globalization, in the sense of increasing international commerce over long distances, has been going on since human beings made their way out of Africa and spread themselves far and wide. Trade between China and the Mediterranean seems to have been taking place at least 3,000 years ago. (We know this through chemical analysis of silk found in the hair of an Egyptian mummy interred around 1000 BCE; the silk was identified as almost certainly from China.) The long history of long-distance commerce does cast an aura of inevitability over globalization.

But the spread of international commerce has not taken shape outside of human control. Globalization takes many forms; its history has variously involved colonial control, spheres of influence, and forms of regulated trade.

The current era of globalization was quite consciously planned by the U.S. government and U.S. business during and after World War II. They saw the United States replacing the British Empire as the dominant power among capitalist countries. But in place of 19th century-style colonial control, they looked to a "free trade" regime to give U.S. firms access to resources and markets around the world. While U.S. business and the U.S. government did not achieve the "free trade" goal immediately, this has been what they have promoted over the last 65 years.

This U.S.—sponsored form of globalization has given great advantage to U.S. business. And it has put many U.S. workers in direct competition with more poorly paid workers elsewhere in the world, who are often denied the right to organize and have little choice but to work long hours in often unsafe conditions. U.S. business can make its profits off these workers elsewhere—often by sub-contracting to local firms. But there is nothing inevitable about this set-up.

Furthermore, there are ways to counter these developments. Just as the current global economic arrangements were created by political decisions, they can be altered by political decisions. Two examples:

- The development of better social programs in the United States would put workers here in a stronger bargaining position, regardless of global competition. With universal health care (a "single-payer" system), for instance, U.S. workers would be in a better position to leave a bad job or turn down a bad offer.

- Rebuilding the labor movement is essential for placing U.S. workers in a stronger bargaining position in relation to their employers. Equally important, stronger unions would give workers more leverage in the political arena, where many decisions about the nature of global commerce are made.

No, we may not be able to create the same labor movement of decades past. However, lest one think that the decline of the labor movement has been itself inevitable in the face of globalization, consider some of the political decisions that have undermined labor's strength:

- The National Labor Relations Board has not done its job. In the '50s, '60s, and early 1970s, fewer than one in ten union elections were marred by illegal firings of union organizers. By the early 1980s, over 30% of union elections involved illegal firings. While the figure declined to 16% by the late 1990s, it was back up to 25% in the early 2000s.

- Or consider the minimum wage. Even with the recent increase of the federal minimum wage to $7.25 per hour, adjusted for inflation it is still below what it was in the 1960s and 1970s.

These are crucial political decisions that have affected organized labor, wage rates, and jobs. But they were not inevitable developments.

It would be folly to think that the changes in the global economy have not affected economic conditions in the United States, including the position of organized labor. But it would also be folly to assume that conditions in the United States are inevitably determined by the global economy. Political action matters.

(Caveat: Advocating a "different shape" for globalization is not a call for protectionism. It is possible to engage in world commerce and protect the interest of U.S. workers without resorting to traditional protectionism. But that is a topic for another day.) ❑

Article 5.6

THE ASSAULT ON LABOR IN CANANEA, MEXICO

BY ANNE FISCHEL AND LIN NELSON

September/October 2010

> *The actions taken in collusion between Grupo México and the Mexican government are an outrage. And if they can crush this very effective, independent union ... all independent unions in Mexico are at risk. And then other countries that are watching can say, "Well, if they can do it there, we can do it here too." And so I think that ... a union that is fighting for safe working conditions, fighting for decent treatment of the ... workers in those mines, if we can't stand behind that as a global labor movement, we're in trouble.*
>
> —Leo Gerard, president, United Steelworkers Union

On the night of June 6, 2010, more than 3,000 federal and 500 state police descended on the city of Cananea, Mexico (population 32,000), 30 miles south of the Arizona-Mexico border, where Section 65 of the Union of Miners and Metallurgical Workers (the Mineros) has been on strike for three years. They drove workers out of the mine, pursued them to the union hall, and gassed all who took refuge inside, including women and children. Several people were injured in the melee and at least five miners were arrested.

The attack on the workers of Cananea was a bitter turn in the prolonged David-and-Goliath struggle between a proud union and a powerful transnational copper mining company, Grupo México, backed by a neoliberal Mexican government. The miners are striking to restore health and safety protections guaranteed by their union contract and to mitigate environmental damage to their region and community. More fundamentally, they are fighting for the survival of independent Mexican unions—for the power to organize, and protect workers and their communities from corporate abuse.

Fighting for the Right to Health and the Right to Strike

> *Grupo México doesn't respect the lives or the dignity of workers. It doesn't invest in safety or in reducing pollution. It is not interested in the hygiene of its worksites and it is not interested in rights or collective agreements.*
>
> —Napoleón Gómez Urrutia, general secretary, Union of Miners
> and Metallurgical Workers

The Mineros union is at the forefront of an international movement defending workers and communities against neoliberal incursions. Although the U.S. media has largely ignored the Mineros' struggle, the strike has drawn global support from unions, including the United Steelworkers, the main union at Grupo México's U.S. plants. Steelworkers president, Leo Gerard, was quick to denounce the Mexican government's action, calling it "a reign of terror for the workers."

Grupo México became notorious in 2006 for its role in the Pasta de Conchos mining disaster in Coahuila, Mexico, in which 65 members of the Mineros union were killed. In the months leading up to the massive explosion in the mine, workers repeatedly warned of dangerous conditions, including a build-up of explosive methane gas. They were ignored by the company and by regulating agencies charged with overseeing mine safety in Mexico. On February 19, 2006, the mine blew up. Napoleón Gómez Urrutia, general secretary of the Mineros, accused Grupo México of "industrial homicide," and called for an investigation. Gómez was already well known for his opposition to neoliberal labor reforms and his focus on international labor solidarity. Under his leadership the Mineros forged alliances with the Steelworkers (United States and Canada) and with Grupo's key union at its Peruvian mines, the Federation of Metal Workers of Peru.

After Gómez Urrutia denounced the state's complicity in the Pasta de Conchos explosion, Calderón's government removed him from his leadership post. Gómez was charged with mishandling union funds and forced to flee to Canada, where he now lives as a guest of the Steelworkers. After an independent audit by a Swiss accounting firm exonerated Gómez and the union, Mexican courts threw out the charges and Gómez was officially reinstated as general secretary. Despite this, the government continued to seek his extradition, but Canada repeatedly refused. The Mineros refused to accept government control of their union and have re-elected Gómez Urrutia six times. In the United States, the AFL-CIO denounced Gómez' ouster as part of "the continuing suppression of the independent labor movement ... by the Mexican government."

In Cananea the Mineros have been on strike since July 2007, when 1,300 workers walked off their jobs citing dangerous health and safety conditions and contract violations that threaten the health and safety of the community. The violations were thoroughly documented by the Maquila Health and Safety Support Network (MHSSN), a bi-national group of occupational health experts who toured the mine in fall 2007. Among their findings: piles of silica dust, which can cause silicosis and lung cancer; dismantled dust collectors; and inadequate ventilation systems, respirators, and auditory equipment. MHSSN's report documents "a workplace being deliberately run into the ground" where workers are "exposed to high levels of toxic dusts and acid mists, operate malfunctioning and poorly maintained equipment, and work in ... dangerous surroundings."

Since then Grupo México and the union have waged a prolonged legal battle, as the company sought repeatedly to have the strike declared invalid. Under Mexican constitutional law, strikes must be honored unless invalidated by the courts; as long as union workers are striking, companies cannot hire replacement workers or resume production. In January 2008, the courts briefly sided with the company, and police ousted the workers from the mine. Helicopters bombed strikers with tear gas; police beat them with clubs; 20 miners were injured. The next day the court reversed its position and upheld the strike, forcing Grupo México to withdraw from the mine.

In February 2010, two and a half years into the struggle, the Supreme Court again declared the strike invalid, and terminated the union's contract. Mexico's Political Coordination Board, a governing body of the National Chamber of Deputies, urged the government to "avoid the use of public force against the strike movement" and instead consider revoking Grupo México's ownership of the Cananea mine concession "given their persistent refusal to resolve, by means of dialogue and negotiation, the strike that this mine's workers maintain." The Board called for a 30-day cooling-off period followed by negotiations. Looking broadly at the struggles against Grupo México at all its mining sites in Mexico, it called for a "legal, comprehensive and fair solution to the Cananea, Sonora, Sombrerete, Zacatecas, and Taxco, Guerrero miners' striking conflicts, within a frame of respect to the rights of unions' autonomy, strike, collective hiring, safety and hygiene and all other labor rights." Hoping that the Political Coordination Board's recommendations would win out, the workers continued to press their demands.

Imposing a Company Union on a Community

In May 2010, we traveled to Cananea with a delegation of labor educators and activists to meet union members and the Women's Front (the Frente) that works in solidarity with them. We stayed in the homes of mining families, met with union and Frente leaders, and were taken on a tour of the vast open pit mine. During the tour we saw for ourselves some of the conditions that impelled the miners to strike. We talked with Cananea's mayor about the state of the city's economy and with the head of the local hospital about Grupo México's problematic health and safety record. We returned to the United States prepared to support the growing movement of global solidarity that has coalesced around the Mineros. Two weeks later the government sent in the police, rupturing the constitutional protections that undergird Mexican labor law.

In a 2008 report the International Metalworkers Federation wrote, "The line between the Mexican government and Grupo México has remained blurry since Calderón took office ... and the two have worked in concert to plan and execute the assault on los Mineros." In fact, Mexico's ruling party, the Partido del Acción Nacional (PAN), has long pursued an openly neoliberal agenda. One of President Calderón's legislative priorities was to fundamentally restructure the relationships between labor, capital, and the state. Since winning the presidency for the first time in 2000, the PAN has championed the dismantling of contractual protections for workers. In Mexico, the process is known as "flexibilization," which allows companies to hire temporary and part-time workers without benefits or job security, and subcontract out jobs previously held by unionized workers. Grupo México has played a leading role in implementing flexibilization; as the Mineros explained to us, all of the union locals at Grupo's mines have been under assault, and several have been replaced by a *sindicato blanco*, a company union. In the days following the police incursion at Cananea, Grupo announced that all the strikers were welcome to return to work, as long as they agreed to join the *sindicato blanco*. With the mine secured, Grupo México, Minister of Labor Javier Lozano, and Sonora Governor Guillermo Padres quickly unveiled a new partnership: Grupo México will invest $120 million to rebuild and expand the mine, while the state will invest almost $440 million in new infrastructure and aid for economic development in Cananea.

Cananea's Place in Mexican History

The struggle for workers' rights is not new to Cananea. The city holds a special place in Mexican history. In June 1906, Mexican miners walked off the job, demanding equal pay with their U.S. co-workers. Their U.S. employer sent for Arizona vigilantes who fired into a crowd of striking miners, killing 23. The massacre in Cananea created outrage throughout Mexico and helped start the Revolution of 1910. The city is proud of its revolutionary and working-class history. Visitors are welcomed by a sign, "Cananea: the Proletarian City," and in one of the older neighborhoods, the "Neighborhood of the Martyrs of Cananea," streets are named for miners who died in the 1906 struggle. To millions of Mexicans, Cananea symbolizes their nation's long and incomplete struggle for political and economic independence, while the union is a standard-bearer in the battle for workers' rights.

The rights to organize and strike were written into the Constitution of 1917 and codified into labor law in 1931. The Mexican Constitution also charges the government with safeguarding resources essential to national development. Mining is high on the list, as are railroads and oil. In the 1960s, the government purchased the Cananea mine from its U.S. owner in accordance with Constitutional law. But in 1988, facing a debt crisis and a rapidly devaluing currency, then-President Salinas agreed to privatize state-owned industry. The concession to operate Cananea was auctioned off to a group of wealthy cronies, who created what is now Grupo México. While Grupo México is a relatively young company, its origins lie with one of the oldest U.S. miners, the American Smelting and Refining Company, or ASARCO (see box).

Undermining Health, Wasting the Environment

Environment is the last thing that Grupo Mexico cares about. We see the destroyed mountains; we see the contamination; the acids in the atmosphere, the dust which is toxic to the people. [But] all GrupoMexico wants is the metal. To destroy, take the profits and leave the city in ruins, that is what they want.
—Dr. Luis Calderón, medical director, El Ronquillo Hospital, Cananea

When Grupo acquired the Cananea mine in 1989, it immediately began to dismantle the historic social contract with the workers and the community. It closed the Workers

---

Grupo México and ASARCO: A Case Study of a Corporate Shape-shifter

Grupo México began as ASARCO Mexicana. From its 1880s beginnings ASARCO operated mines in Mexico. ASARCO helped open Mexico to U.S. investment and economic control. ASARCO's mines produced fabulous wealth for its U.S. owners, while ASARCO's railroads trekked Mexico's ore across the border to ASARCO's smelters and refineries. At one time ASARCO had over 95 U.S. mines, smelters, and refineries, as well as holdings in Mexico, Chile, Peru, Australia, the Philippines, and the Congo.

In 1998, plagued by aging plants, contaminated sites, and the plunging price of copper, ASARCO put itself on the market and was purchased by its former Mexican affiliate. In 2002 ASARCO sold its lucrative Peruvian subsidiary, Southern Peru Copper, to its new owner, shifting its most potent assets across the border to Mexico. In 2005, ASARCO filed for Chapter 11 bankruptcy, citing lack of assets and environmental liabilities as the primary causes. The most prolonged and complex environmental bankruptcy in U.S. history was finally concluded in late 2009, when the company settled its claims and Grupo México regained control, over the strenuous objections of the Steelworkers. This closely watched bankruptcy left many communities struggling to complete remediation projects with modest funds; Texas State Senator Eliot Shapleigh called it an environmental test case for corporate polluters, while the Government Accounting Office warned of a precedent that could encourage corporations to use bankruptcy to evade the public trust.

After ASARCO was sold to Grupo México, workers at the Hayden, Arizona, plant complained about inadequate training for employees working with industrial chemicals and hazardous equipment. Workers reported that stocks of safety equipment were consistently low, and even gloves and toilet paper were often unavailable. In interviews conducted in summer 2006, workers told of accidents caused by inadequate training, fingers lost because of poor lockout procedures, broken limbs, and a co-worker who was electrocuted when the power was improperly shut down. The local union's president, Tony Mesa, told us, "You're like a number; you can be replaced. That's not part of the agreement when you hired on that I'm going to leave part of my fingers here or I'm going to leave my arm or my leg or my life."

Grupo México now proposes to consolidate ASARCO and Southern Copper Corporation into a single entity. This Mexican-U.S.-Peruvian conglomerate is well-engineered for today's global economic landscape, able to shift assets and investments across borders, dedicated to eliminating obstacles to profits, and relying on international financial instruments and compliant governments for backup. It is this corporate shape-shifter, and the threat it represents to workers and communities, that the Mineros are fighting in Cananea.

Clinic, a well-equipped hospital run by the union and subsidized by the company, where miners and their families received treatment, including maternity and pediatric care. This left only the Ronquillo Hospital, a tiny, aging medical center owned and administered by the company. In 2008, in the midst of the strike, company officials summoned hospital personnel and announced the closure of the hospital. The company refused to pay for gasoline to transport dialysis patients to Hermosillo, four hours away; instead, hospital employees had to ask passersby for donations to buy gasoline. The community was left without access to health care. Dr. Calderón, the hospital's medical director, said, "They are stingy. They are exploiting a very rich mineral and there are positive things they could do to support the people. Instead Grupo Mexico has taken away all the benefits we used to receive in Cananea." The state of Sonora has since reopened the hospital, though at a very basic level of service.

During our visit the Mineros warned of the dangers that mine wastes pose to Cananea's air and water supply and to the region's watershed. The town is bordered on the northwest by the ever-expanding mine and on the east by a valley filling up with mine waste. Cananea maps show the valley area as a leachate lake, or reservoir, into which chemicals used to separate copper from its impurities are drained. Mountains of mine wastes, known as "halis" or tailings, loom on the outskirts of the city. When the winds blow, the top layers of the tailings drift through town, often ending up as a fine powder inside residents' homes. We were told that on windy days the sky is grey and thick, and waste materials blow as far north as the Arizona border. Local historian Arturo Rodriquez Aguero says, "On a bad day, you can't see the mountains at all." Increasingly the town is being swallowed up as the mine and the leachate lake continue to expand.

When Grupo took over the mine it promised to provide electricity and water to the community as the government and previous corporate owners had done. Instead, the company refused to pay the town's electrical bills and demanded exclusive use of the majority of town wells. This left the city with an inadequate water supply and distribution system. The city is building new wells, but this will take time; for now, the majority of residents use the Sonora River, which is contaminated by mine wastes, for their household needs, including drinking water—or purchase purified water, if they can afford it.

There is growing concern about the movement of mine wastes through the San Pedro River watershed, which begins in Cananea and flows 140 miles north to its confluence at Winkleman, Arizona, site of an ASARCO smelter. The San Pedro has one of the most diverse bird populations in the United States, including 100 species of breeding birds and 300 species of migrating birds. Agustín Gómez-Álverez reports, "Acid mining drainage from mine tailings is currently reaching a tributary of the San Pedro River with heavy metals and sulfates in water and sediments." Cadmium, copper, iron, manganese, lead and zinc have become fluid parts of the regional ecosystem.

"With the Support of Our Friends"

The Minero's strike has been broken, at least temporarily, but the struggle continues. The attack in Cananea is only the first wave in the corporate/state onslaught against workers' rights and unions in Mexico. Eleven days after the government sent in the police, Gammon Gold, a Canadian company, fired 397 union workers at its Mexican mine, citing the "relentless distractions of union labor disruptions." According to the *Financial Post*, the company said the Labor Ministry's support of Grupo México has "emboldened other miners to take decisive action against the union."

As Grupo's profits mount ($337 million in the last quarter), the Mineros continue to fight. They rely on the support of a growing international movement. The Steelworkers union has a steady presence in Cananea and is working with the Mineros to create an international alliance to strengthen workers' rights. The International Federation of Chemical, Energy and Mine Workers has sent delegations to Cananea. The International Metal Workers Foundation has published two white paper reports about the Mineros' struggle; the IMF supports the findings of the independent International Tribunal on Trade Union Rights, which met for over a year to consider the growing crisis of labor in Mexico. In its May 2010 report, the Tribunal questioned "the illegal sentence that has terminated the employment relationship ... between workers and the company." The Tribunal condemned the "partiality" of the Mexican government which appeared "as if acting on behalf of employers," and expressed concern about "the continuing use of force to end labor disputes." It concluded, "Repeated use of force and abuse of the law could lead to social upheaval and social unrest, and to the closure of legal avenues to resolve labor problems."

On July 9, the Superior Court of Justice of the Federal District of Mexico dismissed the arrest warrant against Napoleon Gómez Urrutia, removing any legal base for a case against him. And amidst the frenzy of the World Cup in South Africa, the National Congress of Mineworkers and the Coalition of South African Trade Unions mobilized an international demonstration of support for the Cananea miners. These signals of support give hope to the Mineros in their ongoing struggle. Sergio Lozano, secretary of the Cananea local told us, "You help us overcome the barrier of the border. In the past this didn't happen so much. It makes a big difference."

Just as in 1906, the miners of Cananea are standing against the abuses of unregulated corporate power backed by a compliant state. As a recent email from a union member stated, "We have lost a battle, but our struggle continues. We remain hopeful that with the international support of our friends and allies, we can persist and win."

Postscript

On August 11 [2010], two months after the federal police seized the mine, the Ninth District Judge in Sonora ruled that the Mineros' strike was still in existence and once again legally recognized. The judge found that the federal Attorney General and Secretary of Public Security had the authority to send police to inspect mine installations, but not to remove the strikers. The judge has granted a temporary injunction barring Grupo Mexico's replacement workers and the police from the mine until a permanent court ruling can be made. At least one replacement worker died in a mining accident and an estimated 25 have been injured on the job. As this article goes to press 800 miners and their supporters are waiting outside the gates to once again take control of the mine. ❏

Sources: Judy Ancel, "Mexican Government Threatens to Open Mine by Force," *The Cross Border Network*, June 2010; Barr, Heather et. al., "Workplace Health and Safety Survey and Medical Screening of Miners at Grupo México's Copper Mine, Cananea, Sonora, Mexico, *Maquiladora Health and Safety Support Network*, www.igc. org/mhssn, October 5–8, 2007; Garrett Brown, "Genuine Worker Participation—An Indispensable Key to Effective Global OHS," *New Solutions: A Journal of Occupational and Environmental Health*, 2009; Garrett Brown, "International OHS Through the

Looking Glass of the Global Economy," *EHS Today*, January 2008; Gómez-Álvarez, Augustín, et al. "Estimation of potential pollution from mine tailings in the San Pedro River (1993-2005), Mexico-U.S. border," *Environmental Geology*, vol. 57, #7, 2009; "Hasta La Victoria: Napoleon Gómez Speaks," speech to ITUC, June 29, 2010, www. mua.org.au; International Metalworkers' Federation, "Report of IMF Fact Finding Mission to Mexico," July 2006, www.solidaritycenter.org; International Metalworkers' Federation, "An Injury to One: The Mexican Miners' Struggle for Union Independence." March 2008, www.imfmetal.org; International Metalworkers' Federation, "International Tribunal on Freedom of Association condemns Mexican government policies," www. imfmetal.org; Interview with Dr. Calderón, El Ronquillo Hospital, Cananea, Mexico, May 2010; Interview with Tony Mesa, Phoenix, Arizona, July 2006; Mara Kardas-Nelson, Lin Nelson, and Anne Fischel, "Bankruptcy as Corporate Makeover: ASARCO demonstrates how to evade environmental responsibility," *Dollars & Sense*, May/June 2010; Gerald Markowitz and David Rosner, "Deceit and Denial: The Deadly Politics of Industrial Pollution," UC Press, 2002; Ingrid Zubieta, "Cananea Copper Mine: Is it Safe for Workers?" NIEHS presentation, 2009; Ingrig Zubieta et al., "Cananea Copper Mine: An International Effort to Improve Working Conditions in Mexico," *International Journal of Occupational and Environmental Health*, 2009.

Chapter 6

MIGRATION

Article 6.1

THE RIGHT TO STAY HOME
Transnational communities are creating new ways of looking at citizenship and residence that correspond to the realities of migration.

BY DAVID BACON
September/October 2008

For almost half a century, migration has been the main fact of social life in hundreds of indigenous towns spread through the hills of Oaxaca, one of Mexico's poorest states. That's made migrants' rights, and the conditions they face, central concerns for communities like Santiago de Juxtlahuaca. Today the right to travel to seek work is a matter of survival. But this June in Juxtlahuaca, in the heart of Oaxaca's Mixteca region, dozens of farmers left their fields, and weavers their looms, to talk about another right—the right to stay home.

In the town's community center two hundred Mixtec, Zapotec, and Triqui farmers, and a handful of their relatives working in the United States, made impassioned speeches asserting this right at the triannual assembly of the Indigenous Front of Binational Organizations (FIOB). Hot debates ended in numerous votes. The voices of mothers and fathers arguing over the future of their children echoed from the cinderblock walls of the cavernous hall. In Spanish, Mixteco, and Triqui, people repeated one phrase over and over: *el derecho de no migrar*—the right to *not* migrate. Asserting this right challenges not just inequality and exploitation facing migrants, but the very reasons why people have to migrate to begin with. Indigenous communities are pointing to the need for social change.

About 500,000 indigenous people from Oaxaca live in the United States, including 300,000 in California alone, according to Rufino Dominguez, one of FIOB's founders. These men and women come from communities whose economies are totally dependent on migration. The ability to send a son or daughter across the border to the north, to work and send back money, makes the difference between eating chicken or eating salt and tortillas. Migration means not having to manhandle a wooden plough behind an ox, cutting furrows in dry soil for a corn crop that can't be sold for what it cost to plant it. It means that dollars arrive in the mail when kids need shoes to go to school, or when a grandparent needs a doctor.

Seventy-five percent of Oaxaca's 3.4 million residents live in extreme poverty, according to EDUCA, an education and development organization. For more than two decades, under pressure from international lenders, the Mexican government has cut spending intended to raise rural incomes. Prices have risen dramatically since price controls and subsidies were eliminated for necessities like gasoline, electricity, bus fares, tortillas, and milk.

CITIZENSHIP, POLITICAL RIGHTS, AND LABOR RIGHTS

Citizenship is a complex issue in a world in which transnational migrant communities span borders and exist in more than one place simultaneously. Residents of transnational communities don't see themselves simply as victims of an unfair system, but as actors capable of reproducing culture, of providing economic support to families in their towns of origin, and of seeking social justice in the countries to which they've migrated. A sensible immigration policy would recognize and support migrant communities. It would reinforce indigenous culture and language, rather than treating them as a threat. At the same time, it would seek to integrate immigrants into the broader community around them and give them a voice in it, rather than promoting social exclusion, isolation, and segregation. It would protect the rights of immigrants as part of protecting the rights of all working people.

Transnational communities in Mexico are creating new ways of looking at citizenship and residence that correspond more closely to the reality of migration. In 2005 Jesús Martínez, a professor at California State University in Fresno, was elected by residents of the state of Michoacán in Mexico to their state legislature. His mandate was to represent the interests of the state's citizens living in the United States. "In Michoacán, we're trying to carry out reforms that can do justice to the role migrants play in our lives," Martínez said. In 2006 Pepe Jacques Medina, director of the Comité Pro Uno in Los Angeles' San Fernando Valley, was elected to the Federal Chamber of Deputies on the ticket of the left-leaning Party of the Democratic Revolution (PRD) with the same charge. Transnational migrants insist that they have important political and social rights, both in their communities of origin and in their communities abroad.

The two parties that control the Mexican national congress, the Institutional Revolutionary Party (PRI) and the National Action Party (PAN), have taken steps to provide political rights for migrants. But while Mexico's congress voted over a decade ago to enfranchise Mexicans in the United States, it only set up a system to implement that decision in April 2005. They imposed so many obstacles that in the 2006 presidential elections only 40,000 were able to vote, out of a potential electorate of millions.

While it is difficult for Mexicans in the United States to vote in Mexico, they are barred from voting in the United States altogether. But U.S. electoral politics can't remain forever immune from expectations of representation, and they shouldn't. After all, the slogan of the Boston Tea Party was "No taxation without representation"; those who make economic contributions have political rights. That principle requires recognition of the legitimate social status of everyone living in the United States. Legalization isn't just important to migrants—it is a basic step in the preservation and extension of democratic rights for all people. With and without

Raquel Cruz Manzano, principal of the Formal Primary School in San Pablo Macuiltianguis, a town in the indigenous Zapotec region, says only 900,000 Oaxacans receive organized health care, and the illiteracy rate is 21.8%. "The educational level in Oaxaca is 5.8 years," Cruz notes, "against a national average of 7.3 years. The average monthly wage for non-governmental employees is less than 2,000 pesos [about $200] per family," the lowest in the nation. "Around 75,000 children have to work in order to survive or to help their families," says Jaime Medina, a reporter for Oaxaca's daily *Noticias*, "A typical teacher earns about 2200 pesos every two weeks [about $220]. From that they have to purchase chalk, pencils and other school supplies for the children." Towns like Juxtlahuaca don't even have waste water treatment. Rural communities rely on the same rivers for drinking water that are also used to carry away sewage.

visas, 34 million migrants living in the United States cannot vote to choose the political representatives who decide basic questions about wages and conditions at work, the education of their children, their health care or lack of it, and even whether they can walk the streets without fear of arrest and deportation.

Migrants' disenfranchisement affects U.S. citizens, especially working people. If all the farm workers and their families in California's San Joaquin Valley were able to vote, a wave of living wage ordinances would undoubtedly sweep the state. California's legislature would pass a single-payer health plan to ensure that every resident receives free and adequate health care. If it failed to pass, San Joaquin Valley legislators, currently among the most conservative, would be swept from office.

When those who most need social change and economic justice are excluded from the electorate, the range of possible reform is restricted, not only on issues of immigration, but on most economic issues that affect working people. Immigration policy, including political and social rights for immigrants, are integral parts of a broad agenda for change that includes better wages and housing, a national healthcare system, a national jobs program, and the right to organize without fear of being fired. Without expanding the electorate, it will be politically difficult to achieve any of it. By the same token, it's not possible to win major changes in immigration policy apart from a struggle for these other goals.

Anti-immigrant hysteria has always preached that the interests of immigrants and the native born are in conflict, that one group can only gain at the expense of the other. In fact, the opposite is true. To raise wages generally, the low price of immigrant labor has to rise, which means that immigrant workers have to be able to organize effectively. Given half a chance, they will fight for better jobs, wages, schools, and health care, just like anyone else. When they gain political power, the working class communities around them benefit too. Since it's easier for immigrants to organize if they have permanent legal status, a real legalization program would benefit a broad range of working people, far beyond immigrants themselves. On the other hand, when the government and employers use employer sanctions, enforcement, and raids to stop the push for better conditions, organizing is much more difficult, and unions and workers in general suffer the consequences.

The social exclusion and second-class status imposed by guestworker programs only increases migrants' vulnerability. De-linking immigration status and employment is a necessary step to achieving equal rights for migrant workers, who will never have significant power if they have to leave the country when they lose their jobs. Healthy immigrant communities need employed workers, but they also need students, old and young people, caregivers, artists, the disabled, and those who don't have traditional jobs.

"There are no jobs here, and NAFTA [the North American Free Trade Agreement] made the price of corn so low that it's not economically possible to plant a crop anymore," Dominguez asserts. "We come to the U.S. to work because we can't get a price for our product at home. There is no alternative." Without large-scale political change, most communities won't have the resources for productive projects and economic development that could provide a decent living.

Because of its indigenous membership, FIOB campaigns for the rights of migrants in the United States who come from those communities. It calls for immigration amnesty and legalization for undocumented migrants. FIOB has also condemned the proposals for guestworker programs. Migrants need the right to work, but "these workers don't have labor rights or benefits," Dominguez charges. "It's like slavery."

At the same time, "we need development that makes migration a choice rather than a necessity—the right to not migrate," explains Gaspar Rivera Salgado, a professor at UCLA. "Both rights are part of the same solution. We have to change the debate from one in which immigration is presented as a problem to a debate over rights. The real problem is exploitation." But the right to stay home, to not migrate, has to mean more than the right to be poor, the right to go hungry and be homeless. Choosing whether to stay home or leave only has meaning if each choice can provide a meaningful future.

In Juxtlahuaca, Rivera Salgado was elected as FIOB's new binational coordinator. His father and mother still live on a ranch half an hour up a dirt road from the main highway, in the tiny town of Santa Cruz Rancho Viejo. There his father Sidronio planted three hundred avocado trees a few years ago, in the hope that someday their fruit would take the place of the corn and beans that were once his staple crops. He's fortunate—his relatives have water, and a pipe from their spring has kept most of his trees, and those hopes, alive. Fernando, Gaspar's brother, has started growing mushrooms in a FIOB-sponsored project, and even put up a greenhouse for tomatoes. Those projects, they hope, will produce enough money that Fernando won't have to go back to Seattle, where he worked for seven years.

This family perhaps has come close to achieving the *derecho de no migrar*. For the millions of farmers throughout the indigenous countryside, not migrating means doing something like what Gaspar's family has done. But finding the necessary resources, even for a small number of families and communities, presents FIOB with its biggest challenge.

Rivera Salgado says, "we will find the answer to migration in our communities of origin. To make the right to not migrate concrete, we need to organize the forces in our communities, and combine them with the resources and experiences we've accumulated in 16 years of cross-border organizing." Over the years FIOB has organized women weavers in Juxtlahuaca, helping them sell their textiles and garments through its chapters in California. It set up a union for rural taxis, both to help farming families get from Juxtlahuaca to the tiny towns in the surrounding hills, and to provide jobs for drivers. Artisan co-ops make traditional products, helped by a cooperative loan fund.

The government does have some money for loans to start similar projects, but it usually goes to officials who often just pocket it, supporters of the ruling PRI, which has ruled Oaxaca since it was formed in the 1940s. "Part of our political culture is the use of *regalos*, or government favors, to buy votes," Rivera Salgado explains. "People want *regalos*, and think an organization is strong because of what it can give. It's critical that our members see organization as the answer to problems, not a gift from the government or a political party. FIOB members need political education."

But for the 16 years of its existence, FIOB has been a crucial part of the political opposition to Oaxaca's PRI government. Juan Romualdo Gutierrez Cortéz, a school teacher in Tecomaxtlahuaca, was FIOB's Oaxaca coordinator until he stepped down at the Juxtlahuaca assembly. He is also a leader of Oaxaca's teachers union, Section 22 of the National Education Workers Union, and of the Popular Association of the People of Oaxaca (APPO).

A June 2006 strike by Section 22 sparked a months-long uprising, led by APPO, which sought to remove the state's governor, Ulises Ruíz, and make a basic change in development and economic policy. The uprising was crushed by Federal armed intervention, and dozens of activists were arrested. According to Leoncio Vásquez, an FIOB activist in Fresno, "the lack of human rights itself is a factor contributing to migration from Oaxaca and Mexico, since it closes off our ability to call for any change." This spring teachers again occupied the central plaza, or *zócalo*, of the state capital, protesting the same conditions that sparked the uprising two years ago.

In the late 1990s Gutierrez was elected to the Oaxaca Chamber of Deputies, in an alliance between FIOB and Mexico's left-wing Democratic Revolutionary Party (PRD). Following his term in office, he was imprisoned by Ruíz' predecessor, José Murat, until a binational campaign won his release. His crime, and that of many others filling Oaxaca's jails, was insisting on a new path of economic development that would raise rural living standards and make migration just an option, rather than an indispensable means of survival.

Despite the fact that APPO wasn't successful in getting rid of Ruíz and the PRI, Rivera Salgado believes that "in Mexico we're very close to getting power in our communities on a local and state level." FIOB delegates agreed that the organization would continue its alliance with the PRD. "We know the PRD is caught up in an internal crisis, and there's no real alternative vision on the left," Rivera Salgado says. "But there are no other choices if we want to participate in electoral politics. Migration is part of globalization," he emphasizes, "an aspect of state policies that expel people. Creating an alternative to that requires political power. There's no way to avoid that." ❑

Article 6.2

"THEY WORK HERE, THEY LIVE HERE, THEY STAY HERE!"

French immigrants strike for the right to work—and win.

BY MARIE KENNEDY AND CHRIS TILLY

July/August 2007

France has an estimated half-million undocumented immigrants, including many from France's former colonies in Africa. The *sans-papiers* (literally, "without papers"), as the French call them, lead a shadowy existence, much like their U.S. counterparts. And as U.S. immigrants did in 2006 with rousing mass demonstrations, the French undocumented have recently taken a dramatic step out of the shadows. But the *sans-papiers* did it in a particularly French way: hundreds of them occupied their workplaces.

Snowballing Strikes

The snowflake that led to this snowball of sit-in strikes was a November immigration law, sponsored by the arch-conservative government of President Nicolas Sarkozy, that cracked down on family reunification and ramped up expulsions of unauthorized immigrants. The law also added a pro-business provision permitting migration, and even "regularization" of undocumented workers, in occupations facing labor shortages. The French government followed up with a January notice to businesses in labor-starved sectors, opening the door for employers to apply to local authorities for work permits for workers with false papers whom they had "in good faith" hired. However, for low-level jobs, this provision was limited to migrants from new European Union member countries. Africans could only qualify if they were working in highly skilled occupations such as science or engineering—but not surprisingly, most Africans in France are concentrated in low-wage service sector jobs.

At that point, African *sans-papiers* took matters into their own hands. On February 13, Fodie Konté of Mali and eight co-workers at the Grande Armée restaurant in Paris occupied their workplace to demand papers. All nine were members of the Confédération Générale du Travail (CGT), France's largest union federation, and the CGT backed them up. In less than a week, Parisian officials agreed to regularize seven of the nine, with Konté the first to get his papers.

The CGT and *Droits Devant!!* (Rights Ahead!!), an immigrant rights advocacy group, saw an opportunity and gave the snowball a push. They escorted Konté and his co-workers to meetings and rallies with other undocumented CGT workers, where they declared, "We've started it, it's up to you to follow." Small groups began to do just that. Then on April 15, fifteen new workplaces in Paris and the surrounding region sprouted red CGT flags as several hundred "irregular" workers held sit-ins. At France's Labor Day parade on May 1, a contingent of several thousand undocumented, most from West African countries such as Mali, Senegal, and Ivory Coast, were the stars.

But local governments were slow to move on their demands, so with only 70 workers regularized one month into the sit-ins, another 200 *sans-papiers* upped the ante on May 20 by taking over twenty more job sites. Still others have joined the strike since. As of early July, 400 former strikers have received papers (typically one-year permits), and the CGT estimates that 600 are still sitting tight at 41 workplaces.

Restaurants, with their visible locations on main boulevards, are the highest profile strike sites. But strikers are also camping out at businesses in construction, cleaning, security, personal services, and landscaping. Though the movement reportedly includes North Africans, Eastern Europeans, and even Filipinos, its public presence has consisted almost entirely of sub-Saharan Africans, a stunning indication of the degree of racial segregation in immigrant jobs. Strikers are overwhelmingly men, though the female employees of a contract cleaning business, Ma Net, made a splash when they joined the strike on May 26, and groups representing domestics and other women workers began to demonstrate around the same time.

"To Go Around Freely..."

The *sans-papiers* came to France by different means. Some overstayed student or tourist visas. Others paid as much as 7,500 euros ($12,000) to a trafficker to travel to the North African coast, clandestinely cross by boat to Spain, and then find their way to France. Strike leader Konté arrived in Paris, his target, two long years after leaving Mali. A set of false papers for 200 euros, and he was ready to look for work.

But opportunities for the undocumented are, for the most part, limited to jobs with the worst pay and working conditions. The French minimum wage is 8.71 euros an hour (almost $13), but strikers tell of working for 3 euros or even less. "With papers, I would get 1,000 euros a month," Issac, a Malian cleaner for the Quick restaurant chain who has been in France eleven years, told *Dollars & Sense*. "Without papers, I get 300." Even so, he and many others send half their pay home to families who depend on them. Through paycheck withholding, the *sans-papiers* pay taxes and contribute to the French health care and retirement funds. But "if I get sick, I don't have any right to reimbursement," said Camara, a dishwasher from Mali. He told *L'Humanité*, the French Communist Party newspaper, how much he wished "to go around freely." "In the evening I don't go out," he said. "When I leave home in the morning, I don't even know if I will get home that night. I avoid some subway stations" that are closely monitored by the police.

When asked how he would reply to the claim that the undocumented are taking jobs from French workers, Issac replied simply, "We are French workers—just without any rights. Yes, we're citizens, because France owned all of black Africa!"

Business Allies

The surprise allies in this guerrilla struggle for the right to work are many of the employers. When workers seized the Samsic contract cleaning agency in the Paris suburb of Massy, owner Mehdi Daïri first called the police. When they told him there was nothing they could do, he pragmatically decided to apply for permits for his 300-plus employees. "It's in everybody's best interest," he told *Le Monde*, the French daily newspaper. "Their action is legitimate. They've been here for years, working, contributing to the social security system, paying taxes, and we're satisfied with their work." He even has his office staff make coffee for the strikers every morning.

Though some businesses have taken a harder line against the strikers, the major business associations have called for massive regularization of their workforces. According to *L'Humanité*, André Dauguin, president of the hotel operators association, is demanding that 50,000 to 100,000 undocumented workers be given papers. Didier Chenet, president of another association of restaurant and hotel enterprises, declared that with 20,000 jobs going unfilled in these sectors, the *sans-papiers* "are not taking jobs away from other workers."

For the CGT, busy with defensive battles against labor "reforms" such as cutbacks in public employees' pensions, the strike wave represents a step in a new direction. The core of the CGT remains white, native-born French workers. As recently as the 1980s, the Communist Party, to which the CGT was then closely linked, took some controversial anti-immigrant stands. Raymond Chauveau, the general secretary of the CGT's Massy local, acknowledged to *Le Monde* that some union members still have trouble understanding why the organization has taken up this issue. But he added, "Today, these people are recognized for what they are: workers. They are developing class consciousness. Our role as a union is to show that these people are not outside the world of work." While some immigrant rights groups are critical of the CGT for suddenly stepping into the leadership of a fight other groups had been pursuing for years, it is hard to deny the importance of the labor organization's clout.

Half Empty or Half Full?

With only 400 of 1,400 applications for work permits granted four months into the struggle, the CGT is publicly voicing its impatience at the national government's insistence that local authorities make each decision on a case-by-case basis rather than offering broader guidelines. But Chauveau said he is proud that they have compelled the government to accept regularization of Africans in low-end jobs, broadening the opening beyond the intent of the 2007 law. And on its website, the CGT boasted that the *sans-papiers* "have compelled the government to take its first steps back, when that had seemed impossible since the [May 2007] election of Nicolas Sarkozy." Perhaps even more important for the long term is that class consciousness Chauveau mentioned. This is "a struggle that has changed my life," stated Mamadou Dembia Thiam of Senegal, a security guard who won his work authorization in June. "Before the struggle, I was really very timid. I've changed!" Changes like that seem likely to bring a new burst of energy to the struggling French labor movement. ❑

Resources: Confédération Générale du Travail, www.cgt.fr; Droits Devant!!, www.droitsdevant.org.

Article 6.3

MADE IN ARGENTINA
Bolivian Migrant Workers Fight Neoliberal Fashion

BY MARIE TRIGONA
January/February 2007

Dubbed "the Paris of the South," Buenos Aires is known for its European architecture, tango clubs, and *haute couture*. But few people are aware that Argentina's top fashion brands employ tens of thousands of undocumented Bolivian workers in slave-labor conditions. In residential neighborhoods across Buenos Aires, top clothing companies have turned small warehouses or gutted buildings into clandestine sweatshops. Locked in, workers are forced to live and work in cramped quarters with little ventilation and, often, limited access to water and gas. The *Unión de Trabajadores Costureros* (Union of Seamstress Workers—UTC), an assembly of undocumented textile workers, has reported more than 8,000 cases of labor abuses inside the city's nearly 400 clandestine shops in the past year. Around 100,000 undocumented immigrants work in these unsafe plants with an average wage—if they are paid at all—of $100 per month.

According to Olga Cruz, a 29-year-old textile worker, slave-labor conditions in textile factories are systematic. "During a normal workday in a shop you work from 7 a.m. until midnight or 1 a.m. Many times they don't pay the women and they owe them two or three years' pay. For not having our legal documents or not knowing what our rights are in Argentina, we've had to remain silent. You don't have rights to rent a room or to work legally."

Another Bolivian textile worker, Naomi Hernández, traveled to Argentina three years ago in hopes of a well-paying job. "I ended up working in a clandestine sweatshop without knowing the conditions I would have to endure. For two years I worked and slept in a three-square-meter room along with my two children and three sewing machines my boss provided. They would bring us two meals a day. For breakfast a cup of tea with a piece of bread and lunch consisting of a portion of rice, a potato, and an egg. We had to share our two meals with our children because according to my boss, my children didn't have the right to food rations because they aren't workers and don't yield production." She reported the subhuman conditions in her workplace and was subsequently fired.

Diseases like tuberculosis and lung complications are common due to the subhuman working conditions and constant exposure to dust and fibers. Many workers suffer from back injuries and tendonitis from sitting at a sewing machine 12 to 16 hours a day. And there are other hazards. A blaze that killed six people last year brought to light abusive working conditions inside a network of clandestine textile plants in Buenos Aires. The two women and four children who were killed had been locked inside the factory.

The situation of these workers shows that exploitation of migrant labor is not just a first-world/third-world phenomenon. The system of exploitative subcontracting of migrant workers that has arisen in U.S. cities as a result of neoliberal globalization also occurs in the countries of the global south—as does organized resistance to such exploitation.

Survival for Bolivian Workers

Buenos Aires is the number one destination for migrants from Bolivia, Paraguay, and Peru, whose numbers have grown in the past decade because of the declining economic conditions in those countries. More than one million Bolivians have migrated to Argentina since 1999; approximately one-third are undocumented.

Even when Argentina's economy took a nosedive in the 1990s, Bolivians were still driven to migrate there given their homeland's far more bleak economic conditions. Over two-thirds of Bolivians live in poverty, and nearly half subsist on less than a dollar a day. For decades, migration of rural workers (44% of the population) to urban areas kept many families afloat. Now, facing limited employment opportunities and low salaries in Bolivia's cities, many workers have opted to migrate to Argentina or Brazil.

Buenos Aires' clandestine network of sweatshops emerged in the late 1990s, following the influx of inexpensive Asian textile imports. Most of the textile factory owners are Argentine, Korean, or Bolivian. The workers manufacture garments for high-end brands like Lacár, Kosiuko, Adidas, and Montage in what has become a $700 million a year industry.

In many cases workers are lured by radio or newspaper ads in Bolivia promising transportation to Buenos Aires and decent wages plus room and board once they arrive. Truck drivers working for the trafficking rings transport workers in the back of trucks to cross into Argentina illegally.

For undocumented immigrants in Argentina, survival itself is a vicious cycle. The undocumented are especially susceptible to threats of losing their jobs. Workers can't afford to rent a room; even if they could, many residential hotel managers are unwilling to rent rooms to immigrants, especially when they have children.

Finding legal work is almost impossible without a national identity card. For years, Bolivian citizens had reported that Alvaro Gonzalez Quint, the head of Bolivia's consulate in Buenos Aires, would charge immigrants up to $100—equivalent to a textile worker's average monthly pay—to complete paperwork necessary for their documentation. The Argentine League for Human Rights has also brought charges against Gonzalez Quint in federal court, alleging he is tied to the network of smugglers who profit from bringing immigrants into Argentina to work in the sweatshops.

A New Chapter in Argentina's Labor Struggles

Argentina has a notable tradition of labor organizing among immigrants. Since the 19th century, working-class immigrants have fought for basic rights, including Sundays off, eight-hour workdays, and a minimum wage. The eight-hour workday became law in 1933, but employers have not always complied. Beginning with the 1976-1983 military dictatorship, and continuing through the neoliberal 1990s, many labor laws have been altered to allow flexible labor standards. University of Buenos Aires economist Eduardo Lucita, a member of UDI (Economists from the Left), says that although the law for an eight-hour workday stands, the average workday in Argentina is 10 to 12 hours. "Only half of workers have formal labor contracts; the rest are laboring as subcontracted workers in the unregulated, informal sector. For such workers there are no regulations for production rates and lengths of a workday—much less criteria for salaries." The average salary for Argentines is only around $200 a month, in contrast to the minimum of $600 required to meet the basic needs of a family of four.

Today, the extreme abuses in the new sweatshops have prompted a new generation of immigrant workers to organize.

"We have had to remain silent and accept abuse. I'm tired of taking the blows. We are starting to fight, *compañeros*; thank you for attending the assembly." These are the words of Ana Salazar at an assembly of textile workers that met in Buenos Aires on a Sunday evening last April. The UTC formed out of a neighborhood assembly in the working class neighborhood of Parque Avalleneda. Initially, the assembly was a weekly social event for families on Sundays, the only day textile workers can leave the shop. Families began to gather at the assembly location, situated at the corner of a park. Later, because Argentina's traditional unions refuse to accept undocumented affiliates, the workers expanded their informal assembly into a full-fledged union.

Since the factory fire that killed six on March 30, 2006, the UTC has stepped up actions against the brand-name clothing companies that subcontract with clandestine sweatshops. The group has held a number of *escraches*, or exposure protests, outside fashion makers' offices in Buenos Aires to push the city government to hold inspections inside the companies' textile workshops. Workers from the UTC also presented legal complaints against the top jean manufacturer Kosiuko.

At a recent surprise protest, young women held placards: "I kill myself for your jeans," signed, "a Bolivian textile worker." During the protest, outside Kosiuko's offices in the exclusive Barrio Norte neighborhood, UTC presented an in-depth research report into the brand's labor violations. "The Kosiuko company is concealing slave shops," said Gustavo Vera, member of the La Alemeda popular assembly. "They disclosed false addresses to inspectors and they have other workshops which they are not reporting to the city government." The UTC released a detailed list of the locations of alleged sweatshops. Most of the addresses that the Kosiuko company had provided turned out to be private residences or stores.

To further spotlight large brand names that exploit susceptible undocumented workers, the UTC held a unique fashion show in front of the Buenos Aires city legislature last September. "Welcome to the neoliberal fashion show—Spring Season 2006," announced the host, as spectators cheered—or jeered—the top brands that use slave labor. Models from a local theatre group paraded down a red carpet in brands like Kosiuko, Montagne, Porte Said, and Lacar, while the host shouted out the addresses of the brands' sweatshops and details of subhuman conditions inside shops.

"I repressed all of my rage about my working conditions and violations of my rights. Inside a clandestine workshop you don't have any rights. You don't have dignity," said Naomi Hernández, pedaling away at a sewing machine during the "fashion show."

After the show, Hernández stood up in front of the spectators and choked down tears while giving testimony of her experience as a slave laborer in a sweatshop: "I found out what it is to fight as a human being." She says her life has changed since joining the UTC.

Inspection-Free Garment Shops

To date, the union's campaign has had some successes. In April of 2006, the Buenos Aires city government initiated inspections of sweatshops employing Bolivians and Paraguayans; inspectors shut down at least 100. (Perhaps not surprisingly, Bolivian consul Gonzalez Quint has protested the city government's moves to regulate sweatshops, arguing that the measures discriminate against Bolivian employers who run some of the largest textile shops.) But since then, inspections have been suspended and many clothes manufacturers have simply moved their sweatshops to the suburban industrial belt or to new locations in the city. The UTC has reported that other manufacturers force workers to labor during the night to avoid daytime inspections.

Nestor Escudero, an Argentine who participates in the UTC, says that police, inspectors, and the courts are also responsible for the documented slave-labor conditions inside textile factories. "They bring in illegal immigrants to brutally exploit them. The textile worker is paid 75 cents for a garment that is later sold for $50. This profit is enough to pay bribes and keep this system going."

Since 2003, thousands of reports of slave-labor conditions have piled up in the courts without any resolution. In many cases when workers have presented reports to police of poor treatment, including threats, physical abuse, and forced labor, the police say they can't act because the victims do not have national identity cards.

Seeing their complaints go unheeded is sometimes the least of it. Escudero has confirmed that over a dozen textile workers have received death threats for reporting to media outlets on slave-labor conditions inside the textile plants. Shortly after the UTC went public last spring with hundreds of reports of abuses, over a dozen of the union's representatives were threatened. And in a particularly shocking episode, two men kidnapped the 9-year-old son of José Orellano and Monica Frías, textile workers who had reported slave-labor conditions in their shop. The attackers held the boy at knifepoint and told him to "tell your parents that they should stop messing around with the reports against the sweatshops." The UTC filed criminal charges of abandonment and abuse of power against Argentina's Interior Minister Aníbal Fernández in November for not providing the couple with witness protection.

The Road Ahead

Although the Buenos Aires city government has yet to make much headway in regulating the city's sweatshops, the UTC continues to press for an end to sweatshop slavery, along with mass legalization of immigrants and housing for immigrants living in poverty. Organizing efforts have not been in vain. In an important victory, the city government has opened a number of offices to process immigration documents free of charge for Bolivian and Paraguayan citizens, circumventing the Bolivian Consulate.

The UTC has also proposed that clandestine textile shops be shut down and handed over to the workers to manage them as co-ops and, ultimately, build a cooperative network that can bypass the middlemen and the entire piece-work system. Already, the Alameda assembly has joined with the UTC to form the Alameda Workers' Cooperative as an alternative to sweatshops. Nearly 30 former sweatshop workers work at the cooperative in the same space where the weekly assemblies are held.

Olga Cruz now works with the cooperative sewing garments. She says that although it's a struggle, she now has dignity that she didn't have when she worked in one of the piece-work shops. "We are working as a cooperative, we all make the same wage. In the clandestine shops you are paid per garment: they give you the fabric and you have to hand over the garment fully manufactured. Here we have a line system, which is more advanced and everyone works the same amount."

Fired for reporting on abusive conditions at her sweatshop, Naomi Hernández has also found work at the cooperative. "We are freeing ourselves, that's what I feel. Before I wasn't a free person and didn't have any rights," said Hernández to a crowd of spectators in front of the city legislature. She sent a special message and invitation: "Now we are fighting together with the Alameda cooperative and the UTC. I invite all workers who know their rights are being violated to join the movement against slave labor." ❑

Resources: To contact UTC activists at La Alameda assembly in Parque Avellaneda, email: asambleaparqueavellaneda@hotmail.com. To see videos of recent UTC actions, go to: www. revolutionvideo.org/agoratv/secciones/luchas_obreras/costureros_utc.html; www.revolutionvideo. org/agoratv/secciones/luchas_obreras/escrache_costureros.html.

Article 6.4

THE RISE OF MIGRANT WORKER MILITANCY

IMMANUEL NESS
September/October 2006

Testifying before the Senate immigration hearings in early July, Mayor Michael Bloomberg affirmed that undocumented immigrants have become indispensable to the economy of New York City: "Although they broke the law by illegally crossing our borders or overstaying their visas, and our businesses broke the law by employing them, our city's economy would be a shell of itself had they not, and it would collapse if they were deported. The same holds true for the nation." Bloomberg's comment outraged right-wing pundits, but how much more outraged would they be if they knew that immigrant workers, beyond being economically indispensable, are beginning to transform the U.S. labor movement with a bold new militancy?

After years of working in obscurity in the unregulated economy, migrant workers in New York City catapulted themselves to the forefront of labor activism beginning in late 1999 through three separate organizing drives among low-wage workers. Immigrants initiated all three drives: Mexican immigrants organized and struck for improved wages and working conditions at greengroceries; Francophone African delivery workers struck for unpaid wages and respect from labor contractors for leading supermarket chains; and South Asians organized for improved conditions and a union in the for-hire car service industry. (In New York, "car services" are taxis that cannot be hailed on the street, only arranged by phone.) These organizing efforts have persisted, and are part of a growing militancy among migrant workers in New York City and across the United States.

Why would seemingly invisible workers rise up to contest power in their workplaces? Why are vulnerable migrant workers currently more likely to organize than are U.S.-born workers? To answer these questions, we have to look at immigrants' distinct position in the political economy of a globalized New York City and at their specific economic and social niches, ones in which exploitation and isolation nurture class consciousness and militancy.

Labor Migration and Industrial Restructuring

New immigrant workers in the United States, many here illegally, stand at the crossroads of two overwhelming trends. On one hand, industrial restructuring and capital mobility have eroded traditional industries and remade the U.S. political economy in the last 30 years in ways that have led many companies to create millions of low-wage jobs and to seek vulnerable workers to fill them. On the other hand, at the behest of international financial institutions like the International Monetary Fund, and to meet the requirements of free-trade agreements such as NAFTA, governments throughout the global South have adopted neoliberal policies that have restructured their economies, resulting in the displacement of urban workers and rural farmers alike. Many have no choice but to migrate north.

A century ago the United States likewise experienced a large influx of immigrants, many of whom worked in factories for their entire lives. There they formed social networks across ethnic lines and developed a class consciousness that spurred the organizing of unions; they made up the generation of workers whose efforts began with the fight for the eight-hour day around the turn of the last century and culminated in the great organizing victories of the 1930s and 1940s across the entire spectrum of mining and manufacturing industries.

Today's immigrants face an entirely different political-economic landscape. Unlike most of their European counterparts a century ago, immigration restrictions mean that many newcomers to the United States are now here illegally. Workers from Latin America frequently migrate illegally without proper documentation; those from Africa, Asia, and Europe commonly arrive with business, worker, student, or tourist visas, then overstay them.

The urban areas where many immigrants arrive have undergone a 30-year decline in manufacturing jobs. The growing pool of service jobs which have come in their stead tend to be dispersed in small firms throughout the city. The proliferation of geographically dispersed subcontractors who compete on the basis of low wages encourages a process of informalization—a term referring to a redistribution of work from regulated sectors of the economy to new unregulated sectors of the underground or informal economy. As a result, wages and working conditions have fallen, often below government-established norms.

Although informal work is typically associated with the developing world—or Global South—observers are increasingly recognizing the link between the regulated and unregulated sectors in advanced industrial regions. More and more the regulated sector depends on unregulated economic activity through subcontracting and outsourcing of work to firms employing low-wage immigrant labor. Major corporations employ or subcontract to businesses employing migrant workers in what were once established sectors of the economy with decent wages and working conditions.

Informalization requires government regulatory agencies to look the other way. For decades federal and state regulatory bodies have ignored violations of laws governing wages, hours, and workplace safety, leading to illegally low wages and declining workplace health and safety practices. The process of informalization is furthered by the reduction or elimination of protections such as disability insurance, Social Security, health care coverage, unemployment insurance, and workers compensation.

By the 1990s, substandard jobs employing almost exclusively migrant workers had become crucial to key sectors of the national economy. Today, immigrants have gained a major presence as bricklayers, demolition workers, and hazardous waste workers on construction and building rehab sites; as cooks, dishwashers, and busboys in restaurants; and as taxi drivers, domestic workers, and delivery people.

Employers frequently treat these workers as self-employed. They typically have no union protection and little or no job security. With government enforcement shrinking, they lack the protection of minimum-wage laws and they have been excluded from Social Security and unemployment insurance.

These workers are increasingly victimized by employers who force them to accept 19th-century working conditions and sub-minimum wages. Today, New York City, Los Angeles, Miami, Houston, and Boston form a nexus of international labor migration, with constantly churning labor markets. As long as there is a demand for cheap labor, immigrants will continue to enter the United States in large numbers. Like water, capital always flows to the lowest level, a state of symmetry where wages are cheapest.

In turn, the availability of a reserve army of immigrant labor provides an enormous incentive for larger corporations to create and use subcontracting firms. Without this workforce, employers in the regulated economy would have more incentive to invest in labor-saving technology, increase the capital-labor ratio, and seek accommodation with unions.

New unauthorized immigrants residing and working in the United States are ideal workers in the new informalized sectors: Their undocumented legal status makes them more tractable since they constantly fear deportation. Undocumented immigrants are less likely to know about, or demand adherence to, established labor standards, and even low U.S. wages represent an improvement over earnings in their home countries.

Forging Migrant Labor Solidarity

The perception that new immigrants undermine U.S.-born workers by undercutting prevailing wage and work standards cannot be entirely dismissed. The entry of a large number of immigrants into the underground economy unquestionably reduces the labor market leverage of U.S.-born workers. But the story is more complicated. In spite of their vulnerability, migrant workers have demonstrated a willingness and a capacity to organize for improvements in their wages and working conditions; they arguably are responding to tough conditions on the job with greater militancy than U.S.-born workers.

New York City has been the site of a number of instances of immigrant worker organizing. In 1998, Mexicans working in greengroceries embarked on a citywide organizing campaign to improve their conditions of work. Most of the 20,000 greengrocery workers were paid below $3.00 an hour, working on average 72 hours a week. Some did not make enough to pay their living expenses, no less send remittances back home to Mexico. Following a relentless and coordinated four-year organizing campaign among the workers, employers agreed to raise wages above the minimum and improve working conditions. Moreover, the campaign led state Attorney General Eliot Spitzer to establish a Greengrocer Code of Conduct and to strengthen enforcement of labor regulations.

In another display of immigrant worker militancy, beginning in 1999 Francophone African supermarket delivery workers in New York City fought for and won equality with other workers in the same stores. The workers were responsible for bagging groceries and delivering them to affluent customers in Manhattan and throughout the city. As contractors, the delivery workers were paid no wage, instead relying on the goodwill of customers in affluent neighborhoods to pay tips for each delivery.

The workers were employed in supermarkets and drug stores where some others had a union. Without union support themselves, delivery workers staged a significant strike and insurrection that made consumers aware of their appalling conditions of work. In late October, workers went on strike and marched from supermarket to supermarket, demanding living wages and dignity on the job. At the start of their campaign, wages averaged less than $70 a week. In the months following the strike the workers all won recognition from the stores through the United Food and Commercial Workers that had earlier neglected to include them in negotiations with management. The National Employee Law Project, a national worker advocacy organization, filed landmark lawsuits against the supermarkets and delivery companies and won backwage settlements as the courts deemed them to be workers—not independent contractors in business for themselves.

Immigrant workers have organized countless other campaigns, in New York and across the country. How do new immigrants, with weak ties to organized labor and the state, manage to assert their interests? The explanation lies in the character of immigrant work and social life; the constraints immigrant workers face paradoxically encourage them to draw on shared experiences to create solidarity at work and in their communities.

The typical migrant worker can expect to work twelve-hour days, seven days a week. When arriving home, immigrant workers frequently share the same apartments, buildings, and neighborhoods. These employment ghettos typify immigrant communities across the nation. Workers cook for one another, share stories about their oppressively long and hard days, commiserate about their ill treatment at work, and then go to sleep only to start anew the next day.

Migrant women, surrounded by a world of exploitation, typically suffer even more abuse their male counterparts, suffering from low wages, long hours, and dangerous conditions. Patterns of gender stratification found in the general labor market are even more apparent among migrant women workers. Most jobs in the nonunion economy, such as construction and driving, are stereotypically considered "men's work." Women predominate in the garment industry, as domestic and child care workers, in laundries, hotels, restaurants, and ever more in sex work. A striking example of migrant women's perilous work environment is the massive recruitment of migrant women to clean up the hazardous materials in the rubble left by the collapse of the World Trade Center without proper safety training.

Isolated in their jobs and communities, immigrant workers have few social ties to unions, community groups, and public officials, and few resources to call upon to assist them in transforming their workplaces. Because new immigrants have few social networks outside the workplace, the ties they develop on the job are especially solid and meaningful—and are nurtured every day. The workers' very isolation and status as outsiders, and their concentration into industrial niches by employers who hire on the basis of ethnicity, tend to strengthen old social ties, build new ones, and deepen class solidarity.

Immigrant social networks contribute to workplace militancy. Conversely, activism at work can stimulate new social networks that can expand workers' power. It is through relationships developed on the job and in the community that shared social identities and mutual resentment of the boss evolves into class consciousness and class solidarity: migrant workers begin to form informal organizations, meet with coworkers to respond to poor working conditions, and take action on the shop floor in defiance of employer abuse.

Typically, few workplace hierarchies exist among immigrants, since few reach supervisory positions. As a result, immigrant workers suffer poor treatment equally at the hands of employers. A gathering sense of collective exploitation usually transforms individualistic activities into shared ones. In rare cases where there are immigrant foremen and crew leaders, they may recognize this solidarity and side with the workers rather than with management. One former manager employed for a fast-food sandwich chain in New York City said: "We are hired only to divide the workers but I was really trying to help the workers get better pay and shorter hours."

Migrant workers bring social identities from their home countries, and those identities are shaped through socialization and work in this country. In cities and towns across the United States, segmentation of migrant workers from specific countries reinforces ethnic, national, and religious identities and helps to form other identities that may stimulate solidarity. Before arriving in the United States, Mexican immigrant workers often see themselves as peasants but not initially as "people of color," while Francophone Africans see themselves as Malian or Senegalese ethnics but not necessarily "black." Life and work in New York can encourage them to adopt new identifications, including a new class consciousness that can spur organizing and militancy.

Once triggered, organizing can go from workplace to workplace like wildfire. When workers realize that they can fight and prevail, this creates a sense of invincibility that stimulates militant action that would otherwise be avoided at all costs. This demonstration effect is vitally important, as was the case in the strikes among garment workers and coal miners in the history of the U.S. labor movement.

"Solidarity Forever" vs. "Take This Job and Shove It"

The militancy of many migrant workers contrasts sharply with the passivity of many U.S.-born workers facing the same low wages and poor working conditions. Why do most workers at chain stores and restaurants like Wal-Mart and McDonalds—most of whom were born in the United States—appear so complacent, while new immigrants are often so militant?

Migrants are not inherently more militant or less passive. Instead, the real workplace conditions of migrant workers seem to produce greater militancy on the job. First, collective social isolation engenders strong ties among migrants in low-wage jobs where organizing is frequently the only way to improve conditions. Because migrants work in jobs that are more amenable to organizing, they are highly represented among newly unionized workers. Strong social ties in the workplace drive migrants to form their own embryonic organizations at work and in their communities that are ripe for union representation. Organizing among migrant workers gains the attention of labor unions, which then see a chance to recruit new members and may provide resources to help immigrant workers mobilize at work and join the union.

Employers also play a major role. Firms employing U.S. workers tend to be larger and are often much harder to organize than the small businesses where immigrants work. In 2003, the Merriam-Webster dictionary added the new word McJob, defined as "a low-paying job that requires little skill and provides little opportunity for advancement." The widely accepted coinage reflects the relentless 30-year economic restructuring creating low-end jobs in the retail sector.

Organizing against Home Depot, McDonalds, Taco Bell, or Wal-Mart is completely different from organizing against smaller employers. Wal-Mart uses many of the same tactics against workers that immigrants contend with: failure to pay overtime, stealing time (intentionally paying workers for fewer hours than actually worked), no health care, part-time work, high turnover, and gender division of labor. The difference is that Wal-Mart has far more resources to oppose unionization than do the smaller employers who are frequently subcontractors to larger firms. But Wal-Mart's opposition to labor unions is so forceful that workers choose to leave rather than stay and fight it out. Relentless labor turnover mitigates against the formation of working class consciousness and militancy.

The expanding non-immigrant low-end service sector tends to produce unskilled part-time jobs that do not train workers in skills that keep them in the same sector of the labor market. Because jobs at the low end of the economy require little training, workers frequently move from one industry to the next. One day a U.S.-born worker may work as a sales clerk for Target, the next day as a waiter at Olive Garden. Because they are not stuck in identity-defined niches, U.S. workers change their world by quitting and finding a job elsewhere, giving them less reason to organize and unionize.

The fact that U.S.-born workers have an exit strategy and migrant workers do not is a significant and important difference. Immigrant workers are more prone to take action to change their working conditions because they have far fewer options than U.S.-born workers. Workers employed by companies like Wal-Mart are unable to change their conditions, since they have little power and will be summarily fired for any form of dissent. If workers violate the terms of Wal-Mart's or McDonalds' employee manual by, say, arriving late, and then are summarily fired, no one is likely to fend for them, as is usually the case among many migrant workers. While migrant workers engage in direct action against their employers to obtain higher wages and respect on the job, U.S. workers do not develop the same dense connections in labor market niches that forge solidarity. Employers firing new immigrants may risk demonstrations, picket lines, or even strikes.

Immigrant workers are pushed into low-wage labor market niches as day laborers, food handlers, delivery workers, and nannies; these niches are difficult if not impossible to escape. Yet immigrant workers relegated to dead-end jobs in the lowest echelons of the labor market in food, delivery, and car service work show a greater eagerness to fight it out to improve their wages and conditions than do U.S. workers who can move on to another dead-end job.

The Role of Unions

Today's labor movement is in serious trouble; membership is spiraling downward as employers demand union-free workplaces. Unionized manufacturing and service workers are losing their jobs to low-wage operations abroad. Unions and, more importantly, the U.S. working class, are in dire straits and must find a means to triumph over the neoliberal dogma that dominates the capitalist system.

As organizing campaigns in New York City show, migrant workers are indispensable to the revitalization of the labor movement. As employers turn to migrant labor to fill low-wage jobs, unions must encourage and support organizing drives that emerge from the oppressive conditions of work. As the 1930s workers' movement demonstrates, if conditions improve for immigrants, all workers will prosper. To gain traction, unions must recognize that capital is pitting migrant workers against native-born laborers to lower wages and improve profitability. Although unions have had some success organizing immigrants, most are circling the wagons, disinterested in building a more inclusive mass labor movement. The first step is for unions to go beyond rhetoric and form a broad and inclusive coalition embracing migrant workers. ❏

Chapter 7

ECONOMIC DEVELOPMENT

Article 7.1

WORLD HISTORY AND ECONOMIC DEVELOPMENT
Lessons from New Comparisons of Europe and East Asia

BY RAVI BHANDARI AND KENNETH POMERANZ
August 2009

Development prescriptions that assume that the rest of the world can (or should) mimic a stylized North Atlantic path to the modern world dominated the 1950s to 1970s, with limited success. The neo-liberal prescriptions of the last 30 years were no better at creating long-term dynamism, and often imposed horrific social costs.

Most of the success stories of post-1945 development are clustered in East Asia: Taiwan, South Korea, Hong Kong, Singapore, and (with more caveats), coastal China. Among other things, almost the entire *net* reduction in global poverty numbers during the last 30 years has occurred in China, which largely ignored the "Washington Consensus" on development strategy. This geographic clumping has encouraged discussion of an "East Asian development path." Sometimes this is said to derive from 20th century corporatist institutions, sometimes from supposedly timeless "Asian values" of discipline and respect for education; but none of these are sufficiently "East Asian" to explain very much.

A new comparative history of economic development yields different lessons. It highlights differences in political-economic relations between cores and peripheries and differential access to fossil fuels in explaining why the most dynamic regions in the West out-distanced their East Asian counterparts in the 19th century, casting particular doubt on arguments that focus on allegedly more perfect markets in the West. A second theme is the role of labor-intensive industries, often based in the countryside and employing people from households still connected to agriculture (creating relatively low rates of both urbanization and proletarianization). This period of catch-up growth unfolds with less growth of landlessness and less inequality than in most of the industrializing West. However, in China (by far the biggest East Asian country) we also see problems related to trade-dependence, resource shortages, and environmental degradation. These problems have made the indefinite extension of this path highly unlikely, and have engendered familiar strategies—socially and environmentally disquieting—for China's interior.

Comparative-Historical Theories of Development

Recent scholarship suggests a rough comparability in living standards between advanced areas in 18th century China and those in Europe. This allows us to use China to raise questions about Europe, and its 19th century breakthrough to sustained per capita growth. If the divergence in economic performance was quite late, it makes untenable any simple contrast between Western growth and non-Western stagnation. It also means that any explanation resting on cultural or institutional differences (which preceded the divergence by centuries) face a new burden of proof. We must either explain why some difference that was not particularly advantageous earlier became so later, or find offsetting disadvantages that fell away at a particular point, rather than looking only for "advantages" within Europe.

By contrast, most social science in both the Marxist and Weberian traditions was born from contemplation of a West that (briefly) held the world's only industrial societies, and took Western Europe as the standard of "real" historical change; other places were examples of failed, absent, or deviant development. The "new world history," or "California School," of which the work discussed here forms a part, does not deny that this approach yielded many insights, but suggests that reciprocal comparisons may be more valuable today: comparisons in which we also ask, "Why wasn't England the Yangzi Delta or the Kinai—wealthy agro-commercial areas with lots of handicrafts that did not initiate large-scale energy-intensive manufacturing?" Such comparisons are useful for separating the necessary and the contingent in North Atlantic growth; many structures happened to be in place as the West industrialized, and were adapted to serve that process—e.g. financial markets originally designed mostly to finance war were also useful for financing new technologies like railways that required lots of patient capital—but it does not follow that they were necessary to the process. Reciprocal comparisons allow us to take more seriously the possibilities that other societies had advantages as well as disadvantages, and to see the possibilities for transformative change that draws upon, rather than simply overcoming, indigenous institutions and expectations.

Others have taken these elements and combined them in other ways. André Gunder Frank, for instance, shared the emphasis here on the relative prosperity of early modern East Asia—indeed, he went much further, suggesting that Europe did not become more prosperous until the middle of the 19th century—and also used it to raise doubts about whether Western institutions were more conducive to growth. He also questioned the significance of any differences in local institutions, favoring an exclusive significance on the dynamics of a world system. Others, such as R. Bin Wong and Jack Goldstone, have differed from the analysis here in the opposite direction, focusing more or less exclusively on reciprocal comparisons while minimizing (at least for the pre-1850 period) the significance of trans-continental connections (including violent ones) and questions of resource endowments and extraction that will figure prominently in later parts of this essay.

But all of us have concluded that the evidence is inconsistent with any assertion that early modern European culture or economic institutions led directly to superior economic performance, much less that they were both necessary and sufficient for the creation of modernity.

Early Modern Economies and the Origins of the Great Divergence

An emerging consensus among European economic historians has moved away from seeing industrialization as a British-centered "Big Bang." Instead, they put industrialization back into its historical context: in long processes of slowly-growing markets, division of labor, many small innovations, and gradual accumulation. The gradual market-driven growth thus highlighted was crucial, but it didn't differentiate Europe from East Asia. Smithian dynamics worked just as well in much of China and Japan, but didn't transform basic possibilities—eventually, highly developed areas everywhere came up against serious resource constraints, in part because commercialization and proto-industrialization accelerated population growth. Britain ultimately needed not only technology and institutions, but also the Americas, coal, and various favorable conjunctures. In Flanders and even Holland, proto-industrialization and productive commercial agriculture led to results more like China's Yangzi Delta or Japan's Kinai region than like England.

Some readers may object to comparing regions within China and Japan to European countries, but China more closely resembles all of Europe than any one European country in its range of environments, living standards and so on. The Yangzi Delta (with about 31.5 million people in 1770, exceeding France plus the Low Countries), the empire's most developed region, can be compared to Britain (or Britain plus the Netherlands) in terms of its prosperity and its position within a larger system. The rice-exporting, cloth-importing Middle Yangzi might be better compared to Poland. Such comparisons illuminate parallels and differences in the structuring of inter-regional relationships within world areas, and relate economic development to larger contexts, rather than searching within each region for its "key to success" or "fatal flaw."

In an influential version of the gradualist story, Jan DeVries has placed the Industrial Revolution within a larger "*industrious* revolution"—a concept which helps resolve a paradox. The grain-buying power of European day wages fell sharply between 1430 and 1550, and took centuries to regain 1430 levels. Yet death inventories from 1550 on show ordinary people slowly gaining more possessions. These trends can be reconciled because people worked more hours per year for money, allowing them to buy both more non-food goods and stable amounts of increasingly expensive bread. Leisure probably decreased—though this is hard to pin down—and people certainly spent less time making goods for their own households. Instead, they specialized more and bought more, including many goods (baked bread, manufactured candles, etc.) which "saved time" on domestic chores.

Chinese trends were similar. The rice-buying power of day wages generally fell in late imperial times, but nutritional standards do not seem to have fallen, or to have been inferior to Europe's. Average Chinese caloric intake in the late 1700s appears to compare well with Europe (and that of the Yangzi Delta with England); China probably led in vitamin intake; and most surprisingly, protein consumption in the Delta and England seems to have been comparable, at least for the vast majority of both societies. Rough nutritional parity is also suggested by Chinese life expectancies, which were comparable to England's (and thus above Continental Europe's) until at least 1750. Moreover, while Chinese birth rates (contrary to mythology) appear to have been no higher than European ones between 1550 and 1850, the rate of population growth was the same or slightly higher, suggesting that Chinese death rates were the same or lower.

There is abundant anecdotal evidence that the consumption of "non-essentials" by ordinary Chinese was rising modestly between about 1500 and 1750, much as it was in Western Europe. Quantitative estimates for various commodities suggest that in most cases China circa 1750 stacked up well against Europe, and the Yangzi Delta fairly well against England. Yangzi Delta labor productivity in the largest sector of all 18th century economies—agriculture—was 90% of England's as late as 1820, leaving both far ahead of almost all of Continental Europe. Total factor productivity was much higher in the Yangzi Delta, because of greatly superior land productivity. In the second largest sector, textiles, the earnings per day of Yangzi Delta producers exceeded those of their English counterparts even in the late 18th century, though the beginnings of mechanization must have caused their productivity to fall behind by then.

The Yangzi Delta may not have stacked up quite as well overall against England as it did sector by sector, because the mix of sectors was different. Lacking much in the way of ores, forest, fossil fuels, or even waterpower (being essentially flat), the Delta had less of its labor force in energy-intensive industry. For example, using one 1704 data set, charcoal was 20 times as costly relative to labor in Canton as it was in London, though real wages were roughly equal. And while the Delta's long-distance trade was very large, it was, as we shall see, leveling off by the late 1700s.

Generally speaking, though, the economic performance of these two regions was surprisingly similar. Europe-China comparisons are more difficult to do than those for England and the Yangzi Delta, because conditions varied much more and statistics are less reliable; but the data we have also suggest fairly close comparability in 1750 and perhaps 1800.

But another feature of East Asian cores was strikingly different from the early modern West (and probably South Asia). From the 16th century on, a growing percentage of rural European workers (whether in agriculture or other occupations) were proletarians—people who owned no means of production and worked for wages. In the most advanced parts of 18th century Europe they became a majority. In China, however (and, for different reasons, also Japan), proletarians were under 10% of the 18th century rural population; almost every household either owned some land or had secure tenancy. On the positive side, this reflected both hard-won customary rights and the state's desire for a peasantry sufficiently independent to be ruled without going through local magnates. More negatively, it reflected very low reproduction rates among those who were proletarianized. Since sex-selective infanticide and neglect skewed male/female ratios, and a few elite males had concubines as well as wives, the poorest men rarely married. (This was perhaps their most intense social grievance; it disappeared for a while after the Revolution, but has reappeared due to sex-selective abortion.)

Given secure tenure, even full-time tenants earned more than twice as much as rural wage laborers. Since urban unskilled wages were very close to rural ones, the poor had little incentive to head for the cities. They were much better off heading for the frontier, where gaining access to land was relatively easy: average incomes were lower, but the chance for a newcomer to reach that average was much better. Consequently, the large non-agricultural labor force in areas like the Lower Yangzi remained embedded in farm households, which produced both agricultural commodities and light manufactures for sale. The resulting economy produced relatively high average incomes, some cushion against market fluctuations, and probably less inequality than in the early modern West, but it needed a continued frontier (both to trade with and to send migrants to), and it produced fewer of the urban agglomeration effects that *may* have been important to early industrial innovation.

Parity did not last. In the 19th century, output and specialization soared in Europe, while in China, per capita non-grain consumption probably declined: 1900 figures for cloth, sugar, and tobacco, for instance, are below even conservative estimates for 1750.

Much of the difference was ecological, but not because "population pressure" was necessarily producing more serious problems within Chinese core areas than in cores of Europe. Dry-farming areas in North China seem to have been maintaining the soil as well as those in England circa 1800; nutrient balances in South China's paddy rice regions (where periodic inundation provided nutrients that supplemented impressive applications of recycled human and animal wastes) would compare very favorably to anything in Europe. Even for wood supply and deforestation there was no clear Western European advantage circa 1750, despite its much sparser population. China used fuel very efficiently, and was actually better off in certain ways than Western Europe, where deforestation, sandstorms, and other signs of environmental stress were all increasing in the 18th century. Still, high fuel prices mattered, since they made people in China unlikely to try substituting heat energy for labor.

One can find some signs of serious problems and of relatively stable conditions in cores at both ends of Eurasia, and the research available leaves many gaps; however, the current state of our understanding no longer supports older, taken-for-granted notions that because they were more densely populated, East Asian cores must have been worse off than European ones in the 18th century. On the whole, the current research seems to suggest rough comparability. What is clear, however, is that in the early 19th century—when both population and per capita consumption were growing as never before in Western Europe—some ecological variables, such as forested area, underwent a surprising stabilization, after declining considerably amidst the much slower growth of the early modern period. In China, by contrast, ecological problems accelerated despite a slowdown in population growth and a probable stagnation or even decline of per capita consumption.

The basic explanation of this ecological divergence appears to be twofold. One is the English transition to fossil fuels. This required new technology, but also luck. Before railways, most of China's coal deposits were far too many land-locked miles away from its core regions to be economical, regardless of any breakthroughs in extraction and use. In England, by contrast, early deforestation and abundant coal outcroppings in places accessible to London caused widespread early use of this less-preferred fuel, but production would have stalled at early 18th century levels without steam engines to pump water from deeper mines. Early steam engines, meanwhile, were so inefficient that for roughly a century their only use was at the pithead, where fuel was virtually free (fuel prices throughout the early modern world were largely driven by transport costs). But once the engines had *some* use, they were worth tinkering with, eventually reaching a point where they revolutionized transport and opened a new world of cheap, energy-intensive production.

Secondly, Western Europe benefited from a surge in imports of various land-intensive products from less developed areas, especially in the Americas. As demand for food, fiber, building materials, and fuel (Malthus' "four necessities") mounted, cores everywhere had to acquire some of these land-intensive products by trading with peripheries that wanted the manufactures, especially textiles, that cores produced.

But that trade tended to run into one of two problems. Where families in the peripheral areas were largely free to allocate their own labor, export booms stimulated population growth through natural increase and/or immigration. Over time, some labor switched into handicrafts, reducing exportable surpluses of raw materials and demand for imported manufactures. The Middle and Upper Yangzi, North China, and other Chinese hinterlands followed this path around 1750-1850, and what had been by far the world's largest long-distance staple trades declined. Moreover, the terms of trade shifted against manufactures: a bolt of medium-quality cloth bought roughly half as much rice in 1850 as in 1750. Core regions felt the pinch: the Yangzi Delta population stagnated while that of China overall was doubling.

In peripheries with less flexible institutions, such as Eastern Europe, these trade-dampening dynamics were weaker. Few people migrated in, people could not switch into handicrafts on any great scale, and since cash crop producers were often coerced, export booms did not necessarily increase their birth or survival rates. But such regions also responded less to external demand for their primary products in the first place. Thus, the Baltic trade had reached a plateau by 1650 at a fraction the size of China's long distance staple trades.

The Americas, however, were different. Smallpox and other disasters depopulated the region, and most of the new labor force were either slaves, purchased from abroad, or indentured whites transported by land-owners in order to generate exports to Europe. Moreover, plantations in particular often became highly specialized; thus slaves, despite their poverty, were a significant market for coarse cloth and other low-end manufactures. Consequently, the circum-Caribbean slave region (from Brazil to what became the U.S. South) was in some important ways the first "modern" periphery, with large bills to pay for imported capital goods (in this case human ones) and a market for some mass consumer goods. Combined with its ecological bounty, this meant that, unlike most Eurasian peripheries, the Americas kept expanding as a source of land-intensive exports.

Thus, contrary to conventional wisdom, Western Europe broke through resource constraints partly because markets in its peripheries *weren't* unencumbered. They were actually freer in East Asia, which led to a more equal dispersion of proto-industry and an ecological cul-de-sac. One reason for China's declining per capita consumption after about 1750 was a shift in population distribution: as the still relatively prosperous Yangzi Delta went from being about 16% of China to being 9% (and 6% by 1950), hinterlands had much more weight in Chinese aggregates. And while living standards in some hinterlands may have kept creeping upwards, others, as we shall see, declined drastically.

Europe in a Chinese Mirror

Once we stop explaining the bottlenecks China hit as due to peculiar pathologies, we can see more clearly the importance of an unexpected relaxing of land constraints— both through coal and through the Americas—in enabling parts of Northwestern Europe to gain population, specialize more in manufacturing, and consume more per capita without raw material prices soaring. Even in 1830—before the great mid-century boom in North American grain, meat, and timber exports, and when its sugar consumption per capita was just 20% of what it would be by 1900—replacing Britain's New World imports with local products would have required about 23 million acres (mostly to substitute for cotton). This exceeds even E.A. Wrigley's estimate of the additional forest acres that would have been needed to replace the coal boom—and either number roughly matches Britain's total arable land plus pastureland. Thus, positive resource shocks, only partly due to technology, allowed England to stretch ecological constraints that might otherwise have slowed its growth, much as the filling up of China's interior hobbled the Yangzi Delta.

In China, ecological problems mounted in the 19th century—not primarily in cores, but in areas like the over-logged Northwest and Southwest, the North China plain, and alongside rivers whose beds rose as highland forest clearance increased erosion. These problems were exacerbated, as we will see, by a decline in transfer payments from richer regions that had been used in large part for environmental management. In short, though European and Chinese cores had much in common, they were hitched to very different peripheries: filling up, turning to handicrafts, hitting ecological constraints, and exporting fewer primary products in China; and vastly expanded, ecologically rich, and outward-oriented in the Americas.

So colonies (and former colonies) mattered a lot—not necessarily because they yielded especially high profits, as dependency models have claimed, but because they were a special *kind* of trading partner—one which allowed European cores to change labor and capital into land-saving imports in a way that expanded trade closer to home couldn't.

East Asia from the Great Divergence to a (Partial) New Convergence

After recovering from mid-19th century shocks, Japan's economy began to grow faster than ever, benefiting both from new technologies (which were adapted to internal conditions) and from new trading partners with different factor endowments. China had a much rougher late 19th and early 20th century. But it is also true that, after suffering huge mid-century disasters—in part because its state was much weaker than Japan's—China's wealthiest regions also resumed economic growth, benefiting from some technological changes and from new trading opportunities that to some extent replaced the primary products, markets for light manufactures, and outlets for emigration once provided by internal hinterlands. Rice from Southeast Asia, for instance, helped to feed much of the Yangzi Delta and rapidly growing Shanghai, replacing lost shipments from the interior; Guangdong and Fujian soon imported rice, too. Timber and other land-intensive products were imported to coastal areas, while old and new light manufactures—cloth, straw mats, cane chairs, cigarettes, and patent medicines—were exported, along with people. It was some of China's hinterlands that had a hundred-year crisis.

Some internal regions, like the Middle Yangzi, gradually recovered to pre-1850 levels after the mid-19th century rebellions and then reached a plateau. Others, such as North China, declined dramatically, with ecological and political problems reinforcing each other. The Chinese state was battered both by rebellion and by foreign incursions. As it began to recover, its priorities shifted to reflect a more dangerous environment. Defending and developing relatively prosperous and now contested coastal regions became a top priority. Conversely, less attention was devoted to an older "reproductive" statecraft: using revenues from rich regions to underwrite flood control, emergency granaries, irrigation, and other efforts to stabilize family farming and Confucian society in poorer, more ecologically fragile areas. For instance, the state sharply reduced its massive subsidies (between 10% and 20% of all government spending from 1820-1850) for flood control and water transport on the Yellow River and Grand Canal (the canal having been superseded by railways and coastal steamships). The savings were largely diverted to paying indemnities for lost wars and attempts at military modernization. Subsidies for deep wells in semi-arid regions disappeared, even though the water table was falling as population grew.

Thus, certain interior regions suffered simultaneously from being pushed into near-autarchy as long-distance internal trade declined, from population growth, and from a loss of state assistance with worsening environmental problems. Floods, droughts and violence all increased dramatically. (That the late 19th century had especially severe El Niños didn't help.) By contrast, new imports and increased government attention helped stabilize at least some ecological challenges closer to the coast, and levels of violence were much lower there.

Thus, this period provided a strong foretaste of a phenomenon much noted in recent decades: an economic decoupling of coastal and interior China, as the coast became more oriented toward external trading partners and once-crucial inter-regional transfer payments declined. Under these circumstances, coastal China—both the parts seized by imperialists (Taiwan, Hong Kong, the treaty ports, and more briefly Manchuria) and the rest—achieved substantial per capita growth in the early 20th century, despite huge problems. Enough of this growth reached ordinary people for some social indicators to improve: for instance, the average height of railway labor recruits from the Lower Yangzi increased at almost Japanese rates from around 1890-1937. Much of this was powered by growth in rural industry, which adapted new technologies but built in many other ways on historical precedents. In Jiangsu province (which included Shanghai), almost half of manufacturing output still occurred in villages on the eve of World War II. However, interior regions experienced little or even negative growth, much greater social unrest, and a shredding of what had been, by pre-modern standards, a relatively effective safety net. Xia Mingfang has estimated that roughly 1.2 million Chinese died in famines between 1644 and 1796, while 38 million died from 1875-1937—almost all of them in the North and Northwest.

It is therefore not surprising that Maoist political economy, while undoubtedly revolutionary in many ways, in other ways recalled certain tasks and even solutions from the high Qing era. In some sense collectivization made everyone a proletarian, but in another, every rural household was guaranteed access to farm work where, like smallholders or secure tenants, they earned incomes based on their average, not their marginal, product. Subsequent de-collectivization made the comparison to Qing tenures even stronger, though it is now being undermined as farmland as seized for various development projects. (More modest land reforms also preceded industrial booms in Japan, Taiwan, and South Korea.) Massive (if sometimes counterproductive) efforts were made to industrialize the countryside, rather than assuming that higher living standards would have to come from moving people out of the countryside. Migration to cities essentially stopped by 1960. Funds were again directed from wealthier to poorer regions, and (despite the disasters of the Great Leap) emphasis was placed on subsistence security for poor people and fragile regions. The per capita growth rates are unimpressive next to post-1978 achievements, but the social gains were dramatic: literacy soared and life expectancy nearly doubled between 1950 and 1976. So was the creation of infrastructure, including a crucial tripling of China's irrigated area, almost all of it in the North and Northwest.

An enormous amount changed after 1978, but it's also important to notice what did not. Rural industry, which added 130 million jobs before its job creation leveled off (as it became more capital-intensive) in the mid-1990s, was in many ways a more important engine of growth than the more glamorous reorganization of urban economies. Despite rapid urban growth, China remains more rural than other comparably industrial countries (just barely more urban than England in 1840). The diversification of rural economic activities means that by 2000 more than two-thirds of rural income came from non-agricultural activities, about the same level Taiwan reached circa 1980. (In India, by contrast, the figure is about 45%, and in South Korea 20%.) In the more successful parts of the countryside, families with local land-leasing rights also provide much of the industrial work force; indeed, villages often insure that as many native households as possible have some stake in the more lucrative parts of the local economy before any migrants are employed in good jobs. Though this model is now fraying in many ways, it is worth reiterating some of its achievements: enormous poverty reduction and labor-absorption, vastly fewer semi-legal urban slums than in most of the developing world, and so on.

If we look at things regionally, we again see familiar patterns. This rural industrialization is again very concentrated in coastal areas (though it takes in a bit more of the coast than before); as of a few years ago, over half of rural industrial value added came from three provinces. And, as the export boom suggests, those areas are again more oriented towards a wider world than towards the rest of China. China's ratio of foreign trade to GDP now far exceeds the highest levels reached in Japanese history. Both exports and imports play a role here, as coastal China is importing hugely increased amounts of oil, metals, raw cotton, lumber, and so on—just as Japan, Taiwan, and Korea have come to do. Despite those imports, however, coastal China's economy is still far less resource-intensive than that of the interior: for instance, energy use per dollar of GDP in Jiangsu, Zhejiang, and Guangdong is about 40% of what it is in Gansu and Xinjiang.

And there's the rub—or rather, rubs. Being six times the population of Japan, Korea, and Taiwan, China can't ever import the quantities of primary products per capita that the other countries do. Internally, the rapid growth of inland/coastal and urban/rural inequalities is both a problem in itself and a threat to the basic development model. Incomes in rural areas that remain heavily agricultural now lag so far behind those in other areas that guaranteed access to land is no longer enough to keep people in the countryside (the rural population stopped growing in absolute terms in 1996, just about when rural industry stopped adding significant numbers of jobs). Despite still-significant barriers, net rural-urban migration is now approaching 20 million per year. Here China seems to be following Japanese trends, with a 50-year lag; after remaining relatively rural for its level of industrialization until the 1950s, Japan then began two decades of extremely rapid urbanization at the same time that it moved strongly into higher value-added industries. But when Japan began this push, its unemployment rate was 2%, so that even as the cities bulged, everyone found jobs. China's situation is very different, and its success at avoiding massive peri-urban slums will be hard to sustain. And the prospects for the West absorbing a further surge in manufactured imports from Asia are much murkier than in the 1950s.

One result has been the "Go West" initiative: a massive, government-led campaign to jumpstart economic development through mining, hydropower construction, and other capital-intensive, resource-oriented projects in Western China, to generate primary products for the East. Han Chinese migration to these areas (long restricted to avoid provoking ethnic resentment) is now being subsidized to fill skilled jobs. Lakes, mines, and so on—previously off-limits for various reasons—are now being opened, often over local (and sometimes international) opposition. In general, a long-standing paternalism towards minorities here (which, granted, has been slowly weakening for some time) is now being decisively pushed aside. And this initiative also carries huge ecological risks: removing trees at high elevations where re-growth is slow, quick and dirty mining, diversion of water from the Himalayan glaciers and annual snow melt (some of which currently goes to South and Southeast Asia), and so on. Perhaps half the hydroelectric dams built in West China since 1949 are now silted up, and some new ones are expected to provide power for only 20 years.

In one sense, "Go West" is an effort to stitch the country together, increasing interdependence and reducing economic (and perhaps ethnic) differences. In other ways, it may exacerbate differences. The coastal economy is increasingly semi-private—only 20% of industry remains truly state-owned in many coastal provinces—and the new rich are playing an increasing role in providing local services, as elites in rich areas traditionally did. The West, meanwhile, is seeing a revival of state (often military)-led development, with 60-80% of industry state-owned and far fewer high status jobs outside the state sector. Thus, it is not hard to imagine growing regional differences in social and political orientation as well as in living standards. Rather than a projection of the "East Asian" development seen on the coast across more of the Chinese landscape, developments in the interior (especially the far west) seem to have more in common with colonial or "internal colonial" styles of development.

Conclusion

A comparative history of development casts further doubt on the unique advantages of North Atlantic paths to the modern world; it reminds us that more laborintensive (and less resource-intensive) "East Asian" paths accounted for much of the world's economic growth during both the period before 1800 and the period since 1945, and may sometimes offer a less socially-disruptive transition to modernity. They should be taken as seriously as models drawn from North Atlantic experiences, not pigeonholed as a regionally specific curiosity. But the East Asian path is no panacea, either—when projected onto the gigantic scale represented by China, it eventually runs up against massive social and environmental problems of its own.

We still do not know how to have cores without hinterlands. ❑

Sources: For reasons of both length and style, the footnotes have been removed from this paper. Sources (and a more fully developed version of the argument) can be found in a series of publications by Kenneth Pomeranz, including: *The Great Divergence: China, Europe and the Making of the Modern World Economy*, Princeton University Press, 2000; "Beyond the East-West Binary: Resituating Development Paths in the Eighteenth Century World," *Journal of Asian Studies*, May, 2002; "Is There an East Asian Development Path? Long-Term Comparisons, Constraints, and Continuities," *Journal of the Economic and Social History of the Orient*, 2001; "Standards of Living in 18th Century China: Regional Differences, Temporal Trends, and Incomplete Evidence," in Robert Allen, Tommy Bengtsson, and Martin Dribe, eds., *Standards of Living and Mortality in Pre-Industrial Times*, Oxford University Press, 2005; "Chinese Development in Long-run Perspective," *Proceedings of the American Philosophical Society*, March, 2008.

Article 7.2

MEASURES OF GLOBAL POVERTY

BY ARTHUR MacEWAN
January/February 2008

Dear Dr. Dollar:

I hear all kinds of views about poverty in the developing world from different corners of the media. One minute you can get the impression that a huge swell is lifting everyone up and that millions of people in Asia are no longer in poverty. Then from a different source you get the impression that poverty is deepening and getting worse—the pictures of the kids with swollen bellies, etc. What's the reality?
—*William Chin, Randolph, Mass.*

The reality of poverty, like many other "realities," is elusive! There are disputes over how to define poverty, and, even when we can agree on a definition, there are disputes over how to measure poverty. However, one aspect of the poverty reality is fairly clear: there are still a great many very poor people in the world.

One widely used standard used to measure poverty is $2 per day—that is, people whose income is less than $2 per day are considered "in poverty." And people are viewed as in "extreme poverty" if their income is less than $1 per day. By these standards, in 2004 about 2.5 billion people, 39% of the world's 6.4 billion people, were in poverty, and 969 million were in extreme poverty.

This standard, however, requires a bit of explanation. The $2/day and the $1/day are based on what people could buy in 1990. Translated into today's prices, these figures would be about $3.20/day and $1.60/day. Also, these amounts are defined in terms of real purchasing power, not in terms of actual exchange rates. Thus $1.60 per day represents what a person could buy with that amount in the United States, not what could be bought in a low-income country if the $1.60 were exchanged for the local currency. Generally the latter would be substantially more than the former.

The World Bank makes annual attempts to update the figures on how many people are in poverty and how many are in extreme poverty by these standards. According to the Bank, there has been some substantial progress in the last fifteen years. By the Bank's count, the number of people in extreme poverty dropped from 1.25 billion in 1990 to below a billion in 2004—or from 24% of the world's people to its 2004 figure of 15%. The absolute number below $2/day fell only slightly in this period, from 2.6 billion to 2.5 billion, but this was a drop from 49% to 39% of the population (because the population increased).

The World Bank's appraisal of the situation, however, is open to dispute. To begin with, there are always problems in measuring what happens to people's incomes over time, because prices change. While the Bank adjusts for price changes, it does not do so adequately. To measure what happens in a country, the bank uses price changes for that country as a whole. It seems, however, that the prices of the goods that the poor buy have generally risen more rapidly than prices for the society as a whole. Thus the Bank's estimates of poverty reduction are probably overstated.

Furthermore, as the Bank recognizes, its picture of overall progress for the world obscures some very great differences between countries. By the $2/day and $1/day standard, the last fifteen years have seen great progress in China and India, two countries that together account for more than one-third of the world's population and which have grown quite rapidly. Other parts of the world, especially much of sub-Saharan Africa and parts of Latin America, have not done so well.

But there is a bigger difficulty. The $2/day and $1/day definitions of extreme poverty and poverty are, at best, a questionable way to frame the problem. It is misleading to define the poverty line simply in absolute terms, as the value of a certain quantity of goods and services that people must purchase to meet their basic needs (as represented by the $2/day and $1/day cutoffs). Raising people's absolute incomes is important and leads to improvements in nutrition, shelter, longevity, and general well-being. But there is more to poverty than an absolute level of income.

Poverty is a social status, a relation among people, and our standard of what it means to be in poverty varies across societies and over time. As a society's economy grows, its standard of "need" changes, and thus the meaning of poverty changes. For example, as an economy grows, more work takes place away from the home, and thus people's need for transportation increases. Also, as incomes rise, people's standards of what they need in terms of food, clothing, shelter, and everything else change.

Roughly speaking, we can think of a society's standard of needs as determined by what the people in the middle have. If so, people are in poverty when their level of income is far below what the people in the middle have. This means that poverty is greatly affected by the distribution of income. In two societies where the absolute income of the bottom segment (say the bottom 20%) is the same, poverty will be greater in the society where income distribution is more unequal because in that society the bottom segment will be further from the norm and thus more lacking in that society's socially determined needs.

In China and India, in particular, the countries responsible for large reductions in poverty by the $2/day measure, income inequality has increased dramatically in recent decades. Thus, if we define poverty as a certain distance (in income terms) form the middle, it is possible that there are more people in poverty in China and India than there were twenty years ago, in spite of rapid economic expansion. And China and India are not unusual. Over the last few decades, many countries have seen rising inequality.

Even if one accepts the absolute poverty definition—the $2/day and $1/day standards—rising inequality makes the reduction of poverty with economic growth much less than it would be if, along with growth, income distribution were improving. The problem is that the World Bank and much of the U.N. effort to "make poverty history" largely ignore the issue of income distribution. For example, land redistribution is not on the table in World Bank and U.N. programs, yet unequal land holdings are at the foundation of the lack of income and political power experienced by the poor in many parts of the world. Or another example: the Bank and the United Nations tout education as a cure-all for poverty, but they give no consideration to the ways inequalities of income and political power restrict the emergence of effective school programs.

Whether one emphasizes the absolute or relative concept of poverty—or takes both into account—it is doubtful that much progress can be attained while ignoring the underlying issues of power and social structure that create and maintain poverty. ❏

Article 7.3

MICROCREDIT AND WOMEN'S POVERTY

Granting this year's Nobel Peace Prize to microcredit guru Muhammad Yunus affirms neoliberalism.

BY SUSAN F. FEINER AND DRUCILLA K. BARKER
November/December 2006

The key to understanding why Grameen Bank founder and CEO Muhammad Yunus won the Nobel Peace Prize lies in the current fascination with individualistic myths of wealth and poverty. Many policy-makers believe that poverty is "simply" a problem of individual behavior. By rejecting the notion that poverty has structural causes, they deny the need for collective responses. In fact, according to this tough-love view, broad-based civic commitments to increase employment or provide income supports only make matters worse: helping the poor is pernicious because such aid undermines the incentive for hard work. This ideology is part and parcel of neoliberalism.

For neoliberals the solution to poverty is getting the poor to work harder, get educated, have fewer children, and act more responsibly. Markets reward those who help themselves, and women, who comprise the vast majority of microcredit borrowers, are no exception. Neoliberals champion the Grameen Bank and similar efforts precisely because microcredit programs do not change the structural conditions of globalization—such as loss of land rights, privatization of essential public services, or cutbacks in health and education spending—that reproduce poverty among women in developing nations.

What exactly is microcredit? Yunus, a Bangladeshi banker and economist, pioneered the idea of setting up a bank to make loans to the "poorest of the poor." The term "microcredit" reflects the very small size of the loans, often less than $100. Recognizing that the lack of collateral was often a barrier to borrowing by the poor, Yunus founded the Grameen Bank in the 1970s to make loans in areas of severe rural poverty where there were often no alternatives to what we would call loan sharks.

His solution to these problems was twofold. First, Grameen Bank would hire agents to travel the countryside on a regular schedule, making loans and collecting loan repayments. Second, only women belonging to Grameen's "loan circles" would be eligible for loans. If one woman in a loan circle did not meet her obligations, the others in the circle would either be ineligible for future loans or be held responsible for repayment of her loan. In this way the collective liability of the group served as collateral.

The Grameen Bank toasts its successes: not only do loan repayment rates approach 95%, the poor, empowered by their investments, are not dependent on "handouts." Microcredit advocates see these programs as a solution to poverty because poor women can generate income by using the borrowed funds to start small-scale enterprises, often home-based handicraft production. But these enterprises are almost all in the informal sector, which is fiercely competitive and typically unregulated, in other words, outside the range of any laws that protect workers or ensure their rights. Not surprisingly, women comprise the majority of workers in the informal economy and are heavily represented at the bottom of its already-low income scale.

Women and men have different experiences with work and entrepreneurship because a gender division of labor in most cultures assigns men to paid work outside the home and women to unpaid labor in the home. Consequently, women's paid work is constrained by domestic responsibilities. They either work part time, or they combine paid and unpaid work by working at home. Microcredit encourages women to work at home doing piecework: sewing garments, weaving rugs, assembling toys and electronic components. Home workers—mostly women and children—often work long hours for very poor pay in hazardous conditions, with no legal protections. As progressive journalist Gina Neff has noted, encouraging the growth of the informal sector sounds like advice from one of Dickens' more objectionable characters.

Why then do national governments and international organizations promote microcredit, thereby encouraging women's work in the informal sector? As an antipoverty program, microcredit fits nicely with the prevailing ideology that defines poverty as an individual problem and that shifts responsibility for addressing it away from government policy-makers and multilateral bank managers onto the backs of poor women.

Microcredit programs do nothing to change the structural conditions that create poverty. But microcredit *has* been a success for the many banks that have adopted it. Of course, lending to the poor has long been a lucrative enterprise. Pawnshops, finance companies, payday loan operations, and loan sharks charge high interest rates precisely because poor people are often desperate for cash and lack access to formal credit networks. According to Sheryl Nance-Nash, a correspondent for Women's eNews, "the interest rates on microfinance vary between 25% to 50%." She notes that these rates "are much lower than informal money lenders, where rates may exceed 10% per month." It is important for the poor to have access to credit on relatively reasonable terms. Still, microcredit lenders are reaping the rewards of extraordinarily high repayment rates on loans that are still at somewhat above-market interest rates.

Anecdotal accounts can easily overstate the concrete gains to borrowers from microcredit. For example, widely cited research by the Canadian International Development Agency (CIDA) reports that "Women in particular face significant barriers to achieving sustained increases in income and improving their status, and require complementary support in other areas, such as training, marketing, literacy, social mobilization, and other financial services (e.g., consumption loans, savings)." The report goes on to conclude that most borrowers realize only very small gains, and that the poorest borrowers benefit the least. CIDA also found little relationship between loan repayment and business success.

However large or small their income gains, poor women are widely believed to find empowerment in access to microcredit loans. According to the World Bank, for instance, microcredit empowers women by giving them more control over household assets and resources, more autonomy and decision-making power, and greater access to participation in public life. This defense of microcredit stands or falls with individual success stories featuring women using their loans to start some sort of small-scale enterprise, perhaps renting a stall in the local market or buying a sewing machine to assemble piece goods. There is no doubt that when they succeed, women and their families are better off than they were before they became micro-debtors.

But the evidence on microcredit and women's empowerment is ambiguous. Access to credit is not the sole determinant of women's power and autonomy. Credit may, for example, increase women's dual burden of market and household labor. It may also increase conflict within the household if men, rather than women, control how loan moneys are used. Moreover, the group pressure over repayment in Grameen's loan circles can just as easily create conflict among women as build solidarity.

Grameen Bank founder Muhammad Yunus won the Nobel Peace Prize because his approach to banking reinforces the neoliberal view that individual behavior is the source of poverty and the neoliberal agenda of restricting state aid to the most vulnerable when and where the need for government assistance is most acute. Progressives working in poor communities around the world disagree. They argue that poverty is structural, so the solutions to poverty must focus not on adjusting the conditions of individuals but on building structures of inclusion. Expanding the state sector to provide the rudiments of a working social infrastructure is, therefore, a far more effective way to help women escape or avoid poverty.

Do the activities of the Grameen Bank and other micro-lenders romanticize individual struggles to escape poverty? Yes. Do these programs help some women "pull themselves up by the bootstraps"? Yes. Will micro-enterprises in the informal sector contribute to ending world poverty? Not a chance. ❑

Sources: Grameen Bank, grameen-info.org; "Informal Economy: Formalizing the Hidden Potential and Raising Standards," ILO Global Employment Forum (Nov. 2001), www-ilo-mirror. cornell.edu/public/english/employment/geforum/informal.htm; Jean L. Pyle, "Sex, Maids, and Export Processing," World Bank, *Engendering Development; Engendering Development Through Gender Equality in Rights, Resources, and Voice* (Oxford University Press, 2001); Naila Kabeer, "Conflicts Over Credit: Re-Evaluating the Empowerment Potential of Loans to Women in Rural Bangladesh," *World Development* 29 (2001); Norman MacIsaac, "The Role of Microcredit in Poverty Reduction and Promoting Gender Equity," South Asia Partnership Canada, Strategic Policy and Planning Division, Asia Branch Canada International Development Agency (June, 1997), www.acdi-cida.gc.ca/index-e.htm.

Article 7.4

FAIR TRADE AND FARM SUBSIDIES
How Big a Deal? Two Views

November/December 2003; updated, October 2009

In September of 2003, the global free-trade express was derailed—at least temporarily—when the World Trade Organization talks in Cancún, Mexico, collapsed. At the time, the inconsistency of the United States and other rich countries—pressing poor countries to adopt free trade while continuing to subsidize and protect selected domestic sectors, especially agriculture—received wide attention for the first time. Where does ending agricultural subsidies and trade barriers in the rich countries rank as a strategy for achieving global economic justice? Dollars & Sense *asked progressive researchers on different sides of this question to make their case.*

MAKE TRADE FAIR

BY GAWAIN KRIPKE

Trade can be a powerful engine for economic growth in developing countries and can help pull millions of people out of poverty. Trade also offers an avenue of growth that relies less than other development strategies on the fickle charity of wealthy countries or the self-interest of multinational corporations. However, current trade rules create enormous obstacles that prevent people in developing countries from realizing the benefits of trade. A growing number of advocacy organizations are now tackling this fundamental problem, hoping to open a route out of poverty for tens of millions of people who have few other prospects.

Why Trade? Poor countries have few options for improving the welfare of their people and generating economic growth. Large debt burdens limit the ability of governments in the developing world to make investments and provide education, clean water, and other critical services. Despite some recent progress on the crushing problem of debt, only about 15% of the global South's $300 billion in unpayable debt has been eliminated.

Poor countries have traditionally looked to foreign aid and private investment to drive economic development. Both of these are proving inadequate. To reach the goals of the United Nations' current Millenium Development campaign, including reducing hunger and providing universal primary education, wealthy countries would have to increase their foreign aid from a paltry 0.23% of GDP to 0.7%. Instead, foreign aid flows are stagnant and are losing value against inflation and population growth. In 2001, the United States spent just 0.11% of GDP on foreign aid.

Likewise, although global foreign direct investment soared to unprecedented levels in the late 1990s, most developing countries are not attractive to foreign investors. The bulk of foreign private investment in the developing world, more than 76%, goes to ten large countries including China, Brazil, and Mexico. For the majority of developing countries, particularly the poorest, foreign investment remains a modest contributor to economic growth, on a par with official foreign aid. Sub-Saharan Africa, with the highest concentration of the world's poor, attracted only $14 billion in 2001.

In this environment, trade offers an important potential source of economic growth for developing countries. Relatively modest gains in their share of global trade could yield large benefits for developing countries. Gaining an additional 1% share of the $8 trillion global export market, for example, would generate more revenue than all current foreign aid spending.

But today, poor countries are bit players in the global trade game. More than 40% of the world's population lives in low-income countries, but these countries generate only 3% of global exports. Despite exhortations from the United States and other wealthy countries to export, many of the poorest countries are actually losing share in export markets. Africa generated a mere 2.4% of world exports of goods in 2001, down from 3.1% in 1990.

Many factors contribute to the poorest countries' inability to gain a foothold in export trade, but the core problem is that the playing field is heavily tilted against them. This is particularly true in the farm sector. The majority of the global South population lives in rural areas and depends on agriculture for survival. Moreover, poverty is concentrated in the countryside: more than three-quarters of the world's poorest people, the 1.1 billion who live on less than one dollar a day, live in rural areas. This means that agriculture must be at the center of trade, development, and poverty-reduction strategies throughout the developing world.

Two examples demonstrate the unfair rules of the global trading system in agriculture: cotton and corn.

"It's Not White Gold Anymore". Cotton is an important crop in Central and West Africa. More than two million households depend directly on the crop for their livelihoods, with millions more indirectly involved. Despite serious social and environmental problems that have accompanied the expansion of cotton cultivation, cotton provides families with desperately needed cash for health care, education, and even food. The cotton crop can make a big difference in reducing poverty. For example, a 2002 World Bank study found a strong link between cotton prices and rural welfare in Benin, a poor West African country.

Cotton is important at a macroeconomic level as well; in 11 African countries, it accounts for more than one-quarter of export revenue. But since the mid-1990s, the cotton market has experienced chronic price depression. Though prices have rebounded in recent months, they remain below the long-term average of $0.72 a pound. Lower prices mean less export revenue for African countries and lower incomes for African cotton farmers.

But not for U.S. cotton farmers. Thanks to farm subsidies, U.S. cotton producers are insulated from the market and have produced bumper crops that depress prices worldwide. The global price of cotton is 20% lower than it would be without U.S. subsidies, according to an analysis by the International Cotton Advisory Committee. Oxfam estimates that in 2001, as a result of U.S. cotton subsidies, eight countries in Africa lost approximately $300 million—about one-quarter of the total amount the U.S. Agency for International Development will spend in Africa next year.

Dumping on Our Neighbor. Mexico has been growing corn (or maize) for 10,000 years. Today, nearly three million Mexican farmers grow corn, but they are facing a crisis due to sharply declining prices. Real prices for corn have fallen 70% since 1994. Poverty is widespread in corn-growing areas like Chiapas, Oaxaca, and Guerrero. Every year, large numbers of rural Mexicans leave the land and migrate to the cities or to the United States to try to earn a living.

The price drops are due to increased U.S. corn exports to Mexico, which have more than tripled since 1994. These exports result in large part from U.S. government policies that encourage overproduction. While Mexican farmers struggle to keep their farms and support their families, the United States pours up to $10 billion annually into subsidies for U.S. corn producers. By comparison, the entire Mexican government budget for agriculture is $1 billion. Between 2000 and 2002, a metric ton of American corn sold on export markets for $20 less than the average cost to produce it. The United States controls nearly 70% of the global corn market, so this dumping has a huge impact on prices and on small-scale corn farmers in Mexico.

To be fair, the Mexican government shares some of the responsibility for the crisis facing corn farmers. Although the North American Free Trade Agreement (NAFTA) opened trade between the United States and Mexico, the Mexican government voluntarily lowered tariffs on corn beyond what was required by NAFTA. As NAFTA is fully phased in, though, Mexico will lose the option of raising tariffs to safeguard poor farmers from a flood of subsidized corn.

What do Poor Countries Want? Cotton and corn illustrate the problems that current trade regimes pose for developing countries and particularly for the world's poorest people. African countries want to engage in global trade but are crowded out by subsidized cotton from the United States. The livelihood of Mexican corn farmers is undermined by dumped U.S. corn. In both of these cases, and many more, it's all perfectly legal. WTO and NAFTA rules provide near impunity to rich countries that subsidize agriculture, and increasingly restrict developing countries' ability to safeguard their farmers and promote development.

How much do subsidies and trade barriers in the rich countries really cost the developing world? One study estimates that developing countries lose $24 billion annually in agricultural income—not a trivial amount. In today's political climate, it's hard to see where else these countries are going to find $24 billion to promote their economic development.

The benefits of higher prices for farmers in the developing world have to be balanced against the potential cost to consumers, both North and South. However, it's important to remember that many Northern consumers actually pay more for food *because of* subsidies. In fact, they often pay twice: first in higher food costs, and then in taxes to pay for the subsidies. Consumers in poor countries will pay more for food if farm commodity prices rise, but the majority of people who work in agriculture will benefit. Since poverty is concentrated in rural areas, the gains to agricultural producers are particularly important.

However, some low-income countries are net food importers and could face difficulties if prices rise. Assuring affordable food is critical, but this goal can be achieved much more cheaply and efficiently than by spending $100 billion on farm subsidies in the rich countries. The World Bank says that low-income countries that depend on food imports faced a net agricultural trade deficit of $2.8 billion in 2000-2001. The savings realized from reducing agricultural subsidies could easily cover this shortfall.

Each country faces different challenges. Developing countries, in particular, need flexibility to develop appropriate solutions to address their economic, humanitarian, and development situations. Broad-stroke solutions inevitably fail to address specific circumstances. But the complexity of the issues must not be used as an excuse for inaction by policy-makers. Failure to act to lift trade barriers and agricultural subsidies will only mean growing inequity, continuing poverty, and endless injustice.

Sources: Xinshen Diao, Eugenio Diaz-Bonilla, and Sherman Robinson, "How Much Does It Hurt? The Impact of Agricultural Trade Policies on Developing Countries," International Food Policy Research Institute, Washington, D.C., 2003; "Global Development Finance: Striving for Stability in Development Finance," World Bank, 2003; Lyuba Zarksy and Kevin Gallagher, "Searching for the Holy Grail? Making FDI Work for Sustainable Development," Tufts Global Development and Environment Institute/WWF, March 2003; Oxfam's website on trade issues, www.maketradefair.com.

FALSE PROMISES ON TRADE

BY DEAN BAKER AND MARK WEISBROT

Farmers throughout the Third World are suffering not from too much free trade, but from not enough. That's the impression you get from most media coverage of the recent World Trade Organization (WTO) meetings in Cancún. The *New York Times*, *Washington Post*, and other major news outlets devoted huge amounts of space to news pieces and editorials arguing that agricultural subsidies in rich countries are a major cause of poverty in the developing world. If only these subsidies were eliminated, and the doors to imports from developing countries opened, the argument goes, then the playing field would be level and genuinely free trade would work its magic on poverty in the Third World. The media decided that agricultural subsidies were the major theme of the trade talks even if evidence indicated that other issues—for example, patent and copyright protection, rules on investment, or developing countries' right to regulate imports—would have more impact on the well-being of people in those countries.

There is certainly some element of truth in the argument that agricultural subsidies and barriers to imports can hurt farmers in developing countries. There are unquestionably farmers in a number of developing countries who have been undersold and even put out of business by imports whose prices are artificially low thanks to subsidies the rich countries pay their farmers. It is also true that many of these subsidy programs are poorly targeted, benefiting primarily large farmers and often encouraging environmentally harmful farming practices.

However, the media have massively overstated the potential gains that poor countries might get from the elimination of farm subsidies and import barriers. The risk of this exaggeration is that it encourages policy-makers and concerned non-governmental organizations (NGOs) to focus their energies on an issue that is largely peripheral to economic development and to ignore much more important matters.

To put the issue in perspective: the World Bank, one of the most powerful advocates of removing most trade barriers, has estimated the gains from removing all the rich countries' remaining barriers to trade in manufactured and farm products *and* ending agricultural subsidies. The total estimated gain to low- and middle-income countries, when the changes are phased in by 2015, is an extra 0.6% of GDP. In other words, an African country with an annual income of $500 per person would see that figure rise to $503 as a result of removing these barriers and subsidies.

Simplistic Talk on Subsidies. The media often claim that the rich countries give $300 billion annually in agricultural subsidies to their farmers. In fact, this is not the amount of money paid by governments to farmers, which is actually less than $100 billion. The $300 billion figure is an estimate of the excess cost to consumers in rich nations that results from all market barriers in agriculture. Most of this cost is attributable to higher food prices that result from planting restrictions, import tariffs, and quotas.

The distinction is important, because not all of the $300 billion ends up in the pockets of farmers in rich nations. Some of it goes to exporters in developing nations, as when sugar producers in Brazil or Nicaragua are able to sell their sugar in the United States for an amount that is close to three times the world price. The higher price that U.S. consumers pay for this sugar is part of the $300 billion that many accounts mistakenly describe as subsidies to farmers in rich countries.

Another significant misrepresentation is the idea that cheap imports from the rich nations are always bad for developing countries. When subsides from rich countries lower the price of agricultural imports to developing countries, consumers in those countries benefit. This is one reason why a recent World Bank study found that the removal of *all* trade barriers and subsidies in the United States would have no net effect on growth in sub-Saharan Africa.

In addition, removing the rich countries' subsidies or barriers will not level the playing field—since there will still often be large differences in productivity—and thus will not save developing countries from the economic and social upheavals that such "free trade" agreements as the WTO have in store for them. These agreements envision a massive displacement of people employed in agriculture, as farmers in developing countries are pushed out by international competition. It took the United States 100 years, from 1870 to 1970, to reduce agricultural employment from 53% to under 5% of the labor force, and the transition nonetheless caused considerable social unrest. To compress such a process into a period of a few years or even a decade, by removing remaining agricultural trade barriers in poor countries, is a recipe for social explosion.

It is important to realize that in terms of the effect on developing countries, low agricultural prices due to subsidies for rich-country farmers have the exact same impact as low agricultural prices that stem from productivity gains. If the opponents of agricultural subsidies consider the former to be harmful to the developing countries, then they should be equally concerned about the impact of productivity gains in the agricultural sectors of rich countries.

Insofar as cheap food imports might have a negative impact on a developing country's economy, the problem can be easily remedied by an import tariff. In this situation, the developing world would gain the most if those countries that benefit from cheap imported food have access to it, while those that are better served by protecting their domestic agricultural sector are allowed to impose tariffs without fear of retaliation from rich nations. This would make much more sense, and cause much less harm, than simply removing all trade barriers and subsidies on both sides of the North-South economic divide. The concept of a "level playing field" is a false one. Mexican corn farmers, for example, are not going to be able to compete with U.S. agribusiness, subsidies or no subsidies, nor should they have to.

It is of course good that such institutions as the *New York Times* are pointing out the hypocrisy of governments in the United States, Europe, and Japan in insisting that developing countries remove trade barriers and subsidies while keeping some of their own. And the subsidy issue was exploited very skillfully by developing-country governments and NGOs at the recent Cancún talks. The end result—the collapse of the talks—was a great thing for the developing world. So were the ties that were forged among countries such as those in the group of 22, enabling them to stand up to the rich countries. But the WTO remedy of eliminating subsidies and trade barriers across the board will not save developing countries from most of the harm caused by current policies. Just the opposite: the removal of import restrictions in the developing world could wipe out tens of millions of farmers and cause enormous economic damage.

Avoiding the Key Issues. While reducing agricultural protection and subsidies just in the rich countries might in general be a good thing for developing countries, the gross exaggeration of its importance has real consequences, because it can divert attention from issues of far more pressing concern. One such issue is the role that the IMF continues to play as enforcer of a creditors' cartel in the developing world, threatening any country that defies its edicts with a cutoff of access to international credit. One of the most devastated recent victims of the IMF's measures has been Argentina, which saw its economy thrown into a depression after the failure of a decade of neoliberal economic policies. The IMF's harsh treatment of Argentina last year, while it was suffering from the worst depression in its history, is widely viewed in the developing world as a warning to other countries that might deviate from the IMF's recommendations. One result is that Brazil's new president, elected with an overwhelming mandate for change, must struggle to promote growth in the face of 22% interest rates demanded by the IMF's monetary experts.

Similarly, most of sub-Saharan Africa is suffering from an unpayable debt burden. While there has been some limited relief offered in recent years, the remaining debt service burden is still more than the debtor countries in that region spend on health care or education. The list of problems that the current world economic order imposes on developing countries is long: bans on the industrial policies that led to successful development in the West, the imposition of patents on drugs and copyrights on computer software and recorded material, inappropriate macroeconomic policies imposed by the IMF and the World Bank. All of these factors are likely to have far more severe consequences for the development prospects of poor countries than the agricultural policies of rich countries. ❏

Sources: Elena Ianchovichina, Aaditya Mattoo, and Marcelo Olareaga, "Unrestricted Market Access for Sub-Saharan Africa: How much is it worth and who pays," (World Bank, April 2001); Mark Weisbrot and Dean Baker, "The Relative Impact of Trade Liberalization on Developing Countries," (Center for Economic and Policy Research, June 2002).

Update: As of July 2008, the WTO negotiations have failed to reach an agreement, particularly on the issue of farm subsidies. Developing countries, especially India and China, demanded a deeper cut in the farm subsidies provided to U.S. and EU farmers and a much lower threshold for special safeguard mechanism for farmers in the developing countries. Meanwhile, developed countries, especially the United States, were not ready to budge from their position of reducing annual farm subsidies from $18 billion to $14.5 billion. The EU countries spend a total of $280 billion to support domestic farmers, while the official development assistance by the OECD countries to the developing world was $80 billion in 2004).

The IMF and the World Bank pushed the agenda of the structural adjustment program in more than 70 countries. The resulting decline in government spending has forced the farmers of the developing countries to deal with the mounting costs of cultivation. This, coupled with the vagaries of world farm-products prices (thanks to the Northern protectionism) has been driving the farmers in the South to much despair and hopelessness, and in the case of some 190,753 Indian farmers, suicide.

—Arpita Banerjee

Article 7.5

HOW TO MAKE MUD COOKIES

A traditional Haitian remedy for hunger pangs could be a path to riches.

BY MAURICE DUFOUR
July/August 2008

Mud cookies are all the rage in Haiti today—a rage sparked by soaring food prices. The cookies, a traditional remedy for hunger pangs and a source of calcium for pregnant women, have become a staple because food is simply unaffordable for impoverished Haitians. With food prices showing no signs of leveling off, more and more Haitians are likely to rely on the biscuits for their nutritional needs—and the rage is likely to grow.

The cookies are easy to make. The main ingredient, an edible clay from Haiti's Central Plateau, is abundant, and salt and vegetable shortening are added in quantities that vary according to affordability. The cookies are then left out in the sun to bake. Besides being filling, they are dirt-cheap.

At least they have been up until now. The clay that is used to make the cookies is rapidly going up in price due to increasing demand. It now costs about five dollars to make 100 cookies, so even the "cookie jar" is out of reach of many Haitians, who make an average of about two dollars a day.

While it may seem that Haitians have reached rock bottom, they may, in fact, be sitting on a gold mine. Through the alchemy of comparative advantage, their sludge-filled biscuits could become their most valuable commodity, propel the country into the ranks of rich nations, and even provide a lasting solution to world hunger. After all, the logic of shifting more resources into the production of these biscuits is as "impeccable" as Lawrence Summers' argument for moving dirty industries from rich to poor countries.

Think of it. Clever marketers could label the exported cookies "organic" and "low-cal." Publicity campaigns could make favorable comparisons with Twinkies in terms of nutritive value without violating any truth-in-advertising regulations. Bakeries could diversify their offerings: mud pastries, mud quiches, mud rolls, mud scones, and so on. Franchising could be hugely lucrative. Soon, door-to-door deliveries of no-dough donuts could displace Dunkin' Donuts' delicacies. To steal market share from the famous franchise, marketers could mimic the name of the chain: how about "Muck-in-Donuts"? Sales experts from McDonald's could be brought in to coach vendors on the correct way of saying, "Would you like flies with that?"

It's a win-win situation, really. Haiti could climb out of poverty through increased export revenues, and businesses could even boost revenue by selling their carbon credits, since the baking process relies exclusively on solar energy. Production costs would subsequently come down, making the cookies more affordable.

If the IMF could then coax other Third World countries into producing their own varieties of mud cookies for export, the global supply of cookies would expand, and the price would drop even further. A cheap global supply of mud cookies would help to alleviate hunger throughout the global South. The United States would then be able to pare down its food aid to poor countries, freeing up money to spend on worthier pursuits, like bringing peace to Iraq. And, instead of handing out candies to Iraqi children, American soldiers could be distributing Haitian-made cookies, at a fraction of the cost.

Copyrighting the recipe would be unnecessary. Step-by-step instructions can easily be found in cookbooks such as Milton Friedman's *Capitalism and Freedom* or Freidrich von Hayek's *The Road to Serfdom*. An abridged version follows:

Start by pouring dollops of any cheap American grain—say, rice—into any poor country—say, Haiti. The imported grain should be heavily seasoned with subsidies from the U.S. government. While pocketing millions in subsidies, be sure to sing the praises of "free" trade, peppering your verses with denunciations of government interference in markets. If the intended importing country resists, turn up the heat, withholding crucial loans until its leader agrees to cut tariffs on American grain imports. The flood of cheap imports will undercut domestic grain production, push local farmers deeper into poverty, and make a formerly self-sufficient country dependent on grain imports. Check to make sure that enough bags of imported U.S. rice are labeled "foreign aid." Reassure impoverished Haitian farmers with the old saying that expresses the great virtue of open markets: "A rising tide lifts all goats."

To ensure Haitians get a balanced diet, you can add some "greens" in the form of grain-based biofuels, like ethanol. The biofuels should also be generously seasoned with subsidies from the U.S. government (this could also be followed by condemnations of the market distortions caused by government interference). Ramping up biofuel production will drive global food prices up even more. Fortunately, the mud cookie industry has been well established by now.

Sit back and watch as the Haitians simmer with rage. Don't let the crisis boil over, though. If food riots erupt, toss in some troops with orders to crack open a few heads. After all, you can't make an omelette without breaking eggs! To prevent the American public from getting squeamish at the sight of blood-filled streets in Haiti, get CNN to focus its attention on the Dalai Lama. Before long, a collective feeling of detachment will set in; images of a corpulent laughing Buddha will draw public attention away from the skeletons walking the streets of Cité Soleil. Eventually, the Caribbean pressure cooker will move to the back burner all by itself. Mud cookies will continue to sell like hotcakes.

Critics may start linking your recipe to rising food prices, so it is now time to blame out-of-control "Asian demand," another way of saying the Chinese should not be eating as many hamburgers as North Americans. Then claim that bad weather and bad harvests have left the global food pantry practically empty. Ignore the fact that per capita consumption of beef in the United States is about seven times greater than China's. Disregard the fact that half the rise in corn demand in the past three years has been due to ethanol production. Also overlook the Canadian government's recent decision to pay hog farmers $50 million to kill 150,000 pigs in order to raise the price of pork. Trust us—there's a real food shortage out there.

Don't remove your apron just yet. Flip through the cookbook of the Michael Milken Culinary Institute, where you'll find other "quick 'n easy dough" recipes. (The now-defunct institute, better known for cooking the books than for publishing cookbooks, remains an inspiration for many pinstriped pastry pros on Wall Street.)

The main ingredient for fast dough—grain futures—can be purchased at any commodity futures exchange. You'll need to buy huge quantities if you want to make lots of dough. But through leveraging, this shouldn't be a problem—you'll be using other people's money. Leaven with the nostrums of laissez-faire and watch your mix turn into a soufflé. This is market efficiency working its magic.

As the soufflé inflates, global grain prices will swell, along with the bellies of Haitian children. But at least unemployment on the island will come down as bakeries add more shifts to meet the demand for their cookies. Ignore the accusations of speculation and price manipulation; what you are doing is greasing the markets, otherwise known as "hedging." (You may want to use short(en)ing for grease, but only if you are sure the soufflé will deflate fairly soon.) To absolve yourself of any responsibility for escalating food costs, invoke "Asian demand" anew.

You can now pass the apron on to the head chef—U.S. agribusiness. The chef will assure the starving masses that only he can feed the world. Already bloated from subsidies, he will take advantage of government-granted monopolies—patent-protected genetically modified crops—to further tighten his grip over global food production. This he will do while delivering encomiums to unfettered markets.

Pay no attention to the epidemic of farmer suicides in India; they have nothing to do with the debt-inducing purchases of fertilizers and pesticides that must be used along with the costly patent-protected genetically modified seeds. Remind yourself that the subcontinent could become a huge market for Haiti's cookies. If the price of the mud cookies subsequently begins to soar, you can blame "Asian demand" once again. ❑

Article 7.6

REFORMING LAND REFORM
Land reform is back in the international spotlight.

BY RAVI BHANDARI AND ALEX LINGHORN
July/August 2009

L and lies at the heart of many of the world's most compelling contemporary issues: from climate change to armed conflict, from food security to social justice. Since the turn of the millennium, land issues have reclaimed center stage in national and international development debates, which increasingly focus on access to land in promoting economic growth and alleviating poverty.

The distribution of agricultural land in many poor countries is profoundly inequitable, giving rise to social tension, impaired development and extreme poverty. These exploitative imbalances are legacies of colonialism and institutionalized feudalism, posing serious threats to future prosperity and sustainable peace in many poor agrarian societies. Donor-driven development projects focusing on land governance have sought to impose market-led capitalist ideals, further polarizing power and marginalizing the poor. Exacerbating this dire situation are new commercial pressures on land, rapidly transforming it into a commodity to be traded between international banks, multinational companies, governments and speculators. Looming large is the paradigm-shifting presence of globalization, reinforced by international financial institutions seeking to unilaterally impose their macro-economic policies. This toxic blend of national feudalism and international hegemony has placed the world's poor agrarian societies in a perilous predicament. For one sixth of the world's population, nearly a billion farmers, without security of land ownership, the situation is grave. Confronted with this menacing dystopia, it has become increasingly urgent to assess the ways in which land is owned, accessed and regulated.

What is Land Reform?

Land reform is the process of transforming prevailing policies and laws that govern land ownership and access with the aim of instituting a more equal distribution of agricultural land while improving productivity. It can take the form of relatively benign tinkering with land tenure and administration systems or escalate to wholesale redistribution of land from rich to poor. Land reform, also known as agrarian reform, rarely occurs in isolation and is generally accompanied by structural changes to the agricultural sector to assist economic transformation.

The concept of land reform is far from new; since the time of the Roman Empire, nation states have been unable to resist tampering with land ownership and agricultural labor relations. In the last century, no less than 55 countries initiated programs of redistributive land reform, with many more altering their rural land ownership systems. Since the 1950s, powerful international institutions, such as the United Nations and the World Bank, have promoted western forms of private tenure in many developing countries, through the introduction of individualization, titling and registration programs. Their goal was to hasten capitalist transformation by securing land for progressive farmers while hoping that the disenfranchised landless would gain employment in urban industries. Capitalism's litigious obsession with private property rights has proved incongruous in the context of many developing countries which operate customary land ownership systems, where indigenous groups have traditional rights over land they have occupied for centuries.

Despite international interference, the early period of land reform (1950s–1970s) was characterized by nation states seeking to equitably reallocate resources from those who own the land to those who work the land, in a bid to redress historical imbalances and enhance development. These "land to the tiller" programs were particularly prevalent in post-colonial South America, where high levels of landlessness and gross inequity in land holdings exist. Reformation led to state-owned collectivized farming in China, the USSR and Cuba, while locally owned collectives prevailed in Mexico, Honduras and El Salvador. Overall these reforms failed, with a few notable successes clustered in East Asia. In many cases, land became concentrated in the hands of the state and, in feudal countries, real reform failed to materialize from the rhetoric. China's land reform was directly responsible for a famine that killed over 40 million people.

Land reform entered a new phase in the 1980s and 1990s, with widespread de-collectivization and a new approach, so-called "market-assisted land reform." This neo-liberal orthodoxy, set forth and funded by the World Bank, aims to redistribute land by facilitating a land market of "willing buyers" and "willing sellers." The World Bank provides the buyers with loans, who are then required to pay full market price and display the clear intention of maximizing productivity. These land markets generously rewarded the rich, who often took the opportunity to offload marginal land, and created an enormous debt burden on the poor. Aided by the World Bank's coercive advocacy, marked-assisted land reform supplanted state-led redistributive land reform as the dominant paradigm.

Since its inception almost 30 years ago, market-led land reform has largely been a failure. In the process of dehumanizing and commoditizing land, it contributed to a rise in landlessness and exacerbated and entrenched the gap between rich and poor. Its fundamental flaws lie in its failure to address existing inequalities or appreciate the gamut of issues associated with land in developing countries—issues such as poverty, conflict, minority and gender discrimination, and environmental degradation. Land, too, is the foundation for enjoying basic human rights. Farmers excluded from land ownership in poor agrarian societies are condemned to a life of extreme poverty and exploitation. In some countries, basic livelihood needs such as access to potable water and firewood, or education and even citizenship, are denied to those without land ownership certificates.

The rise in landlessness and inequality, both corollaries of failed land reform, has fuelled tensions across rural societies and contributed to conflict. In Nepal's case, failed land reform led to a decade-long civil war. In response, landless farmers' organizations have begun to establish themselves into powerful social movements to challenge the status quo and demand their rights to land. Governments and international institutions have finally begun to realize that authentic land reform is a prerequisite to alleviating poverty and achieving sustainable peace and economic prosperity.

All Eyes on Nepal

Nepal is one of the most relevant countries today for contemporary debate on land reform. Nepal made global headlines in 2001 when the crown prince embarked on a murderous rampage through the palace in Kathmandu, slaughtering the king and queen and most of the royal family before killing himself. However, it is the deeper question of land ownership in relation to political and economic power that is actually shaping developments in Nepal, as in so many other poor, agrarian countries around the globe.

This small, mountainous nation, landlocked and sandwiched between the giants of China and India, is home to 30 million people. It is one of the world's poorest countries, with half the population living below the poverty line. The dramatic topography renders 80% of the land uncultivable, yet three-quarters of the population depend on agriculture for their livelihood, one-third of whom are marginal tenants and landless farmers.

Nepal's pattern of land ownership is the corollary of over 200 years of autocratic monarchy, with successive kings treating the land as their personal property, distributing large tracts to military leaders, officials and family members, in lieu of salaries or as gifts. This feudal system deliberately precluded ordinary people from owning land and ensured their continued position as agricultural servants. Non-farmer elites began to accumulate considerable land holdings as a form of security and status, precipitating the now well-established class structure of landlordism: a dismal system whereby those who work the land have little ownership of it.

Landlessness affords no status in communities and disenfranchises millions from their basic human rights. Without a land certificate, people are denied access to many government services such as banking, electricity, telephone service, and potable water. The landless are further victimized by non-government services, preventing them from keeping livestock and prohibiting them from accessing community forestland.

Nepal's land governance was subject to capricious rulers until the first land act was introduced in 1964. In response to a fledgling land rights movement initiated by tenant farmers, the monarchy introduced the act with the aim of "showing a human face." It imposed land ceilings with redistribution of the surplus to needy farmers and pledged to end the ritual of offering vast land grants to royal favorites.

In practice, ceilings were not enforced, little land was redistributed, and landlords, rather than tenants, often benefited. No further significant land reform measures occurred for the next 30 years; the 1964 Land Act remains at the center of Nepal's land reform legislation even today.

The People's Movement of 1990 reintroduced multi-party democracy to the Kingdom of Nepal, bringing new hope. In 1996, amendments to the original land act stipulated that any tenant farmer who had cultivated a piece of land continuously for three or more years would be given the right of tenancy and the right to receive half the land they farmed. As the majority of tenants were unregistered, landlords reacted predictably by evicting them from their land and refusing to grant secure tenancy contracts. In a country as poorly developed as Nepal, where it can

---

A COMMUNITY-LED APPROACH TO LAND REFORM

An innovative model for land reform is rising from the ashes of market-led agendas and centralized state bureaucracies, one loosely termed "community-based land reform." Borrowing from success stories over the past half century and incorporating new insights into sustainable rural development, the model offers a democratized, devolved approach that involves communities in the planning, implementation, and ongoing management of land reform.

In this model, each rural community is authorized to control its own land relations, including redistribution, working within a clear set of parameters laid out by the state. Governments typically fear relinquishing power, but it is precisely through this process of devolution that the majority poor can be included, empowered, and mobilized to ensure the effectiveness and sustainability of the reform. This bottom-up approach is often more cost-effective than top-down methods because of its potential to harness the administrative powers of existing local institutions (in Nepal's case, Village Development Committees). Plus, accurate data on land ownership, tenancy, and other factors such as idle land—an important starting point for any reform program—is more likely to emerge from community-level institutions. Devolved reform offers more room for flexibility across varying ecological zones and social contexts, while locally tested pilot schemes can provide valuable feedback.

Community-led reform is not simply a development buzzword or the latest fad. It has proven success, notably, the elected Land Committees that facilitated Japan's successful reform. Landless populations are pressing for greater inclusion, rightly asserting that they hold the knowledge required to design the most viable model for land reform. Even the World Bank has admitted that "greater community involvement" may be required; the bank now describes market-assisted land reform as only one "option."

take many days to walk to the nearest road, and many more to reach a centralized bureaucracy, these amendments served to formally terminate tenancy rights for over half a million families.

The World Bank's mission to proselytize market-assisted land reform had by now reached Nepal. The bank proposed establishing a Land Bank to assist the poor in buying land from the rich. Matching willing buyers with willing sellers is an expensive and difficult process and leaves the door wide open to multi-level corruption. The concept of landless farmers borrowing huge sums of money to purchase land from feudal elites who had not acquired their lands through fair means did little to imbue a sense of justice.

It is clear from experiences in many other countries that international financial institutions (IFIs) such as the World Bank are not interested in pursuing an equitable and sustainable system of land access and ownership, nor are they concerned with enabling landless farmers to lead respectable lives and contribute fully to the socioeconomic and political life of their country. They persistently overlook the long-term benefits of providing secure access to land for the rural poor despite documentary evidence of poverty reduction, increased agricultural productivity, stimulation of the rural economy, and conflict prevention.

Land ceilings also came under attack from the World Bank, which criticized the Philippines, for instance, for implementing "land ownership ceilings [which] restrict the functioning of land markets." Of course, this is the intention of land ceilings. Instead of helping an impoverished farmer to invest in the land, create a livelihood, and improve production, World Bank policies opt to facilitate that farmer in selling it to someone in a better position. In Nepal, so far, the Land Bank has remained on the table, postponed by years of conflict and civil society resistance.

Land reform policies in Nepal have failed to significantly redistribute land, improve agricultural productivity, or realign socioeconomic power imbalances.

LAND GRAB IN MADAGASCAR

In 2008, Daewoo Logistics of South Korea reached a now-infamous deal with the Madagascan government to lease 1.3 million hectares of land (over half the island's cultivable land) on which to grow food for the South Korean domestic market. Madagascar is part of the World Food Program, from which it receives food for the 600,000 people who live at subsistence level. Not a single grain from the Daewoo deal was to remain on the island. Farmers and opposition leaders rose up and took to the streets to demonstrate their disapproval, claiming that the people were losing control of their land, which would also be destroyed by Daewoo's mass deforestation plans. The land minister eventually rejected the deal; nonetheless, it was the last straw for a population increasingly betrayed by its government. The country has now plunged into crisis, with security forces killing over 100 antigovernment protesters and the situation likely to end only by coup or referendum.

The main reason for this lies in the conflicts of interest of decision makers. Government leaders are closely tied to landlords, if they are not landlords themselves. This corrupt nexus of power has ensured the continued failure of land reform and the perpetuation of a feudal society. The primary result of imposing land ceilings was concealment of ownership; the primary result of land records reform was authenticating elite ownership; the primary result of tenancy registration was eviction; and the primary result of modernization was abuse of customary rights.

The increasing dispossession of the majority poor and the escalating autocracy of the king led Nepal into a decade of civil war with the opposition Maoists, from 1996 to 2006. Land reform was the rallying cry of the Maoists, who declared themselves the saviors of the poor and enemies of feudalism, colonialism, and foreign imperialism.

Over the next decade, the Maoists came to control over half the country's rural areas and, with public and political opinion turning against the monarchy, the war ended with the signing of the Comprehensive Peace Accord in 2006, paving the way for multi-party elections. The Maoists swept to victory in the 2008 election, confounding the international community but not Nepalese voters. Under intense popular pressure, the king was forced to abdicate and a new Federal Republic of Nepal was declared on May 28, 2008. The People's Movement played a significant role in the Maoist victory and that same civil society is clamoring for the Maoist-led government to deliver on its promises of land reform.

The land rights movement in Nepal has built a significant democratic power base in the form of the National Land Rights Forum, which has over 1.6 million landless members. The organization has developed a major groundswell of momentum to bolster its lobbying and policy advocacy. The movement is united, democratic, people-led, inclusive and peaceful, and should serve as a role model for land rights movements across the world. Nepal's land rights movement pursues a rights-based approach, advocating the intrinsic link between land rights and the fundamental human rights of subsistence, protection, participation and identity. This leverages existing international conventions, laws and constitutions that protect fundamental rights and is an effective way to ensure a framework for land reform which will address the structural causes of poverty. They claim it is the duty of nation states to devise inclusive policies which allow citizens to participate fully in society and not to abandon them to inequitable power structures and a free market system which will ride roughshod over their economic, social and cultural rights.

India also offers examples of successful people-centered movements that are peaceful and community-led. Sustained democratic pressure from India's civil society succeeded in putting land reform on the official agenda. The Janadesh rally in October 2007 witnessed 25,000 people marching 340 kilometers from Madhya Pradesh to Delhi to pressure the government into forming a national land reforms commission, which it duly did.

While it is vital to keep land reform firmly under the political spotlight, it is also essential not to politicize land rights movements. Farmers' organizations in

Indonesia became polarized between political parties, each pursuing separate or competing interests, which proved to be a major obstacle to implementing successful land reform. It is critical that land rights movements remain firmly in the hands of the landless farmers, where they are most effective. A sustainable and successful land rights movement needs to be led by those whose future security depends upon its success. The role of civil-society organizations and non-governmental organizations is to support landless farmers in creating a solid institutional base and strong dynamic leadership while facilitating access to government policy-making forums, at local and national levels.

Civil society pressure has led Nepal's Maoist government to embark upon a "revolutionary" program of scientific land reform. Exactly how revolutionary or scientific it will be remains open to conjecture. Following two weeks of mass demonstrations by the land rights movement, the government recently established a Scientific Land Reform Commission to investigate available options and provide concrete recommendations. They have pledged to adopt an inclusive approach closely involving landless people in the process and to end feudal control over land once and for all.

Land Reform in Context

The redistribution of land, either through awarding new land to the landless or granting ownership rights to existing occupants, must not be seen as the final stage in the process but rather the initial stage in creating a viable and sustainable model to ensure livelihood stability and enhanced productivity. In many developing countries there is a trend towards abandoning, selling, or mortgaging awarded lands, often to raise money for medical expenses or because of a lack of credit to finance production. The combined pressures of increasing land prices and a dearth of government-support services has been the main catalyst for selling awarded lands. Without the necessary support systems, deprived farmers will understandably focus on solving their immediate food and economic security problems, reversing the land reform process and undermining the whole basis of a sustainable livelihood model.

In Indonesia, the government places certain obligations upon land reform beneficiaries to ensure a positive outcome: the land must be owner-cultivated and production must increase within two years. Negligent beneficiaries have their land expropriated without compensation. Such conditions are only reasonable if the newly entitled farmers are provided with the support they need, including improved infrastructure and access to markets, accompanied by financial, technical, and social services. Few governments or non-governmental organizations are committed to, or even capable of, providing the necessary support during this critical post-claim period.

The Philippines leads the way in rural support services, having established post-harvest facilities and continuous agricultural and enterprise development which focuses on community capacity building and rural infrastructure and finance.

Studies show that when agrarian reform is implemented properly and integrated support services are provided, farmers have higher incomes and invest in their farms more intensively. The examples of Japan, Korea, and Taiwan demonstrate that land reform is not only a social justice measure, but also the foundation for mobilizing agrarian societies towards rural, and, ultimately, urban industrialization.

In the case of Nepal, where broader macroeconomic policies do not support agriculture in general or small-scale producers in particular, land reform alone will not bring substantial income gains to the poor or a reduction in poverty and inequality. Indeed, if the macroeconomic context is adverse to agriculture—if, for example, exchange rate overvaluation and trade policies make agricultural imports too cheap for local growers to compete—then to encourage the poor to seek a living in farming is to lure them into debt and penury. A holistic approach to land reform must therefore be adopted to ensure viable and sustainable benefits.

Nepal is in the process of integrating into regional and global trading platforms that require a series of profound economic policy commitments. As a member of the World Trade Organization (WTO), Nepal has a legal obligation to align its economic policy with global requirements. The landless, near landless, and smallholders face an uncertain future in this era of globalization; Nepal must learn from the experiences of other developing countries that have courted the global players, adopted their policies, and paid the price. Succumbing blindly to globalization's holy trinity of privatization, liberalization, and deregulation is tantamount to self-sacrifice at its altar.

Land reform, and protective measures against unfair trade practices, must be in place before Nepal ventures into any international commitments to open its markets and resource wealth to international speculators. Indeed, the revenues of many transnational companies now far exceed those of the countries in which they operate. Such a concentration of lightly regulated power in international profit-seeking hands is ominous for small producers and even more so for the most marginalized members of agrarian societies. While genuine community-based agricultural investment is to be welcomed, the neocolonial pacts favored by foreign investors pose a serious threat to tenure security and to marginal farmers, many of whom could be pushed out of food production and forced to join the ranks of the rural hungry or city slum dwellers.

In 1995, Indonesia signed the Agreement on Agriculture with the WTO and agreed to open its markets. Liberalization of the domestic market for agricultural commodities spelled calamity for peasant farmers. International free trade agreements are not made with the intention of strengthening poor farmers' land rights. Furthermore, small-scale agricultural production simply cannot compete in a global market controlled by multinational corporations. Developed countries continue to bolster their agricultural export products with significant state subsidies while protecting their domestic market with prohibitive tariffs. Indonesia has since become the largest recipient of food in the world and is experiencing a startling rate of natural resource exploitation; deforestation currently occurs at the equivalent of 300 football fields every hour.

The WTO believes it is better for countries to buy food at the international market with money obtained from exports rather than attempting self-sufficiency; this paves the way for monoculture and contract farming while creating a precarious reliance on imports for basic food commodities. International trade is a natural phenomenon, but a significant degree of autonomy must be maintained; dependence on imports for basic needs such as food is dangerous. Strengthening agricultural self-sufficiency is especially important to developing countries that do not have the resources to sustain expensive food imports long-term.

Monoculture of cash crops in Indonesia has caused landlessness and has made small-scale farmers dependent on expensive agricultural inputs such as high-yield seed varieties, chemical fertilizers, and pesticides, which are often imported. Furthermore, these farming methods compromise ecological integrity and, as has been witnessed in Bangladesh and Indonesia, can lead to large-scale environmental degradation.

The repercussions of IFI interventions in developing countries, namely greater exploitation and inequality, illustrate the danger of imposing a capitalist model upon semi-feudal systems. International trade policies and programs in Indonesia, which were aimed at strengthening the position of agricultural exporters, proved to be overly discriminatory and served to weaken the bargaining position of local farmers. Large corporations were expected to develop farmers' institutions, but instead they exploited them by creating crop-buying monopsonies while forming cartels to raise the prices of their own products.

To accompany market liberalization, IFIs seek to impose the use of modern technology on agrarian societies. If this is not implemented diligently and judiciously, it leads to growth in rural unemployment. In Indonesia, the imposition of modern technology achieved just this, most notably among women, who were evicted from the land and became a pool of cheap labor for multi-national corporations—the same corporations that benefited most from the technology.

The deregulation that IFIs press for must not be carried out too hastily. Without a prior improvement in infrastructure to accompany the dismantling of para-state apparatuses, marginal areas will be alienated. This was seen in sub-Saharan Africa, where only those farmers close to urban centers benefited from the influx of private trade.

Commercialization of Land and the Last Great Global Land Grab

In addition to the globalization of trade, there are new, powerful commercial pressures for landless and marginalized farmers to contend with. Catalyzed by soaring food prices in 2008 and compounded by worldwide financial uncertainty, import-reliant, often oil-rich countries have begun scrambling to secure food sources for their domestic markets, in what has been called "the last great global land grab." Concurrent with this is the rampant growth of subsidized biofuel production to meet ambitious renewable fuel targets in the West, and the inception of carbon trading, which places a commercial value on standing forests and rangelands. Extractive mining and "ecotourism" add to the perilous predicament for vulnerable landless and marginal farmers.

The scramble for land often occurs in countries with a weak legal framework where farmers are not protected by secure land tenure systems. This results in the fertile land of the world's poorest countries becoming privatized and concentrated, creating a direct threat to food sovereignty, local production, and rural livelihoods. The increase in biofuel production is certain to intensify competition for land between indigenous forest users, land-poor farmers, agribusinesses, and financial speculators.

It is clear that potential foreign investment should be carefully analyzed to assess the full impact on the community as compared with the investors' financial interests before any deals are made. Sound investment should be accompanied by skills and knowledge sharing with local communities to establish foundations for long-term cooperation. The exploitation of natural resources for the sole purpose of shareholder gain is unsustainable.

The new REDD (Reduced Emissions from Deforestation and Degradation) scheme, which will offer developing countries financial incentives for preserving biomass stocks in standing forests, is an opportunity for states to define forest tenure and create community-based benefit-sharing mechanisms. Similarly, sustainable tourism can be used to reinforce community governance over biodiversity as a conservation strategy.

Land reform is a pressing issue shared by many developing countries that are shackled by entrenched inequities in land access and ownership. Highly unequal land ownership breeds social tension and political unrest and inhibits economic growth. While each developing country faces its own particular land related issues, some common themes prevail: the lack of political will to formulate and implement effective land reform, entrenched inequitable power structures, exclusive legal systems, poor dissemination of information, and the age-old millstones of corruption and excessive bureaucracy. Across the board, authorities are seen to be rich in rhetoric and poor in deed.

The rising discontent among landless and small-holder farmers has forced open an ideological debate between neo-liberalism, centralized elite domination, and pro-people policy making. The majority rural poor have begun to find their voice, and Nepal's civil war will act as a warning that their land grievances can quickly turn to violence.

Today, the worldwide financial crisis is threatening aid from the West and causing the demand for exports to shrink. Both factors render the billions of dollars of potential investment from multinational corporations and food-hungry, oil-rich nations enormously tempting to impoverished states. Governments must not be lured into exclusive market mechanisms that generate ever greater inequalities and create a profoundly negative effect upon community governance, food sovereignty, and peace building. Effective redistributive land reform, ensuring secure tenancy and ownership systems for marginal farmers, must occur in poor agrarian societies before opening their doors to global trade. The primary responsibility of all governments is to protect the basic human rights of their citizens, paying special attention to the poorest and most vulnerable.

Land reform is beginning to emerge from the vortex of market-led ideology to find itself at the epicenter of topical discourses on poverty alleviation, sustainable rural development, conflict transformation, food security, and fundamental human rights. IFIs continue to push reforms that consolidate and authenticate inequity, but land rights organizations are now enjoying a higher profile with increasing solidarity from a wide variety of state and non-state actors.

It is abundantly clear that the best approaches to land reform are those that integrate security, livelihood, resource management, and community empowerment. Land reform must redistribute land widely enough to preclude any dominant land-owning class and be accompanied by a support structure to sustain productivity. The expansion of rural markets that will follow will generate growth and this will lead to stable peace and national development. All eyes are on Nepal to see if the Maoist government seizes the unique chance to institute such an innovative, rational, and scientific process of land reform. ❑

Acknowledgement: We wish to thank our research assistant, Nabaraj Subedi, for his invaluable help in contributing to this article and the editors of Dollars & Sense for recognizing the importance of the current global debates on land reform and tenure security as a key policy issue for the 21st century.

Sources: Ravi Bhandari, "The Peasant Betrayed: Towards a Human Ecology of Land Reform in Nepal," in Roy Allen (ed.) *Human Ecology Economics: A New Framework for Global Sustainability*; Ravi Bhandari, "The Significance of Social Distance in Sharecropping Efficiency: The Case of Rural Nepal," *Journal of Economic Studies*, September, 2007; Ravi Bhandari, "Searching for a Weapon of Mass Production in Nepal: Can Market-Assisted Land Reform Live Up to its Promise?" *Journal of Developing Societies*, June 2006; Community Self-Reliance Centre Nepal, *Land and Tenurial Security Nepal*, 2008; Elizabeth Fortin, "Reforming Land Rights: The World Bank and the Globalization of Agriculture," *Social and Legal Studies*, 2005; Lorenzo Cotula, *Fuelling Exclusion? The Biofuels Boom and Poor People's Access to Land*, International Institute for Environment and Development, 2008; International Land Coalition, *Land and Vulnerable People in a World of Change*, Global Bioenergy Partnership, 2008; International Land Coalition, *Secure Access to Land for Food Security*, UNDP-OGC, November 24, 2008; Alex Linghorn, "Land Reform: An International Perspective," *Land First*, July 2008; Alex Linghorn, "Commercial Pressures on Land," *Land First*, April 2009; Oxfam International, *Another Inconvenient Truth: How Biofuel Policies are Deepening Poverty and Accelerating Climate Change*, 2008; Rights and Resources Initiative, *Seeing People Through Trees: Scaling Up Efforts to Advance Rights and Address Poverty, Conflict, and Climate Change*, 2008.

Article 7.7

LABOR RADICALISM AND POPULAR EMANCIPATION
The Egyptian uprising continues.

BY STEPHEN MAHER
November/December 2011

In mid-August, the eminent Marxist philosopher Slavoj Žižek wrote, "Unfortunately, the Egyptian summer of 2011 will be remembered as marking the end of revolution, a time when its emancipatory potential was suffocated." Indeed, the forcible clearing of protestors from Tahrir Square, the outlawing of labor strikes, and the imprisonment of thousands by the military that was taking place as Žižek wrote did not bode well for the revolution. In the months since his words were published, things have not gotten much better: the military has reinstated Mubarak's Emergency Law, the International Monetary Fund has issued grim predictions for Egypt's economic performance as interest rates soar, and Moody's has again downgraded Egypt's bond rating and that of several of its major banks. Meanwhile, the Islamists, marginalized in the earlier days of the revolutionary uprising, have returned, well organized and poised to play a significant part in the constitution-writing process that will commence following the upcoming elections.

Yet since the overthrow of Mubarak, industrial actions against low wages and poor working conditions have persisted, and a multitude of new, independent labor unions have been formed. In recent weeks, a new wave of labor strikes has exploded across the country on a scale "not seen since the earliest weeks of the revolution," as the *Washington Post* put it. But in view of the monumental challenges they face, what can these ongoing labor and leftist popular political movements still hope to accomplish? Is the revolution doomed, as Žižek suggests, or is a brighter future, and a truly radical social transformation, away from the domination of Egyptian society by capital, still within reach for Egypt?

Rise to Rebellion

The years leading up to the overthrow of Hosni Mubarak saw the development of a democratic social movement unprecedented in the history of the modern Middle East. This movement developed partly in resistance to the neoliberal policies imposed after a 1991 debt restructuring by the Egyptian state in collaboration with the International Monetary Fund (IMF) and the World Bank. The "reforms" consisted of the familiar neoliberal package: liberalized capital flows, deregulation and privatization of industries, and the gutting of the national health care and education systems along with the retreat of the state from other areas of social provision. As Marxist theorist David Harvey has argued, "the evidence strongly suggests that the neoliberal turn is in some way and in some degree associated with the restoration or reconstruction of the power of economic elites." Egypt's neoliberal transformation was no exception, with the breakdown of the powerful nationalist solidarity that held sway during the presidency of Gamal Abdel Nasser, followed by the ascendance of a powerful bourgeoisie linked to global capitalism. Despite increased production and strong GDP growth—between 4% and 7% per year—much of the new wealth was concentrated into the hands of Egypt's ruling class, while workers were left with barely enough to eat and social services for the poor were degraded or eliminated outright.

These programs were accelerated after 2004 with the inauguration of the "reform cabinet" of Ahmad Nazif. But alongside this push grew fierce resistance: between 2004 and 2010, there were more than 3,000 labor actions in Egypt, as workers exercised leverage from within the labor process against the ruling class and an authoritarian, unresponsive state apparatus. A sudden spike in inflation (which doubled in 2009), partly spurred by the liquidity that flooded the market as a result of the U.S. Federal Reserve's $2 trillion Quantitative Easing program, exacerbated the social crisis as the pitifully low wages paid out to Egyptian workers proved inadequate to meet basic needs. Egyptian society—beginning with the workers in the factories—was increasingly pushed toward revolutionary social transformation. The spread of high technology linked together workers in the industrial towns and an urban youth movement chafing under the authoritarian state apparatus, expanding conceptions of the revolutionary potential for the future. An 18-day popular uprising, which eventually saw millions gather in Cairo's central Tahrir Square, led on February 11 to the resignation of Hosni Mubarak, the suspension of the constitution, the repeal of the dreaded Emergency Law (which effectively circumvented all constitutional protections) and the transfer of power to the Egyptian army under the auspices of the Supreme Council of the Armed Forces (SCAF).

Reaction and Normalization

Despite Mubarak's resignation, large-scale protests and labor actions continued across Egypt. Such ongoing actions have made clear that the uprising is fundamentally social: it seeks to challenge not just the leadership of one individual, but rather an entire social-institutional order. Concern that the movement could turn explicitly anti-capitalist and lead to a more radical transformation of Egyptian society led the IMF to cloak its proposed post-revolution loan programs—negotiated in secret with Mubarak-appointed finance minister Samir Radwan—behind claims of "social justice" and an "orderly transition" to democratic rule. Meanwhile, after supporting Mubarak until his final days in office, the United States hurriedly expressed its support for the revolutionary movement, which it claimed had achieved its goals and urged the activists to return home and get back to work.

But soon after Mubarak's resignation, 5,000 employees from the Tawhid wa-Nur department store chain descended on Cairo, winning a 12-hour workday and a significant pay increase. Then, on March 3, planned protests against newly appointed

Prime Minister Ahmad Shafiq, widely viewed to be a member of Mubarak's old guard, caused him to resign, replaced by Essam Sharaf. Ongoing industrial actions also forced the army to permit the organization of independent labor unions. But by the end of March, ongoing mass demonstrations across the country led the Egyptian cabinet to order a law criminalizing all strikes and protests, which were made punishable by huge fines or imprisonment.

Still, the revolutionaries were not deterred. On April 1, "Save the Revolution Day," tens of thousands again filled Tahrir in defiance of the new measures. Massive protests continued on May 27 in opposition to the repression of SCAF, in particular the practice of subjecting civilians to military trials. The ongoing demonstrations forced SCAF to hastily announce on June 30 that it would reject all loans from the IMF and World Bank, which had been negotiated by Finance Minister Radwan just three weeks previously. This powerful mass movement was able to retain its momentum throughout July, before the military forcibly cleared Tahrir in early August. After arresting thousands of demonstrators, by September SCAF had reinstated the despised Emergency Law, one of the primary targets of the revolution.

Slowly but surely, the U.S.-backed Egyptian military and the ruling elite to which it is intimately connected seemed to consolidate their grip on power, ensuring that Egypt would remain closely linked to global capitalism and stay within the U.S. imperial system. Harsh repression, aimed at stifling a democratic social transformation and solidifying the hegemony of the army and the bourgeoisie, proceeded even as the show trial of Mubarak and a few of his closest associates got underway. Designed to demobilize the population and create the impression that justice has been achieved and "the system is working," the trial of Mubarak is perhaps the most effective measure the SCAF has taken so far toward the goal of preserving the existing social order.

Dark Clouds

Thorough the maintenance of a debt cycle, international capital keeps Egypt on a short leash. The establishment of a self-reinforcing cycle of debt means that as Egypt needs constant access to new credit in order to service its long-term obligations, the government will have to do whatever is necessary to keep new loans coming in. The result is a net *outflow* of capital from Egypt to international lenders. Between 2000 and 2009, net transfers on Egypt's long-term debt (the difference between received loans and debt payments) reached $3.4 billion. In the same period, Egypt's debt *grew* by 15%, despite the fact that it repaid a total of $24.6 billion in loans. This self-reinforcing cycle of dependency, which redistributes billions from Egypt's poor to Western financiers, gives these institutions tremendous leverage over Egypt's government. This, despite the fact that much of this debt is what is referred to as "odious" debt, contracted by an unelected dictatorship with the encouragement of the IMF, World Bank, and others. Mubarak's inner circle and the capitalist class were enriched to the tune of billions of dollars, while millions of Egyptians were kept in desperate poverty.

Keeping the economy open to foreign investment by eliminating trade barriers and capital controls is another way Egyptian dependence on foreign capital is maintained, establishing what is often referred to as a "virtual parliament." If the Egyptian government does not serve the interests of capital, Western investors can literally defund the country by rapidly withdrawing capital, thereby driving up interest rates and destroying the Egyptian currency. Not surprisingly, the maintenance of liberalized capital flows is a key demand made on the new Egyptian government, likewise tied to the continued extension of aid and credit, as the Egyptian business class warns the ongoing revolutionary movement of the dangers of capital flight. Ominously, Moody's Investor Service downgraded its rating for five major Egyptian banks, a move certain to provoke a reaction in international markets. Further liberalization and privatization, on the other hand, would almost certainly improve such ratings.

The downgrades bode ill for Egypt's ability to borrow on international markets. With Egypt in danger of bankruptcy, Egyptian finance minister Hazem el Beblawi has suggested that Egypt would again consider returning to the IMF for a loan, regardless of the popular outrage sparked by the deal made by his predecessor. Beblawi has already concluded a deal for $400 million from the World Bank to finance various public works projects, and Saudi Arabia and the United Arab Emirates have sought to preserve the rule of Egypt's capitalist class by lending Egypt $5 billion in budget support, and to finance new infrastructure projects. By soaking up unemployment through the implementation of Keynesian programs and making financing available for capitalistic activities, these loans seek to stabilize an Egyptian capitalism whose future—in the face of a massive new labor uprising—seems uncertain at best.

An IMF report on the Egyptian economy issued in late September further clarified the dark clouds on Egypt's horizon, projecting just 1.5% growth in 2011, mildly recovering to 2.5% in 2012. Gaping budget deficits, as the state seeks to buy off dissent and agitation for a more radical transformation by increasing the wages of public sector workers, are meeting with soaring interest rates that led the Cairo Central Bank to halt the sale of two- and three-year bonds on September 19. On September 22, Egypt gained $1.3 billion through the sale of six-month and one-year bonds, but at an average interest rate of 13.9%. Even at this astronomical interest rate, government borrowing risked crowding out private investment, according to the IMF report, which suggested that Egypt might have to return to the IMF after all in order to meet its budgetary shortfall.

A New Explosion

During Mubarak's rule, the only labor organization permitted to operate was the regime-dominated General Federation of Trade Unions, which supported the neoliberal agenda and worked to keep labor in line with state and ruling-class objectives. Before the uprising, labor organizers risked arrest, imprisonment, and torture to organize workers underground, but since the resignation of Mubarak labor organization has exploded: 130 new unions have been formed in the past seven months. In recent weeks, laborers from a broad swath of Egyptian society have taken advantage of the gains of the revolution, with a tidal wave of strikes engulfing the country on an unprecedented scale. While Mubarak never hesitated to obstruct labor action by deploying brute force, today's empowered strikers confront the state and the bourgeoisie with demands to reverse many of the neoliberal measures and redistribute the vast wealth that was concentrated in the hands of the upper classes in the neoliberal era.

Doctors staging sit-ins at hospitals are demanding better pay and insisting on a trebling of health spending in order to reverse the neoliberal gutting of what was once a strong public-health system. Striking teachers demanding the restructuring of the educational system to include classes on democracy and human rights, pay increases, and the firing of the education minister have forced the total or partial shutdown of 85% of Egyptian schools. Transit workers, demanding better pay, have brought the Cairo metro system to a screeching halt. Dockworkers at the port of Ain Al Sokhna are also refusing to work, disrupting trade with the Far East. This growing class consciousness, and willingness to confront the authorities, is taking hold of ever-wider segments of Egyptian society, and now, according to a *Washington Post* report, "appears to be spreading to private factories and farms, fueled by the breaking of a barrier of fear that served to curb union activity here for decades." As Abdel Aziz El Bialy, deputy director of the Independent Teachers' Union, put it: "This is a social revolution to complete the political revolution."

The Road Ahead

Given the organizational head start of the Islamists, the upcoming parliamentary elections are likely to bring victories to such conservative social forces, which will give them a tremendous hand in the constitution-writing process that will follow. The Islamists, who were an integral component of social stability during the Mubarak regime, are likely to accept the privilege of the army and the ruling class in exchange for increased ideological dominance. But as this tremendous labor uprising makes clear, the Egyptian people do not want the restoration of economic growth based on the gross exploitation of poorly paid workers by the owners of capital. Egypt has already been through that, with much of the vast wealth produced by workers in the neoliberal period simply concentrated in the hands of the bourgeoisie. Indeed, the IMF and World Bank issued one glowing assessment after another on Egypt's economic performance during the period of its neoliberal transformation (including one issued just days before the beginning of the uprising), which saw social inequalities grow to unprecedented heights amid severe state repression of labor and other dissent.

The purpose of the revolution was not to preserve market stability and assuage global capitalism; on the contrary, capitalist exploitation of labor in factory towns like Mahalla was the target of the uprising in the first place. A true, democratic social transformation is possible for Egypt, but this means discarding the advice and interests of capitalists, local and international, and their affiliates and agents. It means the democratic management of production and social life, the construction of a society in which despair and unemployment are impossible and true human flourishing is the foremost social goal, not the senseless accumulation of capital. In other words, the revolution must seek a true social transformation: one that puts an end to the exploitation of the workers and the violent deprivation of the poor and brings about genuine democratic management of social and political life. Such a radical social transformation will not be looked upon kindly by global capitalism and those at its head. But, again in the words of Slavoj Žižek, "liberation hurts." ❑

Sources: Slavoj Žižek. "Shoplifters of the World Unite," *London Review of Books*, August 19, 2011; Slavoj Žižek and Eric Dean Rasmussen, "Liberation Hurts: An Interview with Slavoj Žižek," *Electronic Book Review*, July 1, 2004; Anthony Faiola, "Egypt's Labor Movement Blooms in Arab Spring," *Washington Post*, September 25, 2009; David Harvey, *A Brief History of Neoliberalism*, Oxford University Press, 2005; Ismail Arslan, World Bank Independent Evaluation Group, *Egypt, Positive Results From Knowledge Sharing and Modest Lending: An IEG Country Assistance Evaluation, 1999-2007*, World Bank Publications, 2009; Adam Morrow and Khaled Moussa al-Omrani "Economists Blame 'Neo-liberalism' for Region's Woes," *Inter Press Service*, January 18, 2010; Walter Armbrust, "A Revolution Against Neoliberalism?" Al-Jazeera English, February 24, 2011; "The Struggle For Worker Rights in Egypt," The Solidarity Center, February, 2010 (www.solidaritycenter.org/files/pubs_egypt_wr.pdf); "IMF agrees to $3bn Egypt loan for post-Mubarak transition," Bloomberg, June 5, 2011; Anand Gopal, "Egypt's Cauldron of Revolt," *Foreign Policy*, February 16, 2011; Steve Hendrix and William Wan, "Egyptian prime minister Ahmed Shafiq resigns ahead of protests," *Washington Post*, March 3, 2011; Yassin Gaber, "Egypt workers lay down demands at new trade union conference," *Al-Ahram,* March 3, 2011; Klaus Enders, "Egypt: Reforms Trigger Economic Growth," IMF Middle East and Central Asia Department, February 13, 2008; Abigail Hauslohner, "Has the Revolution Left Egypt's Workers Behind?" Time Magazine, June 23, 2011; "Tens of Thousands attend 'Save the Revolution' Day," Al-Ahram, April 1, 2011; "Tens of thousands of Tahrir protesters demans swift justice in 'Second Friday of Anger'," *The Daily News Egypt*, May 27, 2011; Edmund Blair, "Egypt says will not need IMF, World Bank funds," Reuters, June 25, 2011; Malika Bilal, "Egypt: An incomplete revolution," *Al-Jazeera English*, August 19, 2011; Shahira Amin, "Activists fight revival of emergency law," CNN, September 19, 2011; "IMF: Egypt economy to grow just 1.5 per cent in 2011," *Al Ahram*, September 21, 2011; Alaa Shahine, "Arabs May Buy Egypt Debt to Cut Highest Yield Since 2008," *Bloomberg Businessweek*, September 23, 2011; Tim Falconer, "Moody's Downgrades Egypt's Ratings," *Wall Street Journal*, March 16, 2011; "Standard & Poor's Downgrades Egypt Debt Rating," CBS/AP, February 1, 2011; Tarek El-Tablawy, "Moody's downgrades five Egyptian banks," *The Daily News Egypt*, February 3, 2011; Sharif Abdel Kouddous, "Hot Teachers," *Foreign Policy*, September 21, 2011; Michael Robbins and Mark Tessler, "What Egyptians mean by democracy," *Foreign Policy*, September 20, 2011; International Monetary Fund, "Arab Republic of Egypt—2010 Article IV Consultation Mission, Concluding Statement," Cairo, February 16, 2010.

Chapter 8

NATURAL RESOURCES AND THE ENVIRONMENT

Article 8.1

GENETIC ENGINEERING AND THE PRIVATIZATION OF SEEDS

BY ANURADHA MITTAL AND PETER ROSSET
March/April 2001

In 1998, angry farmers burned Monsanto-owned fields in Karnataka, India, starting a nationwide "Cremate Monsanto" campaign. The campaign demanded that biotech corporations like Monsanto, Novartis, and Pioneer leave the country. Farmers particularly targeted Monsanto because its field trials of the "terminator gene"—designed to prevent plants from producing seeds and so to make farmers buy new seed each year—created the danger of "genetic pollution" that would sterilize other crops in the area. That year, Indian citizens chose Quit India Day (August 9), the anniversary of Mahatma Gandhi's demand that British colonial rulers leave the country, to launch a "Monsanto Quit India" campaign. Ten thousand citizens from across the country sent the Quit India message to Monsanto's Indian headquarters, accusing the company of colonizing the food system.

In recent years, farmers across the world have echoed the Indian farmers' resistance to the biotech giants. In Brazil, the Landless Workers' Movement (MST) has set out to stop Monsanto soybeans. The MST has vowed to destroy any genetically engineered crops planted in the state of Rio Grande do Sul, where the state government has banned such crops. Meanwhile, in September 2000, more than 1,000 local farmers joined a "Long March for Biodiversity" across Thailand. "Rice, corn, and other staple crops, food crops, medicinal plants and all other life forms are significant genetic resources that shape our culture and lifestyle," the farmers declared. "We oppose any plan to transform these into genetically modified organisms."

Industrial Agriculture I: The Green Revolution

For thousands of years, small farmers everywhere have grown food for their local communities—planting diverse crops in healthy soil, recycling organic matter, and following nature's rainfall patterns. Good farming relied upon the farmer's accumulated knowledge of the local environment. Until the 1950s, most Third World agriculture was done this way.

The "Green Revolution" of the 1960s gradually replaced this kind of farming with monocultures (single-crop production) heavily dependent on chemical fertilizers, pesticides, and herbicides. The industrialization of agriculture made Third World countries increase exports to First World markets, in order to earn the foreign exchange they needed to pay for agrochemicals and farm machinery manufactured in the global North. Today, as much as 70% of basic grain production in the global South is the product of industrial farming.

The Green Revolution was an attempt by northern countries to export chemical- and machine-intensive U.S.-style agriculture to the Third World. After the Cuban revolution, northern policymakers worried that rampant hunger created the basis for "communist" revolution. Since the First World had no intention of redistributing the world's wealth, its answer was for First World science to "help" the Third World by giving it the means to produce more food. The Green Revolution was to substitute for the "red."

During the peak Green Revolution years, from 1970 to 1990, world food production per capita rose by 11%. Yet the number of people living in hunger (averaging less than the minimum daily caloric intake) continued to rise. In the Third World—excluding China—the hungry population increased by more than 11%, from 536 to 597 million. While hunger declined somewhat relative to total Third World population, the Green Revolution was certainly not the solution for world hunger that its proponents made it out to be.

Not only did the Green Revolution fail to remedy unequal access to food and food-producing resources, it actually contributed to inequality. The costs of improved seeds and fertilizers hit cash-poor small farmers the hardest. Unable to afford the new technology, many farmers lost their land. Over time, the industrialization of agriculture contributed to the replacement of farms with corporations, farmers with machines, mixed crops with monocultures, and local food security with global commerce.

Industrial Agriculture II: The New Biorevolution

The same companies that promoted chemical-based agriculture are now bringing the world genetically engineered food and agriculture. Some of the leading pesticide companies of yesterday have become what today are euphemistically called "life sciences companies"—Aventis, Novartis, Syngenta, Monsanto, Dupont, and others. Through genetic engineering, these companies are now converting seeds into product-delivery systems. The crops produced by Monsanto's Roundup-Ready brand seeds, for example, tolerate only the company's Roundup brand herbicide.

The "life sciences" companies claim that they can solve the environmental problems of agriculture. For example, they promise to create a world free of pesticides by equipping each crop with its own "insecticidal genes." Many distinguished agriculture scientists, corporate bigwigs, and economists are jumping on the "biotechnology" bandwagon. They argue that, in a world where more than 830 million people go to bed hungry, biotechnology provides the only hope of feeding our burgeoning population, especially in the Third World.

In fact, since genetic engineering is based on the same old principles of industrial agriculture—monoculture, technology, and corporate control—it is likely to exacerbate the problems of ecological and social devastation:

- As long as chemical companies dominate the "life sciences" industry, the biotechnology they develop will only reinforce intensive chemical use. Corporations are currently developing plants whose genetic traits can be turned "on" or "off" by applying an external chemical, as well as crops that die if the correct chemical—made by the same company—is not applied.
- The biotechnology industry is releasing hundreds of thousands of genetically engineered organisms into the environment every year. These organisms can reproduce, cross-pollinate, mutate, and migrate. Each release of a genetically engineered organism is a round of ecological Russian roulette. Recently, Aventis' genetically engineered StarLink corn, a variety approved by the U.S. Department of Agriculture only for livestock consumption, entered the food supply by mixing in grain elevators and cross-pollination in the field.
- With the advent of genetic engineering, corporations are using new "intellectual property" rights to stake far-reaching claims of ownership over a vast array of biological resources. By controlling the ownership of seeds, the corporate giants force farmers to pay yearly for seeds they once saved from each harvest to the next planting. By making seed exchanges between farmers illegal, they also limit farmers' capacity to contribute to agricultural biodiversity.

The False Promise of "Golden Rice"

The biotech industry is taking great pains to advertise the humanitarian applications of genetic engineering. "[M]illions of people—many of them children—have lost their sight to vitamin A deficiency," says the Council for Biotechnology Information, an industry-funded public relations group. "But suppose rice consumers could obtain enough vitamin A and iron simply by eating dietary staples that are locally grown? … Biotechnology is already producing some of these innovations." More than $10 million was spent over ten years to engineer vitamin A rice—hailed as the "Golden Rice"—at the Institute of Plant Sciences of the Swiss Federal Institute of Technology in Zurich. It will take millions more and another decade of research and development to produce vitamin A rice varieties that can actually be grown in farmers' fields.

In reality, the selling of vitamin A rice as a miracle cure for blindness depends on blindness to lower-cost and safer alternatives. Meat, liver, chicken, eggs, milk, butter, carrots, pumpkins, mangoes, spinach and other leafy green vegetables, and many other foods contain vitamin A. Women farmers in Bengal, an eastern Indian state, plant more than 100 varieties of green leafy vegetables. The promotion of monoculture and rising herbicide use, however, are destroying such sources of vitamin A. For example, bathua, a very popular leafy vegetable in northern India, has been pushed to extinction in areas of intensive herbicide use.

The long-run solutions to vitamin A deficiency—and other nutritional problems—are increased biodiversity in agriculture and increased food security for poor people. In the meantime, there are better, safer, and more economical short-run measures than genetically engineered foods. UNICEF, for example, gives high-dose vitamin A capsules to poor children twice a year. The cost? Just two cents per pill.

Intellectual Property Rights and Genetic Engineering

In 1998, Monsanto surprised Saskatchewan farmer Percy Schmeiser by suing him for doing what he has always done and, indeed, what farmers have done for millennia—save seeds for the next planting. Schmeiser is one of hundreds of Canadian and U.S. farmers the company has sued for re-using genetically engineered seeds. Monsanto has patented those seeds, and forbids farmers from saving them.

In recent years, Monsanto has spent over $8.5 billion acquiring seed and biotech companies, and DuPont spent over $9.4 billion to acquire Pioneer Hi-Bred, the world's largest seed company. Seed is the most important link in the food chain. Over 1.4 billion people—primarily poor farmers—depend on farm-saved seed for their livelihoods. While the "gene police" have not yet gone after farmers in the Third World, it is probably only a matter of time.

If corporations like Monsanto have their way, genetic technology—like the so-called "terminator" seeds—will soon render the "gene police" redundant. Far from being designed to increase agricultural production, "terminator" technology is meant to prevent unauthorized production—and increase seed-industry profits. Fortunately, worldwide protests, like the "Monsanto Quit India" campaign, forced the company to put this technology on hold. Unfortunately, Monsanto did not pledge to abandon "terminator" seeds permanently, and other companies continue to develop similar systems.

Future Possible

From the United States to India, small-scale ecological agriculture is proving itself a viable alternative to chemical-intensive and bioengineered agriculture. In the United States, the National Research Council found that "alternative farmers often produce high per acre yields with significant reductions in costs per unit of crop harvested," despite the fact that "many federal policies discourage adoption of alternative practices." The Council concluded that "federal commodity programs must be restructured to help farmers realize the full benefits of the productivity gains possible through alternative practices."

Another study, published in the *American Journal of Alternative Agriculture*, found that ecological farms in India were just as productive and profitable as chemical ones. The author concluded that, if adopted on a national scale, ecological farming would have "no negative impact on food security," and would reduce soil erosion and the depletion of soil fertility while greatly lessening dependence on external inputs.

The country where alternative agriculture has been put to its greatest test, however, is Cuba. Before 1989, Cuba had a model Green Revolution-style agricultural economy (an approach the Soviet Union had promoted as much as the United States). Cuban agriculture featured enormous production units, using vast quantities of imported chemicals and machinery to produce export crops, while the country imported over half its food.

Although the Cuban government's commitment to equity and favorable terms of trade offered by Eastern Europe protected Cubans from undernourishment, the collapse of the East bloc in 1989 exposed the vulnerability of this approach. Cuba plunged into its worst food crisis since the revolution. Consumption of calories and protein dropped by perhaps as much as 30%. Nevertheless, today Cubans are eating almost as well as they did before 1989, with much lower imports of food and agrochemicals. What happened?

Cut off from imports of food and agrochemicals, Cuba turned inward to create a more self-reliant agriculture based on higher crop prices to farmers, smaller production units, urban agriculture, and ecological principles. As a result of the trade embargo, food shortages, and the opening of farmers' markets, farmers began to receive much better prices for their products. Given this incentive to produce, they did so, even without Green Revolution-style inputs. The farmers received a huge boost from the reorientation of government education, research, and assistance toward alternative methods, as well as the rediscovery of traditional farming techniques.

While small farmers and cooperatives increased production, large-scale state farms stagnated. In response, the Cuban government parceled out the state farms to their former employees as smaller-scale production units. Finally, the government mobilized support for a growing urban agriculture movement—small-scale organic farming on vacant lots—which, together with the other changes, transformed Cuban cities and urban diets in just a few years.

Will Biotechnology Feed the World?

The biotech industry pretends concern for hungry people in the Third World, holding up greater food production through genetic engineering as the solution to world hunger. If the Green Revolution has taught us one thing, however, it is that increased food production can—and often does—go hand in hand with more hunger, not less. Hunger in the modern world is not caused by a shortage of food, and cannot be eliminated by producing more. Enough food is already available to provide at least 4.3 pounds of food per person a day worldwide. The root of the hunger problem is not inadequate production but unequal access and distribution. This is why the second Green Revolution promised by the "life sciences" companies is no more likely to end hunger than the first.

The United States is the world's largest producer of surplus food. According to the U.S. Department of Agriculture, however, some 36 million of the country's people (including 14 million children) do not have adequate access to food. That's an increase of six million hungry people since the 1996 welfare reform, with its massive cuts in food stamp programs.

Even the world's "hungry countries" have enough food for all their people right now. In fact, about three quarters of the world's malnourished children live in countries with net food surpluses, much of which are being exported. India, for example, ranks among the top Third World agricultural exporters, and yet more than a third of the world's 830 million hungry people live there. Year after year, Indian governments have managed a sizeable food surplus by depriving the poor of their basic human right to food.

The poorest of the poor in the Third World are landless peasants, many of whom became landless because of policies that favor large, wealthy farmers. The high costs of genetically engineered seeds, "technology-use payments," and other inputs that small farmers will have to use under the new biotech agriculture will tighten the squeeze on already poor farmers, deepening rural poverty. If agriculture can play any role in alleviating hunger, it will only be to the extent that we reverse the existing bias toward wealthier and larger farmers, embrace land reform and sustainable agriculture, reduce inequality, and make small farmers the center of an economically vibrant rural economy. ❑

Article 8.2

FISHERFOLK OUT, TOURISTS IN

Sri Lanka's tsunami reconstruction plans displace devastated coastal residents to make way for tourism industry expansion.

BY VASUKI NESIAH AND DEVINDER SHARMA
July/August 2005

Two days after the south Asian tsunami struck last December, as thousands around him were grappling with its devastating impact, former German chancellor Helmut Kohl was airlifted from the roof of his holiday resort in southern Sri Lanka by the country's air force. Kohl is, of course, among the most elite of tourists, and his privileges are not representative of all tourists. Nonetheless, that aerial exit is symptomatic of the tourist industry's alienation from the local community. His easy flight away from the devastation, at a time when official relief supplies were still to reach the majority of victims, was an early indicator of the interplay between tsunami relief and the tourism industry. Kohl was barely airborne, and the waves barely receding, when plans were already afoot to ensure that the beaches of Sri Lanka were cleared of fisherfolk and rendered pristine for a new wave of tourists.

"Natural" Disasters?

Right from the start, global attention to the tsunami was no doubt heightened by the fact that tourists were among the victims. Reporters conducted their share of riveting tsunami escape interviews in airport departure lounges: first-rate, first-person accounts with first-world tourists. This is not the first time viewers in the rich countries have been plied with images of "natives" being overwhelmed by natural disasters, passively awaiting international humanitarian relief and rescue. Some parts of the globe are just scripted into tragedy and chaos; first-world television screens are accustomed to their loss, their displacement, their overwhelming misery. Against this backdrop, the tales of tourists offered a more newsworthy break from stories that simply echo yesterday's news reports about locals caught up in floods in Bangladesh or mudslides in Haiti.

But while being located in the trajectory of tsunami waves or monsoons is a given, the acute vulnerability of countries like Sri Lanka, Haiti, or Bangladesh to natural disasters only appears spontaneous. It is the socio-political landscape that determines the extent of exposure to adverse impact from such natural disasters. The political economy of exposure to natural disaster is disastrous for those made vulnerable—but not natural. For example, coastal mangrove forests would have contained the fury of the tsunami waves, except that they've been rapidly destroyed in recent years to make way for resorts and industrial shrimp farms. (See sidebar, "The Tsunami and the Mangroves.")

Defining that vulnerability as natural is, however, important to the tourism industry, whose job it is to produce exotic destinations through comparison and contrast. The devastation of repeated natural disasters is simply the "native predicament" in places like Sri Lanka, and one of the principle drives behind western tourism to the global South hinges on that predicament. Tourism often is, after all, a quest for a departure from the everyday of western suburbia—but in a neatly packaged module that insulates the visitor from the actual risks of the locale. Trafficking in that balance of otherness and insulation is the task of the tour masters.

The tsunami penetrated that insulation to some degree. However, even through the bloodletting of the last two decades, tourists visiting Sri Lanka have been remarkably insulated from it all: both from the civil war and from the country's impoverished social and economic circumstances. In fact, on the tourism industry's map, Sri Lanka is an adventure zone whose attraction lies at least partly in those circumstances, which make it a cheap vacation spot, a low-cost listing in a travel catalog of exotic but consumer-friendly destinations.

What Does Tourism Do?

Does the tourist industry simply feed off a pre-existing socio-economic predicament and perhaps even mitigate it, or does the industry exacerbate that predicament and entrench a country like Sri Lanka in an itinerary of peripheral economies served up for tourist consumption?

The argument is not that tourism per se is bad for Sri Lanka. Clearly the broader tradition of tourism and international travel has had a mixed, complex history. For the many who came, surfed, littered, took photographs, bought sex, batik shirts, or barefoot sarongs and left, there are others who ended up engaged by newly discovered solidarities. Even the interface with colonial exploration was double-edged. As political scientist Kumari Jayewardene and others have shown us, we have always had a line of itinerant travelers who washed onto our shore as tourists of one sort or another, only to develop more fundamental commitments to local communities—commitments that then fed into, or even helped catalyze, traditions of dissent and struggles for justice that have had enormous reach in our collective histories.

Such solidarity aside, tourism can be a significant source of revenue, employment, and infrastructure development. It also has a range of indirect effects since tourism generates demand in many sectors; every job created in the tourism industry is said to result in almost ten jobs in other industries, with enhanced demand in areas like agriculture and small industries, a whole spectrum of service-sector employment, and so on—the kind of thing that excites Central Bank policymakers, not to mention the middlemen who profit from those batik shirts and barefoot sarongs, from the increased demand for sex work and other informal sector labor. At a micro level, the jobs generated by the industry have enabled some financial autonomy for some sections of the working poor. Even when pay and working conditions are exploitative, this is an autonomy that may have particular significance for women and other groups who yield less financial decisionmaking power in the "old" economy.

Yet this baby came with a lot of muddy bath water even before the tsunamis washed in. The growth it has generated has often been of an unbalanced kind that worsened the country's financial vulnerability with little accountability to local communities. As they discovered through the shifting fortunes of the ceasefire, the post-9/11 drop in international travel, and recessions in distant lands, communities that work in the tourism industry have a heightened dependence on a fickle, fluctuating transnational market. The majority of the jobs tourism creates in the formal sector are service-sector jobs that are exploitative, badly paid, seasonal, and insecure; these problems are replicated many times over in the industry's large informal sector,

---

THE TSUNAMI AND THE MANGROVES

Since the 1980s, Asia has been plundered by large industrialized shrimp farms that have brought environmentally unfriendly aquaculture to its shores. Nearly 72% of global shrimp farming takes place in Asia, where the World Bank has been its largest funder. Even before the tsunami struck last December, shrimp cultivation, once termed a "rape-and-run" industry by the U.N. Food and Agricultural Organization, had already caused havoc in the region. Shrimp farms are only productive for two to five years. The ponds are then abandoned, leaving behind toxic waste, destroyed ecosystems, and displaced communities that have lost their traditional livelihoods. The whole cycle is then repeated in another pristine coastal area.

Now the shrimp farms—along with rapid tourism development—are also responsible for a share of the death and destruction the tsunami brought. Shrimp farming was expanded at the cost of tropical mangrove forests, which are among the world's most important ecosystems. Mangrove swamps have long been nature's protection for coastal regions, holding back large waves, weathering the impact of cyclones, and serving as a nursery for the three-fourths of commercial fish species that spend part of their life cycle there.

Ecologists tell us that mangroves provide double protection against storms and tsunamis. The first layer of red mangroves with their flexible branches and tangled roots hanging in the coastal waters absorb the first shock waves. The second layer of tall black mangroves then acts like a wall, withstanding much of the sea's fury.

But shrimp farming has continued its destructive spree, eating away more than half of the world's mangroves. Since the 1960s, for instance, aquaculture and industrial development in Thailand have resulted in a loss of over 65,000 hectares of mangroves. In Indonesia, Java has lost 70% of its mangroves, Sulawesi 49%, and Sumatra 36%. At the time the tsunami struck in all its fury, logging companies were busy axing mangroves in the Aceh province of Indonesia to export to Malaysia and Singapore.

In India, mangrove cover has been reduced by over two-thirds in the past three decades. In Andhra Pradesh, more than 50,000 people have been forcibly removed to make way for shrimp farms; throughout the country, millions have been displaced.

Whatever remained of the mangroves in India was cut down by the hotel industry, aided and abetted by the Ministry of Environment and Forests and the Ministry of Industries. Five-star hotels, golf courses, industries, and mansions

ranging from prostitution to handicrafts. Its untrammeled exploitation of the coast has created unsustainable demands on the local environment that have had particularly bad impacts on coastal ecology. Equally pernicious, it has transformed more and more public land such as beaches into private goods, fencing out local residents.

Reconstruction for Whom?

The tragedy is that many of tourism's downsides may be exacerbated by the tsunami reconstruction plans. From Thailand to Sri Lanka, the tourist industry saw the tsunami through dollar signs. The governments concerned were on board from the outset, quickly planning massive subsidies for the tourism industry in ways that

sprung up all along the coast, warnings from environmentalists notwithstanding. These two ministries worked overtime to dilute the Coastal Regulation Zone rules, allowing the hotels to take over even the 500-meter buffer zone that was supposed to be maintained along the beach.

The recent tourism boom throughout the Asia-Pacific region coincided with the destructive fallout from industrial shrimp farms. In the past two decades, the entire coastline along the Bay of Bengal, the Arabian Sea, and the Strait of Malacca in the Indian Ocean, as well as all along the South Pacific Ocean, has witnessed massive investment in hotels and tourism facilities. By 2010, the region is projected to surpass the Americas to become the world's number two tourist destination, with 229 million arrivals.

If only the mangroves were intact, the damage from the tsunami would have been greatly minimized. That's what happened in Bangladesh in 1960, when a tsunami wave hit the coast in an area where mangroves were intact. Not a single person died. These mangroves were subsequently cut down and replaced with shrimp farms. In 1991, thousands of people were killed when a tsunami of the same magnitude hit the same region.

In Tamil Nadu, in south India, Pichavaram and Muthupet, with dense mangroves, suffered low human casualties and less economic damage from the recent tsunami than other areas. Likewise, Myanmar and the Maldives suffered much less from the killing spree of the tsunami because the tourism industry had so far not spread its tentacles to the virgin mangroves and coral reefs surrounding their coastlines. The large coral reef surrounding the Maldives islands absorbed much of the tidal fury, limiting the human loss to a little over 100 dead. Like mangrove swamps, coral reefs absorb the sea's fury by breaking the waves.

Let's weigh the costs and benefits of destroying the mangroves. Having grown tenfold in the last 15 years, shrimp farming is now a $9 billion industry. It is estimated that shrimp consumption in North America, Japan, and Western Europe has increased by 300% within the last 10 years. But one massive wave of destruction caused by this tsunami in 11 Asian countries has exacted a cost immeasurably greater than the economic gain that the shrimp industry claims to have created.

World governments have so far pledged $4 billion in aid, and private relief agencies are spending additional billions. The World Bank gave $175 million right away, and then-World Bank president James Wolfensohn said, "We can go up to even $1 billion to $1.5 billion depending on the needs...." But if only successive presidents of the World Bank had refrained from aggressively promoting ecologically unsound but market friendly economic policies, a lot of human lives and dollars could have been saved.   —Devinder Sharma suggest the most adverse distributive impact. Infrastructure development will be even further skewed to cater to the industry rather than to the needs of local communities. Within weeks of the tsunami, the Alliance for the Protection of National Resources and Human Rights, a Sri Lankan advocacy group, expressed concern that "the developing situation is disastrous, more disastrous than the tsunami itself, if it is possible for anything to be worse than that."

The tsunami arrived at a critical moment in the recent history of Sri Lanka's political economy. Beginning in the late 1970s, Sri Lankan governments of both major parties followed the neoliberal prescriptions to cut tariffs and quotas, privatize, and deregulate more slavishly than many other Asian states. In 2002, the then-ruling center-right UNP issued a major blueprint for continued liberalization, "Regaining Sri Lanka," under the rubric of the "Poverty Reduction Strategy Plans" (PRSPs) that the World Bank and the IMF now require. But public opposition to these policies has intensified over time. In 2004 a center-left coalition won election on an anti-liberalization platform. Once in office, however, the chief party in the coalition appeared unwilling to truly change direction, and the "Regaining Sri Lanka" plan is still very much on the table.

Now, activists are warning that many of the plan's liberalization proposals will be revived and pushed through with little public dialogue and debate, given the emergency powers the government has given itself under cover of tsunami relief and reconstruction. In January, for example, the government revived a plan for water privatization that had earlier been tabled after public opposition. Official reconstruction plans are being prepared by a newly created agency, TAFREN, which a recent statement by a coalition of over 170 civil-society organizations describes as "composed entirely of big business leaders with vested interests in the tourist and construction industries, who are completely unable to represent the interests of the affected communities."

Proposals announced by TAFREN and by various government officials call for the building of multi-lane highways and the wholesale displacement of entire villages from the coast. Coastal lands are to be sliced up into designated buffer zones and tourism zones. The government is preventing those fishing families who wish to do so from rebuilding their homes on the coast, ostensibly because of the risk of future natural disasters; at the same time, it's encouraging the opening of both new and rebuilt beachfront tourist hotels.

The plans are essentially roadmaps for multinational hotel chains, telecom companies, and the like to cater to the tourism industry. Small-scale fishing operations by individual proprietors will become more difficult to sustain as access to the beach becomes increasingly privatized and fishing conglomerates move in. The environmental deregulation proposed in the PRSP will open the door to even more untrammeled exploitation of natural resources. None of the reconstruction planning is being channeled through decision-making processes that are accountable or participatory. Ultimately, it looks like reconstruction will be determined by the deadly combination of a rapacious private sector and government graft: human tragedy becomes a commercial opportunity, tsunami aid a business venture.

Not unpredictably, even the subsidies planned for the tourism industry in the wake of the tsunami are going to the hotel owners and big tour operators, not to the porters and cleaning women who were casual employees in hotels. Many of the local residents who were proprietors or workers in smaller tourism-related businesses, now unemployed, are not classified as tsunami-affected, so they are denied even the meager compensation they should be entitled to. The situation is much worse for the vast informal sector of sex workers, souvenir sellers, and others whose livelihood depended on the tourism industry. If the tsunami highlighted the acute vulnerability that accompanies financial dependence on the industry, the tsunami reconstruction plans look set to exacerbate this vulnerability even further.

A needs assessment study conducted by the World Bank in collaboration with the Asian Development Bank and Japan's official aid agency pegged the loss borne by the tourism industry at $300 million, versus only $90 million for the fishing industry. The ideological assumptions embedded in an assessment methodology that rates a hotel bed bringing in $200 a night as a greater loss than a fisherman bringing in $50 a month have far-reaching consequences. With reconstruction measures predicated on this kind of accounting, we are on a trajectory that empowers the tourism industry to be an even more dominant player than it was in the past, and, concomitantly, one that disempowers and further marginalizes the coastal poor.

Travel and Displacement

Much has been made of the unsightly fishing shanties that will not be rebuilt. Instead, fishing communities are going to be transformed into even more unsightly urban squalor, their residents crowded into "modern" apartment complexes like the sardines they may fish. However, this will be further inland. As they sit on the beach watching the ocean loll onto Lanka's shore, tourists will enjoy the coast in a sanitized, "consumer friendly" environment. Ironically, they may even be sitting in *cadjan* cabanas, a nostalgic nod to the *cadjan* homes of fishing communities of the past—a neatly consumable experience of the exotic without the interference of a more messy everyday.

But perhaps this *is* the new everyday that is proposed: the teeming hordes in designated settlements, a playground for tourists elsewhere. It's a product of the mercantile imagination—the imagination of tourist industry fat cats who will be raking in the tsunami windfall. With the building of planned superhighways, tourists will be able to zoom from airport to beach, shopping mall to spa, while the people who lived in these regions will become less mobile as they are shut out from entire stretches of coastal land. If tourism is about carefully planned displacement from the ordinary for a privileged few, the crossing of boundaries for recreation and adventure, here it is tied to the forced displacement of fishing communities and the instituting of new boundaries that exclude and dispossess. ❑

Article 8.3

THE GLOBAL OIL MARKET
How it operates, why it doesn't work, and who wants to keep it that way.

PAUL CUMMINGS
July/August 2008

Since the United States-led coalition invaded Iraq in March 2003, the price of a barrel of oil has just about quadrupled to around $135. With U.S. oil imports currently totaling 4.5 billion barrels a year, this translates into a staggering $600 billion annual oil bill. Many energy economists predict that oil prices could top $200 a barrel in the near future, particularly if U.S. opposition to Iran's nuclear enrichment program leads to a confrontation, either directly or through surrogate states.

Why are oil prices skyrocketing? Many economists and business analysts like to talk about "the fundamentals": supply (constrained) and demand (strong). They point to rapid economic growth in China and India driving demand. On the supply side, it's the OPEC cartel limiting production while tree-huggers in the United States block the development of new offshore and Alaskan oil supplies.

But other analysts claim the so-called fundamentals tell us little about why oil prices are rising rapidly. Recently the London *Times*'s economy and finance commentator, Anatole Kaletsky, noted that over the past nine months, as the price of oil has doubled, none of the basic determinants of supply or demand has changed much. China's demand growth is in fact slowing, as is the world's demand growth overall. Iraqi oil production is back up to prewar levels. Kaletsky views the current price spikes as symptoms of a classic financial bubble during which, typically, "prices end up bearing almost no relation to the balance of underlying supply and demand."

For now, the experts are displaying a remarkable lack of consensus on whether it's the actions of commodities traders and other financial-market movements or real supply and demand factors that explain the current oil price spike. In any case, the terms "supply" and "demand" are supposed to conjure up images of a free market. But the global oil market is anything but. Even leaving aside the role of financial markets in setting the price of oil, the supply of and demand for oil are heavily shaped by the actions of mammoth multinational oil companies and of governments in both the consuming and producing countries. And while the price of oil is rising fast, causing real pain to consumers, those extra dollars are going straight to the governments of the oil-rich countries and to the major oil companies—*not* to offset the tremendous costs that oil imposes, chiefly on the environment but in multiple other arenas as well.

Supply Management

From the very beginning of the modern oil industry, the supply of oil has been managed by powerful oil companies and the magnates who run them. The first was none other than John D. Rockefeller, who founded Standard Oil in 1870. By 1878 he had gained control of 90% of U.S. oil refining. In the 1880s Rockefeller used his strategic control of refining to build the first vertically integrated oil company, with oil fields, tankers, pipelines, refineries, and retail sales facilities under one corporate roof. By mercilessly undercutting competitors until they were near bankruptcy, and then buying them on the cheap, Standard Oil gained control of over half of the world's then-known oil supply. By the turn of the century Rockefeller had become the richest man in the world, with a fortune valued at around a billion dollars. Then, in 1911, the Supreme Court ruled that Standard Oil was a monopoly and, to create competition, split it into 34 companies, including Esso and Socony, which eventually became Exxon and Mobil, respectively.

Instead of competing, over the next 50 years Exxon, Mobil, and five other giant oil companies (the "majors") essentially formed a cartel. Leveraging their superior technology, production experience, and control of the retail market, the majors engaged in oil colonialism: they pumped and sold oil from a number of developing countries under highly favorable terms, earning vast profits.

In the 1950s, oil-rich countries began nationalizing their oil and training domestic oil technocracies to run the business. The advantages of collusion were no secret to them. In the 1960s Venezuela and Saudi Arabia organized OPEC (the Organization of Petroleum Exporting Countries), a cartel whose explicit purpose was to control the price of oil by regulating supply. By acting together, the oil-rich nations leveled the playing field with the majors and gained a larger share of oil profits.

With this context in mind, let's consider how oil gets to market today. Currently, around 75% of the world's oil is nationalized, managed by state-run oil companies that are monopolies in their own country. These state companies are often their country's largest employer, largest exporter, largest source of hard currency, and largest contributor to state revenue. State oil executives report to political authorities instead of a corporate board, and local political considerations can trump economic factors in their business decisions. For example, state oil companies may site new facilities in poorer communities to spur local economic development. More importantly, nationalized oil earns the money to pay for hospitals, schools, sanitation systems, and roads, projects rarely funded by Western oil corporations. The downside is that oil money all too frequently has been stolen by corrupt rulers or siphoned away to buy expensive weapons—Zaire's Mobutu Sese Seko and Iraq's Saddam Hussein were just two in a long line of oil-funded despots.

State oil ministers set oil production targets taking into consideration both economic and political factors, including current global economic performance, OPEC member production quotas, long-term contracts with oil corporations, International Monetary Fund debt repayment schedules, domestic revenue requirements, the desires of greedy and corrupt rulers, and the cost of oil extraction compared to oil's market price.

Of course, most of the state-owned oil across the globe lies within OPEC, whose policies fundamentally shape supply. The eleven member states of OPEC control over 50% of the world's oil. After both the 1973 Israeli-Arab war and the 1979 Islamic revolution in Iran, OPEC cut oil production, oil prices skyrocketed, cartel members earned hundreds of billions of dollars in windfall profits, and the world economy slid into recession.

Then, in the 1980s, a weak economy and more efficient cars cut oil demand, while newly discovered non-OPEC oil increased supply. OPEC tried to prop up plunging prices by cutting production. In particular, Saudi Arabia cut its output by nearly 8 million barrels per day. When other OPEC members began to cheat on their lower production quotas, the Saudis enforced market discipline by flooding the market with cheap oil, driving many suppliers out of business. With oil supply back under control, prices rose to around $20 a barrel, OPEC's market share was restored, and OPEC production quotas were honored. John D. Rockefeller would have applauded.

In 1990, the first "oil war" was launched when Iraq invaded Kuwait and seized its oil fields. With Iraqi troops poised to attack Saudi Arabia, a U.S.-led coalition drove the Iraqi army out of Kuwait. The Saudis once again demonstrated their market power by pumping enough additional oil to offset the loss of Kuwaiti and Iraqi oil production.

The cartel aims to keep the price of oil high, but it also seeks reasonable stability in the oil market. After all, the lion's share of the petrodollars that OPEC members earn are plowed back into the United States and the other wealthy consuming countries in the form of investments. If oil price volatility begins to damage the U.S. and other industrialized economies, those investments will likely suffer as well. But OPEC's ability to manage supply for the twin goals of profitability and stability is limited. In recent years conflicts in the Middle East, rapidly growing oil demand in China and India, and OPEC's own tendency to overshoot or undershoot planned production levels have all contributed to a more volatile oil market than OPEC perhaps intended.

The remaining 25% of global oil supply comes from fields owned by the majors or by Russia's ostensibly private energy giant Gazprom. This production is more responsive to market signals, but is still influenced by non-price factors such as government tax and environmental policies and Wall Street pressure to report high quarterly earnings.

Perhaps the clearest indicator that the supply of oil is managed and not a simple response to market signals is the curious fact that much of the oil that is brought to market is relatively expensive to produce because of high extraction costs (for instance, deep sea oil), transport costs (Alaskan oil), or refining costs (some of Africa's oil). At the same time, oil that could be brought to market far more cheaply—much of the oil in the Arabian Peninsula, for example—is left in the ground. Saudi oil costs just $1.50 per barrel to produce, while the average production cost of oil outside of the Middle East is $22 per barrel. In a free market, competition would cause the lowest-cost oil to be sold first, since cheap oil can undercut expensive oil. However, in the case of managed supply, producers of cheap oil can hold back their oil, allowing the market price to rise until it exceeds the production price of expensive oil. This means very high profits for the producers of cheap oil, while many energy analysts stimate that consumers are paying twice as much as they would if oil markets were free, Paul Roberts writes in *The End of Oil*.

Retail supplies are influenced by vertically integrated global oil delivery systems—pipelines, supertankers, refineries, delivery tanker trucks, assorted retail sales facilities—which are controlled by the Saudis, Venezuela, and the supermajors (the six largest private oil companies: ExxonMobil, Shell, BP, Chevron, ConocoPhillips, and Total S.A.). Every day 85 million barrels of oil flow to consumers around the world. The massive oil delivery systems are worth a combined $5 trillion dollars and create a large barrier to entry for alternative energy suppliers. Supply can be constrained for other reasons as well, for instance, environmental or other regulations that block expansion or construction of oil pipelines or refineries.

Occasionally a geopolitical or extreme weather event breaks the oil supply system and retail oil prices go through the roof, creating outrageous profits. For example, in the aftermath of Hurricane Katrina, U.S. gasoline prices doubled overnight. The oil industry denied using Katrina to fleece customers, but a 2006 investigation by the Federal Trade Commission found multiple examples of price gouging at the refining, wholesale, and retail levels. Coincidentally, in the last quarter of 2005, the accounting quarter following Katrina, ExxonMobil earned $9.9 billion, the largest quarterly profits ever reported by a U.S. company.

In 2007 oil prices were exploding along with much of Iraq. That year ExxonMobil earned $40.6 billion in profits on $400 billion in revenue, the highest yearly profit ever earned by a public corporation. Amazingly, even this record profit pales in comparison to the 2007 Saudi net oil revenue of $194 billion.

Captive Consumers

The demand for oil is no more a simple result of free-market forces than is the supply. To begin with, energy demand is not created directly by consumers: we do not desire gasoline the way we might desire a new house or a new pair of shoes. Instead, demand is "pulled" by the economy, whose mix of technologies and rate of growth determine how much energy, from oil and other sources, is required to power it. Oil heats tens of millions of homes, offices, and factories and powers 30% of the world's electric generation. Oil is also used as an input in the manufacture of petrochemicals such as plastics.

And, of course, oil moves mountains of raw materials, tons of finished goods, and billions of people every day. The world's armada of oil-fueled vehicles consists of nearly a billion cars, trucks, buses, tractors, bulldozers, ships and airplanes. The troubling reality is that this armada runs only on oil; there is no viable alternative fuel today, and oil companies intend to keep it that way.

Every year the armada grows, moving more people and more stuff over greater distances. Globalization has spread out the production and sales processes over ever-longer international supply chains. U.S. and Canadian commuters drive more and more miles as suburbanization moves home and work farther apart. And the average fuel efficiency of U.S. passenger vehicles *fell* by 5% during the past 20 years, due to aggressive marketing of SUVs and trucks.

Oil companies use their political clout to stop government efforts to increase fuel efficiency. Over the last 20 years, the oil industry has given $200 million to U.S. politicians, mostly Republicans, who believe in free markets but regularly give an invisible helping hand to the oil companies. During those same 20 years, oil lobbyists have rolled back gas mileage standards and created tax subsidies for buying eight-ton Hummers that inhale gas. Oil lobbyists have redirected funding from alternative energy technology to road and bridge repair.

Oil companies have also used their wealth and political power to crush electric powered transportation systems. In the 1920s city-dwellers commuted on electric trolleys, but oil and auto companies wanted to sell them buses and cars. Standard Oil, General Motors, Mack Truck, and Firestone Tire funded a dummy corporation, National City Lines (NCL), to replace trolleys with buses. It didn't matter if NCL lost money; its goal was to create demand for buses, cars, tires, and oil. If it could do so, its parent companies would make a fortune. By 1929 NCL had established its business model and when the Great Depression deepened, over 100 electric utility companies, located in most major cities, were forced to sell their trolley lines at a sharply discounted price to NCL, the only buyer with cash. Once NCL had control, the trolley systems were sold for scrap and within days a new fleet of buses arrived, followed by a tidal wave of cars. In the late 1940s, NCL had served its purpose and was failing. Government lawyers had been investigating NCL, and in 1949 they successfully prosecuted its parent companies for collusion to destroy the nation's trolley system. Each parent company paid a $5,000 fine, which wasn't too bad considering they had made on the order of $100 million in profits from NCL's illegal actions.

By 1990 the Los Angeles basin faced a serious public health problem due to smog from car exhaust. The state of California issued a mandate requiring car companies to develop a zero emission vehicle, or ZEV. Oil and automobile companies launched a full-fledged political campaign to overturn the ZEV mandate, including TV and magazine ads, direct mail, and thousands of calls from phone banks. The ZEV mandate was never enforced and, in 2003, was replaced with a minimal requirement that car companies sell a few gas-electric hybrid cars by 2008. That same year, in a remarkable episode chronicled in the 2006 documentary "Who Killed the Electric Car?," GM was taking back the hundreds of EV1 electric vehicles it had leased to U.S. drivers beginning in 1996. The carmaker assembled most of the EV1s at a site in Arizona where it proceeded to crush them—despite very positive feedback from EV1 lessees, many of whom wanted to purchase and keep the cars. Explanations for GM's decision to halt the EV1 program and destroy the cars vary.

GM says it determined the venture could never be profitable, in part because hoped-for breakthroughs in battery technology did not occur. One thing is certain: the car did become less marketable once California gave in to pressure from the oil and auto industries (including GM) and lifted the ZEV mandate.

In 1994 oil companies attacked Ballard Power Systems for developing a hydrogen fuel cell to power cars. With a game plan similar to the one they'd used to undermine the ZEV mandate, they took out ads decrying the fuel cell, challenged the company's veracity at trade conferences, and questioned its ability to actually bring a viable product to market. Oil companies pointed out that useable hydrogen was in short supply and an entirely new hydrogen refining, delivery, and fueling infrastructure would need to be built at the cost of many billions of dollars. As a result of these attacks Ballard backed off, and further development of its fuel cell was hidden in an internal R&D program for over a decade.

So the demand for oil is driven by economic and social trends far beyond the control of individual consumers, who are stuck, at least in the short term, paying whatever price the oil companies set if they want to fill their tanks and heat their homes.

Finally, it's impossible to get the whole picture of demand for oil without recognizing one very special oil consumer: the U.S. military. Every tank, armored vehicles, truck, humvee, jet, and missile runs on refined oil, as do most ships. In 2007, the U.S. military consumed about 250 million barrels of oil and 2.6 billion gallons of jet fuel, making it the world's single largest fuel-burning entity. Without oil the Army and Marines could not maneuver, the Air Force could not fly, and most of the Navy could not sail. The United States would be a paralyzed superpower, unable to project power throughout the world. Since all the other military forces in the world also run on oil, the ability to cut their oil lifelines is a tremendous strategic advantage in any conflict. These factors make oil more than just another commodity. Oil is a weapon, a strategic commodity, a national security resource; it is not just like wheat or widgets. By the same token, any shift in U.S. foreign policy that reduces the country's military engagements can also represent a sizeable drop in U.S. oil demand.

Multiple Market Failures

Today's global oil market is working well for the major oil companies, their managers, and their shareholders. It is also working well for the oil-producing countries, at least to the extent that they are garnering vast revenues. (Of course, the extent to which these revenues are benefiting ordinary people in the oil-rich countries varies dramatically.)

But the oil market is characterized by many kinds of market failure: the workings of the market are producing less-than-optimal results on multiple levels. For instance, oil price spikes can lead to "demand shocks" that suck money rapidly out of the economies of the oil-importing nations. If the global financial system cannot get this money re-invested and generating demand quickly, the result can be a drop in global demand followed by an economic downturn. According to energy economist Philip Verleger, over the last 50 years there have been six major oil price spikes, each causing economic losses that have totaled more than $1 trillion. Verleger posits that a 20% increase in the price of a barrel of oil results in a 0.5% decline in global economic growth. Based on that formula, the current $100 spike in the price of oil, if sustained, could wind up causing a reversal in the global economy from a baseline of 2% growth to a 1% contraction.

By and large, Americans have benefited from the fact that the price of oil worldwide is denominated in dollars rather than another currency. Right now, though, the falling value of the dollar against other major currencies is one factor pushing up the price of oil in the United States. Moreover, not only can fluctuations in the value of the dollar affect oil prices; oil market shifts can affect the value of the dollar. Hence, a second type of market failure in the global oil market is the increased "risk premium" that attaches to a whole range of financial transactions when a build-up of petrodollars makes the financial markets worry about an increased risk of either a devaluation of the dollar or a run on the dollar. In both cases the U.S. Federal Reserve may not be able to successfully intervene because trillions of petrodollars are outside of the Fed's control. In general, increased risk is bad for the economy and leads to higher interest rates and slower economic growth.

A third group of oil market failures are environmental. Oil is a dirty business that pollutes the air, water, and earth, often in health-threatening ways. Take oil spills for example. In Ecuador a pipeline runs over the Andes, connecting Ecuador's eastern jungle oil fields to its Pacific coast refinery. When earthquakes or landslides break the pipeline, all the oil between the break and the shut-off valve simply pours out, contaminating a broad swath of the mountain below.

Six thousand miles to the north, Exxon's supertanker, the Valdez, struck Bligh Reef on March 24, 1989, spilling 11 million gallons of oil into Prince William Sound. The oil contaminated 1,500 miles of Alaskan shoreline; nearly 20 years later, local economies dependent on fishing and tourism have still not entirely recovered. There are thousands of similar cases all over the planet.

The mother of all oil market failures is climate change. When oil is converted to energy, it gives off CO_2 which traps heat in the atmosphere and, in large quantity, can alter the climate. The result is a global, cumulative, and intergenerational problem that an increasing number of climate scientists fear may become a crisis of biblical proportions: higher sea levels flooding coastal cities around the globe; droughts, heat waves, pests, and more frequent extreme weather events affecting food supplies and human health.

No matter where CO_2 originates, it spreads quickly through-out the entire atmosphere, and so makes the problem a global one. The longevity of atmospheric CO_2 creates a cumulative problem. Since 1850, our species has dumped so much carbon into the sky that atmospheric CO_2 levels are at their highest point in a million years. That is 500,000,000,000,000 pounds of carbon stuck in the sky, as if the atmosphere were an open sewer! And that longevity makes the problem intergenerational:

it will take the earth 16 generations (400 years) to reabsorb 80% of the CO_2 we emit today, and the remaining 20% will stay in the sky for thousands of years.

Solving climate change begins by realizing that the oil market doesn't have to be managed for the benefit of a small number of extremely rich people. We must also put to rest the canard that oil resources are best allocated by the free market's "invisible hand." Columbia University economist Joseph Stiglitz points out, "the reason that the hand may be invisible is that it is simply not there—or at least that if is there, it is palsied." The public needs to fight to remove the control of oil pricing from the oil corporations and establish an oil market that is more fair and sustainable.

In a sustainable energy market, the price of gasoline and other fossil fuel products should reflect the real costs these energy sources impose—above all, on the environment. That means prices that are higher than what Americans are accustomed to. But a progressive oil agenda would include recapturing that additional revenue and using it to compensate low-income consumers and, especially, to move the economy toward one based on renewable energy. Paying that extra dollar or more a gallon at the pump would feel very different if U.S. consumers knew the money was being spent not to line the pockets of dictators and oil executives, but instead to offset the extra cost for low-income families and, especially, to generously fund myriad projects to put the economy on a green-energy path. ❑

Sources: Sohbet Karbuz, "US military energy consumption: facts and figures," *Energy Bulletin*, May 20, 2007; Chalmers Johnson, "The Arithmetic of America's Military Bases Abroad: What Does It All Add Up To?" www.tomdispatch.com, 2004; OPEC, "World Oil Outlook 2007"; Paul Roberts, *The End of Oil* (Houghton Mifflin, 2005); U.S. Federal Trade Comm., "Investigation of Gasoline Price Manipulation and Post-Katrina Gasoline Price Increases: Report to Congress" (Spring 2006); Eric Noe, "For Oil Giants, Pricey Gas Means Big Profits," ABC News, Jan. 25, 2006; Steven Mufson, "ExxonMobil's Profit in 2007 Tops $40 Billion," *Washington Post*, Feb. 2, 2008; U.S. Energy Information Admin., "OPEC Oil Export Revenues 2007"; Michael Renner, "Five Hundred Million Cars, One Planet—Who's Going to Give?" (Worldwatch Institute, August 2003); Daniel Engber, "How Gasoline Becomes CO2: A gallon turns into 19 pounds?" Slate.com, Nov. 1, 2006; Matthew Kahn, "The Environmental Impact of Suburbanization," *Jrnl of Policy Analysis and Mgmt* 19:4 (Fall 2000); Philip Verleger, "A Collaborative Policy to Neutralize the Economic Impact of Energy Price Fluctuations," Policy paper, June 10, 2003; "The Real Price of Gasoline: An Analysis of the Hidden External Costs Consumers Pay to Fuel Their Automobiles," Int'l Ctr for Technology Assessment, 1998; Joseph Stiglitz, *Making Globalization Work* (W.W. Norton, 2006); Laura Peterson, "Big Oil Wields Ultra Deep Influence," Ctr for Public Integrity, Dec. 2004.

Article 8.4

EVO MORALES' LITHIUM GAMBLE

*Investment in production of a high-tech mineral
could bring about a monumental shift in Bolivia's economy.*

BY ELISSA DENNIS
March/April 2011

> "The industrialization of a raw material is wealth, is dignity, and is sovereignty."
> —*message scrolling along the top of the website of the "Evaporates
> Division" of the Bolivian state mining company COMIBOL (Corporación
> Minera de Bolivia)*

Aspiring to turn the slogan above into reality, president Evo Morales announced last fall that Bolivia will invest $900 million over the next four years in the extraction and industrialization of lithium. The mineral, in growing global demand to produce rechargeable batteries for cell phones, laptops, and especially electric cars, could be the key to the impoverished South American nation's conversion from its centuries-old role as exporter of raw materials to industrialized provider of technology for the 21st century.

While estimates vary dramatically, all agree that the Salar de Uyuni, located in the desolate, harshly cold, 12,000-foot high plateau of Southwest Bolivia, is home to the world's largest reserve of lithium. The Salar is a 3,860-square-mile expanse of white glistening salt, extending down an average of 400 feet beneath the thick crusty surface with alternating layers of mud and brine, a mineral cocktail of magnesium, boron, potassium, and lithium.

In December, Bolivian workers began pumping brine into the first evaporation pool at a pilot plant on the edge of the salt flats, the first tiny step in an ambitious project that would have Bolivia processing and selling 33,000 tons per year of lithium carbonate by 2014. That's about 25% of current world consumption, enough to manufacture batteries for more than seven million of the new all-electric Nissan Leaf. The evaporation process will also produce an annual 770,000 tons of potassium chloride, a key ingredient in fertilizers.

The four-year plan calls for COMIBOL to begin transforming lithium carbonate into batteries for sale on the world market by 2014. That level of industrialization would represent an enormous leap of sophistication for this resource-rich but technology-poor nation. The goal is even more stunning considering that the Morales government is shunning the stream of governmental and corporate suitors from Japan, France, and Korea who have toured the salt flats and signed memoranda of understanding to jointly develop projects for lithium extraction and industrialization. They wanted to just buy the lithium carbonate and take the battery production out of Bolivia, Morales claimed. The "100% state strategy" is designed to keep control of the process and profits from the value-added products in Bolivian hands.

"Bolivia is moving decisively, with much dignity, to change its condition as exporter of raw material to developed countries," Luís Alberto Echazú Alvarado, COMIBOL's national manager of evaporate resources comments by e-mail. "Unlike past eras with neoliberal governments, President Evo Morales has made the decision to industrialize the evaporate resources and add value to our raw materials."

Morales has left the door open a crack for foreign investment, only for the battery technology phase, and only so long as the foreigners collaborate as "partners, not masters," ("*socios, no patrones*") a phrase the president has stressed continuously since his December 2009 landslide re-election, and a distinction that would mark a monumental shift in Bolivia's relationship with the industrialized world.

Magical Metal

Lithium, the lightest metal, has long been used in glass and ceramics, as well as in mood-stabilizing drugs. In recent years, it has garnered significant attention as an excellent material for rechargeable batteries because of its light weight and efficiency in holding a charge. As cell phones, laptops, and a multitude of small electronic devices have proliferated throughout the world, annual lithium production has tripled in the last decade to approximately 132,000 tons of lithium carbonate per year.

But an even bigger boom is on the way. The first 300 Chevy Volts hit U.S. streets in late 2010, grabbing the title of 2011 Motor Trend Car of the Year, with an electric battery powering your first 35 miles and a gas-fueled generator kicking in to keep you on the road for 375 miles. The Leaf—an all-electric vehicle with a range of 100 miles between charges—is coming to a Nissan dealership near you this spring. While previous hybrid cars, like Toyota's popular Prius, use a nickel metal hydride battery, the new generation uses a battery pack made from the lighter, longer-charging lithium carbonate.

Industry producers and analysts see the market for lithium poised to increase by a factor of three, five, or even ten in the next decade, predicting that anywhere from two million to ten million electric vehicles will be cruising the world's highways by 2020. Carmakers in South Korea, Japan, Germany, China, and the United States are spending millions of dollars in the race to enter the market. In the largest single investment in advanced battery technology for hybrid and electric cars ever, the U.S. Department of Energy funded $2.4 billion in grants as part of the 2009 American Recovery and Reinvestment Act to boost U.S. manufacturing capacity for batteries and drive components for electric vehicles.

Raid of Resources

The Salar de Uyuni and the barren wind-swept region around it are remote, yet startlingly entrenched in the global economy. Despite the glistening sparkle of the salt surface and the rich mineral soup below, the Salar currently provides only a meager living to the communities living along its shorelines. In Colchani, on the eastern edge of the salt flat, families scrape at the surface salt with hand shovels and picks, forming three-foot high cones of salt that they transport to their back yards. There they dry it, sprinkle in an iodine powder, and seal it into half-kilogram plastic bags, which they sell whenever a truck comes by to purchase the packages for sale in the national market. Meanwhile, they sell little salt llama figurines and ash trays to tourists on Salar jeep tours.

South of the Salar, along dirt and sand tracks which lead eventually to the Chilean and Argentinian borders, the stark landscape is dotted with tiny mines of lead, tin, and sulfur, each encircled by one or two dozen simple dwellings occupied by desperately poor indigenous Aymara people who work whenever a mine owner decides the mineral's price on the global market merits use of a labor force. Some graze small herds of llamas or grow patches of quinoa. To the west, a sliver of the Atacama Desert, which provides a significant share of the world's current lithium supply, sits between Uyuni and the Pacific Ocean, a painful reminder of the commercially critical sea access Bolivia lost to Chile in the 1880s War of the Pacific.

Strikingly, less than 200 miles to the east of the Salar sits the Cerro Rico of Potosí, the most potent symbol of the exploitation of Latin America's resources to fuel European growth. In the three centuries following the discovery of silver in the "rich hill," at least 8 million indigenous and African slave workers died in its mines. Today, the silver is long gone and the destitute families left behind scrape out a living on the specks of tin, lead, and zinc they find dozens of feet underground. Tourism is the industry in Potosí now; you can get dressed in miner's gear, get yourself a green plastic bag of coca leaves, and crawl down into the stifling mine to deliver dynamite sticks as gifts to the real miners.

Tin took over from silver as the mainstay of the Bolivian economy from roughly the 1880s until prices fell in the 1980s. Today, the nation's economic engine is natural gas, found in the Eastern lowlands of the country primarily populated by a wealthier and lighter-skinned group who have battled with the Morales government over regional allocations of gas profits and most recently the partial re-nationalization of the industry (see "Turning Gas into Development in Bolivia," *Dollars & Sense*, November/December 2006). In 2008, leaders of the natural gas region threatened to secede from the country; amid roadblocks and violence, Morales expelled U.S. Ambassador Philip Goldberg, whose support for the secession movement Morales felt threatened the autonomy of his government.

New Politics, New Economics

A former coca farmer of indigenous Aymara heritage, Evo Morales was swept into power in 2006 on a wave of grassroots protests against the neoliberal policies of previous presidents, whose IMF-dictated structural adjustments led to privatizations and layoffs. In the 2000 "water wars" of Cochabamba, the community successfully defeated efforts by Bechtel to take over its municipal water system and hike water prices by 275%. Two years later the "gas wars" erupted in El Alto, a city of 1 million on the outskirts of La Paz which emerged over the last 30 years as unemployed poor people poured into the capital from previously viable agricultural or mining regions. Street blockades protesting the profit levels of recently privatized companies exporting natural gas through Chile, and calling for the re-nationalization of the gas industry, garnered international attention.

It is in this context of the last decade, as well as the last five centuries, that the confluence of market demand for lithium, the geographic location of the metal in the poor indigenous southwest, and Morales' insistence on going it alone could dramatically transform long-established economic and social power structures. Morales has made it clear that unlike his predecessors, he is not looking for multinational corporations to extract the nation's riches for their own profits and the profits of a small Bolivian elite. Rather, he is seeking a revolutionary transformation of the Bolivian economy to enrich the Bolivian people, especially the indigenous majority who have been most oppressed by past policies.

With a little luck from consistently high natural gas prices, Bolivia has made significant economic progress during the Morales administration. The Bolivian economy grew 3.4% in 2009, the highest rate in South America, with an estimated 4% growth rate in 2010. Higher taxes in the restructured natural gas industry and some redirecting of revenues from regional governments to the federal level have facilitated a popular senior citizen grant and a plethora of social programs. Even the IMF gave kudos to the Morales government for its stabilizing monetary policy, which enabled the government to create comfortable reserves (the government registered a surplus for five straight years) while also expanding the social safety net.

These are enormous successes for the poorest country on the South American continent to build on. But development of large-scale extraction and processing of a new commodity in a region lacking infrastructure, without outside assistance, is a much bigger step. Selecting a rapidly evolving new technology for that first foray into industrialization is a tremendous gamble.

Ready or Not

Bolivia "is a country that doesn't have a single factory that is capable of assembling, from scratch, a TV, telephone, or radio," note the authors of a 2010 report on lithium by the Cochabamba-based Democracy Center. They point out that battery fabrication requires access to input industries like chemical plants to supply the plastics and metal alloys; either the Bolivians would have to create that infrastructure in Bolivia or import the products, either way adding significant complexity and cost. The report's authors suggest that Bolivia might be better off with the "middle ground" of developing simpler lithium batteries for already-established and steadily growing markets such as watches, cell phones, iPods, laptops, and other electronics.

That approach may not have as big an upside potential as the electric car market, but it would be much easier to implement and could serve a growing domestic market.

Juan Carlos Zuleta, a U.S.-trained economist based in Bolivia who has written extensively about lithium, has positioned himself as one of the most vocal critics of the Morales government's plan. He argues that Bolivia does not have the technology to extract and industrialize lithium or the capacity to develop it; by shunning foreign investment, Bolivia is at risk of moving too slowly. "There is no reason to believe that the market will wait for Bolivia," he noted in an e-mail interview. As electric cars are evolving, so are other technologies like zinc-air batteries, methanol and hydrogen; by 2015, when Bolivia says they'll be at full production levels, "the world might have evolved in another direction," he says. "Look for example at China, Taiwan, South Korea, Singapore, and Hong Kong. They are all countries that have developed from strategic partnerships with companies that own technologies. Here the government wants to reinvent the wheel and this is going to take a lot of time."

Zuleta suggests that it would be more efficient for the government to operate with "service contracts" similar to the relationships it has with private oil companies, ensuring that Bolivia is in charge of commercialization and industrialization. Or it could partner with one or two specialized foreign companies to explore and extract jointly, making sure that the partners agree to transfer the technology so that after 10 or 15 years Bolivia could take complete control, with the foreign company as a client for lithium carbonate and the other extracted minerals.

In a series of opinion pieces in the Bolivian press in late 2010, COMIBOL's Echazú refers to critics as "neoliberals" who resent government efforts to eliminate private investment and prevent the looting of Bolivia's natural resources. He dismisses Zuleta's concern about timing, noting that proposals from foreign companies for joint development of the Salar had even longer timelines than COMIBOL's development strategy.

COMIBOL says the research stage is complete, they have patents for extraction technology, and their "100% state" plan is underway. Yet observers note there are issues that have not been fully explored. There are questions of environmental impact, particularly around water usage; drought has already forced some local residents to give up their efforts to grow quinoa or graze llamas. There is also some evidence of toxic contamination in lithium-extracting regions of Chile and Argentina.

COMIBOL's promotional materials offer vague responses to these concerns, saying their process will be environmentally safe and won't drain the region's water supply. "Every project or venture must be developed in harmony with the environment," Echazú responds. "We abide by all the national legislation in this area and we have the permits for our operation."

The new Bolivian Constitution, in addition to strengthening environmental standards, requires consultations with local indigenous communities prior to embarking on a project like this one. So far those "consultas" have produced diverse responses; people are desperate for jobs and for economic activity that benefits the region, but they have been burned many times before by large-scale extractive projects.

The government plan has the support of a local campesino federation which defeated a U.S. company's proposal to extract lithium from the Salar in 1992. But the politics are complex. For 10 days this past April, local residents blocked a railroad between Chile and the San Cristóbal mine, a large open pit zinc and silver mine just southwest of the Salar, which the Japanese corporation Sumitomo took over from a U.S. company in 2009. Residents protested the mine's excessive water usage and mine owners' unkept promises about infrastructure improvements such as roads and electricity upgrades. The protest coincided with an international climate conference in Cochabamba, Morales' high-profile effort to create a progressive alternative to failed talks in Copenhagen the previous winter. Thus these protesters demonstrated not just their animosity to foreign enterprises, but also a willingness to embarrass the president for espousing environmental rhetoric while not regulating abuses in his own back yard.

COMIBOL insists that Bolivia holds 110 million tons of lithium, enough to supply the world for the next 5,000 years. The U.S. Geological Survey acknowledges that Bolivia has the largest lithium reserves worldwide, but with a more modest estimate of 9.9 million tons. Whether or not COMIBOL's claims are exaggerated, supporters and detractors agree that Bolivia's lithium is critical to the future of the rechargeable battery. There will be electric cars without Bolivia's participation, Zuleta predicts, but "it is highly unlikely that there will be an electric car *era*." The opportunity for Bolivia's 10 million people is enormous, and the next couple of years will show whether Morales' gamble is a brilliant strategy or devastating folly. ❏

Sources: Evo Morales Ayma, "Estrategia Nacional de Industrialización de los Recursos Evaporíticos de Bolivia," press conference, October 21, 2010 (evaporiticosbolivia.org); Rebecca Hollender and Jim Shultz, "Bolivia and Its Lithium," a Democracy Center Special Report, May 2010 (democracyctr.org); U.S. Geological Survey, "Lithium," Mineral Commodity Summaries, January 2010 (minerals.usgs.gov); International Monetary Fund, "IMF Executive Board Concludes 2009 Article IV Consultation with Bolivia," Public Information Notice No. 10/09, January 21, 2010 (imf.org).

Article 8.5

CLIMATE ECONOMICS IN FOUR EASY PIECES

Conventional cost-benefit models cannot inform our decisions about how to address the threat of climate change.

FRANK ACKERMAN

November/December 2008

O nce upon a time, debates about climate policy were primarily about the science. An inordinate amount of attention was focused on the handful of "climate skeptics" who challenged the scientific understanding of climate change. The influence of the skeptics, however, is rapidly fading; few people were swayed by their arguments, and doubt about the major results of climate science is no longer important in shaping public policy.

As the climate *science* debate is reaching closure, the climate *economics* debate is heating up. The controversial issue now is the fear that overly ambitious climate initiatives could hurt the economy. Mainstream economists emphasizing that fear have, in effect, replaced the climate skeptics as the intellectual enablers of inaction.

For example, William Nordhaus, the U.S. economist best known for his work on climate change, pays lip service to scientists' calls for decisive action. He finds, however, that the "optimal" policy is a very small carbon tax that would reduce greenhouse gas emissions only 25% below "business-as-usual" levels by 2050—that would, in other words, allow emissions to rise well above current levels by mid-century. Richard Tol, a European economist who has written widely on climate change, favors an even smaller carbon tax of just $2 per ton of carbon dioxide. That would amount to all of $0.02 per gallon of gasoline, a microscopic "incentive" for change that consumers would never notice.

There are other voices in the climate economics debate; in particular, the British government's Stern Review offers a different perspective. Economist Nicholas Stern's analysis is much less wrong than the traditional Nordhaus-Tol approach, but even Stern has not challenged the conventional view enough.

What will it take to build a better economics of climate change, one that is consistent with the urgency expressed by the latest climate science? The issues that matter are big, non-technical principles, capable of being expressed in bumper-sticker format. Here are the four bumper stickers for a better climate economics:

- Our grandchildren's lives are important
- We need to buy insurance for the planet
- Climate damages are too valuable to have prices
- Some costs are better than others

1. Our grandchildren's lives are important.

The most widely debated challenge of climate economics is the valuation of the very long run. For ordinary loans and investments, both the costs today and the resulting future benefits typically occur within a single lifetime. In such cases, it makes sense to think in terms of the same person experiencing and comparing the costs and the benefits.

In the case of climate change, the time spans involved are well beyond those encountered in most areas of economics. The most important consequences of today's choices will be felt by generations to come, long after all of us making those choices have passed away. As a result, the costs of reducing emissions today and the benefits in the far future will not be experienced by the same people. The economics of climate change is centrally concerned with our relationship to our descendants whom we will never meet. As a bridge to that unknowable future, consider our grandchildren—the last generation most of us will ever know.

Suppose that you want your grandchildren to receive $100 (in today's dollars, corrected for inflation), 60 years from now. How much would you have to put in a bank account today, to ensure that the $100 will be there 60 years from now? The answer is $55 at 1% interest, or just over $5 at 5%.

In parallel fashion, economists routinely deal with future costs and benefits by "discounting" them, or converting them to "present values"—a process that is simply compound interest in reverse. In the standard jargon, the *present value* of $100, to be received 60 years from now, is $55 at a 1% *discount rate*, or about $5 at a 5% discount rate. As this example shows, a higher discount rate implies a smaller present value.

The central problem of climate economics, in a cost-benefit framework, is deciding how much to spend today on preventing future harms. What should we spend to prevent $100 of climate damages 60 years from now? The standard answer is, no more than the present value of that future loss: $55 at a discount rate of 1%, or $5 at 5%. The higher the discount rate, the less it is "worth" spending today on protecting our grandchildren.

The effect of a change in the discount rate becomes much more pronounced as the time period lengthens. Damages of $1 million occurring 200 years from now have a present value of only about $60 at a 5% discount rate, versus more than $130,000 at a 1% discount rate. The choice of the discount rate is all-important to our stance toward the far future: should we spend as much as $130,000, or as little as $60, to avoid one million dollars of climate damages in the early twenty-third century?

For financial transactions within a single lifetime, it makes sense to use market interest rates as the discount rate. Climate change, however, involves public policy decisions with impacts spanning centuries; there is no market in which public resources are traded from one century to the next. The choice of an intergenerational discount rate is a matter of ethics and policy, not a market-determined result.

Economists commonly identify two separate aspects of long-term discounting, each contributing to the discount rate.

One component of the discount rate is based on the assumption of an upward trend in income and wealth. If future generations will be richer than we are, they will need less help from us, and they will get less benefit from an additional dollar of income than we do. So we can discount benefits that will flow to our wealthier descendants, at a rate based on the expected growth of per capita incomes. Among economists, the income-related motive for discounting may be the least controversial part of the picture.

Setting aside changes in per capita income from one generation to the next, there may still be a reason to discount a sum many years in the future. This component of the discount rate, known as "pure time preference," is the subject of longstanding ethical, philosophical, and economic debate. On the one hand, there are reasons to think that pure time preference is greater than zero: both psychological experiments and common sense suggest that people are impatient, and prefer money now to money later. On the other hand, a pure time preference of zero expresses the equal worth of people of all generations, and the equal importance of reducing climate impacts and other burdens on them (assuming that all generations have equal incomes).

The Stern Review provides an excellent discussion of the debate, explaining Stern's assumption of pure time preference close to zero and an overall discount rate of 1.4%. This discount rate alone is sufficient to explain Stern's support for a substantial program of climate protection: at the higher discount rates used in more traditional analyses, the Stern program would look "inefficient," since the costs would outweigh the present value of the benefits.

2. We need to buy insurance for the planet.

Does climate science predict that things are certain to get worse? Or does it tell us that we are uncertain about what will happen next? Unfortunately, the answer seems to be yes to both questions. For example, the most likely level of sea level rise in this century, according to the latest Intergovernmental Panel on Climate Change reports, is no more than one meter or so—a real threat to low-lying coastal areas and islands that will face increasing storm damages, but survivable, with some adaptation efforts, for most of the world. On the other hand, there is a worst-case risk of an abrupt loss of the Greenland ice sheet, or perhaps of a large portion of the West Antarctic ice sheet. Either one could cause an eventual seven-meter rise in sea level—a catastrophic impact on coastal communities, economic activity, and infrastructure everywhere, and well beyond the range of plausible adaptation efforts in most places.

The evaluation of climate damages thus depends on whether we focus on the most likely outcomes or the credible worst-case risks; the latter, of course, are much larger.

Cost-benefit analysis conventionally rests on average or expected outcomes. But this is not the only way that people make decisions. When faced with uncertain, potentially large risks, people do not normally act on the basis of average outcomes; instead, they typically focus on protection against worst-case scenarios. When you go to the airport, do you leave just enough time for the average traffic delay (so that you would catch your plane, on average, half of the time)? Or do you allow time for some estimate of worst-case traffic jams? Once you get there, of course, you will experience additional delays due to security, which is all about worst cases: your *average* fellow passenger is not a threat to anyone's safety.

The very existence of the insurance industry is evidence of the desire to avoid or control worst-case scenarios. It is impossible for an insurance company to pay out in claims as much as its customers pay in premiums; if it did, there would be no money left to pay the costs of running the company, or the profits received by its owners. People who buy insurance are therefore guaranteed to get back less than they, on average, have paid; they (we) are paying for the security that insurance provides in case the worst should happen. This way of thinking does not apply to every decision: in casino games, people make bets based on averages and probabilities, and no one has any insurance against losing the next round. But life is not a casino, and public policy should not be a gamble.

Should climate policy be based on the most likely outcomes, or on the worst-case risks? Should we be investing in climate protection as if we expect sea level rise of one meter, or as if we are buying insurance to be sure of preventing a seven-meters rise?

In fact, the worst-case climate risks are even more unknown than the individual risks of fire and death that motivate insurance purchases. You do not know whether or not you will have a fire next year or die before the year is over, but you have very good information about the likelihood of these tragic events. So does the insurance industry, which is why they are willing to insure you. In contrast, there is no body of statistical information about the probability of Greenland-sized ice sheets collapsing at various temperatures; it's not an experiment that anyone can perform over and over again.

A recent analysis by Martin Weitzman argues that the probabilities of the worst outcomes are inescapably unknowable—and this deep uncertainty is more important than anything we do know in motivating concern about climate change. There is a technical sense in which the expected value of future climate damages can be infinite because we know so little about the probability of the worst, most damaging possibilities. The practical implication of infinite expected damages is that the most likely outcome is irrelevant; what matters is buying insurance for the planet, i.e., doing our best to understand and prevent the worst-case risks.

3. Climate damages are too valuable to have prices.

To decide whether climate protection is worthwhile, in cost-benefit terms, we would need to know the monetary value of everything important that is being protected.

Even if we could price everything affected by climate change, the prices would conceal a critical form of international inequity. The emissions that cause climate change have come predominantly from rich countries, while the damages will be felt first and worst in some of the world's poorest, tropical countries (although no one will be immune from harm for long). There are, however, no meaningful prices for many of the benefits of health and environmental protection. What is the dollar value of a human life saved? How much is it worth to save an endangered species from extinction, or to preserve a unique location or ecosystem? Economists have made up price tags for such priceless values, but the results do not always pass the laugh test.

Is a human life worth $6.1 million, as estimated by the Clinton administration, based on small differences in the wages paid for more and less risky jobs? Or is it worth $3.7 million, as the (second) Bush administration concluded on the basis of questionnaires about people's willingness to pay for reducing small, hypothetical risks? Are lives of people in rich countries worth much more than those in poor countries, as some economists infamously argued in the IPCC's 1995 report? Can the value of an endangered species be determined by survey research on how much people would pay to protect it? If, as one study found, the U.S. population as a whole would pay $18 billion to protect the existence of humpback whales, would it be acceptable for someone to pay $36 billion for the right to hunt and kill the entire species?

The only sensible response to such nonsensical questions is that there are many crucially important values that do not have meaningful prices. This is not a new idea: as the eighteenth-century philosopher Immanuel Kant put it, some things have a price, or relative worth, while other things have a dignity, or inner worth. No price tag does justice to the dignity of human life or the natural world.

Since some of the most important benefits of climate protection are priceless, any monetary value for total benefits will necessarily be incomplete. The corollary is that preventive action may be justified even in the absence of a complete monetary measure of the benefits of doing so.

Average Risks or Worst-Case Scenarios?

You don't have to look far to find situations in which the sensible policy is to address worst-case outcomes rather than average outcomes. The annual number of residential fires in the United States is about 0.4% of the number of housing units. This means that a fire occurs, on average, about once every 250 years in each home—not even close to once per lifetime. By far the most likely number of fires a homeowner will experience next year, or even in a lifetime, is zero. Why don't these statistics inspire you to cancel your fire insurance? Unless you are extremely wealthy, the loss of your home in a fire would be a devastating financial blow; despite the low probability, you cannot afford to take any chances on it.

What are the chances of the ultimate loss? The probability that you will die next year is under 0.1% if you are in your twenties, under 0.2% in your thirties, under 0.4% in your forties. It is not until age 61 that you have as much as a 1% chance of death within the coming year. Yet most U.S. families with dependent children buy life insurance. Without it, the risk to children of losing their parents' income would be too great—even though the parents are, on average, extraordinarily likely to survive.

4. Some costs are better than others.

The language of cost-benefit analysis embodies a clear normative slant: benefits are good, costs are bad. The goal is always to have larger benefits and smaller costs. In some respects, measurement and monetary valuation are easier for costs than for benefits: implementing pollution control measures typically involves changes in such areas as manufacturing, construction, and fuel use, all of which have well-defined prices. Yet conventional economic theory distorts the interpretation of costs in ways that exaggerate the burdens of environmental protection and hide the positive features of some of the "costs."

For instance, empirical studies of energy use and carbon emissions repeatedly find significant opportunities for emissions reduction at zero or negative net cost—the so-called "no regrets" options.

According to a long-standing tradition in economic theory, however, cost-free energy savings are impossible. The textbook theory of competitive markets assumes that every resource is productively employed in its most valuable use—in other words, that every no-regrets option must already have been taken. As the saying goes, there are no free lunches; there cannot be any $20 bills on the sidewalk because someone would have picked them up already. Any new emissions reduction measures, then, must have positive costs. This leads to greater estimates of climate policy costs than the bottom-up studies that reveal extensive opportunities for costless savings.

In the medium term, we will need to move beyond the no-regrets options; how much will it cost to finish the job of climate protection? Again, there are rival interpretations of the costs based on rival assumptions about the economy. The same economic theory that proclaimed the absence of $20 bills on the sidewalk is responsible for the idea that all costs are bad. Since the free market lets everyone spend their money in whatever way they choose, any new cost must represent a loss: it leaves people with less to spend on whatever purchases they had previously selected to maximize their satisfaction in life. Climate damages are one source of loss, and spending on climate protection is another; both reduce the resources available for the desirable things in life.

But are the two kinds of costs really comparable? Is it really a matter of indifference whether we spend $1 billion on bigger and better levees or lose $1 billion to storm damages? In the real-world economy, money spent on building levees creates jobs and incomes. The construction workers buy groceries, clothing, and so on, indirectly creating other jobs. With more people working, tax revenues increase while unemployment compensation payments decrease.

None of this happens if the levees are not built and the storm damages are allowed to occur. The costs of prevention are good costs, with numerous indirect benefits; the costs of climate damages are bad costs, representing pure physical destruction. One worthwhile goal is to keep total costs as low as possible; another is to have as much as possible of good costs rather than bad costs. Think of it as the cholesterol theory of climate costs.

In the long run, the deep reductions in carbon emissions needed for climate stabilization will require new technologies that have not yet been invented, or at best exist only in small, expensive prototypes. How much will it cost to invent, develop, and implement the low-carbon technologies of the future?

Lacking a rigorous theory of innovation, economists modeling climate change have often assumed that new technologies simply appear, making the economy inexorably more efficient over time. A more realistic view observes that the costs of producing a new product typically decline as industry gains more experience with it, in a pattern called "learning by doing" or the "learning curve" effect. Public investment is often necessary to support the innovation process in its early, expensive stages. Wind power is now relatively cheap and competitive, in suitable locations; this is a direct result of decades of public investment in the United States and Europe, starting when wind turbines were still quite expensive. The costs of climate policy, in the long run, will include doing the same for other promising new technologies, investing public resources in jump-starting a set of slightly different industries than we might have chosen in the absence of climate change. If this is a cost, many communities would be better off with more of it.

A widely publicized, conventional economic analysis recommends inaction on climate change, claiming that the costs currently outweigh the benefits for anything more than the smallest steps toward reducing carbon emissions. Put our "four easy pieces" together, and we have the outline of an economics that complements the science of climate change and endorses active, large-scale climate protection.

How realistic is it to expect that the world will shake off its inertia and act boldly and rapidly enough to make a difference? This may be the last generation that will have a real chance at protecting the earth's climate. Projections from the latest IPCC reports, the Stern Review, and other sources suggest that it is still possible to save the planet—if we start at once. ❑

Sources: Frank Ackerman, *Can We Afford the Future? Economics for a Warming World*, Zed Books, 2008; Frank Ackerman, *Poisoned for Pennies: The Economics of Toxics and Precaution*, Island Press, 2008; Frank Ackerman and Lisa Heinzerling, *Priceless: On Knowing the Price of Everything and the Value of Nothing*, The New Press, 2004; J. Creyts, A. Derkach, S. Nyquist, K. Ostrowski and J. Stephenson, *Reducing U.S. Greenhouse Gas Emissions: How Much at What Cost?*, McKinsey & Co., 2007; P.-A. Enkvist, T. Naucler and J. Rosander, "A Cost Curve for Greenhouse Gas Reduction," *The McKinsey Quarterly*, 2007; Immanuel Kant, *Groundwork for the Metaphysics of Morals*, translated by Thomas K. Abbot, with revisions by Lara Denis, Broadview Press, 2005 [1785]; B. Lomborg, *Cool It: The Skeptical Environmentalist's Guide to Global Warming*, Alfred A. Knopf, 2007; W.D. Nordhaus, *A Question of Balance: Economic Modeling of Global Warming*, Yale University Press, 2008; F.P. Ramsey, "A mathematical theory of saving," *The Economic Journal* 138(152): 543-59, 1928; Nicholas Stern *et al.*, *The Stern Review: The Economics of Climate Change*, HM Treasury, 2006; U.S. Census Bureau, "Statistical Abstract of the United States." 127th edition. 2008; M.L. Weitzman, "On Modeling and Interpreting the Economics of Catastrophic Climate Change," December 5, 2007 version, www.economics.harvard.edu/faculty/weitzman/files/modeling.pdf.

Article 8.6

KEEP IT IN THE GROUND

An alternative vision for petroleum emerges in Ecuador. But will Big Oil win the day?

BY ELISSA DENNIS
July/August 2010

In the far eastern reaches of Ecuador, in the Amazon basin rain forest, lies a land of incredible beauty and biological diversity. More than 2,200 varieties of trees reach for the sky, providing a habitat for more species of birds, bats, insects, frogs, and fish than can be found almost anywhere else in the world. Indigenous Waorani people have made the land their home for millennia, including the last two tribes living in voluntary isolation in the country. The land was established as Yasuní National Park in 1979, and recognized as a UNESCO World Biosphere Reserve in 1989.

Underneath this landscape lies a different type of natural resource: petroleum. Since 1972, oil has been Ecuador's primary export, representing 57% of the country's exports in 2008; oil revenues comprised on average 26% of the government's revenue between 2000 and 2007. More than 1.1 billion barrels of heavy crude oil have been extracted from Yasuní, about one quarter of the nation's production to date.

At this economic, environmental, and political intersection lie two distinct visions for Yasuní's, and Ecuador's, next 25 years. Petroecuador, the state-owned oil company, has concluded that 846 million barrels of oil could be extracted from proven reserves at the Ishpingo, Tambococha, and Tiputini (ITT) wells in an approximately 200,000-hectare area covering about 20% of the parkland. Extracting this petroleum, either alone or in partnership with interested oil companies in Brazil, Venezuela, or China, would generate approximately $7 billion, primarily in the first 13 years of extraction and continuing with declining productivity for another 12 years.

The alternative vision is the simple but profound choice to leave the oil in the ground. Environmentalists and indigenous communities have been organizing for years to restrict drilling in Yasuní. But the vision became much more real when President Rafael Correa presented a challenge to the world community at a September 24, 2007 meeting of the United Nations General Assembly: If governments, companies, international organizations, and individuals pledge a total of $350 million per year for 10 years, equal to half of the forgone revenues from ITT, then Ecuador will chip in the other half and keep the oil underground indefinitely, as this nation's contribution to halting global climate change.

The Yasuní-ITT Initiative would preserve the fragile environment, leave the voluntarily isolated tribes in peace, and prevent the emission of an estimated 407 million metric tons of carbon dioxide into the atmosphere. This "big idea from a small country" has even broader implications, as Alberto Acosta, former Energy Minister and one of the architects of the proposal, notes in his new book, *La Maldición de la Abundancia (The Curse of Abundance)*. The Initiative is a "punto de ruptura," he writes, a turning point in environmental history which "questions the logic of extractive (exporter of raw material) development," while introducing the possibility of global *"sumak kawsay,"* the indigenous Kichwa concept of "good living" in harmony with nature.

Sumak kawsay is the underlying tenet of the country's 2008 Constitution, which guarantees rights for indigenous tribes and for "Mother Earth." The Constitution was overwhelmingly supported in a national referendum, but putting the document's principles into action has been a bigger challenge. While Correa draws praise for his progressive social programs, for example in education and health care, the University of Illinois-trained economist is criticized for not yet having wrested control of the nation's economy from a deep-rooted powerful elite bearing different ideas about the meaning of "good living." Within this political and economic discord lies the fate of the Yasuni Initiative.

An Abundance of Oil

Ecuador, like much of Latin America, has long been an exporter of raw materials: cacao in the 19th century, bananas in the 20th century, and now petroleum. Shell discovered the heavy, viscous oil of Ecuador's Amazon basin in 1948. In the 1950s, a series of controversial encounters began between the native Waorani people and U.S. missionaries from the Summer Institute of Linguistics (SIL). With SIL assistance, Waorani were corralled into a 16,000-hectare "protectorate" in the late 1960s, and many went to work for the oil companies who were furiously drilling through much of the tribe's homeland.

The nation dove into the oil boom of the 1970s, investing in infrastructure and building up external debt. When oil prices plummeted in the 1980s while interest rates on that debt ballooned, Ecuador was trapped in the debt crisis that affected much of the region. Thus began what Correa calls "the long night of neoliberalism": IMF-mandated privatizations of utilities and mining sectors, with a concomitant decline of revenues from the nation's natural resources to the Ecuadorian people. By 1986, all of the nation's petroleum revenues were going to pay external debt.

After another decade of IMF-driven privatizations, oil price drops, earthquakes, and other natural disasters, the Ecuadorian economy fell into total collapse, leading to the 2000 dollarization. Since then, more than one million Ecuadorians have left the country, mostly for the United States and Spain, and remittances from 2.5 million Ecuadorians living in the exterior, estimated at $4 billion in 2008, have become the nation's second highest source of income.

Close to 40 years of oil production has failed to improve the living standards of the majority of Ecuadorians. "Petroleum has not helped this country," notes Ana Cecilia Salazar, director of the Department of Social Sciences in the College of Economics of the University of Cuenca. "It has been corrupt. It has not diminished poverty. It has not industrialized this country. It has just made a few people rich."

Currently 38% of the population lives in poverty, with 13% in extreme poverty. The nation's per capita income growth between 1982 and 2007 was only 0.7% per year. And although the unemployment rate of 10% may seem moderate, an estimated 53% of the population is considered "underemployed."

Petroleum extraction has brought significant environmental damage. Each year 198,000 hectares of land in the Amazon are deforested for oil production. A verdict is expected this year in an Ecuadorian court in the 17-year-old class action suit brought by 30,000 victims of Texaco/Chevron's drilling operations in the area northwest of Yasuní between 1964 and 1990. The unprecedented $27 billion lawsuit alleges that thousands of cancers and other health problems were caused by Texaco's use of outdated and dangerous practices, including the dumping of 18 billion gallons of toxic wastewater into local water supplies.

Regardless of its economic or environmental impacts, the oil is running out. With 4.16 billion barrels in proven reserves nationwide, and another half billion "probable" barrels, best-case projections, including the discovery of new reserves, indicate the nation will stop exporting oil within 28 years, and stop producing oil within 35 years.

"At this moment we have an opportunity to rethink the extractive economy that for many years has constrained the economy and politics in the country," says Esperanza Martinez, a biologist, environmental activist, and author of the book *Yasuní: El tortuoso camino de Kioto a Quito (Yasuní: The Tortuous Road from Kyoto to Quito)*. "This proposal intends to change the terms of the North-South relationship in climate change negotiations."

Collecting on Ecological Debt

The Initiative fits into the emerging idea of "climate debt." The North's voracious energy consumption in the past has destroyed natural resources in the South; the South is currently bearing the brunt of global warming effects like floods and drought; and the South needs to adapt expensive new energy technology for the future instead of industrializing with the cheap fossil fuels that built the North. Bolivian president Evo Morales proposed at the Copenhagen climate talks last December that developed nations pay 1% of GDP, totaling $700 billion/year, into a compensation fund that poor nations could use to adapt their energy systems.

"Clearly in the future, it will not be possible to extract all the petroleum in the world because that would create a very serious world problem, so we need to create measures of compensation to pay the ecological debt to the countries," says Malki Sáenz, formerly Coordinator of the Yasuní-ITT Initiative within the Ministry of Foreign Relations. The Initiative "is a way to show the international community that real compensation mechanisms exist for not extracting petroleum."

Indigenous and environmental movements in Latin America and Africa are raising possibilities of leaving oil in the ground elsewhere. But the Yasuní-ITT proposal is the furthest along in detail, government sponsorship, and ongoing negotiations. The Initiative proposes that governments, international institutions, civil associations, companies, and individuals contribute to a fund administered through an international organization such as the United Nations Development Program (UNDP). Contributions could include swaps of Ecuador's external debt, as well as resources generated from emissions auctions in the European Union and carbon emission taxes such as those implemented in Sweden and Slovakia.

Contributors of at least $10,000 would receive a Yasuní Guarantee Certificate (CGY), redeemable only in the event that a future government decides to extract the oil. The total dollar value of the CGYs issued would equal the calculated value of the 407 million metric tons of non-emitted carbon dioxide.

The money would be invested in fixed income shares of renewable energy projects with a guaranteed yield, such as hydroelectric, geothermal, wind, and solar power, thus helping to reduce the country's dependence on fossil fuels. The interest payments generated by these investments would be designated for: 1) conservation projects, preventing deforestation of almost 10 million hectares in 40 protected areas covering 38% of Ecuador's territory; 2) reforestation and natural regeneration projects on another one million hectares of forest land; 3) national energy efficiency improvements; and 4) education, health, employment, and training programs in sustainable activities like ecotourism and agro forestry in the affected areas. The first three activities could prevent an additional 820 million metric tons of carbon dioxide emissions, tripling the Initiative's effectiveness.

Government Waffling

These nationwide conservation efforts, as well as the proposal's mention of "monitoring" throughout Yasuní and possibly shutting down existing oil production, are particularly disconcerting to Ecuadorian and international oil and wood interests. Many speculate that political pressure from these economic powerhouses was behind a major blow to the Initiative this past January, when Correa, in one of his regular Saturday radio broadcasts, suddenly blasted the negotiations as "shameful," and a threat to the nation's "sovereignty" and "dignity." He threatened that if the full package of international commitments is not in place by this June, he would begin extracting oil from ITT.

Correa's comments spurred the resignations of four critical members of the negotiating commission, including Chancellor Fander Falconí, a longtime ally in Correa's PAIS party, and Roque Sevilla, an ecologist, businessman, and ex-Mayor of Quito whom Correa had picked to lead the commission. Ecuador's Ambassador to the UN Francisco Carrion also resigned from the commission, as did World Wildlife Fund president Yolanda Kakabadse.

Correa has been clear from the outset that the government has a Plan B, to extract the oil, and that the non-extraction "first option" is contingent on the mandated monetary commitments. But oddly his outburst came as the negotiating team's efforts were bearing fruit. Sevilla told the press in January of commitments in various stages of approval from Germany, Spain, Belgium, France, and Switzerland, totaling at least $1.5 billion. The team was poised to sign an agreement with UNDP last December in Copenhagen to administer the fund. Correa called off the signing at the last minute, questioning the breadth of the Initiative's conservation efforts and UNDP's proposed six-person administrative body, three appointed by Ecuador, two by contributing nations, and one by UNDP. This joint control structure apparently sparked Correa's tirade about shame and dignity.

Correa's impulsivity and poor word choice have gotten him into trouble before. Acosta, another former key PAIS ally, resigned as president of the Constituent Assembly in June 2008, in the final stages of drafting the nation's new Constitution, when Correa set a vote deadline Acosta felt hindered the democratic process for this major undertaking. The President has had frequent tussles with indigenous and environmental organizations over mining issues, on several occasions crossing the line from staking out an economically pragmatic political position to name-calling of "childish ecologists."

Within a couple of weeks of the blowup, the government had backpedaled, withdrawing the June deadline, appointing a new negotiating team, and reasserting the position that the government's "first option" is to leave the oil in the ground. At the same time, Petroecuador began work on a new pipeline near Yasuní, part of the infrastructure needed for ITT production, pursuant to a 2007 Memorandum of Understanding with several foreign oil companies.

If the People Lead...

Amid the doubts and mixed messages, proponents are fighting to save the Initiative as a cornerstone in the creation of a post-petroleum Ecuador and ultimately a post-petroleum world. In media interviews after his resignation, Sevilla stressed that he would keep working to ensure that the Initiative would not fail. The Constitution provides for a public referendum prior to extracting oil from protected areas like Yasuní, he noted. "If the president doesn't want to assume his responsibility as leader...let's pass the responsibility to the public." In fact, 75% of respondents in a January poll in Quito and Guayaquil, the country's two largest cities, indicated that they would vote to not extract the ITT oil.

Martinez and Sáenz concur that just as the Initiative emerged from widespread organizing efforts, its success will come from the people. "This is the moment to define ourselves and develop an economic model not based on petroleum," Salazar says. "We have other knowledge, we have minerals, water. We need to change our consciousness and end the economic dependence on one resource." ❏

Resources: Live Yasuni, Finding Species, Inc. (liveyasuni.org); "S.O.S. Yasuni" (sosyasuni.org); "Yasuni-ITT: An Initiative to Change History," Government of Ecuador, (yasuni-itt.gov.ec).

Chapter 9

THE POLITICAL ECONOMY OF WAR AND IMPERIALISM

Article 9.1

WHY THE EMPEROR HAS NO CLOTHES
America's Spiraling External Debt and the Decline of the U.S. Dollar

BY ANDRE GUNDER FRANK

January 2005 — Centre for Research on Globalisation

U ncle Sam has reneged and defaulted on up to 40% of its trillion-dollar for-eign debt, and nobody has said a word except for a line in *The Economist*. In plain English, that means Uncle Sam runs a worldwide confidence racket with his self-made dollar based on the confidence that he has elicited and received from others around the world, and he is also a deadbeat in that he does not honor and return the money he has received.

How much of our dollar stake we have lost depends on how much we originally paid for it. Uncle Sam let his dollar fall, or rather through his deliberate political economic policies drove it down, by 40%, from 80 cents to the euro to 133 cents. The dollar is down by a similar factor against the yen, yuan, and other currencies. And it is still declining, indeed is apt to plummet altogether.

True, as the dollar has declined, so has the real value that foreigners pay to service their debt to Uncle Sam. But that works only if they can themselves earn in currencies that have increased in value against the dollar. Otherwise, foreigners earn and pay in the same devalued dollars, and even then with some loss from devaluation between the time they got their dollars and the time they repay them to Uncle Sam.

Uncle Sam's debt to the rest of the world already amounts to more than a third of his annual domestic production and is still growing. That alone already makes his debt economically and politically never repayable, even if he wanted to, which he does not. Uncle Sam's domestic, e.g. credit-card, debt is almost 100% of gross domestic product (GDP) and consumption, including that from China. Uncle Sam's federal debt is now $7.5 trillion, of which all but $1 trillion was built up in the past three decades, the last $2 trillion in the past eight years, and the last $1 trillion in the past two years. Alas, that costs more than $300 billion a year in interest, compared with, for example, the $15 billion spent annually on the National Aeronautics and Space Administration (NASA). But no worries: Congress just raised the debt ceiling to $8.2 trillion. To help us visualize, $1 trillion tightly packed up in $1,000 bills would create a pile 100km high.

But nearly half is owed to foreigners. All Uncle Sam's debt, including private household consumer credit-card, mortgage debt, etc., of about $10 trillion, plus corporate and financial, with options, derivatives and the like, and state and local government debt comes to an unvisualizable, indeed unimaginable, $37 trillion, which is nearly four times Uncle Sam's GDP. Only some of that can be managed domestically, but with dangerous limitations for Uncle Sam noted below. That is only one reason I want you to meet Uncle Sam, the deadbeat confidence man, who may remind you of the film *Meet Joe Black*; for as we get to know him better below, we will find that he is also a Shylock, and a corrupt one at that.

The United States is the world's most privileged nation for having the monopoly privilege of printing the world's reserve currency at will and at a cost of nothing but the paper and ink it is printed on. Additionally, his is also the only country whose "foreign" debt is mostly denominated in his own world-currency dollars that he can print at will; while most foreigners' debt is also denominated in the same dollar, but they have to buy it from Uncle Sam with their own currency and real goods. So he simply pays the Chinese and others in essence with these dollars that have no real worth beyond their paper and ink. So especially poor China gives away for nothing at all to rich Uncle Sam hundreds of billions of dollars' worth of real goods produced at home and consumed by Uncle Sam. Then China turns around and trades these same paper dollar bills in for more of Uncle Sam's paper called Treasury Certificate bonds, which are even more worthless, except that they pay a percent of interest.

In an earlier essay, I argued that Uncle Sam's power rests on two pillars only, the paper dollar and the Pentagon. Each supports the other, but the vulnerability of each is also an Achilles' heel that threatens the viability of the other. Since then, Iraq, not to mention Afghanistan, has shown confidence in the Pentagon not to be what it was cracked up to be; and with the in-part-consequent decline in the dollar, so has confidence in it and Uncle Sam's ability to use it to finance his Pentagon's foreign adventures. So far relations with other countries, in particular with China, still favor Uncle Sam, but they also help maintain an image that is deceptive. Consider the following:

> A $2 toy leaving a U.S.-owned factory in China is a $3 shipment arriving at San Diego. By the time a U.S. consumer buys it for $10 at Wal-Mart, the U.S. economy registers $10 in final sales, less $3 import cost, for a $7 addition to the U.S. GDP.

Moreover, ever-clever Uncle Sam has arranged matters so as to earn 9% from his economic and financial holdings abroad, while foreigners earn only 3% on theirs, and among them on their Treasury Certificates only 1% real return. Note that this difference of 6 percentage points is already double what Uncle Sam pays out, and his total 9% take is triple the 3% he gives back. Therefore, although foreign holdings and Uncle Sam's are now about equal, Uncle Sam is still the big net interested winner, just like any Shylock, but no other ever did so grand a business.

But Uncle Sam also earns quite well, thank you, from other holdings abroad, e.g. from service payments by mostly poor foreign debtors. For from his direct investments in foreign property alone, Uncle Sam's profits now equal 50%, and including his receipts from other holdings abroad now are a full 100% of profits derived from all of his own domestic activities combined. These foreign receipts add more than 4% to Uncle Sam's national domestic product.

The productivity hype of president Bill Clinton's "new economy" in the 1990s was limited to computers and information technology (IT), and even that proved to be a sham when the dot-com bubble burst. Also, not only the apparent increase in "profits" but also that of "productivity" were, at the bottom, on the backs of shop-floor, office and sales-floor workers working harder and longer hours and, at the top, the result of innovative accounting shams by Enron and the like. Such factors still compensate for and permit much of Uncle Sam's $600-billion-and-still-rising trade deficit from excess home consumption over what he himself produces. That is what has resulted in the multi-trillion-dollar debt. Exactly how large that debt is Uncle Sam is reluctant to reveal, but what is sure is that it is by far the world's largest, even as net debt to foreigners, after their debt to him is deducted.

How Has All This Come About?

The simple answer is that Uncle Sam, who is increasingly hooked on consumption, not to mention harder drugs, saves no more than 0.2% of his own income. The Federal Reserve's guru and now you see it, now you don't doctor of magic, Alan Greenspan, recently observed that this is so because the richest 20% of Americans, who are the only ones who do save, have reduced their savings to 2%. Yet even these measly savings (other, poorer countries save and even invest 20%, 30%, even 40% of their incomes) are more than counterbalanced by the 6% deficit spending of the government. That is what brings the average saving rate to 0.2%. To maintain that $400-plus-billion budget deficit (more than 3% of national domestic product), which is really more the $600 billion if we count, as we should, the more than $200 billion Uncle Sam "borrows" from the temporary surplus in his own Federal Social Security fund, which he is also bankrupting.

So with this $600-billion-plus budget deficit and the above-mentioned related $600-billion-plus deficit, rich Uncle Sam, and primarily his highest earners and biggest consumers, as well as of course the Big Uncle himself, live off the fat of the rest of the world's land. Uncle Sam absorbs the savings of others who themselves are often much poorer, particularly when their central banks put many of their reserves in world-currency dollars and hence into the hands of Uncle Sam and some also in dollars at home. Their private investors send dollars to or buy dollar assets on Wall Street, all with the confidence that they are putting their wherewithal in the world's safest haven (and that, of course, is part of the above-mentioned confidence racket). From the central banks alone, we are looking at yearly sums of more than $100 billion from Europe, more than $100 billion from poor China, $140 billion from super-saver Japan, and many 10s of billions from many others around the globe, including the Third World. But in addition, Uncle Sam obliges them, through the good offices of their own states, to send their thus literally forced savings to Uncle Sam as well in the form of their "service" of their predominantly dollar debt to him.

His treasury secretary and his International Monetary Fund (IMF) handmaiden blithely continue to strut around the world insisting that the Third- and ex-Second, now also Third-World countries of course continue to service their foreign debts, especially to him. No matter that with interest rates multiplied several times over by Uncle Sam himself after the Fed's Paul Volcker's coup in October 1979, most have already paid off their original borrowings three to five times over. For to pay at all at interest rates that Volcker boosted to 20%, they had to borrow still more at still higher rates until thereby their outstanding foreign debt doubled and tripled, not to mention their domestic debt from which part of the foreign payments were raised, particularly in Brazil. Privatization is the name of the game there and elsewhere, except for the debt. The debt was socialized after it had been incurred mostly by private business, but only the state had enough power to squeeze the greatest bulk of back payments out of the hides of its poor and middle-class people and transfer them as "invisible service payments" to Uncle Sam.

When Mexicans were told to tighten their belts still further, they answered that they couldn't because they had already had to eat their belts. Only Argentina and for a while Russia declared an effective moratorium on debt "service," and that only after political economic policies had destroyed their societies, thanks to Uncle Sam's advisers and his IMF strong arm. Since then, Uncle Sam himself has been blithely defaulting on his own foreign debt, as he already had several times before in the 19th century.

One piece of practical advice came from the premier military strategist Carl von Clausewitz: make the lands you conquer pay for their own conquest and administration. That is of course exactly what Britain did in and with India through the infamous "Home Charges" remitted to London in payment for Britain administering India, which even the British themselves recognized as "tribute" and responsible for much of "The Drain" from India to Britain. How much more efficient yet to let foreign countries' own states administer themselves but by rules set and imposed by Uncle Sam's IMF and then effect a drain of debt service anyway. Actually, the British therein also set the 19th-century precedent of relying on the "imperialism of free trade" with "independent" states as far and as long as possible, using gunboat diplomacy to make it work (which Uncle Sam had already learned to copy by early in the 20th century); and if that was not enough, simply to invade, and if necessary to occupy—and then rely on the Clausewitz rule.

After I wrote the above, I received by e-mail an excerpt from the Democracy Now! website, titled "Confessions of an Economic Hit Man: How the U.S. Uses Globalization to Cheat Poor Countries Out of Trillions":

> We speak with John Perkins, a former respected member of the international banking community. In his book Confessions of an Economic Hit Man he describes how as a highly paid professional, he helped the U.S. cheat poor countries around the globe out of trillions of dollars by lending them more money than they could possibly repay and then take over their economies ...

> **JOHN PERKINS:** Basically what we were trained to do and what our job is to do is to build up the American empire. To bring—to create situations where as many resources as possible flow into this country, to our corporations, and our government, and in fact we've been very successful. We've built the largest empire in the history of the world ... primarily through economic manipulation, through cheating, through fraud, through seducing people into our way of life, through the economic hit men. I was very much a part of that ... I was initially recruited while I was in business school back in the late '60s by the National Security Agency, the nation's largest and least understood spy organization ... and then [it] send[s] us to work for private consulting companies, engineering firms, construction companies, so that if we were caught, there would be no connection with the government ...

> I became its chief economist. I ended up having 50 people working for me. But my real job was deal-making. It was giving loans to other countries, huge loans, much bigger than they could possibly repay. One of the conditions of the loan— let's say a $1 billion to a country like Indonesia or Ecuador—and this country would then have to give 90% of that loan back to a U.S. company, or U.S. companies ... a Halliburton or a Bechtel ... A country today like Ecuador owes over 50% of its national budget just to pay down its debt. And it really can't do it. So we literally have them over a barrel. So when we want more oil, we go to Ecuador and say, "Look, you're not able to repay your debts, therefore give your oil companies your Amazon rain [forests], which are filled with oil." And today we're going in and destroying Amazonian rain forests, forcing Ecuador to give them to us because they've accumulated all this debt ... [We work] very, very closely with the World Bank. The World Bank provides most of the money that's used by economic hit men, it and the IMF.

Last but not least, oil producers also put their savings in Uncle Sam. With the "shock" of oil that restored its real price after the dollar valuation had fallen in 1973, ever-cleverer-by-half Henry Kissinger made a deal with the world's largest oil exporter, Saudi Arabia, that it would continue to price oil in dollars, and these earnings would be deposited with Uncle Sam and partly compensated by military hardware. That deal de facto extended to all of the Organization of Petroleum Exporting Countries (OPEC) and still stands, except that before the war against Iraq that country suddenly opted out by switching to pricing its oil in euros, and Iran threatened do the same. North Korea, the third member of the "axis of evil", has no oil but trades entirely in euros. (Venezuela is a major oil supplier to Uncle Sam and also supplies some at preferential rates as non-dollar trade swaps to poor countries such as Cuba. So Uncle Sam sponsored and financed military commandos from its Plan Colombia next door, promoted an illegal coup and, when that failed, pushed a referendum in his attempt at yet another "regime change"; and now along with Brazil all three are being baptized as yet another "axis of evil").

After writing this, I found that the good (hit) man Mr. Perkins was in Saudi Arabia too:

> Yes, it was a fascinating time. I remember well ... the Treasury Department hired me and a few other economic hit men. We went to Saudi Arabia ... And we worked out this deal whereby the Royal House of Saud agreed to send most of their petrodollars back to the United States and invest them in U.S. government securities. The Treasury Department would use the interest from these securities to hire U.S. companies to build Saudi Arabia—new cities, new infrastructure—which we've done. And the House of Saud would agree to maintain the price of oil within acceptable limits to us, which they've done all of these years, and we would agree to keep the House of Saud in power as long as they did this, which we've done, which is one of the reasons we went to war with Iraq in the first place. And in Iraq we tried to implement the same policy that was so successful in Saudi Arabia, but Saddam Hussein didn't buy. When the economic hit men fail in this scenario, the next step is what we call the jackals. Jackals are CIA-sanctioned people that come in and try to foment a coup or revolution. If that doesn't work, they perform assassinations. Or try to. In the case of Iraq, they weren't able to get through to Saddam Hussein. He had—his bodyguards were too good. He had doubles. They couldn't get through to him. So the third line of defense, if the economic hit men and the jackals fail, the next line of defense is our young men and women, who are sent in to die and kill, which is what we've obviously done in Iraq.

To return to the main issue and call a spade a huge spade, all of the above is part and parcel of the world's biggest-ever Ponzi-scheme confidence racket. Like all others, its most essential characteristic is that it can only continue to pay off dollars and be maintained at the top as long as it continues to receive new dollars at the bottom, voluntarily through confidence if possible and by force if not. (Of course, the Clausewitz formula result in the poorest paying the most, since they are also the most defenseless: so that the ones sitting on/above them pass much of the cost and pain down to them.)

What If Confidence in the Dollar Runs Out?

Things are already getting shakier in the House of Uncle Sam. The declining dollar reduces the necessary dollar inflows, so Greenspan needs to raise interest rates to maintain some attraction for the foreign dollars he needs to fill the trade gap. As a quid pro quo for being reappointed by President George W Bush, he promised to do that only after the election. That time has now arrived, but doing so threatens to collapse the housing bubble that was built on low interest and mortgage—and re-mortgage—rates.

But it is in their house values that most Americans have their savings, if they have any at all. They and this imaginary wealth effect supported over-consumption and the nearly as-high-as-GDP household debt, and a collapse of the housing price bubble with increased interest and mortgage rates would not only drastically undercut house prices, it would thereby have a domino effect on their owners' enormous second and third re-mortgages and credit-card and other debt, their consumption, corporate debt and profit, and investment. In fact, these factors would be enough to plummet Uncle Sam into a deep recession, if not depression, and another Big Bear deflation on stock and de facto on other prices, rendering debt service even more onerous.

Still lower real U.S. investment would reduce its industrial productivity and competitiveness even more—probably to a degree lower than can compensated for by further devaluing the dollar and making U.S. exports cheaper, as is the confident hope of many, probably including the good Doctor. Until now, the apparent inflation of prices abroad in rubles and pesos and their consequent devaluations have been a de facto deflation in terms of the dollar world currency. Uncle Sam then printed dollars to buy up at bargain-basement fire-sale prices natural resources in Russia (whose economy was then run on $100 bills), and companies and even banks, as in South Korea. True, now Greenspan and Uncle Sam are trying again to get other central banks to raise their own interest rates and otherwise plunge their own people into even deeper depression.

So, far beyond Osama bin Laden, al-Qaeda and all the terrorists put together, the greatest real-world threat to Uncle Sam is that the inflow of dollars dries up. For instance, foreign central banks and private investors (it is said that "overseas Chinese" have a tidy trillion dollars) could any day decide to place more of their money elsewhere than in the declining dollar and abandon poor ol' Uncle Sam to his destiny. China could double its per capita income very quickly if it made real investments at home instead of financial ones with Uncle Sam. Central banks, European and others, can now put their reserves in (rising!) euros or even soon-to-be-revalued Chinese yuan. Not so far down the road, there may be an East Asian currency, eg a basket first of ASEAN + 3 (China, Japan, South Korea)—and then + 4 (India). While India's total exports in the past five years rose by 73%, those to the Association of Southeast Asian Nations (ASEAN) rose at double that rate and sixfold to China. India has become an ASEAN summit partner, and its ambitions stretch still further to an economic zone stretching from India to Japan. Not for nothing, in the 1997 East Asian currency and then full economic crisis, Uncle Sam strong-armed Japan not to start a proposed East Asian currency fund that would have prevented at least the worst of the crisis. Uncle Sam then benefited from it by buying devalued East Asian currencies and using them to buy up East Asian real resources, and in South Korea also banks, at bargain-basement reduced-price fire sales. But now, China is already taking steps toward such an arrangement, only on a much grander financial and now also economic scale.

A day after writing the above, I read in *The Economist* (December 11-17, 2004) a report on the previous week's summit meeting of ASEAN + 3 in Malaysia. That country's prime minister announced that this summit should lay the groundwork for an East Asian Community (EAC) that "should build a free-trade area, cooperate on finance, and sign a security pact ... that would transform East Asia into a cohesive economic block ... In fact, some of these schemes are already in motion ... China, as the region's pre-eminent economic and military power, will doubtless dominate ... and host the second East Asia Summit." The report went on to recall that in 1990, Uncle Sam shot down a similar initiative for fear of losing influence in the region. Now it is a case of "Yankee Stay Home."

Or what if, long before that comes to pass, exporters of oil simply cease to price it in ever-devaluing dollars, and instead make a mint by switching to the rising euro and/or a basket of East Asian currencies? Since selling oil for falling dollars instead of rising euros is evidently bad business, the world's largest oil exporters in Russia and OPEC have been considering doing just that. In the meantime, they have only raised the dollar price of oil, so that in euro terms it has remained approximately stable since 2000. So far, many oil exporters and others still place their increased amount of dollars with Uncle Sam, even though he now offers an ever less attractive and less safe haven, but Russia is now buying more euros with some of its dollars.

So also many countries' central banks have begun to put ever more of their reserves into the euro and currencies other than Uncle Sam's dollar. Now even the Central Bank of China, the greatest friend of Uncle Sam in need, has begun to buy some euros. China itself has also begun to use some of its dollars—as long as they are still accepted by them—to buy real goods from other Asians and thousands of tons of iron ore and steel from Brazil, etc. (Brazil's president recently took a huge business delegation to China, and a Chinese one just went to Argentina. They are going after South African minerals too.)

So what will happen to the rich on top of Uncle Sam's Ponzi scheme when the confidence of poorer central banks and oil exporters in the middle runs out, and the more destitute around the world, confident or not, can no longer make their in-payments at the bottom? The Uncle Sam Ponzi Scheme Confidence Racket would—or will?—come crashing down, like all other such schemes before, only this time with a worldwide bang. It would cut the present U.S. consumer demand down to realistic size and hurt many exporters and producers elsewhere in the world. In fact, it may involve a wholesale fundamental reorganization of the world political economy now run by Uncle Sam.

Uncle Sam's Paper Dollar Tiger Poses A Mad Geo-Political Catch 22

Of course, crashing the dollar would also in one fell swoop wipe out, that is default, the Uncle Sam debt altogether. Thereby, it would simultaneously also make all foreigners and rich Americans lose the whole of their dollar asset shirt. They are still desperately trying to save as much of it as possible by not going for the crash, that is for broke. That is, they are trying to protect the remainder of their dollar investment shirt by keeping their dollar life sustaining pump going. The whole business of maintaining the Uncle Sam Ponzi Scheme poses the world's biggest and craziest Catch-22 since MAD, and it is just about as mad.

This dissolution of the Uncle Sam Ponzi Scheme will be costly and the greatest costs will as usual probably be dumped on the poorest who are least able to bear these costs, but who are also least able to protect themselves from being forced to do so. And the historically necessary transition out from under the Uncle Sam run doughnut world can bring the entire world into the deepest depression ever. Only East Asia is in a relatively good position to save itself from being pulled—or pushed—to the bottom, but even then also after paying a high cost for this transition—toward itself!

However, the world is facing an even MADer global geo-political and military Catch 22. It remains the great unknown and perhaps unknowable. How will Uncle Sam react as a Paper [money] Tiger that is wounded by a crash of the Ponzi Scheme Confidence Racket from which he and millions of un-knowing Uncle Sammies have lived the good life? To compensate for less bread and civil rights but more "Patriotic" acts at home, a more chauvinist Uncle Sam can provide a World War III circus abroad. A crash of the dollar will pull the financial rug out from under, and discourage his foreign victims from continuing to pay for new Pentagon adventures abroad. But some more wars may still be possible with the weapons he would still have and some more Military Keynesian government deficit spending at home. That could well—nay horribly—be the cost to the world of the current policies to "defend Freedom and Civilization." The Super Catch 22 is that almost nobody other than Osama bin Laden wants to run that risk.

Recall how much the transition to Uncle Sam cost: a 30 Year War from 1914 to 1945 with the intervening second Great Depression in a century that cost 100 million lives lost to war, more than in all previous world history combined, not to mention the literally [hundreds?] of millions who suffered and died from unnecessary starvation and disease. Or that the previous transition to the British Major Bull cost the Napoleonic Wars, the Great Depression of 1873-95, colonialism and semi-colonialism and their human costs. The latter coincided with the most pronounced El Niño climatic changes in two centuries, which ravaged Indians, Chinese, and many others with famines. But these were in turn magnified by the Imperial Colonial powers who used them in their own interests, e.g. increased export of wheat from India especially during years of famine.

The parallels with today, including even taking advantage of renewed El Niños a century later, are too horrifying and guilt generating for hardly anybody to make. They include Uncle Sam's IMF imposed "structural adjustment" that obliges Mexican peasants to have already eaten the belt that the IMF wants them to tighten still further. Three million dead and still counting in Rwanda and Burundi, and then some in neighbouring Congo, came after IMF imposed strictures and the cancellation primarily by Uncle Sam of the Coffee Agreement that had sustained its price for these producers. And now—nay since the CIA murder of Lumumba and the elevation of Kosavubu in Katanga in 1961, indeed since the King of Belgium's private reserve of the Congo in the 19th century, we get the scramble for and production and sale there of gold for Uncle Sam's Fort Knox, and now also titanium so that we can communicate by mobile cell phone, diamonds for ever, and so on.

Uncle Sam also took advantage of yet another strong El Niño event that ravaged South East Asia, and especially Indonesia, simultaneously with the post 1997 financial crisis that Uncle Sam deliberately parlayed into an economic depression. It was so great that it swept out of office President Suharto whom Uncle Sam had installed there thirty years earlier with his CIA coup against the popular father of Indonesian independence, Sukarno. That had cost at least half a million but also an estimated up to one million lives that Suhartu took directly plus the poverty generated by the infamous "Berkeley Mafia" that he installed to run the Indonesian economy into the ground.

The parallels with the past also include environmental degradation, and the shift of ecological damage from the rich who generate it to the poor Third World who bears its greatest burden. And of course we should not forget World War III [the third after the second *and* fought in the Third World] that Daddy Bush began against Iraq in 1991

Yet there are also others in the world who do not (yet?) feel all that caught up in the Catch 22. Calculatedly just before this year's 2004 Uncle Sam election, one of them said so out loud in a video broadcast to the world. It seems to have been least publicly noted by its principal addressee Uncle Sam, who should have been the most interested party: For it was none other than bin Laden himself who announced that he is "going to bankrupt the Uncle Sam!" In view of the deliberate Uncle Sam blindness to the shakiness of his real world foundation abroad, so massive a collapse abroad may not be more difficult to arrange than it was to topple its Twin Tower symbol at home. ❏

Sources: "Blaming 'Undervalued' Yuan Wins Votes," Asia Times Online, February 26, 2004; "Yankee Stay Home," *The Economist*, December 11-17, 2004; Gerard Dumenil and Dominique Levy, "The Economics of Uncle Sam Imperialism at the Turn of the 21st Century" *Review of International Political Economy*, October, 2004.

Article 9.2

SYNERGY IN SECURITY
The Rise of the National Security Complex

BY TOM BARRY
March/April 2010

In his January 17, 1961 farewell address, President Dwight D. Eisenhower cautioned: "In the councils of government, we must guard against the acquisition of unwarranted influence, whether sought or unsought, by the military-industrial complex."

Five decades later, this complex, which Eisenhower defined as the "conjunction of an immense military establishment and a large arms industry," is no longer new. And while Eisenhower's warning is still pertinent, the scale, scope, and substance of the complex have changed in alarming ways. It has morphed into a new type of public-private partnership—one that spans military, intelligence, and homeland-security contracting, and might be better called a "national security complex."

Not counting the supplemental authorizations for the wars in Iraq and Afghanistan, current levels of military spending are, adjusting for inflation, about 45% higher than the military budget when Eisenhower left office. Including the Iraq and Afghanistan war budgets, military spending stands about 30% higher, adjusted for inflation, than any of the post-WWII highpoints—Korea, Vietnam, and the Reagan build-up in the 1980s. Private military contracting, which constituted about half of the Pentagon's spending in the 1960s, currently absorbs about 70% of the Department of Defense (DoD) budget. No longer centered exclusively in the Pentagon, outsourcing to private contractors now extends to all aspects of government. But since 2001, the major surge in federal outsourcing has occurred in the "intelligence community" and in the new Department of Homeland Security (DHS).

Since Sept. 11, 2001, a vastly broadened government-industry complex has emerged—one that brings together all aspects of national security. Several interrelated trends are responsible for its formation and explosive growth: 1) the dramatic growth in government outsourcing since the early 1990s, and particularly since the beginning of the George W. Bush administration, 2) the post-Sept. 11 focus on homeland security, 3) the wars in Iraq and Afghanistan, 4) the Bush-era surge in intelligence budget and intelligence contracts, and 5) the cross-agency focus on information and communications technology.

The term "military-industrial complex" no longer adequately describes the multi-headed monster that has emerged in our times. The industrial (that is, big business) part of the military-industrial complex has become ever more deeply integrated into government—no longer simply providing arms but also increasingly offering their services on the fronts of war and deep inside the halls of government—commissioned to carry out the very missions of the DoD, DHS, and intelligence agencies. In the national security complex, it is ever more difficult to determine what is private sector and what is public sector—and whose interests are being served.

Different Departments, Same Companies

In 2008, the federal government handed out contracts to the private sector totaling $525.5 billion—up from $209 billion in 2000. That's about a quarter of the entire federal budget. The DoD alone accounts for about $390 billion, or nearly three-quarters of total federal contracts.

The living symbol of the new national security complex is Lockheed Martin, whose slogan is "We Never Forget Who We're Working For." That's the U.S. government—sales to which account for more than 80% of the company's revenues, with most of the balance coming from international weapons sales and other security contracts facilitated by Washington. In addition to its sales of military hardware, Lockheed is the government's top provider of IT services and systems integration (see Table 1).

Whether it is military operations, interrogations, intelligence gathering, or homeland security, the country's "national security" apparatus is largely in the same hands. Various components of the U.S. national-security state are divvied up among different federal bureaucracies. But increasingly, the main components are finding a common home within corporate America. Corporations such as Lockheed Martin, Boeing, L-3 Communications, and Northrop Grumman have the entire business—military, intelligence, and "homeland security"—covered.

Lockheed Martin, Northrop Grumman, and Boeing led the top ten military contractors in 2008 (see Table 2).

The 2003 creation of the Department of Homeland Security has helped spawn an explosion of new companies, and new divisions of existing companies, providing "homeland security" products and services. Before President Bush created DHS in

TABLE 1:
TOP TEN GOVERNMENT CONTRACTORS, 2008

Lockheed Martin	$34,785,141,737
Boeing	$23,784,593,887
Northrop Grumman	$18,177,546,625
BAE Systems	$16,137,793,437
General Dynamics	$15,992,669,588
Raytheon	$14,663,608,137
United Technologies	$8,927,106,729
L-3 Communications	$7,597,574,871
KBR	$5,995,025,351
SAIC	$5,945,115,101

Source: USAGovernmentSpending.gov

the wake of Sept. 11, the agencies that would be merged into the new department did very little outsourcing. From less than 1% of federal contracts (as a total dollar amount) in 2000, outsourcing by DHS has quadrupled as a portion of federal contracting from 2003 to 2009.

Although DHS contracts with scores of new companies, its top contractors are all leading military contractors that have established "homeland security" divisions and subsidiaries.

The top ten DHS contractors in 2008 were Lockheed Martin, Northrop Grumman, IBM, L-3 Communications, Unisys, SAIC, Boeing, Booz Allen Hamilton, General Electric, and Accenture, all leading military contractors. Other major military contractors among the top 25 DHS contractors include General Dynamics, Fluor, and Computer Sciences Corp (see Table 3).

There is no public list of corporations that contract for U.S. intelligence agencies. But based on company press releases and filings with the Securities and Exchange Commission, Tim Shorrock concludes in his new book *Spies for Hire* that the top five intelligence contractors are probably Lockheed Martin, Northrop Grumman, SAIC, General Dynamics, and L-3 Communications. Other major contractors include Booz Allen Hamilton, CACI International, DRS Technologies, and ManTech International, also leading military contractors.

Within the past eight years—since Sept. 11, 2001—the intelligence budget has soared, rising from an estimated $30 billion in 2000 to an estimated $66.5 billion today. Intelligence agencies have channeled most of the new funding to private contractors, both major companies like CACI and thousands of individual contractors. Private contracts now account for about 70% of the intelligence budget. Intelligence community sources told the *Washington Post* that private contractors constituted

TABLE 2: TOP TEN DoD CONTRACTORS, 2008	
Lockheed Martin	$29,363,894,334
Northrop Grumman	$23,436,442,251
Boeing	$21,838,400,709
BAE Systems	$16,227,370,773
Raytheon	$13,593,610,345
General Dynamics	$13,490,652,077
United Technologies	$8,283,275,612
L-3 Communications	$6,675,712,135
KBR	$5,997,147,425
Navistar Int'l	$4,761,740,206

Source: USAGovernmentSpending.gov

"a significant majority" of analysts working at the new National Counterterrorism Center, which provides the White House with terrorism intelligence.

The major military contractors are now moving their headquarters from their production centers, often in California and Texas, to the Washington Beltway in pursuit of more intelligence, military, and homeland security contracts. The gleaming Beltway office buildings of the security corporations are now the most visible symbol of this national security complex.

Boots on the Ground, Computers in Cubicles

Another feature of this evolving, ever-expanding complex is that all the U.S. government departments involved in national security—DoD, State Department, DHS, and intelligence—are outsourcing the boots-on-the-ground components of their missions through the use of private security and military provider firms. Companies such as ArmourGroup (which includes Wackhenhut), DynCorp, MPRI, and Xe (formerly Blackwater Worldwide) have injected the private sector directly into the public sector through their work as interrogators, military trainers, prison guards, intelligence agents, and war-fighters.

Five dozen of these security contractors have organized themselves into the International Peace Operations Association (IPOA). After Blackwater came under worldwide scrutiny for its massacre of unarmed Iraqis in central Baghdad on Sept. 17, 2007, the firm left IPOA, whose code of conduct for "peacekeeping" operations it

TABLE 3: TOP TEN HOMELAND SECURITY DEPARTMENT CONTRACTORS, 2008	
Boeing	$591,048,628
IBM	$486,219,723
Accenture Ltd	$392,700,978
General Dynamics	$391,294,040
Integrated Coast Guard Systems (Northrop Grumman/ Lockheed Martin joint venture)	$386,344,211
Unisys	$367,722,670
SAIC	$362,403,533
L-3 Communications	$329,431,785
Lockheed Martin	$294,412,822
Booz Allen Hamilton	$242,899,612

Source: USAGovernmentSpending.gov

had flagrantly ignored. Blackwater created a new association of private military contractors called Global Peace and Security Operations—conveniently without any potentially embarrassing code of conduct.

Private contractors are not only on the frontlines of war and clandestine operations, but have also penetrated the national security bureaucracy itself. Reacting to a March 2008 GAO report on conflicts of interest within the Pentagon, Frida Berrigan of the New America Foundation's Arms and Security Initiative observed that alarming numbers of "cubicle mercenaries" are now working within federal bureaucracies as administrators, contract managers, intelligence analysts, and cybersecurity chiefs. No longer does the "large arms industry" that Eisenhower warned about just peddle goods like weapons and missiles, it also sells itself through its services.

Common Dominators of the New Complex: Information and Security

Private contractors are also in control of the core of the complex's information and intelligence systems. Information and communications technology is the fastest-growing sector in government contracting. The DHS's expanding involvement in cybersecurity, information systems, and electronic identification programs, for example, is adding billions of dollars annually to the national security boom.

Lockheed Martin led the ranks of information technology (IT) contractors in 2008, followed by Boeing and Northrop Grumman. Although IT contracts are expanding rapidly, there are few new entrants to the list of top IT providers to the government. Among the top 100 IT contractors, there were just twelve new entrants, as traditional military giants dominated the list (see Table 4).

TABLE 4:
TOP TEN FEDERAL IT AND SYSTEMS INTEGRATION CONTRACTORS, 2009

Lockheed Martin	$14,983,515,367
Boeing	$10,838,231,984
Northrop Grumman	$9,947,316,207
General Dynamics	$ 6,066,178,545
Raytheon	$ 5,942,575,316
KBR	$5,467,721,429
SAIC	$4,811,194,880
L-3 Communications	$4,236,653,555
Computer Sciences	$3,435,767,906
Booz Allen Hamilton	$2,779,421,015

Source: Washington Technology, Eagle Eye Publishers Inc., and Houlihan Lokey

One of the largest sources of federal contracting at DHS has been the EAGLE (Enterprise Acquisition Gateway for Leading Edge Solutions) IT program, which awarded $8.2 billion in contracts in the past three years. Among the leading contractors are CACI, Booz Allen Hamilton, Lockheed Martin, SAIC, Northrop Grumman, General Dynamics, and BAE Systems—all major military contractors. Most of the EAGLE IT bonanza is in the form of "indefinite-delivery, indefinite quantity contracts" that provide generous operating room for IT firms to determine their own solutions to DHS' vast IT and cybersecurity requirements.

The major military corporations have quickly formed new branches to focus on these new opportunities outside of their traditional core contracts with the Pentagon. This year, for example, Northrop Grumman created a new Information Systems division to seek military, homeland security, and intelligence IT contracts. Recognizing the interest in the Obama administration in cyber-security and information war, corporations such as Booz Allen Hamilton and Hewlett-Packard, among others, have created new cybersecurity divisions or subsidiaries. Similarly, the new administration's focus on transnational disease has led military companies such as General Dynamics to acquire medical subsidiaries.

Revolving-Door Security Consultants

Another manifestation of the new national security complex is the rise of a new series of consulting agencies that act as an interface between government and their clients. That's an easy connection for such companies as the Chertoff Group, Ridge Global, and RiceHadley Group, since all their principals recently left government, where they had presided over the unprecedented wave of outsourcing.

Two of these national security agencies are headed by the DHS's first two secretaries, Michael Chertoff and Tom Ridge, while the newest group brings together Condoleezza Rice and Stephen Hadley, who only a year ago were serving as secretary of state and national security adviser, respectively.

When announcing his group's formation, Chertoff boasted, "Our principals have worked closely together for years, as leaders of the Department of Defense, the Department of Homeland Security, the Department of Justice, the National Security Agency and the CIA." Indeed, a leading member of this new group is former CIA director Michael Hayden (2005-2009), who also directed the National Security Agency (1999-2005). Others include former DHS deputy Paul Schneider (who was head of acquisitions for NSA and the U.S. Navy prior to his position at DHS); Admiral Jay Cohen (Ret.), who was DHS director of science and technology and previously the Navy's technology chief; and Charlie Allen, who was the intelligence chief at DHS and, according to Michael Chertoff, "pretty much head of everything you could be for the CIA."

The Chertoff Group has now hooked up with Blue Star Capital, a transatlantic investment company specializing in mergers and acquisitions in the security business. In its announcement of the new partnership, Blue Star emphasized their joint interest in "generating opportunities" across the national security spectrum—"in the homeland security, defense, and intelligence markets."

Chertoff himself applauded the value of the merger: "I believe there are many areas of opportunity within the Homeland Security, Intelligence and Defense sectors where the synergies between Blue Star and the Chertoff Group will provide real value."

Taking Back Security

The "unwarranted influence" that concerned Eisenhower during the Cold War now pervades national politics and is rarely questioned. Nor has there been any evaluation of the achievements of the increasingly privatized national security complex. In his 2010 State of the Union address, President Obama talked about the need for fiscal restraint, but exempted "national security" from the planned spending freeze. Despite manifold evidence of vast waste and scandalous profiteering in the security apparatus—to say nothing of "unnecessary wars"—the president didn't see fit to scale back the security agencies. By failing to do so, he has all but guaranteed that the outsourcing bonanza will continue. With "national security" off limits for budget cuts, Obama signaled that safeguarding the nation against the "unwarranted influence" and "rise of misplaced power" will not be priorities for this administration.

As major corporations such as Lockheed Martin and security consulting agencies such as the Chertoff Group extend their corporate tentacles into the intelligence, military, and homeland security terrains, the greater threat they pose. The corporate penetration of all the government's information-gathering, communications, intelligence, and data systems undermines democratic governance. The new corporate domination of data-mining, communications, and cybersecurity systems—with little or no government oversight —threatens individual liberty and privacy. This also creates a powerful vested interest in a large and growing "national security" apparatus—and one that is deeply integrated with the top echelons of the intelligence agencies, military, and other parts of this secretive state-within-the-state.

In the end, it's not the contractors that are the central problem with the national security complex—it's the outsourcers, that is, the elected politicians and the government administrators they appoint or confirm. The contractors are working to maximize profits, and are answerable mainly to company shareholders. The outsourcers, however, are ultimately answerable, at least in principle, to the public. What is at stake is who really controls public policy—a democratically accountable government, or an unaccountable fusion of governmental and corporate power. ❏

Sources: Center for Defense Information, "Military Budgets 1946-2009,"; Center for Arms Control and NonProliferation, "2008-2009 U.S. Defense Spending Highest Since WWII," Feb. 20, 2008; FedSpending, org, a project of OMB Watch; USASpending.gov; Tim Shorrock, *New Spies for Hire: The Secret World of Intelligence Outsourcing*, 2008; FY2009 Intelligence Budget, GlobalSecurity.org; F.J. Hillhouse, "Outsourcing Intelligence," *The Nation*, July 24, 2007; Walter Pincus, "Lawmakers Want More Data on Contracting Out Intelligence," *Washington Post*, May 7,

2006: David Horowitz, ed., *Corporations and the Cold War*, 1969; GAO, "Defense Contracting: Army Case Study Delineates Concerns with Use of Contractors as Contract Specialists," March 2008; Frida Berrigan, "Military Industrial Complex 2.0," TruthOut, Sept. 14, 2008; "2009 Top 100," Washington Technology; DHS, Enterprise Solutions Office, EAGLE contracts; *Global Homeland Security 2009-2019*, VisionGain, June 23, 2009; Chertoff Group web pages, chertoffgroup.com; Homeland Security & Defense Business Council web pages, homelandcouncil. org; Chalmers Johnson, "Military Industrial Complex: It's Much Later Than You Think," AntiWar. com, July 28, 2008; Allison Stanger, *One Nation Under Contract: The Outsourcing of American Power and the Future of Foreign Policy* (Yale University Press, 2009); Project on Government Oversight (POGO); Deborah Avant, *The Market for Force: The Consequences of Privatizing Security* (Cambridge University Press, 2005); Center for Public Integrity, "Making a Killing: The Business of War," 2002, "The Shadow Pentagon," 2004; Peter Singer, *Corporate Warriors* (Cornell University Press, 2003).

Article 9.3

ON THE JASMINE REVOLUTION

Tunisia's political economy exemplifies a region in transition.

BY FADHEL KABOUB

March/April 2011

The success of the revolutions in Tunisia and Egypt, which put an end to two of the most oppressive police states in the Middle East, continues to spark similar popular uprisings across the region. Despite the different institutional structures, geopolitical roles, and military capabilities across the region, the experience in Tunisia, whose uprising sparked the rest, exemplifies what most countries in the region have experienced since their independence from European colonialism, and can shed some light onto their likely post-revolution paths.

In January, Tunisia succeeded in toppling the 23-year Ben Ali regime via a popular grassroots revolt against injustice, corruption, and oppression. The protesters' demands in what has been dubbed the "Jasmine Revolution" were very straightforward: jobs, freedom, and dignity. Like all revolutions, the Tunisian revolution was not an overnight event but rather a long process that can be dissected into four distinct phases with important economic consequences: the neoliberal phase that started in the 1980s with the introduction of World Bank-sponsored economic policies; the plutocracy phase which began in the early 2000s with the rise of the Trabelsi-Ben Ali business empire; the uprising phase which began after the self-immolation of Mohammed Bouazizi on December 17, 2010; and finally the ongoing reconstruction phase which began after the departure of Zine El Abidine Ben Ali on January 14, 2011.

The 1980s neoliberal phase began as Tunisia's external debt soared. Its economy faced high unemployment, low currency reserves, bad harvests, decline in oil revenues, and closure of European labor market outlets for Tunisian immigrants. Like many developing countries, Tunisia was subjected to the World Bank and IMF structural adjustment program: in 1985, aggressive austerity measures led to food riots killing at least 100 people. As the crisis intensified, Ben Ali was appointed interior minister in 1986 and later prime minister in 1987. He then took over as president in a bloodless coup d'état on November 7, 1987. His immediate agenda was two-fold: crush the opposition and forge ahead with structural adjustment policies. Opposition party leaders were arrested, tortured, jailed, killed, or exiled. On the economic front, the government began privatizing state-owned enterprises, promoting free-trade zones, supporting export-oriented industries, and capitalizing on the growth of the tourism industry. Despite robust economic growth rates in the 1990s, unemployment remained stubbornly high, and socioeconomic indicators began to show signs of rising income inequality and deterioration of the economic status of the middle class.

The plutocracy phase began in the early 2000s. While the Trabelsi-Ben Ali clan was amassing billions of dollars in business deals, corruption ravaged the economy, and the Tunisian middle class slid further down the income ladder. Highly educated youth were facing humiliating life conditions and long-term unemployment with little to no hope for a better future. After more than a decade of clearing all opposition forces from the political arena and affirming Ben Ali's grip on the political and security apparatus, Leila Trabelsi, Ben Ali's second wife, expanded her First Lady duties to include securing business deals for her family. The Trabelsi-Ben Ali clan built a gigantic business empire in less than a decade. They secured quasi-monopoly deals in industries such as banking, telecommunications, media, real estate, and retail. Their aggressive and violent approach alienated even the traditional business class, which was forced to sell to or work for the Trabelsi-Ben Ali clan or face serious consequences. Banks were coerced into extending more than $1.7 billion in credit to the Trabelsi-Ben Ali clan without any repayment guarantees.

The uprising phase that followed was intense, well focused, and effective, taking only 23 days to put an end to 23 years of Ben Ali's rule. The leaderless youth movement was spontaneous, secular, fearless, and determined to put an end to an era of repression, theft, and humiliation. In a day-long general strike on January 14, the Tunisian economy was brought to a complete standstill, and men and women from all walks of life joined the protesters to unseat Ben Ali.

The reconstruction phase began as soon as Ben Ali fled the country. It is the most labor-intensive phase and it requires active participation from all facets of Tunisian society. Tunisians have faced the challenge of institutionalizing democracy head-on with popular demands to dissolve Ben Ali's RCD ruling party, free all political prisoners, rewrite the constitution, seize all the Trabelsi-Ben Ali assets, and most importantly, cleanse all socio-economic and government institutions of corrupt RCD loyalists.

While Tunisians are forging ahead with radical constitutional, judicial, and democratic reforms, they will still face a major economic challenge: unemployment among the highly educated youth. The Jasmine Revolution's achievements thus far are commendable, but the revolution will be incomplete without full employment as a means of achieving true social justice.

The challenges after Egypt's revolution are more serious than Tunisia's. The Egyptian military is very large and owns much of the country's industrial and business infrastructure; it also plays a significant role in protecting the American and Israeli interests in the region. A truly democratic civilian government in Egypt will very likely want a military that is more disengaged from the political and economic arena. Egypt is also facing a more serious economic challenge, with mass unemployment and poverty in a population that is eight times larger than that of Tunisia.

While watching events unfold in Libya, Yemen, Bahrain, and beyond, one cannot help but wonder about the extent to which a revolutionary domino effect is likely to sweep the entire region, and its significance for the political economy of the Middle East and its relationship with the United States and Europe. It is clear that there is a critical mass of empowered and fearless youth whose movements are supported by labor advocates, human rights activists, and democratic voices. The challenge, however, is to create lasting radical economic and political changes that will ensure a successful post-revolution reconstruction phase.

Western powers must also recognize that a double-standard policy cannot be an effective way of promoting peace and security in the region. The threat of an Iranian-like anti-Western Islamic revolution is simply not plausible today, so one cannot use the anti-terrorism Bush-Cheney rhetoric to justify Western support for oppressive regimes. It is the actions taken by post-revolution movements in conjunction with the reaction of the West to these events that will determine whether the Jasmine Revolution was a turning point in world history or just a footnote in the history of the region. ❑

Article 9.4

THE TRUE COST OF OIL

What are the military costs of securing "our" oil?

BY ANITA DANCS
May/June 2010

When Americans pull up to the pump, the price they pay for a gallon of gas does not begin to reflect the true costs of extracting, transporting, and burning that gallon of fuel.

Most people know that burning fossil fuels contributes to climate change. Every time we drive our cars, we are sending greenhouse gases into the air, which trap radiation and warm the earth's surface. The more the earth warms, the more costly the consequences.

But as bad as the costs of pollution and global warming are, as taxpayers we pay another cost for oil. Each year, our military devotes substantial resources to securing access to and safeguarding the transportation of oil and other energy sources. I estimate that we will pay $90 billion this year to secure oil. If spending on the Iraq War is included, the total rises to $166 billion.

This year, the U.S. government will spend $722 billion on the military, not including military assistance to other countries, space exploration, or veterans' benefits. Defending American access to oil represents a modest share of U.S. militarism.

Calculating the numbers isn't straightforward. Energy security, according to national security documents, is a vital national interest and has been incorporated into military objectives and strategies for more than half a century. But military documents do not attach a dollar figure to each mission, strategy, or objective, so figuring out which military actions relate to oil requires plowing through various documents and devising methodologies.

The U.S. military carves the world up into regions—Europe, Africa, the Pacific, the Middle East, South America and North America—each with its own command structure, called a "unified combatant command." I arrived at my estimate of military spending related to securing oil by tracing U.S. military objectives and strategies through these geographic commands and their respective fleets, divisions, and other units. I only considered conventional spending, excluding spending on nuclear weapons, which is not directly related to securing access to resources.

U.S. Central Command has an "area of responsibility" which stretches from the Arabian Gulf region through Central Asia and was specifically created in 1980 during the Carter administration because of the region's oil reserves. Two-thirds of the world's oil reserves and nearly half of natural gas supplies reside within these twenty countries. Aside from joint training exercises with oil-producing nations, securing oil fields, and a host of other oil-related tasks, the command closely monitors the

Strait of Hormuz. Nearly half of all oil transported throughout the world passes through this chokepoint, which has been periodically threatened with disruptions. I estimate about 15% of conventional military spending is directed at supporting the missions and strategies of Central Command, and three-quarters of that spending is related to securing and transporting oil from and through the region, as shown in Table 1.

U.S. Pacific Command ensures transportation of oil, specifically through the Strait of Malacca, one of the two most important strategic oil chokepoints. Fifteen million barrels of oil per day flow from the Middle East and West Africa to Asia. This oil is particularly important to another oil-dependent country—Japan, an important American ally in the region. Pacific Command is the largest of all the commands, covering half of the globe. It is also responsible for the largest number of troops and is an important provider of training and troops to U.S. Central Command. Given information on bases, assigned troops and other indicators, I estimate that about 35% of conventional military spending is required for missions and strategies for this command and about 20% of that amount is needed for securing the transport of energy throughout the region.

U.S. European Command and U.S. Africa Command also have resources devoted to securing access to energy. Initially formed to protect Western Europe against Soviet aggression, European Command is currently postured to project power toward the energy-rich areas of the Caspian Sea, the Caucasus, and the Middle East. Alongside NATO, European Command is increasingly focused on energy security in Europe, especially since the revision of NATO's Strategic Concept in 1999. Finally, the command was also responsible for overseeing the set-up of the newest command, U.S. Africa Command, which was motivated by competition for newly discovered oil reserves. I estimate that around 25% of the military budget is devoted to military strategies relating to Europe and Africa, and of that, about two-fifths can be attributed to securing oil and energy supplies.

TABLE 1: SECURING ACCESS TO OIL IN FY2010 (IN BILLIONS OF DOLLARS)

Geographic Combatant Command	Percentage of Total Conventional Military Spending	Share of Conventional Military Spending	Percentage Estimated for Securing Oil	Dollar Estimate for Securing Oil
Central Command	15%	$44.7	75%	$33.5
European Command	30%	$89.4	40%	$35.8
Pacific Command	35%	$104.3	20%	$20.9
Northern & Southern Command	20%	$59.6	0%	$0
Subtotal				$90.2
Iraq War				$76.1
Total				**$166.3**

U.S. Northern Command and U.S. Southern Command are responsible for North and South America and the surrounding waters. While Canada, Mexico, and Venezuela rank in the top five countries from which the United States imports oil, I could not find definitive activities connected with either Northern or Southern Command that would justify inclusion in the estimate.

Dividing the military budget according to geographic regions and reviewing activities in those regions leads me to conclude that about $90 billion will be spent this year for securing access to and the transport of oil and other energy supplies.

But that number does not include the vast sums spent on the Iraq War. In spite of the Bush administration's claims that the United States invaded Iraq because of weapons of mass destruction, evidence points to oil. Since World War II and historic meetings between President Roosevelt and the leader of Saudi Arabia, U.S. policy interests have been focused on establishing a stronghold in the region. Prior to the invasion, the Bush administration had already made plans for the oil industry, and currently, the military surrounds and secures the oil fields.

Since 2003, the Iraq War has cost U.S. taxpayers three-quarters of a trillion dollars, as shown in Table 2. Though spending will decline this year, including the Iraq War brings total spending on securing access to oil to $166 billion. Other analysts might point to the strategic importance of Afghanistan in a resource-rich region, but spending on that prolonged war and occupation is not included in this analysis.

Recently, President Obama appeased the oil industry by opening large parts of the East Coast, Gulf waters, and elsewhere to drilling. But this shortsighted policy would only lessen our dependence on foreign oil by a trivial amount. Moreover, if production were increased, oil prices may drop and the average American may choose to drive more. Bring back the Hummer.

Instead, the $166 billion that we are spending right now on the military could subsidize and expand public transport, weatherize homes, and fund

TABLE 2: COST OF THE IRAQ WAR	
Fiscal Year	Cost of Iraq War (in billions)
2003 (half)	$53.0
2004	75.9
2005	85.5
2006	101.6
2007	130.8
2008	141.1
2009	94.8
2010 (estimated)	76.1
Total Through 2010	$758.8

Source: Based on Belasco, A. "The cost of Iraq, Afghanistan, and Other Global War on Terror Operations since 9/11" Congressional Research Service, RL 33110, September 28, 2009.

research on renewable energy. Typically, the federal government invests only $2.3 billion in renewable energy and conservation each year. Even the stimulus bill, which contained an unprecedented amount of spending for renewable energy and conservation, pales in comparison with military spending. Stimulus spending included $18.5 billion for energy efficiency and renewable energy programs, $8 billion in federal loan guarantees for renewable-energy systems, and $17.4 billion for modernization programs such as the "smart" electricity grid, which will reduce electricity consumption. While these healthy federal investments—spent over several years—will encourage a move away from fossil fuels, strategic military operations securing access to those climate-changing resources will continue to dominate our taxpayer dollar.

Put all these numbers in perspective: The price of a barrel of oil consumed in the United States would have to increase by $23.40 to offset military resources expended to secure oil. That translates to an additional 56 cents for a gallon of gas, or three times the federal gas tax that funds road construction.

If $166 billion were spent on other priorities, the Boston public transportation system, the "T," could have its operating expenses covered, with commuters riding for free. And there would still be money left over for another 100 public transport systems across the United States. Or, we could build and install nearly 50,000 wind turbines. Take your pick. ❏

Sources: Energy Information Administration (eia.doe.gov). These estimates are refined and updated from an earlier paper, Anita Dancs with Mary Orisich and Suzanne Smith, "The Military Cost of Securing Energy," National Priorities Project (nationalpriorities.org), October 2008.

Article 9.5

HAITI'S FAULT LINES: MADE IN THE U.S.A.

BY MARIE KENNEDY AND CHRIS TILLY
March/April 2010

T he mainstream media got half the story right about Haiti. Reporters observed that Haiti's stark poverty intensified the devastation caused by the recent earthquake. True: hillside shantytowns, widespread concrete construction without rebar reinforcement, a grossly inadequate road network, and a healthcare system mainly designed to cater to the small elite all contributed mightily to death and destruction.

But what caused that poverty? U.S. readers and viewers might be forgiven for concluding that some inexplicable curse has handed Haiti corrupt and unstable governments, unproductive agriculture, and widespread illiteracy. Televangelist Pat Robertson simply took this line of "explanation" to its nutty, racist conclusion when he opined that Haitians were paying for a pact with the devil.

But the devil had little to do with Haiti's underdevelopment. Instead, the fingerprints of more mundane actors—France and later the United States—are all over the crime scene. After the slave rebellion of 1791, France wrought massive destruction in attempting to recapture its former colony, then extracted 150 million francs of reparations, only fully paid off in 1947. France's most poisonous legacy may have been the skin-color hierarchy that sparked fratricidal violence and still divides Haiti.

While France accepted Haiti once the government started paying up, the United States, alarmed by the example of a slave republic, refused to recognize Haiti until 1862. That late-arriving recognition kicked off a continuing series of military and political interventions. The U.S. Marines occupied Haiti outright from 1915 to 1934, modernizing the infrastructure but also revising laws to allow foreign ownership, turning over the country's treasury to a New York bank, saddling Haiti with a $40 million debt to the United States, and reinforcing the status gap between mulattos and blacks. American governments backed the brutal, kleptocratic, two-generation Duvalier dictatorship from 1957-86. When populist priest Jean-Bertrand Aristide was elected president in 1990, the Bush I administration winked at the coup that ousted him a year later. Bill Clinton reversed course, ordering an invasion to restore Aristide, but used that intervention to impose the same free-trade "structural adjustment" Bush had sought. Bush II closed the circle by backing rebels who re-overthrew the re-elected Aristide in 2004. No wonder many Haitians are suspicious of the U.S. troops who poured in after the earthquake.

Though coups and invasions grab headlines, U.S. economic interventions have had equally far-reaching effects. U.S. goals for the last 30 years have been to open Haiti to American products, push Haiti's self-sufficient peasants off the land, and redirect the Haitian economy to plantation-grown luxury crops and export assembly, both underpinned by cheap labor. Though Haiti has yet to boost its export capacity, the first two goals have succeeded, shattering Haiti's former productive capacity. In the early 1980s, the U.S. Agency for International Development exterminated Haiti's hardy Creole pigs in the name of preventing a swine flu epidemic, then helpfully offered U.S. pigs that require expensive U.S.-produced feeds and medicines. Cheap American rice imports crippled the country's breadbasket, the Artibonite, so that Haiti, a rice exporter in the 1980s, now imports massive amounts. Former peasants flooded into Port-au-Prince, doubling the population over the last quarter century, building makeshift housing, and setting the stage for the current catastrophe.

In the wake of the disaster, U.S. aid continues to have two-edged effects. Each aid shipment that flies in U.S. rice and flour instead of buying and distributing local rice or cassava continues to undermine agriculture and deepen dependency. Precious trucks and airstrips are used to marshal U.S. troops against overblown "security threats," crowding out humanitarian assistance. The United States and other international donors show signs of once more using aid to leverage a free-trade agenda. If we seek to end Haiti's curse, the first step is to realize that one of the curse's main sources is...us. ❏

Chapter 10

GLOBAL ECONOMIC CRISIS

Article 10.1

PUTTING THE "GLOBAL" IN THE GLOBAL ECONOMIC CRISIS

BY SMRITI RAO
November/December 2009

There is no question that the current economic crisis originated in the developed world, and primarily in the United States. Much of the analysis of the crisis has thus focused on institutional failures within the United States and there is, rightly, tremendous concern here about high rates of domestic unemployment and under-employment. But after three decades of globalization, what happens in the United States does not stay in the United States; the actions of traders in New York City will mean hunger for children in Nairobi. We now know what crisis looks like in the age of globalization and it is not pretty.

This crisis is uniquely a child of the neoliberal global order. For developing countries the key elements of neoliberalism have consisted of trade liberalization and an emphasis on exports; reductions in government social welfare spending; a greater reliance on the market for determining the price of everything from the currency exchange rate to water from the tap; and, last but not least, economy-wide privatization and deregulation. In each case, the aim was also to promote cross-border flows of goods, services, and capital—and, to a far lesser degree, of people.

Despite Thomas Friedman's assertions of a "flat" world, this age of globalization did not in fact eliminate global inequality. Indeed if we exclude China and India, inequality between countries actually increased during this period. The globalization of the last 30 years was predicated upon the extraction by the developed world of the natural resources, cheap labor, and, in particular, capital of the developing world, the latter via financial markets that siphoned the world's savings to pay for U.S. middle-class consumption. What could be more ironic than the billions of dollars in capital flowing every year from developing countries with unfunded domestic needs to developed countries, which then failed to meet even their minimum obligations with respect to foreign aid? Africa, for example, has actually been a net creditor to the United States for some time, suggesting that the underlying dynamic of the world economy today is not that different from the colonialism of past centuries.

These "reverse flows" are partly the result of attempts by developing countries to ward off balance-of-payment crises by holding large foreign exchange reserves. Within the United States, this capital helped sustain massive borrowing by households, corporations, and governments, exacerbating the debt bubble of the last eight years. Meanwhile, the global "race to the bottom" among developing-county exporters ensured that the prices of most manufactured goods and services remained low, taking the threat of inflation off the table and enabling the U.S. Federal Reserve to keep interest rates low and facilitate the housing bubble.

Now that this debt bubble has finally burst, it is no surprise that the crisis has been transmitted back to the global South at record speed.

Measuring the Impact

A country-by-country comparison of the growth in real (i.e., inflation-adjusted) GDP from 2007 to 2008 against the average annual growth of the preceding three years (2005-2007) gives us a picture of the differential impact of the economic crisis—at least in its early stages—on various countries. Consistent data are available for 178 developed and developing countries.

Overall, GDP growth for these 178 countries was down by 1.3 percentage points in 2008 compared to the average for 2005-2007. Of course, the financial crisis only hit in full force in September 2008, so the 2009 data will give us a more complete picture of the impact of the crisis. The International Monetary Fund (IMF) estimates that global GDP will decline in 2009 for the first time since World War II. Currently, the IMF is expecting a 1.4% contraction this year. According to the International Labor Organization, global unemployment increased by 10.7 million in 2008, with a further increase of 19 million expected in 2009 by relatively conservative estimates. As a result, the number of people living in poverty will increase by an estimated 46 million this year according to the World Bank.

The initial impact in 2008 was greatest in Eastern Europe and Central Asia: six of the ten countries with the steepest declines in real GDP growth were from the Eastern Europe/Central Asia region (see Table 1). Joined by Ireland, this is a list of global high-fliers—countries with very high rates of growth (before 2008, that is) that had globalized rapidly and enthusiastically in the last decade and a half. Singapore of course was an early adopter of globalization, touted by the IMF as a model for other small countries, while Seychelles has depended heavily on international tourism. Myanmar would seem to be the exception to this pattern of intensive globalization, given its political isolation. From an economic perspective, however, this was a country whose economic growth depended heavily on the rising prices of its commodity exports (natural gas and gems).

Indeed, if we rank these 178 countries by the share of their GDP represented by exports before the crisis, we find a correlation between dependence on exports and steeper declines in GDP growth. The 50 most export-dependent countries actually saw larger declines in GDP in 2008 than those less dependent on exports (see Table 2). Likewise with certain other key markers of neoliberal globalization.

That globalizers appear to be most affected by the crisis is no accident. It turns out that each of the three primary channels through which the crisis has been transmitted from the United States to other countries is a direct outcome of the policy choices that developing countries were urged and sometimes coerced into making—with assurances that this particular form of globalization was the best way to build a healthy and prosperous economy (see Figure 1 for a summary).

**FIGURE 1: THE CURRENT CRISIS AND IMF POLICIES:
MAKING THE LINKS**

Lowered exports, remittances ("openness")

+

Outflows of portfolio capital ("openness" + no capital controls)

=

Depreciating currencies (floating exchange rates)

=>

Worsening current account balances/debt burdens

X

Falling flows of FDI and development aid

X

"Inflation targeting" and "fiscal restraint"

Transmission Channels of the Crisis

Lowered exports and remittances. The recession in the United States and Europe has hit exports from the developing world hard. Globally, trade in goods and services did rise by 3% in 2008, but that was compared to 10% and 7% in the previous two years. Trade is expected to decline by a sharp 12% in 2009. The United States, the world's most important importer, has seen imports drop by an unprecedented 30% since July 2008. For countries ranging from Pakistan to Cameroon, this has meant lower foreign exchange earnings, slower economic growth, and higher unemployment.

Meanwhile, for many developing countries, the emphasis on export promotion meant the increasing export not of goods and services but of people, who sought work in richer countries and sent part of their earnings back home. Remittance flows from temporary and permanent migrants accounted for 25% of net inflows of private capital to the global South in 2007. These flows are also affected by the crisis, although they have proved more resilient than other sources of private capital.

Migrant workers in construction, in particular, find that they are no longer able to find work and send money back home, and countries in Latin America have seen sharp declines in remittance inflows. However, as Indian economist Jayati Ghosh points out, women migrants working as maids, nurses, and nannies in the West have not been as hard hit by the recession. This has meant that remittance flows to countries with primarily female migrants, such as Sri Lanka and the Philippines, are not as badly affected. The Middle Eastern countries that are important host countries for many Asian migrants have also been relatively shielded from the crisis. As a result, for the developing world as a whole, remittances actually rose in 2008. Because other private capital flows declined sharply post-crisis, remittances accounted for 46% of net private capital inflows to the developing world in 2008.

Outflows of portfolio capital. In the boom years up to 2007, developing countries were encouraged to liberalize their financial sectors. This meant removing regulatory barriers to the inflow (and outflow) of foreign investors and their money. While some foreign investors did buy factories and other actual physical assets in the developing world, a substantial portion of foreign capital came in the form of portfolio capital—short-term investments in stock and real estate markets. Portfolio capital is called "hot money" for a reason: it tends to be incredibly mobile, and its mobility has been enhanced by the systematic dismantling of various government restrictions ("capital controls") that formerly prevented this money from entering or leaving countries at the volume and speed it can today.

Table 1: Steepest Declines in Economic Growth

Top ten countries by decline in 2008 real GDP growth vs. 2005-07 annual average.		
	Country	Change in 2008 real GDP growth compared to 2005-07 average(in percentage points)
1	Latvia	−15.56
2	Azerbaijan	−14.44
3	Estonia	−12.26
4	Georgia	−8.42
5	Myanmar	−8.32
6	Ireland	−8.30
7	Seychelles	−7.62
8	Armenia	−6.85
9	Singapore	−6.66
10	Kazakhstan	−6.57

Source: Author's calculations based on data from World Development Indicators online, World Bank, June 2009.

Around the time of the collapse of Bear Stearns in the United States in early 2008, various global financial powerhouses began pulling their money out of developing-country markets. The pace of the pullout only accelerated after the crash that September. One consequence for developing countries was a fall in their stock market indices, which in turn depressed growth. Another was that as foreign investors converted their krona, rupees, or rubles into dollars in order to leave, the value of the local currency got pushed down.

The IMF has long touted the virtues of allowing freely floating exchange rates, where market forces determine the value of each currency. In the aftermath of the financial crisis, this meant a sharp depreciation in the value of many local currencies relative to the dollar. This in turn meant that every gallon of oil priced in dollars would cost that many more, say, rupees. Similarly, any dollar-denominated debt a country held became harder to repay. The dollar cost of imports and debt servicing went up, just as exports and remittances—the ability to earn those dollars—were falling. Predictably, countries with floating (i.e., market-determined) exchange rates were harder hit in 2008 (see Table 3).

Table 2: Exports and Foreign Investment

Change in 2008 real GDP growth compared to 2005-07 average (in percentage points) for countries ranked by:		
	Export share of GDP	FDI share of GDP
Average for top 50 countries	−2.25	−1.85
Average for countries ranked 51-100	−1.50	−1.70
Average for the remaining countries	−0.88	−1.07
Total number of countries	167	171

Table 3: Exchange Rate and Fiscal Policy

Average change in 2008 real GDP growth compared to 2005-07 average (in percentage points) for country groupings:			
Exchange Rate Policy		Fiscal Policy	
Countries with fixed exchange rate	−1.19	Countries with no inflation targeting	−1.18
Countries with managed float or other mixed policy	−1.19	Countries with inflation targeting	−2.35
Countries with freely floating exchange rate	−2.04		
Total number of countries	178		171

Sources: Author's calculations based on data from World Development Indicators online, World Bank, June 2009 and De Facto Classification of Exchange Rate Regimes and Monetary Policy Frameworks as of April 31, 2008, IMF.

Falling flows of FDI and development aid. Meanwhile, one other source of foreign exchange, foreign investment in actual physical assets such as factories (known as foreign direct investment, or FDI), is stagnant and likely to fall as companies across the world shelve expansion plans. The signs of vulnerability are evident in the fact that countries most dependent upon FDI inflows (as a percentage of GDP) between 2005 and 2007 suffered greater relative GDP declines in 2008 (see Table 2).

Developed countries are also cutting back on foreign aid budgets, citing the cost of domestic stimulus programs and reduced tax revenues. Such cuts particularly affect the poorest countries. With the economic slowdown their governments are losing domestic tax and other revenues, so falling aid flows are likely to hurt even more. The importance of continued aid flows can be seen in the fact that higher levels of aid per capita from 2005 to 2007 were actually associated with more mild drops in GDP growth in 2008 (see Table 2). This may be partly due to the fact that these countries already had low or negative rates of GDP growth so that 2008 declines appear smaller relative to that baseline. Nevertheless, aid flows appear to have protected the most vulnerable countries from even greater economic disaster. In fact the so-called HIPC group (highly indebted poor countries) actually saw an increase of one percentage point in GDP growth rates when compared to the 2005-2007 average.

Both FDI and aid work their way into and out of economies more slowly, so we may have to wait for 2009 data to estimate the full impact of the crisis via this channel.

The simultaneous transmission of the crisis through these three channels has left developing countries reeling. What makes the situation even worse is that unlike developed countries, developing countries are unlikely to be able to afford generous stimulus packages (China is an important exception). Meanwhile, the IMF and its allies, rather than supporting developing-country governments in their quest to stimulate domestic demand and investment, are hindering the process by insisting on the same old policy mix of deficit reductions and interest rate hikes. In an illustration of how ruinous this policy mix can be, countries that had followed IMF advice and adopted "inflation targeting" before the crisis suffered greater relative GDP declines once the crisis hit (see Table 3).

The tragedy of course is that while the remnants of the welfare state still protect citizens of the developed world from the very worst effects of the crisis, developing countries have been urged for two decades to abandon the food and fuel subsidies and public sector provision of essential services that are the only things that come close to resembling a floor for living standards. They were told they didn't need that safety net, that it only got in the way; now, of course, they are free to fall.

For those unwilling to let this tragedy unfold, this is the time to apply pressure on developed-country governments to maintain aid flows. Even more importantly, this is the time to apply pressure on the IMF and the other multilateral development banks, and on their supporters in the halls of power, so that they offer developing countries a genuine chance to survive this crisis and begin to rebuild for the future.

It is worth recalling that the end of the previous "age of globalization," signaled by the Great Depression, led to a renewed role for the public sector the world over and an attempt to achieve growth alongside self-reliance. In the years after World War II, led by Latin America, newly independent developing countries attempted to prioritize building a domestic producer and consumer base. In the long run, perhaps this crisis will result in a similar rethinking of the currently dominant model of development. In the short run, however, the world seems ready to stand by and watch while the poor and vulnerable in developing countries, truly innocent bystanders, suffer. ❏

Sources: Dilip Ratha, Sanket Mohapatra, and Ani Silwal, "Migration and Development Brief 10," Migration and Remittances Team, Development Prospects Group, World Bank, July 13, 2009; Atish R. Ghosh et al. 2009, "Coping with the Crisis: Policy Options for Emerging Market Countries," IMF Staff Position Note, SPN/09/08, April 23, 2009; World Bank, "Swimming Against the Tide: How Developing Countries Are Coping with the Global Crisis," Background Paper prepared by World Bank Staff for the G20 Finance Ministers and Central Bank Governors Meeting, Horsham, United Kingdom on March 13-14, 2009; Jayati Ghosh, "Current Global Financial Crisis: Curse or Blessing in Disguise for Developing Countries?" Presentation prepared for the IWG-GEM Workshop, Levy Economics Institute, New York, June 29-July 10, 2009.

Article 10.2

W(H)ITHER THE DOLLAR?

The U.S. trade deficit, the global economic crisis, and the dollar's status as the world's reserve currency.

BY KATHERINE SCIACCHITANO

For more than half a century, the dollar was both a symbol and an instrument of U.S. economic and military power. At the height of the financial crisis in the fall of 2008, the dollar served as a safe haven for investors, and demand for U.S. Treasury bonds ("Treasuries") spiked. More recently, the United States has faced a vacillating dollar, calls to replace the greenback as the global reserve currency, and an international consensus that it should save more and spend less.

At first glance, circumstances seem to give reason for concern. The U.S. budget deficit is over 10% of GDP. China has begun a long-anticipated move away from Treasuries, threatening to make U.S. government borrowing more expensive. And the adoption of austerity measures in Greece—with a budget deficit barely 3% higher than the United States—hovers as a reminder that the bond market can enforce wage cuts and pension freezes on developed as well as developing countries.

These pressures on the dollar and for fiscal cut-backs and austerity come at an awkward time given the level of public outlays required to deal with the crisis and the need to attract international capital to pay for them. But the pressures also highlight the central role of the dollar in the crisis. Understanding that role is critical to grasping the link between the financial recklessness we've been told is to blame for the crisis and the deeper causes of the crisis in the real economy: that link is the outsize U.S. trade deficit.

Trade deficits are a form of debt. For mainstream economists, the cure for the U.S. deficit is thus increased "savings": spend less and the bottom line will improve. But the U.S. trade deficit didn't balloon because U.S. households or the government went on a spending spree. It ballooned because, from the 1980s on, successive U.S. administrations pursued a high-dollar policy that sacrificed U.S. manufacturing for finance, and that combined low-wage, export-led growth in the Global South with low-wage, debt-driven consumption at home. From the late nineties, U.S. dollars that went out to pay for imports increasingly came back not as demand for U.S. goods, but as demand for investments that fueled U.S. housing and stock market bubbles. Understanding the history of how the dollar helped create these imbalances, and how these imbalances in turn led to the housing bubble and sub-prime crash, sheds important light on how labor and the left should respond to pressures for austerity and "saving" as the solution to the crisis.

Gold, Deficits, and Austerity

A good place to start is with the charge that the Federal Reserve triggered the housing bubble by lowering interest rates after the dot-com bubble burst and plunged the country into recession in 2001.

In 2001, manufacturing was too weak to lead a recovery, and the Bush administration was ideologically opposed to fiscal stimulus other than tax cuts for the wealthy. So the real question isn't why the Fed lowered rates; it's why it was able to. In 2000, the U.S. trade deficit stood at 3.7% of GDP. Any other country with this size deficit would have had to tighten its belt and jump-start exports, not embark on stimulating domestic demand that could deepen the deficit even more.

The Fed's ability to lower interest rates despite the U.S. trade deficit stemmed from the dollar's role as the world's currency, which was established during the Bretton Woods negotiations for a new international monetary system at the end of World War II.

A key purpose of an international monetary system—Bretton Woods or any other—is to keep international trade and debt in balance. Trade has to be mutual. One country can't do all the selling while other does all the buying; both must be able to buy and sell. If one or more countries develop trade deficits that persist, they won't be able to continue to import without borrowing and going into debt. At the same time, some other country or countries will have corresponding trade surpluses. The result is a global trade imbalance. To get back "in balance," the deficit country has to import less, export more, or both. The surplus country has to do the reverse.

In practice, economic pressure is stronger on deficit countries to adjust their trade balances by importing less, since it's deficit countries that could run out of money to pay for imports. Importing less can be accomplished with import quotas (which block imports over a set level) or tariffs (which decrease demand for imports by imposing a tax on them). It can also be accomplished with "austerity"—squeezing demand by lowering wages.

Under the gold standard, this squeezing took place automatically. Gold was shipped out of a country to pay for a trade deficit. Since money had to be backed by gold, having less gold meant less money in domestic circulation. So prices and wages fell. Falling wages in turn lowered demand for imports and boosted exports. The deficit was corrected, but at the cost of recession, austerity, and hardship for workers. In other words, the gold standard was deflationary.

Bretton Woods

The gold standard lasted until the Great Depression, and in fact helped to cause it. Beyond the high levels of unemployment, one of the most vivid lessons from the global catastrophe that ensued was the collapse of world trade, as country after country tried to deal with falling exports by limiting imports. After World War II, the industrialized countries wanted an international monetary system that could correct trade imbalances without imposing austerity and risking another depression. This was particularly important given the post-war levels of global debt and deficits, which could have suppressed demand and blocked trade again. Countries pursued these aims at the Bretton Woods negotiations in 1944, in Bretton Woods, New Hampshire.

John Maynard Keynes headed the British delegation. Keynes was already famous for his advocacy of government spending to bolster demand and maintain employment during recessions and depressions. England also owed large war debts to the United States and had suffered from high unemployment for over two decades. Keynes therefore had a keen interest in creating a system that prevented the build-up of global debt and avoided placing the full pressure of correcting trade imbalances on debtor countries.

His proposed solution was an international clearing union—a system of accounts kept in a fictitious unit called the "bancor." Accounts would be tallied each year to see which countries were in deficit and which were in surplus. Countries with trade deficits would have to work to import less and export more. In the meantime, they would have the unconditional right—for a period—to an "overdraft" of bancors, the size of the overdraft to be based on the size of previous surpluses. These overdrafts would both support continued imports of necessities and guarantee uninterrupted global trade. At the same time, countries running trade surpluses would be expected to get back in balance too by importing more, and would be fined if their surpluses persisted.

Keynes was also adamant that capital controls be part of the new system. Capital controls are restrictions on the movement of capital across borders. Keynes wanted countries to be able to resort to macroeconomic tools such as deficit spending, lowering interest rates, and expanding money supplies to bolster employment and wages when needed. He worried that without capital controls, capital flight—investors taking their money and running—could veto economic policies and force countries to raise interest rates, cut spending, and lower wages instead, putting downward pressure on global demand as the gold standard had.

Keynes's system wouldn't have solved the problems of capitalism—in his terms, the problem of insufficient demand, and in Marx's terms the problems of overproduction and under-consumption. But by creating incentives for surplus countries to import more, it would have supported global demand and job growth and made the kind of trade imbalances that exist today—including the U.S. trade deficit—much less likely. It would also have taken the pressure off deficit countries to adopt austerity measures. And it would have prevented surplus countries from using the power of debt to dictate economic policy to deficit countries.

At the end of World War II, the United States was, however, the largest surplus country in the world, and it intended to remain so for the foreseeable future. The New Deal had lowered unemployment during the Depression. But political opposition to deficit spending had prevented full recovery until arms production for the war restored manufacturing. Many feared that without continued large U.S. trade surpluses and expanded export markets, unemployment would return to Depression-era levels.

The United States therefore blocked Keynes' proposal. Capital controls were permitted for the time being, largely because of the danger that capital would flee war-torn Europe. But penalties for surplus countries were abandoned; pressures remained primarily on deficit countries to correct. Instead of an international clearing union with automatic rights to overdrafts, the International Monetary Fund (IMF) was established to make short-term loans to deficit countries. And instead of the neutral bancor, the dollar—backed by the U.S. pledge to redeem dollars with gold at $35 an ounce—would be the world currency.

Limits of the System

The system worked for just over twenty-five years, not because trade was balanced, but because the United States was able and willing to recycle its huge trade surpluses. U.S. military spending stayed high because of the U.S. cold-war role as "global cop." And massive aid was given to Europe to rebuild. Dollars went out as foreign aid and military spending (both closely coordinated). They came back as demand for U.S. goods.

At the same time, memory of the Depression created a kind of Keynesian consensus in the advanced industrial democracies to use fiscal and monetary policy to maintain full employment. Labor movements, strengthened by both the war and the post-war boom, pushed wage settlements and welfare spending higher. Global demand was high.

Two problems doomed the system. First, the IMF retained the power to impose conditions on debtor countries, and the United States retained the power to control the IMF.

Second, the United States stood outside the rules of the game: The larger the world economy grew, the more dollars would be needed in circulation; U.S. trade deficits would eventually have to provide them. Other countries would have to correct their trade deficits by tightening their belts to import less, exporting more by devaluing their currencies to push down prices, or relying on savings from trade surpluses denominated in dollars (known as "reserves") to pay for their excess of imports over exports. But precisely because countries needed dollar reserves to pay for international transactions and to provide cushions against periods of deficits, other countries would need to hold the U.S. dollars they earned by investing them in U.S. assets. This meant that U.S. dollars that went out for imports would come back and be reinvested in the United States. Once there, these dollars could be used to finance continued spending on imports—and a larger U.S. trade deficit. At that point, sustaining world trade would depend not on recycling U.S. surpluses, but on recycling U.S. deficits. The ultimate result would be large, destabilizing global capital flows.

The Crisis of the 'Seventies

The turning point came in the early 'seventies. Europe and Japan had rebuilt from the war and were now export powers in their own right. The U.S. trade surplus was turning into a deficit. And the global rate of profit in manufacturing was falling. The United States had also embarked on its "War on Poverty" just as it increased spending on its real war in Vietnam, and this "guns and butter" strategy—an attempt to quell domestic opposition from the civil right and anti-war movements while maintaining global military dominance—led to high inflation.

The result was global economic crisis: the purchasing power of the dollar fell, just as more and more dollars were flowing out of the United States and being held by foreigners.

What had kept the United States from overspending up to this point was its Bretton Woods commitment to exchange dollars for gold at the rate of $35 an ounce. Now countries and investors that didn't want to stand by and watch as the purchasing power of their dollar holdings fell—as well as countries that objected to the Vietnam War—held the United States to its pledge.

There wasn't enough gold in Ft. Knox. The United States would have to retrench its global military role, reign in domestic spending, or change the rules of the game. It changed the rules of the game. In August 1971, Nixon closed the gold window; the United States would no longer redeem dollars for gold. Countries and individuals would have to hold dollars, or dump them and find another currency that was more certain to hold its value. There was none.

The result was that the dollar remained the global reserve currency. But the world moved from a system where the United States could spend only if could back its spending by gold, to a system where its spending was limited only by the quantity of dollars the rest of the world was willing to hold. The value of the dollar would fluctuate with the level of global demand for U.S. products and investment. The value of other currencies would fluctuate with the dollar.

Trading Manufacturing for Finance

The result of this newfound freedom to spend was a decade of global inflation and crises of the dollar. As inflation grew, each dollar purchased less. As each dollar purchased less, the global demand to hold dollars dropped—and with it the dollar's exchange rate. As the exchange rate fell, imports became even more expensive, and inflation ratcheted up again. The cycle intensified when OPEC—which priced its oil in dollars—raised its prices to compensate for the falling dollar.

Owners of finance capital were unhappy because inflation was eroding the value of dollar assets. Owners of manufacturing capital were unhappy because the global rate of profit in manufacturing was dropping. And both U.S. politicians and elites were unhappy because the falling dollar was eroding U.S. military power by making it more expensive.

The response of the Reagan administration was to unleash neoliberalism on both the national and global levels—the so-called Reagan revolution. On the domestic front, inflation was quelled, and the labor movement was put in its place, with high interest rates and the worst recession since the Depression. Corporate profits were boosted directly through deregulation, privatization, and tax cuts, and indirectly by attacks on unions, unemployment insurance, and social spending.

When it was over, profits were up, inflation and wages were down, and the dollar had changed direction. High interest rates attracted a stream of investment capital into the United States, pushing up demand for the currency, and with it the exchange rate. The inflows paid for the growing trade and budget deficits—Reagan had cut domestic spending, but increased military spending. And they provided abundant capital for finance and overseas investment. But the high dollar also made U.S. exports more expensive for the rest of the world. The United States had effectively traded manufacturing for finance and debt.

Simultaneously, debt was used as a hammer to impose neoliberalism on the Third World. As the price of oil rose in the seventies, OPEC countries deposited their growing trade surpluses—so-called petro-dollars—in U.S. banks, which in turn loaned them to poor countries to pay for the soaring price of oil. Initially set at very low interest rates, loan payments skyrocketed when the United States jacked up its rates to deal with inflation. Third World countries began defaulting, starting with Mexico in 1981. In response, and in exchange for more loans, the U.S.-controlled IMF imposed austerity programs, also known as "structural adjustment programs."

The programs were similar to the policies in the United States, but much more severe, and they operated in reverse. Instead of pushing up exchange rates to attract finance capital as the United States had done, Third World countries were told to devalue their currencies to attract foreign direct investment and export their way out of debt. Capital controls were dismantled to enable transnational corporations to enter and exit at will. Governments were forced to slash spending on social programs and infrastructure to push down wages and demand for imports. Services were privatized to create opportunities for private capital, and finance was deregulated.

Policies dovetailed perfectly. As the high dollar hollowed out U.S. manufacturing, countries in the Global South were turned into low-wage export platforms. As U.S. wages stagnated or fell, imports became cheaper, masking the pain. Meanwhile, the high dollar lowered the cost of overseas production. Interest payments on third world debt—which continued to grow—swelled the already large capital flows into the United States and provided even more funds for overseas investment.

The view from the heights of finance looked promising. But Latin America was entering what became known as "the lost decade." And the United State was shifting from exporting goods to exporting demand, and from recycling its trade surplus to recycling its deficit. The world was becoming dependent on the United States as the "consumer of last resort." The United States was becoming dependent on finance and debt.

Consolidating Neoliberalism

The growth of finance in the eighties magnified its political clout in the nineties. With the bond market threatening to charge higher rates for government debt, Clinton abandoned campaign pledges to invest in U.S. infrastructure, education, and industry. Instead, he balanced the budget; he adopted his own high-dollar policy, based on the theory that global competition would keep imports cheap, inflation low, and the living standard high—regardless of sluggish wage growth; and he continued deregulation of the finance industry—repealing Glass-Steagall and refusing to regulate derivatives. By the end of Clinton's second term, the U.S. trade deficit had hit a record 3.7% of GDP; household debt had soared to nearly 69% of GDP and financial profits had risen to 30% of GDP, almost twice as high as they had been at any time up to the mid 1980s.

Internationally, Clinton consolidated IMF-style structural adjustment policies under the rubric of "the Washington Consensus," initiated a new era of trade agreements modeled on the North American Free Trade Agreement, and led the charge to consolidate the elimination of capital controls.

The elimination of capital controls deepened global economic instability in several ways.

First, eliminating restrictions on capital mobility made it easier for capital to go in search of the lowest wages. This expanded the globalization of production, intensifying downward pressure on wages and global demand.

Second, removing capital controls increased the political power of capital by enabling it to "vote with its feet." This accelerated the deregulation of global finance and—as Keynes predicted—limited countries' abilities to run full-employment policies. Regulation of business was punished, as was deficit spending, regardless of its purpose. Low inflation and deregulation of labor markets—weakening unions and making wages more "flexible"—were rewarded.

Finally, capital mobility fed asset bubbles and increased financial speculation and exchange rate volatility. As speculative capital rushed into countries, exchange rates rose; as it fled, they fell. Speculators began betting more and more on currencies themselves, further magnifying rate swings. Rising exchange rates made exports uncompetitive, hurting employment and wages. Falling exchange rates increased the competitiveness of exports, but made imports and foreign borrowing more expensive, except for the United States, which borrows in its own currency. Countries could try to prevent capital flight by raising interest rates, but only at the cost of dampening growth and lost of jobs. Lacking capital controls, there was little countries could do to prevent excessive inflows and bubbles.

Prelude to a Crash

This increased capital mobility, deregulation, and speculation weakened the real economy, further depressed global demand, and greatly magnified economic instability.

From the eighties onward, international financial crises broke out approximately every five years, in countries ranging from Mexico to the former Soviet Union.

By far the largest crisis prior to the sub-prime meltdown took place in East Asia in the mid-nineties. Speculative capital began flowing into East Asia in the mid nineties. In 1997, the bubble burst. By the summer of 1998, stock markets around the world were crashing from the ripple effects. The IMF stepped in with $40 billion in loans, bailing out investors but imposing harsh conditions on workers and governments. Millions were left unemployed as Asia plunged into depression.

When the dust settled, Asian countries said "never again." Their solution was to build up large dollar reserves—savings cushions—so they would never have to turn to the IMF for another loan. To build up reserves, countries had to run large trade surpluses. This meant selling even more to the United States, the only market in the world able and willing to run ever-larger trade deficits to absorb their exports.

In addition to further weakening U.S. manufacturing, the Asia crisis set the stage for the sub-prime crisis in several ways.

First, as capital initially fled Asia, it sought out the United States as a "safe haven," igniting the U.S. stock market and nascent housing bubbles.

Second, the longer-term recycling of burgeoning Asian surpluses ensured an abundant and ongoing source of capital to finance not only the mounting trade deficit, but also the billowing U.S. consumer debt more generally.

Third, preventing their exchange rates from rising with their trade surpluses and making their exports uncompetitive required Asian central banks to print money, swelling global capital flows even more.

Between 1998 and 2007, when the U.S. housing bubble burst, many policy makers and mainstream economists came to believe this inflow of dollars and debt would never stop. It simply seemed too mutually beneficial to end. By financing the U.S. trade deficit, Asian countries guaranteed U.S. consumers would continue to purchase their goods. The United States in turn got cheap imports, cheap money for consumer finance, and inflated stock and real estate markets that appeared to be self-financing and to compensate for stagnating wages. At the same time, foreign holders of dollars bought increasing quantities of U.S. Treasuries, saving the U.S. government from having to raise interest rates to attract purchasers, and giving the United States cheap financing for its budget deficit as well.

It was this ability to keep interest rates low—in particular, the Fed's ability to lower rates after the stock market bubble collapsed in 2000—that set off the last and most destructive stage of the housing bubble. Lower interest rates simultaneously increased the demand for housing (since lower interest rates made mortgages cheaper) and decreased the returns to foreign holders of U.S. Treasuries. These lower returns forced investors to look for other "safe" investments with higher yields. Investors believed they found what they needed in U.S. mortgage securities.

As Wall Street realized what a lucrative international market they had, the big banks purposefully set out to increase the number of mortgages that could be repackaged and sold to investors by lowering lending standards. They also entered into complicated systems of private bets, known as credit default swaps, to insure against the risk of defaults. These credit default swaps created a chain of debt that exponentially magnified risk. When the bubble finally burst, only massive stimulus spending and infusions of capital by the industrialized countries into their banking systems kept the world from falling into another depression.

Deficit Politics

The political establishment—right and center—is now licking its chops, attacking fiscal deficits as if ending them were a solution to the crisis. The underlying theory harks back to the deflationary operation of the gold standard and the conditions imposed by the IMF: Government spending causes trade deficits and inflation by increasing demand. Cutting spending will cut deficits by diminishing demand.

Like Clinton before him, Obama is now caving in to the bond market, fearful that international lenders will raise interest rates on U.S. borrowing. He has created a bi-partisan debt commission to focus on long-term fiscal balance—read: cutting Social Security and Medicare—and revived "PAYGO," which requires either cuts or increases in revenue to pay for all new outlays, even as unemployment hovers just under 10%.

By acquiescing, the U.S. public is implicitly blaming itself for the crisis and offering to pay for it twice: first with the millions of jobs lost to the recession, and again by weakening the safety net. But the recent growth of the U.S. budget deficit principally reflects the cost of cleaning up the crisis and of the wars in Iraq and Afghanistan. Assumptions of future deficits are rooted in projected health-care costs in the absence of meaningful reform. And the U.S. trade deficit is driven mainly by the continued high dollar.

The economic crisis won't be resolved by increasing personal savings or enforcing fiscal discipline, because its origins aren't greedy consumers or profligate governments. The real origins of the crisis are the neoliberal response to the crisis of the 1970s—the shift from manufacturing to finance in the United States, and the transformation of the Global South into a low-wage export platform for transnational capital to bolster sagging profit rate. The U.S. trade and budget deficits may symbolize this transformation. But the systemic problem is a global economic model that separates consumption from production and that has balanced world demand—not just the U.S. economy—on debt and speculation.

Forging an alternative will be the work of generations. As for the present, premature tightening of fiscal policy as countries try to "exit" from the crisis will simply drain global demand and endanger recovery. Demonizing government spending will erode the social wage and undermine democratic debate about the public investment needed for a transition to an environmentally sustainable global economy.

In the United States, where labor market and financial deregulation have garnered the most attention in popular critiques of neoliberalism, painting a bulls-eye on government spending also obscures the role of the dollar and U.S. policy in the crisis. For several decades after World War II, U.S. workers benefited materially as the special status of the dollar helped expand export markets for U.S. goods. But as other labor movements throughout the world know from bitter experience, it's the dollar as the world's currency, together with U.S. control of the IMF, that ultimately provided leverage for the United States to create the low-wage export model of growth and financial deregulation that has so unbalanced the global economy and hurt "first" and "third" world workers alike.

Looking Ahead

At the end of World War II, John Maynard Keynes proposed an international monetary system with the bancor at its core; the system would have helped balance trade and avoid the debt and deflation in inherent in the gold standard that preceded the Great Depression. Instead, Bretton Woods was negotiated, with the dollar as the world's currency. What's left of that system has now come full circle and created the very problems it was intended to avoid: large trade imbalances and deflationary economic conditions.

For the past two and a half decades, the dollar enabled the United States to run increasing trade deficits while systematically draining capital from some of the poorest countries in the world. This money could have been used for development in the Global South, to replace aging infrastructure in the United States, or to prepare for and prevent climate change. Instead, it paid for U.S. military interventions, outsourcing, tax cuts for the wealthy, and massive stock market and housing bubbles.

This mismanagement of the dollar hasn't served the long-term interests of workers the United States any more than it has those in of the developing world. In domestic terms, it has been particularly damaging over the last three decades to U.S. manufacturing, and state budgets and workers are being hit hard by the crisis. Yet even manufacturing workers in the United States cling to the high dollar as if it were a life raft. Many public sector workers advocate cutting back on government spending. And most people in the United States would blame bankers' compensation packages for the sub-prime mess before pointing to the dismantling of capital controls.

After suffering through the worst unemployment since the Depression and paying for the bailout of finance, U.S. unions and the left are right to be angry. On the global scale, there is increased space for activism. Since the summer of 2007, at least 17 countries have imposed or tightened capital controls. Greek workers have been in the streets protesting pension cuts and pay freezes for months now. And a global campaign has been launched for a financial transactions tax that would slow down speculation and provide needed revenue for governments. Together, global labor and the left are actively rethinking and advocating reform of the global financial system, the neoliberal trade agreements, and the role and governance of the International Monetary Fund. And there is increasing discussion of a replacement for the dollar that won't breed deficits, suck capital out of the developing world, impose austerity on deficit countries—or blow bubbles.

Article 10.3

WHO WINS WHEN THE DOLLAR LOSES VALUE?

BY ARTHUR MacEWAN
July/August 2010

Dear Dr. Dollar:

When the dollar loses value in comparison with other currencies, which groups in the United States win and which lose? Do consumers benefit? Does the corporate elite profit? And how does a lower-valued dollar affect the trade deficit?
—*Julia Willebrand, New York, NY*

When the dollar loses value in comparison with other currencies, imports to the United States tend to become more expensive. It takes more dollars to buy, for example, 100 yuan of Chinese goods because it takes more dollars to purchase that amount of yuan. So if you shop a lot at Target or Wal-Mart to buy the low-priced Chinese-made goods, you lose.

However, if you are producing goods for export—for example, U.S.-made semiconductors, software, aircraft, medical equipment, pharmaceutical preparations—then people in other countries will be able to buy your goods at lower prices in terms of their own currencies. In China, it will take less yuan to buy a dollar's worth of the goods you produce; in Europe, it will take less euros. So people in other countries will tend to buy more of the goods you produce. You win.

Higher-priced imports tend to push up prices generally, while lower-priced exports usually mean more jobs in the United States. At a time when inflation is not a threat but we are suffering from a lack of jobs, some loss in the value of the dollar would probably be a good thing.

In recent years, we in the United States have been spending a lot more on goods from abroad than people abroad have been spending on goods from the United States. That difference is the trade deficit. If the dollar falls in value, we can expect that the trade deficit will fall—meaning we would buy less from abroad and people abroad would buy more from us.

A trade deficit, however, has another side. When we import more than we export (each measured in dollars), people abroad are getting more dollars for what they sell to us than they are spending on things that they buy from us. They use these extra dollars to make financial investments (stocks and bonds) or real investments (factories and offices) in the United States. The Chinese government, in particular, has accumulated the dollars that we pay for Chinese goods and has used those dollars to buy U.S. assets. In early 2009, the Chinese central bank held $764 billion in U.S. Treasury bonds, financing a large part of the U.S. government's budget deficit.

If the dollar loses value against other currencies and if, as a result, the trade deficit declines, this means less foreign investment in the United States—i.e., fewer loans from abroad to finance the federal government's debt and also private debt. The result would tend to be an increase of interest rates in the United States. Higher interest rates could reduce real investment in the United States—which could counter the positive jobs impact of the expansion of exports.

But the big losers from rising interest rates could be the banks. They hold huge amounts of Treasury bonds. If interest rates were to rise, the value of those bonds would fall and the banks (and other creditors) could lose billions. For example, on ten-year Treasury bonds, with an increase from 3.5% (roughly the rate in mid-May) to 4.5%, the creditors' bonds would lose about 9% of their value. (That is, a $100 bond returning 3.5% would yield $141.06 in ten years. But at 4.5%, a $90.83 bond would yield $141.06 in ten years. So if interest rates jumped from 3.5% to 4.5%, that $100 bond would be worth only $90.83.)

It is not automatic that a fall in the value of the dollar relative to other currencies would lead to a rise in interest rates. The Federal Reserve could take action (buying more of the Treasury bonds itself) that would keep interest rates down. But this could create other problems—in particular, it could raise the likelihood of inflation.

Some things are pretty clear—a decline in the value of the dollar would lead to higher import prices and an increase in demand for exports. Other impacts depend on a variety of other actions that are difficult to predict—most important, the actions of monetary authorities in the United States and elsewhere.

Beyond the consequences of a loss in the value of the dollar, there are problems that arise from erratic fluctuations in the dollar's value. Over the last two years, the value of the dollar relative to the euro has swung widely, gaining or losing 15% to 20% in these swings. Such gyrations both mess things up and reflect the mess that already exists. ❏

Article 10.4

(ECONOMIC) FREEDOM'S JUST ANOTHER WORD FOR...CRISIS-PRONE

BY JOHN MILLER
September/October 2009

In "Capitalism in Crisis," his May op-ed in the *Wall Street Journal*, U.S. Court of Appeals judge and archconservative legal scholar Richard Posner argued that "a capitalist economy, while immensely dynamic and productive, is not inherently stable." Posner, the long-time cheerleader for deregulation added, quite sensibly, "we may need more regulation of banking to reduce its inherent riskiness."

That may seem like a no-brainer to you and me, right there in the middle of the road with yellow-lines and dead armadillos, as Jim Hightower is fond of saying. But *Journal* readers were having none of it. They wrote in to set Judge Posner straight. "It is not free markets that fail, but government-controlled ones," protested one reader.

And why wouldn't they protest? The *Journal* has repeatedly told readers that "economic freedom" is "the real key to development." And each January for 15 years now the *Journal* tries to elevate that claim to a scientific truth by publishing a summary of the Heritage Foundation Index of Economic Freedom, which they assure readers proves the veracity of the claim.   But the hands of the editors of the *Wall Street Journal* and the researchers from the Heritage Foundation, Washington's foremost right-wing think tank, the Index of Economic Freedom is a barometer of corporate and entrepreneurial freedom from accountability rather than a guide to which countries are giving people more control over their economic lives and over the institutions that govern them.

This January was no different. "The 2009 Index provides strong evidence that the countries that maintain the freest economies do the best job promoting prosperity for all citizens," proclaimed this year's editorial, "Freedom is Still the Winning Formula." But with economies across the globe in recession, the virtues of free markets are a harder sell this year. That is not lost on *Wall Street Journal* editor Paul Gigot, who wrote the foreword to this year's report. Gigot allows that, "ostensibly free-market policymakers in the U.S. lost their monetary policy discipline, and we are now paying a terrible price." Still Gigot maintains that, "the *Index of Economic Freedom* exists to chronicle how steep that price will be and to point the way back to policy wisdom."

What the Heritage report fails to mention is this: while the global economy is in recession, many of the star performers in the Economic Freedom Index are tanking. Fully one half of the ten hardest-hit economies in the world are among the 30 "free" and "mostly free" economies at the top of the Economic Freedom Index rankings of 179 countries.

Here's the damage, according to the IMF. Singapore, the Southeast Asian trading center and perennial number two in the Index, will suffer a 10.0% drop in output this year. Slotting in at number 4, Ireland, the so-called Celtic tiger, has seen its rapid export-led growth give way to an 8.0% drop in output. Number 13 and number 30, the foreign-direct-investment-favored Baltic states, Estonia and Lithuania, will each endure a 10.0% loss of output this year. Finally, the economy of Iceland, the loosely regulated European banking center that sits at number 14 on the Index, will contract 10.6% in 2009.

As a group, the Index's 30 most "free" economies will contract 4.1% in 2009. All of the other groups in the Index ("moderately free," "mostly unfree," and "repressed" economies) will muddle through 2009 with a much smaller loss of output or with moderate growth. The 67 "mostly unfree" countries in the Index will post the fastest growth rate for the year, 2.3%.

So it seems that if the Index of Economic Freedom can be trusted, then Judge Posner was not so far off the mark when he described capitalism as dynamic but "not inherently stable." That wouldn't be so bad, one *Journal* reader pointed out in a letter: "Economic recessions are the cost we pay for our economic freedom and economic prosperity is the benefit. We've had many more years of the latter than the former."

Not to Be Trusted

But the Index of Economic Freedom cannot and should not be trusted. How free or unfree an economy is according to the Index seems to have little do with how quickly it grows. For instance, economist Jeffery Sachs found "no correlation" between a country's ranking in the Index and its per capita growth rates from 1995 to 2003. Also, in this year's report North America is the "freest" of its six regions of the world, but logged the slowest average rate over the last five years, 2.7% per annum. The Asia-Pacific region, which is "less free" than every other region except Sub-Saharan Africa according to the Index, posted the fastest average growth over the last five years, 7.8% per annum. That region includes several of fastest growing of the world's economies, India, China, and Vietnam, which ranked 123, 132, and

ECONOMIC FREEDOM AND ECONOMIC GROWTH IN 2009	
Degree of Economic Freedom	IMF Projected Growth Rate for 2009
"Free" (7 Countries)	-4.54%
"Mostly Free" (23 Counties)	-3.99%
"Moderately Free" (53 Countries)	-0.92%
"Mostly Unfree" (67 Countries)	+2.31%
"Repressed" (69 Counties)	+1.65%
Sources: International Monetary Fund, *World Economic Outlook,: Crisis and Recovery*, April 2009, Tables A1, A2, A3; Terry Miller and Kim R. Holmes, eds., *2009 Index of Economic Freedom*, heritage.org/Index/, Executive Summary.	

145 respectively in the Index and were classified as "mostly unfree." And there are plenty of relatively slow growers among the countries high up in the Index, including Switzerland (which ranks ninth).

The Heritage Foundation folks who edited the Index objected to Sachs' criticisms, pointing out that they claimed "a close relationship" between *changes* in economic freedom, not the *level* of economic freedom, and growth. But even that claim is fraught with problems. Statistically it doesn't hold up. Economic journalist Doug Henwood found that improvements in the index and GDP growth from 1997 to 2003 could explain no more than 10% of GDP growth. In addition, even a tight correlation would not resolve the problem that many of the fastest growing economies are "mostly unfree" according to the Index.

But even more fundamental flaws with the Index render any claim about the relationship between prosperity and economic freedom, as measured by the Heritage Foundation, questionable. Consider just two of the ten components the Economic Freedom Index uses to rank countries: fiscal freedom and government size.

Fiscal freedom (what we might call the "hell-if-I'm-going-to-pay-for-government" index) relies on the top income tax and corporate income tax brackets as two of its three measures of the tax burden. These are decidedly flawed measures even if all that concerned you was the tax burden of the rich and owners of corporations (or the super-rich). Besides ignoring the burden of other taxes, singling out these two top tax rates don't get at effective corporate and income tax rates, or how much of a taxpayer's total income goes to paying these taxes. For example, on paper U.S. corporate tax rates are higher than those in Europe. But nearly one half of U.S. corporate profits go untaxed. The effective rate of taxation on U.S. corporate profits currently stands at 15%, far below the top corporate tax rate of 35%. And relative to GDP, U.S. corporate income taxes are no more than half those of other OECD countries.

Even their third measure of fiscal freedom, government tax revenues relative to GDP, bears little relationship to economic growth. After an exhaustive review, economist Joel Selmrod, former member of the Reagan Treasury Department, concludes that the literature reveals "no consensus" about the relationship between the level of taxation and economic growth.

The Index's treatment of government size, which relies exclusively on the level of government spending relative to GDP, is just as flawed as the fiscal freedom index. First, "richer countries do not tax and spend less" than poorer countries, reports economist Peter Lindhert. Beyond that, this measure does not take into account how the government uses its money. Social spending programs—public education, child-care and parental support, and public health programs—can make people more productive and promote economic growth. That lesson is not lost on Hong Kong and Singapore, number one and number two in the index. They both provide universal access to health care, despite the small size of their governments.

The size-of-government index also misses the mark because it fails to account for industrial policy. This is a serious mistake, because it overestimates the degree to which some of the fastest growing economies of the last few decades, such as Taiwan and South Korea, relied on the market and underestimates the positive role that government played in directing economic development in those countries by guiding investment and protecting infant industries.

This flaw is thrown into sharp relief by the recent report of the World Bank's Commission on Growth and Development. That group studied 13 economies that grew at least 7% a year for at least 25 years since 1950. Three of the Index's "free" and "mostly free" countries made the list (Singapore, Hong Kong, and Japan) but so did three of the index's "mostly unfree" countries (China, Brazil, and Indonesia). While these rapid growers were all export-oriented, their governments "were not free-market purists," according the Commission's report. "They tried a variety of policies to help diversify exports or sustain competitiveness. These included industrial policies to promote new investments."

Still More

Beyond all that, the Index says nothing about political freedom. Consider once again the two city-states, Hong Kong and Singapore, which top their list of free countries. Both are only "partially free" according to Freedom House, which the editors have called "the Michelin Guide to democracy's development." Hong Kong is still without direct elections for it legislatures or its chief executive and a proposed internal security laws threaten press and academic freedom as well as political dissent. In Singapore, freedom of the press and rights to demonstrate are limited, films, TV and the like are censored, and preventive detention is legal.

So it seems that the Index of Economic Freedom in practice tells us little about the cost of abandoning free market policies and offers little proof that government intervention into the economy would either retard economic growth or contract political freedom. In actuality, this rather objective-looking index is a slip-shod measure that would seem to have no other purpose than to sell the neoliberal policies that brought on the current crisis, and to stand in the way of policies that might correct the crisis. ❏

Sources: "Capitalism in Crisis," by Richard A Posner, *Wall Street Journal*, 5/07/09; "Letters: Recessions are the Price We Pay for Economic Freedom," *Wall Street Journal*, 5/19/09/; "Freedom is Still the Winning Formula," by Terry Miller, *Wall Street Journal*, 1/13/09 ; "The Real Key to Development," by Mary Anastasia O'Grady, *Wall Street Journal*, 1/15/08; Terry Miller and Kim R. Holmes, eds., *2009 Index of Economic Freedom*, heritage.org/Index/; Freedom House, "Freedom in the World 2009 Survey," freedomhouse.org; Joel Selmrod and Jon Bakija, *Taxing Ourselves: A Citizen's Guide to the Debate over Taxes*, MIT Press, 2008; International Monetary Fund, *World Economic Outlook,: Crisis and Recovery*, April 2009; Peter H. Lindert, *Growing Public*, Cambridge University Press, 2004; Doug Henwood, "*Laissez-faire* Olympics: An LBO Special Report," leftbusinessobserver.com, March 26, 2005; Jeffrey Sachs, *The End of Poverty: Economic Possibilities for Our Time*, Penguin, 2005.

Article 10.5

THE GIANT POOL OF MONEY

BY ARTHUR MacEWAN
September/October 2009

Dear Dr. Dollar:

On May 9, the public radio program This American Life broadcast an explanation of the housing crisis with the title: "The Giant Pool of Money." With too much money looking for investment opportunities, lots of bad investments were made—including the bad loans to home buyers. But where did this "giant pool of money" come from? Was this really a source of the home mortgage crisis?

—Gail Radford, Buffalo, N.Y.

The show was both entertaining and interesting. A good show, but maybe a bit more explanation will be useful.

There was indeed a "giant pool of money" that was an important part of the story of the home mortgage crisis—well, not "money" as we usually think of it, but financial assets, which I'll get to in a moment. And that pool of money is an important link in the larger economic crisis story.

The giant pool of money was the build-up of financial assets—U.S. Treasury bonds, for example, and other assets that pay a fixed income. According to the program, the amount of these assets had grown from roughly $36 trillion in 2000 to $70 trillion in 2008. That's $70 *trillion*, with a T, which is a lot of money, roughly the same as total world output in 2008.

These financial assets built up for a number of reasons. One was the doubling of oil prices (after adjusting for inflation) between 2000 and 2007, largely due to the U.S. invasion of Iraq. This put a lot of money in the hands of governments in oil-producing countries and private individuals connected to the oil industry.

A second factor was the large build up of reserves (i.e., the excess of receipts from exports over payments for imports) by several low-income countries, most notably China. One reason some countries operated in this manner was simply to keep the cost of their currency low in terms of U.S. dollars, thus maintaining demand for their exports. (Using their own currencies to buy dollars, they were increasing both the supply of their currencies and the demand for dollars; this pushed the price of their currencies down and of dollars up.) But another reason was to protect themselves from the sort of problems they had faced in the early 1980s, when world recession cut their export earnings and left them unable to meet their import costs and pay their debts—thus the debt crisis of that era.

This build-up of dollar reserves by governments (actually, central banks) of other countries was also a result of the budgetary deficits of the Bush administration. Spending more than it was taking in as taxes (after the big tax cuts for the wealthy and with the heavy war spending), the Bush administration needed to borrow. Foreign governments, by buying the U.S. securities, were providing the loans.

Still a third factor explaining the giant pool of financial assets was the high level of inequality within the United States and elsewhere in the global economy. Since 1993, half of all income gains in the United States have gone to the highest-income 1% of households. While the very rich spend a good share of their money on mansions, fancy cars, and other luxuries, there was plenty more money for them to put into investments—the stock market but also fixed-income securities (i.e., bonds).

So there is the giant pool of money or, again, of financial assets.

The financial assets became a problem for two connected reasons. First, in the recovery following the 2001 recession, economic growth was very slow; there were thus very limited real investment opportunities. Between 2001 and 2007, private fixed investment (adjusted for inflation) grew by only 11%, whereas in the same number of years following the recession of the early 1990s, investment grew by 59%.

Second, in an effort to stimulate more growth, the Federal Reserve kept interest rates very low. But the low interest rates meant low returns on financial assets—U.S. government bonds in particular, but financial assets in general. So the holders of financial assets went searching for new investment opportunities, which, as the radio program explained, meant pushing money into high-risk mortgages. The rest, as they say, is history.

So the giant pool of money was the link that tied high inequality, the war, and rising financial imbalances in the world economy (caused in large part by the U.S. government's budgetary policies) to the housing crisis and thus to the more general financial crisis.

Again, check out the *This American Life* episode for the details of how this "link" operated. It's quite a story! ❏

CONTRIBUTORS

Frank Ackerman, a founder of *Dollars & Sense,* is director of the Climate Economics group of the Stockholm Enviroment Institute in Somerville, Mass.

David Bacon is a journalist and photographer covering labor, immigration, and the impact of the global economy on workers.

Tom Barry is a senior policy analyst and director of the TransBorder Project at the Center for International Policy in Washington, D.C.

Dean Baker is an economist and co-director of the Center for Economic and Policy Research (www.cepr.net) in Washington, D.C.

Arpita Banerjee is an economist and independent researcher based in Kolkata, India, and a member of the *Dollars & Sense* collective.

Madeleine Baran is a freelance writer and a graduate student at New York University's Graduate School of Journalism.

Drucilla K. Barker is professor of economics and women's studies at Hollins University. She is co-author of *Liberating Economics: Feminist Perspectives on Families, Work, and Globalization.*

Ravi Bhandari (co-editor of this volume) is the Chevron Endowed Chair of Economics and International Political Economy at Saint Mary's College of California, visiting professor at Tribhuvan University and Kathmandu University's School of Management (KUSOM).

Paul Cummings is a software engineer with a long-standing interest in environmental and social issues.

Anita Dancs is an assistant professor of economics at Western New England College and a staff economist for the Center for Popular Economics.

Maurice Dufour teaches political science and humanities at Marianopolis College in Montreal.

Mark Engler is an analyst with the think tank Foreign Policy In Focus.

Susan F. Feiner is professor of economics and women's studies at the University of Southern Maine. She is co-author of *Liberating Economics: Feminist Perspectives on Families, Work, and Globalization.*

Anne Fischel teaches media and community studies at the Evergreen State College in Olympia, Wash.

Ellen Frank teaches economics at the University of Massachusetts-Boston and is a *Dollars & Sense* Associate. She is the author of *The Raw Deal: How Myths and Misinformation about Deficits, Inflation, and Wealth Impoverish America.*

Andre Gunder Frank, the father of world system theory and dependency theory, was a pioneer in the global analysis of history and social science. He died in 2005 at the age of 76.

Fadhel Kaboub is an assistant professor of economics at Denison University.

Mara Kardas-Nelson is a freelance writer currently based in Cape Town, South Africa. She has written on health, the environment, and human rights for the *Globe & Mail* and the *Mail & Guardian.*

Marie Kennedy is professor emerita of Community Planning at the University of Massachusetts-Boston and visiting professor in Urban Planning at UCLA. She is a member of the board of directors of Grassroots International.

Gawain Kripke is a senior policy advisor at Oxfam America.

Alex Linghorn has worked closely with the land rights movement in Nepal. He is currently a postgraduate at the School of Oriental and African Studies (SOAS), University of London.

Arthur MacEwan, a founder of *Dollars & Sense*, is professor emeritus of economics at the University of Massachusetts-Boston and is a *D&S* Associate.

Stephen Maher is a freelance journalist; he is currently working on his master's degree in international affairs at American University School of International Service, concentrating on U.S. foreign policy in the Middle East.

John Miller is a member of the *Dollars & Sense* collective and teaches economics at Wheaton College.

Anuradha Mittal is a co-director of Food First/The Institute for Food and Development Policy in Oakland, California.

Lin Nelson teaches environmental and community studies at the Evergreen State College in Olympia, Wash.

Vasuki Nesiah is a senior associate at the International Center for Transitional Justice and co-editor of *lines* magazine (www.lines-magazine.org), an online magazine that engages with the political spaces of Sri Lanka and South Asia more broadly.

Immanuel Ness is a professor of political science at Brooklyn College-City University of New York. He is author of *Immigrants, Unions, and the New U.S. Labor Market* and editor of *WorkingUSA: The Journal of Labor and Society*.

Dara O'Rourke is an associate professor of environmental and labor policy at the University of California at Berkeley.

James Petras is an advisor and teacher for the Rural Landless Workers Movement in Brazil and an activist-scholar working with socio-political movements in Latin America, Europe, and Asia.

Robert Pollin teaches economics and is co-director of the Political Economy Research Institute at the University of Massachusetts-Amherst. He is also a *Dollars & Sense* Associate.

Kenneth Pomeranz is a professor of history at the University of California at Irvine and author of *The Great Divergence: China, Europe, and the Making of the Modern World Economy*.

Smriti Rao teaches economics at Assumption College in Worcester, Mass., and is a member of the *Dollars & Sense* collective.

Dan Read is a London-based freelance journalist specializing in human rights and current affairs.

Alejandro Reuss, an economist and historian, is a former editor of *Dollars & Sense* and a *D&S* Associate.

Patricia M. Rodriguez is an assistant professor of politics at Ithaca College.

Peter Rosset is a co-director of Food First/The Institute for Food and Development Policy in Oakland, California.

Katherine Sciacchitano is a former labor lawyer and organizer. She currently teaches at the National Labor College in Silver Spring, Maryland.

Devinder Sharma is a food and trade policy analyst. He chairs the New Delhi-based Forum for Biotechnology & Food Security. Among his works are *GATT to WTO: Seeds of Despair* and *In the Famine Trap.*

Chris Sturr is co-editor of *Dollars & Sense.*

Chris Tilly is director of the Institute for Research on Labor and Employment and professor of urban planning at UCLA and a *Dollars & Sense* Associate.

Marie Trigona is an independent journalist based in Buenos Aires. She is also a member of Grupo Alavío, a direct action and video collective.

Mark Weisbrot is an economist and co-director of the Center for Economic and Policy Research (www.cepr.net) in Washington, D.C.